3/13

SHE-Q

SHE-Q

Why Women Should Mentor Men and Change the World

Michele Takei, PhD

 PRAEGER

AN IMPRINT OF ABC-CLIO, LLC
Santa Barbara, California • Denver, Colorado • Oxford, England

Library of Congress Cataloging-in-Publication Data

Takei, Michele.
    SHE-Q : why women should mentor men and change the world / Michele Takei.
        p. cm.
    Includes bibliographical references and index.
    ISBN 978-1-4408-0406-9 (hbk. : alk. paper) — ISBN 978-1-4408-0407-6 (ebook)
1. Sex differences (Psychology)   2. Women—Psychology.   3. Sex role.
4. Feminism.   I. Title.
    BF692.2.T35   2012
    155.3'3—dc23   2012018789

ISBN: 978-1-4408-0406-9
EISBN: 978-1-4408-0407-6

16   15   14   13   12   1   2   3   4   5

This book is also available on the World Wide Web as an eBook.
Visit www.abc-clio.com for details.

Praeger
An Imprint of ABC-CLIO, LLC

ABC-CLIO, LLC
130 Cremona Drive, P.O. Box 1911
Santa Barbara, California 93116-1911

This book is printed on acid-free paper ∞

Manufactured in the United States of America

For "Dave," a true hero, who allowed me to be myself, for "My Lynnie," a wise woman, who taught me to trust myself, for the wonderful women of New Choices, who taught me that women can do anything, and for all the wise women and good men who are already out there.

Contents

Acknowledgments ix

Introduction xi

1. A Band-Aid Equality 1

2. A World Out of Balance 21

3. How Did We Get Here? 33

4. Women Know and Do Not Know 51

5. Women Are More Rational 77

6. Women Are More Moral 97

7. Women Are the More Creative Sex 115

8. The Real Reason Relationships Fail 125

9. Male Relational Dread 141

10. Confessions of a Male Chauvinist Pig 157

11. Learning How to Be a Man 173

12. Why Men Are Clueless in Relationships 187

13. Her Advanced Knowing Matches New Perspectives 203

14. SHE-Q—The Wisdom of Women 221

15. Mentoring the Masculine 243

16. The New Hero 261

17. A Balanced Future 277

Notes	289
Bibliography	301
Index	307

Acknowledgments

Sincere thanks to my editor, Debbie Carvalko, who seemed to appreciate what I was trying to do even when I first submitted an overgrown and un-wieldy monster of a manuscript in desperate need of editing, cutting, and refinement. Her encouragement was the very thing that kept me on the right track.

And, to Karen Silvestri, who helped me with checking facts, editing, and the many things that one needs to do at the end of a process. Many times her responses to my frantic e-mails that simply said, "Breathe" or "We'll get through this," were just what I needed to hear.

Introduction

This book has been in my mind and in my computer for way too long. I knew much of what I wanted to write long before I ever found research that actually supported it, and it has been thrilling to see what I only sensed was true years ago come into reality.

Having finally completed SHE-Q, I have arrived at a meta-perspective from which to view the interwoven and complex issues of women, men, culture, and how we know what we know. Anything written about women automatically seems to have implications for men and vice versa. In addition, every man and woman is a product of an ever-changing culture. Because there are layers upon layers of beliefs that shape and influence each level of knowing, I was forced to go all the way to the bottom lines in nature to find what true equality really looks like. Because our knowledge is so skewed toward the masculine perspective, this was my only option before I could even begin to understand the real issues that need to be addressed today. What I didn't realize when I started this process was how the implications of imbalance extended far beyond the relationships between men and women to include our earth and our literal future.

Having arrived at this point, the truths that lie at the bottom of the issues included here have all become quite clear. Granted, because patriarchal values have been present since the first written words, it may be hard for a person who has not yet taken this journey to even imagine what a new, more balanced way of thinking would look like. We have a tendency to accept things the way they are because this is the way things have always been.

Traditional knowledge, culture, and values, however, don't have to remain the same. We are entering a whole new era. For thousands of years, males created knowledge based on what they knew, and not surprisingly, it worked in their favor. We believed it because they said it and there was no real way to counter these pronouncements other than disagreeing. Today countless advances enable us to see objectively, for the first time, how incorrect these pronouncements were. So much of what has been attributed to women has not only been wrong, it is and has been mainly reflective of a perverse need to elevate the male and control the female. To make this statement is not male-bashing, but simply to attempt to bring balance to an imbalanced world.

The world is set up on masculine values, and women, as they enter education or employment, are still playing a male game according to male rules. Currently, 100 percent of the time, the masculine Yang quality is valued more highly than the corresponding feminine Yin value—thinking is valued over feeling, separation over connection, and so on. The truth is that women will never truly be equal until we value the feminine Yin qualities of compassion, empathy, foresight, and connectedness, to name just a few, as equally as we value the masculine. The irony is that females are now beating men at their own game.

Currently we see only the tip of the iceberg that will enable women, and require men, to change. Little by little, many of the new ideas that are suggested here already are showing up in culture. For example, women are becoming the richer sex and these new female breadwinners are transforming sex, love, and family. In the 50 short years since the second wave of feminism, the fact that women have become educated and entered the workforce is creating massive role shifts for both men and women that are only now being addressed.

On the personal level of relationships, it appears that men and women will continue to engage in battles as their roles change. She will rise slowly to her level of expertise and he will resent it and try to control her. Without valuing the feminine qualities, however, women will be fighting this battle without ammunition. Interestingly, women will still win—eventually. Their newfound earning power alone will enable them to finally refuse to tolerate the male need to control, and hopefully, men will learn to respond in more supportive ways. Women, however, will be far better armed if they understand the deeper issues. The problems that will arise on the personal level alone will be many, and one can almost hear the cry for further and more specific SHE-Q guidance.

The imbalance, however, has deeper implications that go beyond the personal level to the needs of an imbalanced world. The feminine Yin values include insight, intuition, foresight, embodied wisdom, and whole-brained, big-picture thinking that includes the future of the earth. One could easily argue that the feminine qualities represent the highest and best qualities of human kind. The masculine Yang values represent separation, division, analysis, independence, left-brain thinking, and a need to control. Not surprisingly, the left brain, by its very nature, is highly resistant to change and heavily invested in maintaining its own perspective. These differences in perspective have major implications for our future and the earth. Fracking is a clear example of something that can be viewed from both perspectives. The slick Yang ads assure us that fracking is safe and denies any evidence of pollution and damage. Fracking will create new jobs and more energy they say, and for a moment we forget our gut feeling. We try to believe that they said it was safe until we see the pictures of the toxic, polluted water and the dead wildlife. Because Yang has a history of focusing only on immediate gain with little regard for the future, we need the balance of Yin that considers future generations, explores alternatives, and tries to do what is right for the "many."

Women, the more moral sex who make decisions based on what is best for others, should be the mentors of relationships, the caretakers of the earth, and the leaders of the world. Until then, we should value the qualities of the feminine at least as equally as the masculine. If we continue on the imbalanced male path, we can anticipate a future that is similar to our past, filled with limited personal relationships, wars that cause each country to create ever-increasing stockpiles of weapons, and a depleted and ravaged earth. The problems we face on both the personal and global levels are difficult and complex and can only be understood by returning to the bottom lines of true balance. If we want a future that includes peace and what is best for humanity on all levels, we must finally look to the wisdom and SHE-Q of women.

I hope you will visit the SHE-Q website and feel free to leave your comments on the SHE-Q blog. I also hope that you will complete the questionnaire for women that will be part of the next book entitled, *The Age of Women*.

Enjoy!
Michele (Shelley) Takei

Chapter 1

A Band-Aid Equality

Yin

Female

Yang

Male

Long before I ever became interested in consciousness or how I knew what I knew, I realized that my other-than-conscious mind had been stirring my thoughts without my even knowing it. I kept being presented with strange and foreign ideas that seemed to just bubble up from nowhere. These new and unwanted thoughts entered my consciousness and I was confronted with new ideas I didn't want. I had considered myself a happy wife and mother, and I certainly didn't want to change anything, especially when it came to how I viewed my life. When I look back, however, I realize that period of time was when I actually started to wake up.

It was the early 1970s, and I was a happy housewife and mother of three well-planned children. The children and I were in the kitchen one evening, making Christmas cookies. They were all sitting on the kitchen counter, up to their elbows in dough and sprinkles. My husband, Dave, was in his study, as usual, reading about the meaning of life. Every evening, he typically retired to his study to read philosophy books. I was well aware that he read *real* books about deep philosophical issues, not the fluffy fiction that my friends and I read and talked about among ourselves. Dave had been my college philosophy professor 10 years earlier. Marrying my professor had been a bit of a big deal in the 1960s, but we had settled into an ideal life in small-town, academic suburbia.

My faculty-wife friends and I had a kind of unspoken agreement that part of our roles, as women married to wise, learned men, was to try hard not to saddle our husbands with too much involvement with family related things. Our husbands were, after all, engaged in important intellectual pursuits, and relating to women and children was not the stuff that lofty, philosophical thoughts were made of. When our husbands deigned to spend time with us, leaving their true passions and interests, we were grateful. It never would have occurred to me to try to join our separate worlds in any additional ways. Nor would it have occurred to me to question him. I was quite sure he was living a very meaningful and admirable life and that my role was to support this and uphold my end of the bargain. That is why I was so surprised when I started to hear the little voice.

"Isn't thissssss the meaning of life?" the voice questioned. The electric mixer was on and, at first, I thought that what I was hearing came from the whirring sound of the metal beaters. "Isn't thissssss the meaning of life?" the voice asked again. I blinked as I looked around. The children hadn't heard it. The voice, which sounded a bit like a snake, was coming from inside my head. A little snake had somehow found its way into the garden of my mind, and no one was more surprised than me. I did not like this intruder, but before too long, more questions started coming into my mind. *What is this life that we have together, Dave? What is family to you? Who am I to you? How do you really feel about our children and me? Are we just some burden to you that keeps you from the real meaning of life that you keep searching for in books? Isn't there meaning in our daily life, in family and relationships, too?*

These new thoughts and questions were unsettling my life. I didn't want them, but over the next weeks and months, they would suddenly appear in the Eden of my brain, which had been so happy and unquestioning. Therefore, I did the only thing any normal woman would do to rid myself of such evil thoughts; I started wanting a lobotomy.

It seemed like a perfectly reasonable solution to me. Not a big radical lobotomy—just a small targeted operation that would allow me to go back to being naively happy again. Relaxing in the bathtub, I would imagine pleading my case to a judge and a jury so that some wisdom could be brought to bear on my new dilemma. I thought that maybe a jury would find me innocent of such awful ideas by reason of insanity. Or maybe there would be a very wise person on the jury who could help me better understand what was wrong with me. If my life was being turned upside down by such rebellious notions, surely this same troubling fate was befalling other women. The lobotomy option, I reasoned, would be a blessing for the many women who were as tortured as I was. Questioning our wonderful lives could only lead to unhappiness, right?

I am happy to say, 35 years later, that my brain is still intact. And not just intact, but wise and vibrant and overflowing with insights that often amaze me. I have come a long way from thinking I needed a lobotomy. I am not sure that every little prompting that first knocks on our consciousness is a prelude to what is destined to become a lifelong passion, but looking back, I realize that this was true for me. It was indeed a wake-up call that changed not only my life, but Dave's as well.

In order to answer all the questions that were coming into my mind, I started to become interested in how I knew what I knew, and discovered that there was actually a name for this kind of inquiry. It's called epistemology. Don't be put off by a word that most of us can't even pronounce. Every person in the world has an epistemology, a framework for what they believe, whether they are aware of it or not. I have learned that it is important. One could argue that our epistemological framework—the beliefs we have that inform our lives—is one of the most important things that shapes and drives us. We need beliefs to survive, but most of our beliefs are learned from our environment and not really chosen consciously. Like me, most of us can state what we believe in. All beliefs, however, are rooted in some larger, more basic framework, so it is important not just to know *what* we believe but *why* we believe it. Once we know why we believe what we believe, we are somehow more free.

Few of us actually take thinking to this next level of knowing *why* we believe what we believe or *how* we know what we know. The questioning often starts with little things. I remember, for example, the small but significant example of learning the real truth about Columbus Day. I had grown up believing that Columbus discovered America. It registered almost like a small mental shock when I learned that Columbus could not discover a country when millions of people already lived there. He just happened to be the first *white Anglo-Saxon Protestant male* to come to America and that perspective made all the difference in terms of what was *true*. It was one of the first times I became aware that how I knew what I knew was relative to countless other variables. I started to realize that the *truth* depended on who was writing it—and even reading it. The fact that I was a white Caucasian female would determine, to a large extent, what was true for me. It fascinated me to realize that Truth was relative.

Years later, when I learned that at one time the feminine had been revered and worshiped as the divine principle, I was a little less surprised, having learned to anticipate that most beliefs were just the tip of an iceberg that contained deeper and more real authentic truths. I was still shocked because this time the epistemology about a feminine divinity spoke to me on a much more personal level. At first, I didn't believe it when I heard that the feminine had been revered, thinking that it was a myth like Santa Claus or Amazon women. After some reading and learning, however, the realization that as an adult female I had never even considered the possibility of a feminine divinity stunned me and I began to wonder how it would have changed me had I known.

This wondering prompted me to recall a paper on morality that I had done in graduate school years earlier. Laurence Kohlberg was the expert on this subject and my paper was filled with his quotes. Kohlberg proposed that there were levels of moral development and, further, that females rarely achieved the highest level of morality.[1] I included this fact as truth in the same way I might have stated that one and one is two. It never occurred to me, back then, to question an expert, let alone consider why I, as a female, might be considered morally inferior. I started to become fascinated with how I knew what I knew. When my friends and I talked, we began to focus less on what we had actually learned and more on bottom lines that we felt or sensed were true. I started realizing that having an awareness of how we know what we know enables us to live more consciously and feel more in control of our own lives. It determines how we feel about ourselves and our place in the world. It provides a firmer basis for our thoughts, which further shapes and strengthens our actions.

Knowing what we believe and why we believe it is particularly relevant for women today. There is more information available to us today than ever before. In fact, there is so much information that a new unit of measure, the zettabyte, had to be invented. Further, so much has changed for women in the last 50 years that the rules and roles that once defined women are now obsolete. You may be a woman who has outgrown much of what you learned growing up. You may have heard the call that there could be more to life than what you were living and followed that path into a new and exciting but sometimes lonely world. You may be a woman who still embraces the beliefs of your childhood and feels comfortable with your values. Or, like most women, you may be somewhere in the middle. You have some new thoughts, some old thoughts, and some guilt mixed for good measure. Regardless of where you are, if you are a female, you have probably encountered the concept that you are somehow less than a man. When that happens, how do you react? Do you let it just roll off you because a part of you agrees? Do you get angry and try to fight back? Do you sense that it isn't true but can't really say why?

I have had all of these reactions and these issues and my responses have intrigued me since the day I started to think about them. I was particularly interested in why women were considered to be the lesser sex. I realized that I was one member of a female population who has encountered this concept. Sometimes we are changed instantly by learning something new or perhaps we discover bits of information until we reach a new tipping point. Regardless how it happens, we begin to sense that we are on a path that just seems more real and authentic. I just happened to hear about and then read *The Chalice and the Blade,*[2] and suddenly I had a much larger context for my own religious and spiritual beliefs. The book served as a beginning that led me into exciting, unexplored areas. This immersion into my own process of how I knew what I knew also led me to realize that changes in epistemology don't always come from outside ourselves. These changes can also appear as the still small voice within that manifests in surprising and unbidden ways.

I didn't realize back then that my questions were searching for an epistemological framework. I didn't know then that, even on a personal level, there would be layers upon layers of frameworks and bottom lines involved as I started to get clear on how I knew what I knew. Why, for example, had I believed that what Dave was doing was more important than what I was doing? Why did I feel guilty for the new thoughts that presented themselves? Why did I want to go back to the comfort of my old thoughts? Why is it that I can still mark that day, so long ago, as the beginning of my waking up? The more I tried to figure out this whole issue, the more I realized how many levels there were to it. Many of the layers, I learned later, were related to the concept of equality between males and females. Dave's pursuit of knowledge seemed more important than spending time with family because that is just how it was. Even I had never really thought that family was of primary importance. Then I started wondering, if Truth was relative, what was really true.

Why, for example, at the end of our lives, are our most cherished memories always about relationships and family? Why, if this is true, did relationships seem so much less important than the pursuit of knowledge or the money we made in our daily lives? People rarely remember their paycheck or good grades when they recall life's most stellar moments. They remember the sweet words, the special moments—they remember feeling cherished and loved by those closest to them. Further, why was family more related to what women do, while men were expected to be off doing greater things and pondering wiser thoughts? And, why were almost all of the great thoughts written by men? Did women never have great thoughts? I realized that while they surely did, if we happened to live in a culture that valued certain thoughts over others, we would never even be aware of the great thoughts of the lesser sex. And, why were women considered the lesser sex anyway? My mind thought about these issues all the time, and each thought just seemed to bring up 10 more. Why does our culture revere male values and thoughts more than those of a female? I realized that everything we do or think about—from our childhoods, to how we do in school, what we major in, what jobs we have, our children, the security of our country, what we invest in, what we enjoy and what we believe in—is somehow influenced by whether we are male or female. In each instance, the inquiry will go on and on, and be informed by deeper and deeper layers, which in turn are rooted in even more basic bottom lines.

The Issue of Equality

The bottom line of almost everything we think about, as well as every step along the way, will be based in the concept of the differences between men and women, and more specifically in the issue of equality between them. The truth is that there are only two sexes on this planet, and, historically one has been valued far more highly than the other. Sex or gender is the greatest determinant of who we are, how we feel about ourselves, and how we know ourselves, so the issue of equality matters very much.

But why bring up the issue of equality now—now that most of us feel that it is finally equal? Women won the vote in 1920. We have had a second women's movement for 40 years that seems to have had such a great impact that young females today appear to take equality for granted. The whole issue of equality, however, is both clear and very cloudy, both true and untrue. It is hard to get an accurate picture of where most women are today on this issue. We know that countless women have changed their lives and feel empowered. Others seem not to have changed at all—raising their children the way they were raised, embracing old traditions and rarely questioning what they know.

Statistics can be both good and bad in helping determine where women really are today. On one hand, for example, statistics reveal that one in every three women is or has been sexually abused. Because we have been aware of this for many years, countless efforts to help curb this abuse have been put in place. Surely, one would reason, these statistics would have improved along with our awareness and efforts. And, surely young females today are empowered as the result of having a women's movement. However, other statistics reveal that sexual abuse is more prevalent than ever and, further, that the abuse of teenage girls by their boyfriends has escalated dramatically. Is it equal or not?

Often a famous legal case reveals new statistics. The Laci Peterson case, where eight-months-pregnant Laci was killed by her husband, revealed for the first time that the greatest threat to a pregnant woman and her unborn child is the father of that child. One of the strongest statements to come out of the women's movement was "No means No!" Why then, 40 years later, in 2011, did a bright, young female college student, speaking at the "Anita Hill—20 Years Later Conference," state in her well-articulated speech that college males today appear to believe that "No means Yes and Yes means anal"?

Regardless of the statistics, many women today *sense* that it is equal, or certainly more equal, than it has been. They can still point to inequities in pay and the fact that few women hold the highest positions in companies, but overall, most women appear to believe that finally equality is close to being achieved.

I was among the countless women who had gone back to school and gotten educated, in the 1970s and 1980s; I had majored in psychology as an undergraduate and started taking graduate classes when my youngest child was three. I went to school at night—so that I was able to be home with the children during the day. Starting my masters, I naively expected that the field of psychology would have changed dramatically during the 15 years between undergraduate and graduate training. I was aware that the second wave of feminism, which began in the late 1960s, had been, from the beginning, very critical of psychology, and sadly, I learned that very little had changed in terms of the actual psychology we learned in graduate school.

Prior to the women's movement, psychology focused on the study of men and defined life in masculine terms. Even the word psychology, which originally meant "the study of the soul," had been reinterpreted toward the more masculine "study of the psyche or mind." Psychology linked itself with the medical model as science became more and more dominant. Medical and psychological studies rarely included women and, for the most part, simply generalized statistics to include them. As more women became educated, however, they began recognizing and addressing these problems, and while some changes did occur, they were rarely included as part of general psychological knowledge.

Miriam Greenspan was one of the first women in the field to question the premises of psychology, with her book, *A New Approach to Women & Therapy*.[3] While completing an internship in psychology, she realized that she was actually being taught to help her female clients adapt to their social subordination. Women's difficulties at the time were viewed as the result of their own neuroses. Even in the 1950s, women were expected to be housewives and subservient to men. As women entered the field of psychology, in the 1960s and 1970s, feminists began to sense a major discrepancy between what women really felt and how psychology related to those feelings. Freud's theories still heavily influenced the definition of a healthy woman. While good mental health for men was to become assertive and independent, good mental health for women was measured by their ability to be passive and subservient. Women, therefore, who desired to work or achieve outside of the home were deemed mentally ill because they were unable to adapt to their prescribed roles. They were viewed as trying to compete with men—a concept that was believed, could potentially destroy the moral fabric of society.

The postmodern movement, in the second half of the 20th century, ushered in a deconstruction of Truth, norms, beliefs, and thoughts and served to strongly benefit women. Women began to question the long-held truths of psychology and realized that who gets to decide what is true or "normal" had more to do with gender than it did with real truth. In 1972, Phyllis Chesler wrote *Women and Madness*[4] in which she described how women were pathologized by the psychological theories of the time. She was one of the first women to address the mainly male American Psychological Association (APA) and shocked her audience by asking for one million dollars to help make amends to all the women who had been hurt by the field of psychology. She requested money for all the women who had been labeled, drugged, institutionalized and pathologized for being too assertive for their own good. Both Greenspan and Chesler had awakened to a new way of thinking and responded to their own personal call. Of course, most of the male audience probably believed that Chesler was the perfect example of a woman who was acting pathologically and exchanged knowing looks with each other as if to confirm that this was the most severe case of penis envy that they had ever seen.

While the changes that these early pioneer women lobbied for never actually filtered into what I was being taught in my masters in counseling, nevertheless feminism did have a major impact on the culture for women. In the 1980s, women lobbied the government for funding for programs to help level the academic and professional playing fields between women and men. Recognizing that education was one of the key avenues for equality, programs to help women prepare for schooling and develop greater self-esteem and assertiveness were funded by state and federal dollars.

New Choices

My timing for completing my masters degree and getting a full time job coincided well with the children being in school, and I became the director of a Single Parent and Homemaker program in 1983. The program, called New Choices, was six weeks long and had two major focuses. The guidance portion of the program was designed to help women function at their very best. It included stress management, decision making, and parenting—everything to help the women feel as good about themselves as possible. The career portion included creating a résumé, career testing, and job-shadowing. Most importantly, it provided money for the women to go to school, and close to 100 percent of the New Choices women took advantage of further schooling. Many entered college and became the first wave of returning adult learners. Many of the New Choices student who went to college made the Dean's list. Unlike many typical college-age students, they weren't partying and drinking the night before a test. These women were adults, they were responsible, they completed their assignments, and they studied—some for the first time in their lives. They loved college and the professors loved them. The papers they wrote reflected the wisdom of having lived and learned from life—and often I could not believe what some of them had lived through. I was their teacher, mentor, counselor, and sometimes mother. I taught them many things, but truly, they taught me more than I taught them. Some of them had endured things that I am quite sure I could not have lived through, and yet there they were every morning ready to learn something new and primed to start a new life. More than a thousand remarkable women completed our program during the 12 years that I served as director. When I left to relocate with my husband, the new director of the program was a former New Choices graduate, who had been voted outstanding graduate and delivered the graduation address at both her undergraduate and graduate commencements.

I discovered a doctoral program with a double major in women's studies and transpersonal psychology that I could do while still working full time at New Choices. I had seen so many women follow their dreams; I had to follow my own. It seemed like a perfect fit for me and I was determined to use my doctoral education to get to the bottom lines of all the issues that I had been thinking about and the issues that came up again and again with the New Choices women. The thing that surprised me the most was why the husbands and boyfriends felt so threatened when their partners started New Choices. While there were a few wonderful and supportive spouses, for the most part, the males who were in the women's lives seemed to become incredibly defensive as soon as the women started to take steps to better themselves. They hid or burned the women's books, refused to let them take the cars, and made it hard for them to study. I wanted to get my doctorate in women's studies to learn why there was so little focus on the inner strength of women who had to cope with issues like this on a daily basis. I wanted to learn why it appeared that women developed even more character and strength as a result of their very difficult lives. And, the one thing I really wanted to explore was why all the men were so threatened when their women changed. I saw this happen all the time. Every day was just a different variation of the same theme. Angela came into New Choices one Monday with her arm in a cast. "What happened to you?" we all asked. "Well, I told Jim that if he didn't start treating me better that I was going to leave him after I graduated," she responded.

"Did he break your arm?" we asked. "What happened?" "Well," she responded, "we were in the car when I told him, and he saw a tree and he just crashed the car into the tree. The car is a real mess."

Carrie, who sounded like she had some experience in this area, said, "Don't tell him when you're in the car!" "Yeah," said Angela, "I figured that out. I knew what I said would piss him off, but I didn't think he'd crash his car. He loves that car, so I thought that would be a good time to tell him."

The women all seemed to have a scrappy, gut-level sense of survival. They seem to have learned early on how to read the environment and keep themselves safe. They rarely went as far as Angela did, but even Angela had certain reasoning to her thinking. As I got to know them, I became more and more idealistic about women and what they could do. I actually started to believe that women could do anything and the New Choices women never let me down. In fact, they turned me into a raving optimist when it came to women. I tried to let the world know. I wrote to Oprah and Barbara Walters inviting them to come to see what women could do with just a little help, but never heard back from them. I started my doctorate thinking that surely there would be tons of research being done on how remarkably well women were doing.

Women's Studies

For several years, during my doctoral studies, I was immersed in women's issues at work, at school, and in my own life. I did discover some bottom lines in graduate school, but they sure weren't what I thought they would be.

On a break during my first seminar in women's studies, some of the women in my class were sitting around drinking coffee from cups that said, "Women Are People Too." I should have realized at the beginning of my experience with women's issues that much of what I would be learning would be a challenge. I didn't even understand the message on the cups! Having to state that women were human beings seemed like a desperate attempt to convince oneself. It somehow implied that women weren't real human beings before the women's movement or before there were cups that said so. I understood the point; I just didn't understand why women had to adopt the stance of the victim. Why not just assume that women are strong and resilient like the New Choices women? I was shocked to discover that often the women in New Choices had a far greater sense of themselves than the educated women who were getting their doctorates. Why would men or the rest of the world believe that women were equal if we needed a cup that said we are human to convince us? It often seemed like women's studies almost embraced a male perspective of women. I had mixed feelings about having left my own mug at home that said, "Women Fly When Men Aren't Looking."

I joined the women who were talking about a commercial on sexual harassment that was currently being shown on TV. Many of the women seemed to view it as a big step forward. I remember when I first saw this commercial. I, too, thought it was a good idea to have public service spots on television that addressed sexual harassment. The commercial showed a male and a female in a work setting as he asks her, "If I told you that you had a nice body would you hold it against me?" With each comment the harassing male made, the woman grew smaller and smaller. The commercial ended with a message that sexual harassment was against the law. The commercial made sense, on some level, the first time I saw it, but when I thought more about it, I felt confused. "Why should the *woman* shrink?" I wondered. The message implied that women could be diminished by the words of some jerk. Why should any woman feel somehow less than herself because some man makes a ridiculous comment?

I summoned my courage and asked, "Why should we continue to think that men can put women down and that a woman's self-esteem must be negated by a man's comments?" One woman whipped her head around and said, a little too loudly, "Women might know this, but men still have to get the message!"

"That's true," I said, "but it seems to me that the commercial would be far more effective if it showed the MAN shrinking with each harassing comment he utters. He's the one that is saying words that diminish him, both as a male and as a human being." She closed her mouth and just looked at me.

I was hoping to find a new, more empowered perspective in my doctoral program. However, I learned, once we started class, that the victim issue was still alive and well. The worst thing about a woman viewing herself as a victim is that, by definition, she will never have her own sense of self-esteem. Her sense of self-worth can forever be taken from her by others who perceive her as a victim. Gloria Steinem wrote *Revolution from Within* years after the feminist movement started because she felt that while so many changes had occurred for women, most still had "too little self-esteem to take advantage of hard-won, if still incomplete, opportunities."[5]

Sandra Bartky, one of the well-known feminist writers at the time, provided another perfect example of women locked in the victim mentality. In her often quoted writings on women's psychological oppression, Bartky recounts her experience of being victimized. She recalls walking down the street when men's whistles and catcalls made her know that she was "a nice piece of ass." The men's whistles made her perceive herself the way they viewed her, and she was made to see herself as a piece of ass.[6]

There was something just not right about what she was saying. Surely, I thought to myself, women are stronger than that. I thought of all the women in New Choices. They had been through far worse things than whistles and catcalls and managed to remain strong. It seemed to me that any person would feel like a victim if they believed that others had that strong an effect on them. Victim psychology failed to recognize women's resiliency. Without question women have been victimized. Brutal rapes and well-planned murders, however, are very different than whistles and cat calls.

The issues we grappled with in graduate school were complex and difficult and there were certainly no clear answers. Some feminists felt that we should focus on the rights of *all* women. Papers and books that addressed the issues of American women were often criticized for being too narrow in focus and not accounting for minority women in third world countries. Even books written about problems in America were often written by educated women, who like me, had lived a relatively easy life with enough food, safety and opportunity. What about women of different racial, social, or economic classes who had far less? If an article focused on the importance of allowing women into the workforce, it was quickly pointed out that poor, black women have always worked.

The victim issue was one of the most difficult. Certainly no one thought that women should be victimized in any way, but where should we place our focus in these complex issues? If a woman is victimized, is she always a victim? Was patriarchy imposed on women or did they agree to it and support it? Are there degrees of victimization? Surely, Bartky's victimization was in no way equal to rape or physical abuse.

I choose to focus on women's strengths. The women in New Choices had taught me that they could surmount almost any obstacle and they continually validated my idealism. They may have been victimized, but they could also refuse to view themselves as victims. The issue seemed to be a matter of perception or focus. True, the bottom line is that abuse should not happen. Focusing only on the atrocities, however, often means missing the many stories of courage and who the real victors are. I knew many women who managed to emerge from their ordeals stronger and more confident than they had ever been.

When any group finally becomes conscious of their oppression, a circular argument can result that goes something like, "If you don't see yourself as a victim, then you don't get it. The only way to get it is to see yourself as a victim." Perhaps the women who were insisting that women were victims were, in essence, revictimizing those women who chose to focus on their strengths.

Camille Paglia[7] was a popular example among feminists, who for the most part vilified her. "Camille Paglia is for rape," said one woman loudly during dinner after our seminar. Paglia, a feminist herself, was the first to refer to radical feminists as the lily white, ivory tower women who cry rape at every corner. Her message to young women was to be smarter. Her suggestion to young women was to use their intelligence and good sense to not be drunk in his dorm room at 3:00 A.M. in the morning, and then be shocked when he tried something. Most of the women in our class, however, viewed Paglia as the enemy. "No means No!—under any circumstance! Even if the girl is drunk, she can still be raped!" was the often heard retort.

"Camille Paglia is not for rape," said my friend, Katie, to a small group of women who were having coffee between classes when the topic came up again. "I have her book right here," I said, coming to Katie's support. I knew the exact page of her controversial comment because I had participated in this discussion many times. Paglia says, "If a real rape occurs, I will help lynch the guy from the nearest tree." "No means NO!" the other women at the table said, almost in unison. The whole date rape issue was interesting and complex, but there seemed to be no way to have a discussion about it because all the emotion immediately shut it down.

Later that night, Katie told me about a time when she was accused again of "not getting it" by some women at the college where she taught. "I finally screamed at them," she said. "I get it! I get it! I just don't agree with you! I'm a woman. I live in this country, I'm not a victim and I get it!" She took a deep breath and finished her tea. "I am doing my dissertation on this very issue," she continued. "I think I am doing it because I feel victimized by angry women. I'm a feminist for God's sake. How ironic."

"Part of what I'm researching is the emotionality around the anger. Haven't you wondered if these women were always angry all the time even before they became feminists? The anger thing can affect the quality of your life, and it doesn't just stay directed 'out there' at men. It works its way into your whole life," said Katie.

"Maybe that is the reason that they cannot focus on—or even see—the positive changes that women have made," I added. "They miss the essential element of possible self-transformation. I think I am finally beginning to understand why feminists have such a hard time seeing women as strong and resilient. They would have to change their perception of women—and probably of themselves." "Right," said Katie, "and then, because they don't see other women as capable of overcoming adversity, they fail to see it in themselves and vice versa."

I remembered when I first started learning about the history of women's oppression. I found myself getting angry all the time. So, I remember knowing that I had to provide an answer to the question that was forming in my mind, "Which will die first—me or the patriarchy?" I realized it wasn't going to be the patriarchal system, and then, further realized that I didn't want to spend the rest of my life angry. I think that question and answer served to intensify my interest in bottom lines and I was determined to look for solutions.

There seemed to be little focus on the influence of any personal psychology of women in my doctoral program. General issues and the plight of all women rather than any insight into the psychology of individual women appeared to be the major area of consideration, and it seemed that the strengths of individual women were somehow lost by lumping all women and issues together.

The most difficult thing for me to accept about feminism, however, was the anti-essentialist position—the theory that there are no essential differences between males and females. When the second wave of feminism started, there were four different focuses of feminism. *Radical feminism,* spearheaded by Mary Daly, basically confirmed that the patriarchy is a corrupt and antiquated system based solely on the perpetuation of male power. Radical feminists refused to accept the system and felt that everything about it needed to be changed. *Socialist feminism* recognized that while women had been oppressed, so had all minorities. They hoped to change the structure for everyone. *Cultural feminism* focused on the position called "essentialism" that recognized that women are indeed different from men. Due to the differences between the sexes, females have qualities, attributes, and hormones that make them essentially different from males. They focused on how women differ from men. *Liberal feminism,* which became the most popular and accepted position, appeared to be the opposite of cultural feminism. The liberal feminist position was and still is that women are just like men. Any perceived difference is just the result of social and cultural conditioning. In this perspective, there was no focus on difference, and certainly no focus on women's essential qualities.

All focus, back then and to some extent even today, on differences between the sexes was dropped by liberal feminism, and little or no attention was given to the biological differences between men and women. The bottom line for the feminist position that became popular was that anything a man can do, a woman can also do. In the ultimate irony, I realized that feminists and the position of liberal feminism actually denied and often even despised the feminine qualities. While men have always had difficulty with feminine qualities, it now appeared true that many women also had the same difficulty. The liberal feminist position literally rejected the uniqueness of women.

While I was shocked, at the same time I had to recognize the history that brought women to this strange place. When the second wave of feminism, in the late 1960s, sought its best strategy to finally gain equality, the rejection of distinct feminine qualities appeared to be the best way to proceed. Bright feminists reasoned that it was going to be hard enough for men to make a place for women in their world. Adopting a position that women were just like men was probably the only way that men would allow it. Asking men to accept not only women in their workplace, but also all the possible differences and feminine qualities that women may bring with them, would only make it even harder to gain access.

Second-wave feminists were well aware of an earlier precedent that had actually focused on women's unique and essential differences and how it had, ultimately, been used against them. A hundred years earlier, in the mid-19th century, Susan B. Anthony and Elizabeth Cady Stanton were among the first wave of feminists to suggest that women receive equal treatment. Most scholars of Women's Studies recognize that Stanton was the brain behind the movement. She generated many of the original ideas and wrote most of the speeches for the movement. Stanton, however, had seven children and was often tied to her home. Anthony never married and chose to devote her life to the cause of women's suffrage. While most people associate Anthony with the early women's movement, it was in truth Stanton who first suggested that women be given the vote—six years before she ever met Anthony.

Stanton probably did some of her best thinking while she cared for and rocked her children. With seven children, perhaps the only time she actually had to sit down and think quietly was as she nursed her babies. I like to imagine that she came to wonder why the world thought of women with such degradation, as she sat and rocked and nursed. She realized that much of what fueled the negative perceptions of women came directly from the Bible. After thinking long and hard about this dilemma, she came to understand that unless the foundations of epistemology were changed, we should not even bother to seek the vote for women. She realized, even then, that as long as the degradation and repression of women remained present and justified in our knowing, women would always be considered second-class citizens.

In 1895, she wrote *The Woman's Bible*,[8] which was in reality the same biblical text with the negative attributions to women removed. The powerful act of revising the Bible, which many believed was the direct word of God, however, was enough to cause her and her role in history to be almost erased. Stanton was often frustrated and angry with women who, in her eyes, continued to embrace the very thing that oppressed them. "She believed to the end that real change in woman's condition could be made only by educating the culture to think differently about women."[9] As the 20th century approached, Anthony, who was more focused on getting women the vote, was nevertheless shocked at the growing religious conservatism, especially in the south. At the National American Women Suffrage Association, she told Stanton repeatedly that it was a waste of time to try to change "the barbarisms of 6,000 years ago." She agreed with Stanton that women should question how they know what they know and stated, "If they (women) are going to do without thinking, they had better do without voting." A hundred years later, well known feminist theologian, Elizabeth Fiorenza suggested that Stanton's arguments are still relevant today, and "the Bible was still used to subjugate women; women still believed in their own biblically based subordination; and, finally, reform in the legal system would still be meaningless without simultaneous reform in religion." Anthony urged Stanton to go along with the growing trend and join with the Christian women, but Stanton refused. While the two women remained good friends until the end of their lives, Anthony allied herself with the ever-increasing popularity of the traditional church women, viewing this position as the best way to ensure the vote.

Until her death, Stanton believed that it was imperative for women that the basis of our knowledge, which was dominated by male values and the denigration of the feminine, must be changed. Until the revision of our knowledge occurred, Stanton felt that any strides women made would be compared to and found lacking in relation to the more accepted male truths. She felt that women would simply be playing a male game according to male rules until they valued the feminine qualities unique to their own sex.

A movement called the "Angel of the House" sprang up in the 1860s, seemingly in response to Stanton's suggestion that feminine qualities be acknowledged and appreciated. Women, according to Stanton and her supporters at the time, were deemed the more moral sex. They spoke publicly for the first time as mediums and intuitives about spiritual and philosophical issues. They were respected as the nurturers and caretakers of society. They concerned themselves with the deepest issues around life and death.

However, the inevitable happened. The Angel of the House concepts were soon used against women. The industrial revolution had begun, and the division in the social structure as men worked in the world, also served to put women back in the home where they could function in their "proper" roles as wives, mothers, and nurturers. The patriarchal culture essentially used feminine virtues against women. "You are right," they said to the women who had pushed to have their essential qualities recognized and appreciated. "You women are, indeed, the more moral, caring, and compassionate sex. Therefore, your proper place is in the home raising the children properly and safely and away from the tough, new industrial era." Women did not get the vote until 1920—years after both Stanton and Anthony had died.

The liberal feminists of the second wave appear to have been determined not to experience the same setback as the Angel of the House movement. They looked back at the earlier women's movement and learned from past events. Stanton had embraced the position that, years later, would be referred to as cultural feminism or essentialism. Despite the long-standing difficulty around appreciating feminine qualities, Stanton recognized the deeper philosophical, biological, and psychological errors that would occur as the result of ignoring differences between women and men. She believed that women were indeed different from men and had their own unique attributes. Aware of the problems faced by earlier female pioneers, intelligent women of the second wave of feminism, in homes and academic halls, argued about how best to proceed. Ultimately, they opted for the safest and surest way to win and the position of liberal feminism was accepted. "Let us in," they said. "It's your game, men. We'll play according to your rules."

The bottom line was that the second wave of feminism learned from the first that if they adopted a stance that women are essentially different from men, those qualities would be used against them. Their only option was to drop any focus on difference. Further, in the 1970s and 1980s, much of the sociological research was focused on the importance of the environment and strongly supported the concept that gender roles are learned. Karen, a bright woman in her fifties and fellow student majoring in women's studies, told me late one evening as we discussed the different feminist positions, "I know we had to throw the baby out with the bathwater, but adopting the position that there is no difference between males and females was the only way to ensure success." She sat back and seemed to be remembering how hard the intellectual struggle had been. She took a deep breath and continued.

"There were actually two sides to this problem. It wasn't just recognizing what had been tried and failed in the past for women. The other side of the problem was recognizing the enormity of the male machine. Males had a history of being in charge of everything. All the traditions, all the bottom lines, and even the basis of knowledge are male-based, and have been for at least two thousand years. Do you think they were going to sit back and welcome us and our differences? Do you think they were going to be happy when we took jobs from them or worked alongside them? The problem was that the whole structure of culture was male-based and males were and still are heavily invested in making sure that doesn't change. Males have created a culture that works for them, and have zero need or desire to change it," she said, her voice getting just a little shaky. She stirred her tea, took a drink and continued, "Fortunately, we also had postmodernism in our favor. Countless cultural traditions were being questioned anyway. Truth and Meaning were being deconstructed, and other minorities besides women began saying, 'Hey, that's not my truth.' We feminists used this to our advantage. We knew we had to make some concessions to be allowed into the male world, and dropping the focus on difference just seemed like the best solution."

I took a deep breath and tried to understand. I guess I had never really realized how deeply the culture was based on values that were entirely masculine.

Politically Correct Equality

The veneer of political correctness that seemed to take hold in the 1980's and 90's, appears to be very well timed for males because a large part of this political correctness ensures that we don't focus on the differences between the sexes, and further, that we all pretend that everything is equal for men and women. Just below the surface of this Band-Aid equality, however, is a wealth of information that women today should know. Just because the focus on women's strengths or differences has basically been ignored does not mean that the difference issue has gone away. It is alive and well and still creating problems for women who are trying to articulate new positions. Some women argue that focusing on differences will only perpetuate the stereotype of women as the weaker, more emotional sex. Others fear that women will again be viewed as the caretakers of society and will be stuck in the home and the old roles. Further, feminists argue that women will be prevented from holding positions of power. Others worry that even suggesting that women are more nurturing will continue to justify patriarchal values and the stereotypical views of women. Another side of this complex issue is that compassion and caring do not belong only to women. Men have these qualities too. And further, at the other end of the spectrum, some believe women can be just as ruthless and aggressive as men. Perhaps political correctness reigns because all the issues around difference are so complex. For whatever reason, the current accepted position appears to be that we've had a women's movement, women entered the work force and now it's equal. Women should be happy that things have changed. Don't talk about it.

Why, then, does it not *feel* truly equal to most women? Even without pointing to the facts that women continue to earn less than men do and are still underrepresented in medical research, those areas are only the tip of the iceberg. And, even without fully understanding the problem, women can sense that something is still very wrong with a culture that spends a trillion dollars on war, while cutting spending on social welfare, schools, and women's reproductive rights. Females have been let into the male-based world of education and work, but other than being allowed to play the male game, little else has changed. After years of angry feminism, it appears that we have settled into an uneasy and still unequal truce. Further, a present climate of political correctness has insured that we really don't explore or even talk about any real differences between males and females.

Women are trying to live in a strange world of mirrors where it appears to be equal but really isn't. It is a wonder that more women aren't crazy. We still have a culture and world in which males have denigrated the feminine principle and women have been forced to do the same thing. And, unfortunately, the best qualities of humankind—caring, empathy, compassion, and other qualities long associated with the feminine—have almost been vilified by both women and men.

Chapter 2

A World Out of Balance

Yin	Yang
Women	Men
Less perfect	More perfect
Lens of life	Lens of culture

There are two great primordial principles in the universe. These principles exist in exquisite balance with each other and are responsible for the creation of new life. This equality of value is best represented in the Eastern concept of Yin and Yang. The visual Yin–Yang symbol reflects the natural balance and flow of all opposites. Night flows into day, day flows into night, strength gives way to yielding, which again becomes strong, and so it goes. One quality is never inherently superior to the other and both are to be valued equally. Imagine if it was always sunny. What if it never rained or ever got dark? It may sound wonderful at first, but within days, we would have confused our sleep cycles, which would soon make us crazy. The Earth would experience a drought and plants would die from too little water and too much sun. The whole balance of the world would be disrupted.

Yang represents the masculine principle, Yin, the feminine principle. Together, they represent wholeness and balance. The line that divides them is curved, indicating how one flows into the other. Further, a part of each is present in the other.

Starting with the two great primordial opposites that are present in nature, the qualities of the masculine and the feminine have become associated, over time, with real definitions and the real differences that are reflected in the sexes. The female in almost every species gives birth and nurses and nurtures the young. The male role is to protect the female and their young. It is the difference between the sexes that makes life possible. The perfect balance of Yin and Yang together reveal the inherent wholeness of the Tao, the combination of the two.

Yin	Yang
Feminine	Masculine
Dark	Light
Moon	Sun
Receptive /Passive	Active
Feeling	Thinking
Subjective	Objective
Intuitive	Cognitive
Heart	Head
Process	Product
Synthesis	Analysis

For thousands of generations, the inherent balance that exists in nature also existed between males and females of our species. After a while, however, this natural balance and sense of cooperation between the sexes began to change. Perhaps it was because males are stronger. Our developing culture, in order to advance, had to rely on brute masculine strength as larger animals were hunted and towns were being built. Over time language developed, and we know that an imbalance toward the primacy of masculine values was present in the first written words. As time progressed, the masculine came to be valued over the feminine even in the way we think, learn, and know. We have learned to look through a lens that reflects our more masculine-based culture, not a lens that reflects real and balanced life. All of us have come, unconsciously, to view the feminine as less valuable than the masculine. We over value the masculine qualities to such an extent that this one-sided way of thinking has been internalized and become a part of both our conscious and unconscious knowing.

The Yin and Yang symbol on the cover of this book is somewhat modified in that it is not completely equal. The feminine Yin gold is slightly larger and subsumes the blue Yang—representing the conscious overcorrection into the feminine that is inherent in this book and that is essential to help return us to true balance. The slightly larger feminine, encompassing the masculine, also provides an image that serves to remind us of what we seem to have forgotten—the masculine comes through the feminine.

As the owner of MARI (Mandala Assessment Research Instrument),[1] a whole-brained psychological instrument that is based on symbols and colors, I am highly aware of the importance of both symbol and color because of the accurate intuitive responses they evoke.

The symbol is above the horizon, placing it in the world and consciousness, in the same way that the feminine qualities are now beginning to influence our conscious awareness. The gold shadow on the water serves to represent the newly present feminine influence that is now being sensed in countless other than conscious ways. The whole image is a visual representation of the intent of this book.

The overvaluing of the masculine occurred when various areas of knowledge, such as philosophy and theology, were birthed into existence over the last two or three thousand years. Education today is still based on many of the same left-brained, Platonic principles used when educating young Greek males centuries ago. Historically, our entire knowledge system was developed by males for males. This is why, for example, today we continue to value thinking more than feeling, the knowledge of the head more than the knowing of the heart and objective quantitative research over the subjectivity of a qualitative approach.

Just below today's politically correct veneer, however, lies the real truth about equality. While women today do indeed enjoy greater freedom, this freedom only exists within a male-defined game that is still completely based on male values.

In my quest to better understand the nature of the imbalance or equality between males and females, I began to feel that I was finally getting to the bottom lines of the issue. It was difficult because the concept of true equality seemed so elusive that it was hard to find a model that could be used to even begin with. In my search for a solution, I was forced to go to nature to find what true equality actually looks like. Our entire knowledge base is so imbalanced that the only place to really see or sense true balance is in the concepts of Yin, Yang, and Tao. In nature, these differences exist in exquisite balance and are essential to life. Any culture that is truly equal, then, would similarly reflect an equal valuing of masculine and feminine qualities. This balance is sadly nonexistent in our culture and world, where the masculine quality is more highly valued almost 100 percent of the time. The fact that feminism, similarly, was forced to drop any focus on the Yin qualities of the feminine in order for women to be allowed into the male world only compounded the problem. The feminist approach was in many ways a shortsighted Band-Aid on a much larger cancer that had been imposed on our culture and world. To further add to the problem, females themselves often came to revile the qualities of the feminine. The very fact that women had to ignore Yin values in order to be allowed into the culture reveals how indoctrinated we are by the masculine values and how far we are from any real understanding of the feminine principle.

The real problem associated with equality is twofold. First, is recognizing that the masculine perspective informs the very basis of our knowledge and that this perspective will continue to skew and color virtually everything we know as long as it remains in place. Second, is the fact that because the feminine principle and qualities have been so denigrated, we literally have no idea what the true feminine perspective really is. We must go to the bottom lines of our male-based theories to even begin to understand how and why scientific, religious, and philosophical conceptions of woman's nature have deemed women the lesser sex. We have learned this skewed perspective in our schools, colleges, universities, news programs, families, churches, and social order. We consider it true. This imbalance is so present that it is almost like the air we breathe. It informs and shapes our conscious and even unconscious minds. It colors what is deemed important, what is funded and researched and later determined to be true, which then further reinforces the male-based biases and beliefs. The fields of philosophy, theology, and psychology—all the fields that have informed our deepest sense of meaning for hundreds of years—are based on concepts that deny and belittle the feminine qualities.

Although much of the information came from the earliest classical thinkers, this imbalance became even more acceptable during the era of modernism. The notions and beliefs of women's inherent inferiority, while expressed less obviously today than it was in earlier centuries, still remains a part of the fabric of Western culture. From the classical period to the nineteenth century the fields that most inform our deepest knowing have themselves been informed by this imbalance. Some of these early notions about women are still present but less blatantly obvious today. The more subtle imbalances of today are in many ways more damaging because they are couched in a falsely perceived equality.

While many books have been written on the subject, Nancy Tuana, in *The Less Noble Sex*,[2] does an excellent job of synthesizing the basic concepts that shaped religion, philosophy, and later psychology. She organizes her work around the major feminine stereotype that women are inherently less noble or perfect. Because women are less rational, less moral, and less creative, they must be controlled. Historically, controlling women meant they must be married, or in a relationship with a man, to have any value at all. Sometimes it meant—and still means—that they must bear children of the proper sex, which, of course, is male. Sometimes it means that they must cover their heads, faces, and bodies. Sometimes it means that they can be legally beaten, burned, maimed, and killed. But nobody believes these stereotypes any more—or do they?

Women Are Less Perfect

In Aristotle's time, women were not considered to be fully formed human beings, but rather mutilated males, necessary only for the continuation of the race. Learned men of the time, states Tuana, recognized that males contend for and are selected by females. Therefore, they reasoned, only males evolve and, further, only males are capable of variety and development. Females, who have to spend all their time and energy on incubating, giving birth to and nursing babies, weren't considered to have enough energy left over for their own personal development and therefore remained in a childlike state all of their lives. The male took less time to form his seed and thus had more energy to put toward his own development. This idea wove its way into the idea of the Great Chain of Being—the concept that places God over man, and, ultimately, man over women, children, and animals.

Victorian science of the 19th century proposed that male and female sex roles were the product of a long evolutionary process. They believed that the more advanced a culture was, the more difference there would be between the sex roles of males and females. Anthropologists of the time looked at the various races and determined, not surprisingly, that the European cultures were the most advanced. They also had the most sex role differentiation, unlike Native Americans and other indigenous cultures where the work was more equally shared. Further, since only the males evolved, there was no need to even study the females in any culture, an idea that persisted long into the 20th century.

There were also social implications for believing that sex role differentiation was part of evolution. When the first wave of feminism began in the mid-19th century, women had started speaking publicly for the first time and pushing to be allowed to vote. Scientists, at the time, argued that to give women rights like men would minimize the difference in sex roles and would therefore hinder the evolution of the civilized race. Further, if women left their prescribed roles, they would be responsible for stopping the evolution of the culture.

When scientists had to account for the fact that females mature earlier than males, they said that, unlike men, women started and stopped maturing at an earlier age, suggesting an arrested development in which females retained their infantile qualities. Men, on the other hand, outgrew these infantile qualities and continued to develop more advanced characteristics. The evidence cited was that women had smaller brains and spent more time on fetal development, which took away any energy for intellectual development. For such reasons, they argued, females shouldn't be educated or go to school. It appears that concept is still present today. I actually knew many women who either believed this about themselves or who were the daughters of parents who believed that college was wasted on females. These women, who often got themselves into college and even outperformed their brothers, were still asked the one and only question that seemed to matter to their families: "When are you going to get married and have babies?"

Women Are Less Rational

According to Plato, God originally made man as perfect and this thinking strongly influenced the fields of both theology and philosophy. Some men, however, were unable to control their passions and were reborn into a lower state—as women. Therefore, men are superior, women are inferior. This interpretation had less to do with women's reproductive state than the nature of her soul. Reason was equated with the masculine, passion with the feminine. This didn't mean that women were incapable of being rational. Women who were capable of transcending their feminine emotional states, in other words, of becoming like a man, could become rational if they tried very, very hard. Obviously, from historical records, few women ever achieved this highly desirable state.

These ideas wove their way into religion. Women could be included in God's image, but only when she was together with her own husband, and only through the marriage bond. In many churches, even today, priests still tell brides that they were less than their husbands until marriage made them equal.

For millennia, it has been believed that humans are closest to the image of God through their rational minds, and men, of course, were always deemed to be more rational. This emphasis on rationality led to the witch hunts in the 16th century, when millions of women were burned or killed in other ways because they were considered to be less rational. The women who were burned often worked with herbs, delivered babies, and cured the sick. They were intuitive and often knew instinctually how to solve many problems. Being intuitive, however, often meant not being rational and was therefore devalued and feared, and further the wise women's knowledge was therefore presumed to have come from the devil. Among the tests to determine whether a woman was having relations with the devil was the practice of dunking her. It was a tough test. If she survived the dunking, that alone was proof that the devil was helping her, and she would then be burned for being associated with evil. If she died, she was presumed to have been innocent—and the problem was solved. Not surprisingly, men were starting to take over the medical profession at the time, and something had to be done because women, who had functioned as midwives and healers for centuries, were standing in their way.[3]

Women were especially targeted because their intellectual capacities were thought to be underdeveloped like that of a child. Incapable of comprehending complex spiritual and philosophical matters, women's faith was considered weaker.[4] For this reason, it was believed that women were much more susceptible to witchcraft. Being gullible and impressionable, they were easy prey for the devil. Since it was believed that the passions must be tempered by reason, women's typically inferior rational capacities were considered to be too weak for her to control her passions successfully.

René Descartes declared, "I think, therefore I am," and effectively separated the mind from the body in the 17th century. To be rational, said Descartes, one must be detached from the needs and desires of the body. Further, it was believed that we could only know reality through reason and rationality. Experts at the time agreed that it was harder for women to be detached from their bodies for two reasons: women have periods, and they give birth and nurse their young. Even if men and women had an equal capacity for rationality, it was argued that women are still so controlled by their involvement with their bodies, that it was just far harder for women to be rational. Further, women were handicapped by their social roles. Her social destiny was to be a wife and mother, and these roles prevented her from living a life of the mind. In addition, for a woman to be rational, she would have to become cool, impersonal, distant, and detached—far too many problems for a woman to overcome. Incapable of rational thought, women certainly could not participate in the sciences or philosophy.

Charles Darwin[5] believed that even if every possible effort were made to increase women's intellect, it would still be inferior because biology demanded that men must maintain a higher intellect to control and steer themselves and their families toward greater evolution. Because it was believed that biology was destiny, the male intellect would always be higher than the female intellect. Darwin believed the hierarchy of mental functions ranged from instincts, which are the lowest, to emotions, intuition, imagination, and finally to reason. Animals have instincts. Women are emotional and intuitive. But the imagination that breeds creativity and the mental prowess that leads to reason are the highest mental functions, and only human males possess these advanced qualities.

The 19th century didn't completely discount women's strengths. Society did recognize that females were better at language and skills that required tact and that they had greater love for children. But as in so many other cases, anything women excelled at was considered a lesser value and indicative of women's immaturity and more impressible minds.

Around this time, people began to believe that too much sex would divert energy away from their brains. Women, of course, contributed far more energy to wards reproduction. Therefore, women had to focus more on their reproductive capacities than on intellectual endeavors. Ironically, a century earlier, women were thought to have little or nothing to do with reproduction and were considered mere incubators or fertile ground that nurtured the male-created embryo. The more enlightened Victorians knew better, but in a pattern repeated throughout history, this acknowledgement of female qualities only led to more reasons why women should be denied opportunity. Eminent doctors of the time concluded that educating women could lead to disorders of the female reproductive organs. Several learned men believed that a mere five or six weeks of higher education would cause women to stop menstruating. Further, reproductive disorders related to educating women might result in weak and sickly babies, authorities said. A Victorian doctor suggested that many of the women who had begun asserting themselves as first wave, feminist suffragettes also suffered from uteromania, which made them think they had some sort of important calling and caused them to want to speak publicly. He said that the angle at which the womb was tilted often determined whether a woman was sane or insane.

Women Are Less Moral

The classical view of morality was originally located in the the field of theology, and later, also became a part of philosophy and psychology. Female morality, according to Tuana,[6] was believed to be that while women did have a sense of good and evil, they were less able to control their passions and therefore less likely to choose good. Even today, in some cultures, a woman who has been raped is then killed, as a moral act, by male family members because of the dishonor that her rape brought to the family. In many belief systems women are still held responsible for all the evil in the world. Eve was deceived by the serpent of evil. Easily manipulated, she was inferior to Adam and all men in the moral realm. Pandora was told not to open the box that contained all the evil in the world, but she was weak-willed and couldn't control her impulses. She opened the box and the rest is history. Women act on the basis of their desires, the learned male experts determined, and are even able to control men's actions through the promises or intimations of sex. If women weren't chaste virgins, they were capable of leading innocent men down the garden path to hell.

German philosopher Immanuel Kant[7] proposed that there were universal laws of morality. To be moral, he believed, one had to be able to divorce oneself from personal desire and be able to act out of duty. Women, according to Kant, didn't have to act out of duty because they didn't participate in politics or service of the country. Women aren't immoral, Kant said, they are just amoral and basically incapable of understanding the moral demands that are required for defending the country or leading the family. Jean-Jacques Rousseau,[8] a Genevan philosopher, agreed, specifying that if a woman was to be educated at all, her education must reinforce her modesty.

Sigmund Freud,[9] the father of psychology, entered the scene in the early 20th century with the idea that women are passive and desire to be possessed, which further reveals moral inferiority. According to Freud's theory, women are morally inferior because they never have to develop their superegos or consciences. The formation of conscience comes about when men must resolve the Oedipus complex by fearing castration. Women remain locked at the ego level, displaying defects of character such as narcissism, vanity, and envy. They have a need to be loved rather than to give love and are unable to suppress their instincts. The male is the ideal and the masculine personality represents the completion of ideal human psychological development.

The sense of morality that carried into the 20th century was based on the concepts that humans must work hard at being good and moral, and further, that we can know the good moral life through thinking, following duty, taking virtuous action, and substituting justice for instinct. Morality was thought to be harder for women because they are controlled by their passions, and they don't have to act out of any sense of duty. Lawrence Kohlberg,[10] one of the first to study morality, as separate from the church and as part of psychology, proposed levels of moral thinking. Masculine values of justice and fairness ranked at the top of his proposed hierarchy, a conclusion that colored the field of morality for many years.

For Kohlberg, morality was linked to cognitive development. He thought that to be moral we had to have a moral code, which was based on being able to imagine an ideal. He proposed three basic levels of morality: preconventional, conventional, and postconventional. At the preconventional level, we adopt moral behavior to avoid punishment. Just as children obey their parents, we live morally so that we don't get into trouble.

Most people, according to Kohlberg, function at the next level of conventional morality. We obey the rules of society to please others. The golden rule applies here as we learn to do to others as we hope they will do to us. At this level, morality begins to be internalized. According to Kohlberg, women typically stay at the conventional level because they don't have to concern themselves with the laws and running the country.

At the postconventional level, Kohlberg believes we attain true morality because the control of our conduct is now fully internalized. At this level, we begin to recognize that two seemingly opposing standards can be equally right at the same time. Thus, a person can be punished for stealing medicine that may save a dying spouse, because even though the life of the spouse is important, it is nevertheless against the law to steal.

We see this kind of male perspective on moral issues in some of our most revered spiritual leaders. Gandhi went beyond rules and laws in an effort to save India. He advocated peaceful resistance, and he won. But he also left his family in order to help the country. Buddha similarly left his wife and son in his search for enlightenment. Male morality often had little to do with actual relationships and more to do with an abstract ideal.

Women Are Less Creative

Being creative is associated with giving birth to something—an idea, a work of art, a project, but not a real child. Being uneducated, it is not surprising that women rarely, if ever, got credit for creating artistic works that lasted and were remembered and honored. In reality, however, women were always involved in the literal act of birth, which viewed through the natural lens of life, of course, is the highest act of creativity possible. Not surprisingly, according to Western theology, this creative act of the female, has not only been unacknowledged, but devalued and denigrated as well. Therefore, one of the most important epistemological questions must be— how is it when females bring forth new life, that males came to be viewed as the pinnacle of creation? The early, original group of men who created the concept of the male as the great creator, surely had no idea, at the time, how influential their suggestion would become. The lens of natural, balanced life has been entirely replaced by the lens of a male-based culture.

At one time, women were revered for bringing forth new life. The idea of a Great Mother who gives birth to the world is closely related to what actually happens in nature, and naturally occurs, and the lens of culture, at that time, was an accurate reflection of the lens of life. The goddess was often pictured as pregnant with the world. Her swollen belly is, at the same time, literally the world. The same uterine environment that nurtures the fetus was easily equated to the embryonic cosmos as the birthplace for the world and all human beings.

The process of gestation and birth are similar and natural when applied to the female. Picturing a pregnant male, however, let alone a pregnant male god, is difficult. The early story had to be tweaked to be accepted—so the male god is portrayed as giving birth through his word and breath. In Genesis, there is only a male creative principle, and the notion of an actual birth process plays no role. The male seed, over time, became the primary source of creation. This male seed became so powerful that, at one time, the only role the female had in the whole process was of a mere incubator that simply housed and nurtured it.

Another version of the story of human creation suggests that man is formed out of dust and woman from his rib. Similarly, the story of the birth of Jesus also reflects the primary creative force of the male. Although it is not a birth reversal, the story emphasizes the role of the male in conception. Jesus existed from the beginning of time and was already divinely formed when he was placed in Mary's womb. Mary had little or nothing to do with it.

Therefore, Women Must Be Controlled

Casting the female as less perfect, less creative, less rational, and less moral served to ensure that woman would always stay in her place. At every point in history, men's concepts about women appear to be mostly about control. According to Kant, a woman could inspire a man toward creativity and refinement, but because she could also dominate him, women had to be controlled. A woman under a man's control is a help, said Kant, but a woman out of his control could be his destruction.

The totality and completeness of the inequality, more than any single example, is what started raising red flags for me. For centuries, learned males have proposed theory after theory about how women were less than men in every way, and we have believed this myth.

One would think, however, that there would have been some small consideration of what actually happens in real life. Did men never see the compassion that women so readily displayed and consider that this care might be associated with morality? Did they never consider, as women labored to give birth to their child, that she was in some way, intimately involved? It is hard to imagine, given that there are only two sexes on this earth, that the sex with the power to create the knowledge would so blatantly repress the other. There seems, even today, to be so little awareness of this imbalance, let alone the extent of it; and for this reason, epistemology is so very important especially for women. Surely, if the feminine principle had been included to even a small degree, things would not be so out of balance now. If, for example, just one aspect of the trinity had been feminine, this alone would have made a significant difference for both men and women.

It is depressing to realize that in many parts of the world many of these ideas are still considered true and have carried well into the 20th century. Even in America, in many places, women cannot be priests or hold the highest offices in the church. Religious and political organizations today still attempt to control the reproductive rights of women. In every field, it seems, men have defined themselves as independent and separate from women, while women's purpose has been defined as being dependent on men.

Viewed as secondary, women have been deemed as helpers to men, with helper defined as a person whose main role is to serve the needs of the other. Historically, male experts have agreed that the husband must be able to oversee his wife's conduct. He must govern the marriage relationship and define what she is capable of doing. Beyond giving birth to children, women were of little value in a man's life. Cast as a temptress and the bringer of misery, she could be a helpmate only if her passions were controlled and her energy was channeled into the well-being of the family.

It seems as though this complete imbalance was and is still necessary not just to elevate the male, but also to continually ensure that the female would never challenge it. The female and her feminine qualities had to be devalued in order to keep the male myth vital. She had to be cast in such a poor and inferior light that no one would dare question such a questionable premise.

Chapter 3

How Did We Get Here?

Yin	Yang
Web	Hierarchy
Central role	Peripheral role
Egg	Sperm
Internal	External

How did humans, the only species with cognition and self-awareness, end up being so out of balance with each other? Not only does this imbalance not reflect nature, it reflects an injustice of grave proportions. There are only two human sexes on the earth and yet one sex has completely denigrated and dominated the other. We don't realize this because we are so caught up in the spin that attempts to hide this fact. The spin ranges from small facts like Muslim women who cover themselves actually have more power than Muslim men because they get to control what men see, to the more far-reaching theories of scholars like Ken Wilber[1] who try to convince us that patriarchal values worked as well for women as men, and that women contributed equally to the development of patriarchy. If patriarchy was imposed on women, says Wilber blithely, then women are sheep and men are pigs. To state that females actively participated in creating and accepting patriarchal values that were used against them at a time when stronger males could have brutalized them at every turn, is simply to blame women, not once but twice, and further to confirm that at least some men are pigs indeed.

Few men grapple with the idea of their own importance. Male superiority is a given. In fact, we are so indoctrinated with the present male-based ways of knowing that most of us, men and women alike, just accept things as they are. There had to be a time, however, at some point in history, as the balance between males and females was being lost, that some variation of the following discussion occurred.

The men probably would have been away from their village, the women, the children, and everyday life perhaps for the first time, having to travel farther from the village to hunt. Their venture might have been similar in many ways to the annual deer season rituals in the northern states when men leave their jobs and families to drink, fart, bond, hunt—and if they are lucky, pick up women. As a female who grew up in a small northern Pennsylvania town near a national forest where, right after Thanksgiving, the streets were flooded with pickup trucks and testosterone-fueled males days before deer season, I was well aware of this yearly rite. Our children even had three days off school so that boys could go hunting. During deer and doe season, dead deer were tied to every bumper of every out-of-town vehicle. These visitors appeared to remain in hunting mode even when they exited the woods and came into town, trying to pick up every female they saw in supermarkets, gas stations, and restaurants.

There have to be some similarities between this present ritual and the first time, before language was recorded, when the males of the tribe ventured farther from camp than usual. Having seen signs of larger animals, they probably decided to camp for the night and pursue them early the next morning. Around the fire, they surely talked and the conversation probably went something like this: "Women could never do this. They aren't strong enough to hunt the large elk. We are invaluable to the tribe. Surely, our strength is just as important as the women's ability to give birth. In fact, it is more important. Without meat, we would surely die," said one. As they sat drinking mead into the night, one of the brightest probably righteously suggested the idea of worshipping an invisible father-creator in the sky. "It will never work," countered another. "How can a male give birth?" "We don't understand how lightning works—we'll make it like that—magical and mysterious, like the movement of the planets and the stars" said another, warming to the idea. "We will call him Father Sun," said another. "Yeah," said the first, getting caught up in the enthusiasm. "We are very brave. We should be honored and revered. We should teach the little ones about how strong and wise men are." "That's right!" the others concurred. "I don't like the way the women look at us sometimes," one added. "We shall make the Father an important creator. We shall say that he creates with his words or breath."

No one is sure exactly how they worked it out. Some propose that the concept of a solar messiah that first appeared in Egypt, has been found to have similarly existed in many cultures at the time. We know that, in many ways and for many reasons, men have needed to define themselves in relationship to women. Women bleed for five to seven days and do not die—a small miracle in itself. Men, at least prehistoric males, had no understanding of menses and how women just seemed to know certain things. This feminine knowing often seemed to fill men with fear. It seemed to give women an edge of supernatural magic. Females, it appears, have always had something men want, only men have never been exactly sure what it is.

Men, however, came to realize, once they understood the connection between sex and the birth of their own child, that their physical and spiritual legacy—the child who would carry on his male genes and inherit his property—was entirely dependent on her being only with him. Making this connection appeared to have allayed some of the fear men had about death. Death was easier to understand and accept knowing that his own (male) child would get his property and carry on his legacy. The harder part was controlling her so that he could be sure that the child who got his name and property was really his own.

Countless factors helped the new male perspective take hold. As cultures grew, hierarchies formed naturally. Males were well suited to being at the top of whatever was valued by the culture. Women, whose roles as herbalists, gatherers, and healers had always been closer to nature, lost ground in the hierarchical structure. Some researchers propose that even the development of culture was one way for men to conquer, subjugate, and control nature. As society evolved, culture became a way of rising above nature—and females.

The Balance Shifts

For all these reasons, men began to elevate their status. Perhaps the women, as they began to hear the story change from the great moon goddess who gives birth to the world to the valiant sun god who bravely kills the animals, were at first surprised and maybe even a little interested in the new twist to the story. Perhaps they indulged the men, reasoning that males should have their own stories and that their young sons would probably enjoy them. Perhaps it was as simple as that—the more the men's stories became accepted, the more accepted the men's stories became.

We know women participated willingly when the men from their tribe came to "capture" their young sons and take them away for initiation ceremonies. The women understood that it was necessary for the young males of the tribe to learn the ways of men and separate themselves from their mothers. Perhaps they thought men must make their stories even better so that the boys would better understand. Perhaps one male thought of a good way to raise really strong sons and, at the same time, convince his son's mother: "While we are gone," he said to her carefully, "we will tell the boys how we men are better and stronger than women. We will say that women are not brave. We will say that women are not as smart." Perhaps she rolled her eyes, indulged him, and said, "Go tell your stories."

And perhaps the men began to enjoy these new stories very much and soon they became the stories most often told around the fire, and when women requested the more familiar stories about the mother who gives birth, the men and boys complained that they had heard that story too many times. And most probably as the men retold their stories, the heroes in the stories got braver and bolder and smarter, and the women in the stories got less and less perfect. Surely, then, at one point back then, a woman said to a man, "Enough of these stories. Our sons are saying we are stupid." And the man, because he was much bigger and didn't like her remark, cuffed the outspoken woman on the ear.

And so the stories told around the fire got more and more imbalanced over the period of time when spoken words evolved into written words. We know that this imbalanced masculine perspective was present in the first written documents. The first cuneiform tablets in Egypt, revealing the first written words, speak of Ra, the Sun God, from whom all life comes. The stories were based on what they knew of the world. Ra represented the sun and Set represented the moon or darkness. Because the sun was life giving and necessary for plants to grow, Ra defeated Set every morning. In the evening Set conquered Ra and darkness fell. After a while, gods and goddesses were associated with nature as a way of explaining what the early people did not understand, such as luck, weather, natural disasters, and fate. These first words led to more words, and soon the male story and imbalance was the only story in town. Like all new ideas, the stories appeared to resonate with the prevailing mindset.

Language, Literacy, and the Left Brain

According to Leonard Shlain,[2] in *The Alphabet versus the Goddess,* men have spent the last 150,000 years trying to gain back the power that they lost when women first figured out the connection between sex and pregnancy, and further, learned that they could say no. Once men gained control over the authority of language, what they wrote was based on the primacy of the male perspective.

Shlain confirms that the imbalance between the sexes was present and strengthened when language began. He recognized that language is central to our thinking process and ability to acquire knowledge. Learning to read literally changes the way our brains process the world. When we perceive real objects, says Shlain, our eyes and brain see them directly, similar to the lens of life. Reading about real things removes us by one step in processing that real thing. The person, for example, who reads words about divinity can end up thinking that the words themselves are divine. Once established, the process of being removed from the real thing can take on a life of its own. In some churches, for example, this process is furthered when the priest or minister reads some words and the congregation reads more words. Showing up at church and reading the words can then become the essence of what is spiritual, which can lead to thinking that one church has better words than another church, and this is only a small example in the long process that brought us to the present.

According to Shlain, in every society that learned the written word, the female deity lost ground to the male deity. This happened because the alphabet elevates the left brain at the expense of the right. Individuals use the left brain exclusively to hunt and kill and to read and write. The more people could read and write, the more masculinized the culture became. The right brain, which thinks in images and expresses being, is best explained as a way of meshing feelings with a sense of life. The feelings associated with the more feminine right brain are authentic in that they are felt and sensed. The more masculine left brain is associated with doing and the act of willing. It is linear and is associated with speech, analysis, abstraction, and numbers.

It is no accident, suggests Shlain, that the first book written in an alphabetic text was the Old Testament. Yahweh required that his people read what he had written and forbade making images, and for the first time in history people revered, not a feminine image of a deity, but masculine written words about divinity. According to St. Thomas Aquinas,[3] Eve infected the entire human race with Original Sin. Eve, who was at one time associated with life, was deemed responsible for the death of every human. The same religious pattern was seen in other highly masculinized cultures. Pandora became the pagan stand-in for Eve. She released evil into the world, and having done so, was punished—her punishment being that her husband and father must dominate her. Hera, Athena, and Aphrodite, in their newly forged male-based myths and personas, are portrayed as motherless, having entered the world through a male head or genitals. As we progressed through history, the Greeks revered both bisexuality and homosexuality, and in both cases, the woman was rendered secondary. In Mecca, Arabs embraced an imageless, monotheistic god who was known only through the written word. Under this religion based on words, women were forbidden to even say the words.

Moses was the first wordsmith, who forged not only the concept of one male God, but also the denigration of the feminine. Prior to the Old Testament, women were not prevented from conducting significant sacraments. The first religion based on a book, and all subsequent Western literate religions, however, banned women from officiating over religious ceremonies. The first commandment, "I am the Lord thy God. Thou shall have no other gods before me," announces the disappearance of the goddess and ushers in a change in thinking. This radical sentence, states Schlain, served to be a death knell for the feminine.

The second commandment forbids any images or likenesses—especially those that were nature-related. Not surprisingly, images are associated with the more feminine right brain. Words are the written way to the powerful Father, and a left-brain ban was imposed on right-brain images. The masculine deity created life without any female participation, thoroughly distorting the lens of life. Often it was the act of killing that made the male transcendent. In the Christian story, Mary, the mother of Christ, could only watch helplessly while her son died, and only the father could resurrect his son. The male God now creates new life with word or breath. The female's literal birth act of bringing forth new life becomes denigrated and dirty while the male sperm becomes the primary and active principle. The female was merely the passive vessel that received this great gift. Women were blamed for infertility, and men got the credit for fertility. Original Sin became the cornerstone of Christianity and the grace of God was required to free one from sin. Faith in the words, not virtue or actions, began to be viewed as the way to heaven.

When a culture elevates the written word over relationship with others, patriarchy dominates, writes Shlain. And thus, it comes as no surprise that the printing press helped tilt the balance toward the masculine. Religious wars occurred only in those lands that had printing presses—and the more the literacy, the crueler the war, he writes. Witch hunts, which were women hunts, began in the 15th century. The church-commissioned guide to uncovering the witches was named the *Malleus Maleficarum*—The Hammer of Witches.[4] "All witchcraft comes from carnal lust, which is in women insatiable." Women, with their weaker morals, were sure prey for the devil. This sickness infected the church for hundreds of years as the influence of the printing press grew, and it is estimated that 100,000 to 9 million women were tortured and burned. The witch craze opened the vents for unprecedented misogyny. Rapes increased and rape trials decreased. For the first and only time in history, there were more women than men in jails.

The monastic order also created a strong dichotomy between sexuality and the word. Young men were encouraged to turn their eyes from women and focus on words. Their passion was directed toward knowledge, and the celibate life was considered a far more honorable life than marriage. Monks declared celibacy and read and prayed in silence. Women, of course, were available to clean for them, and not surprisingly, these cleaning ladies frequently gave birth to children who had no support, just as they had no rights. In China, foot-binding of young girls followed shortly after the introduction of the printing press. Ironically, the same linen used for printing was used to bind the feet.

Mary, a compilation of former goddesses, was cast as a virgin—setting her apart from sex and procreation. In fact, many suggest that introducing Mary and a feminine presence into the church structure was the very thing that gave rise to the concept of the devil. The devil was a male but also had many features formerly associated with the Goddess.

The last five hundred years have seen an increase in both reading and violence. Not surprisingly, literacy was literally withheld from women. Men began to shape society and exercise more control in the public sector as it developed, giving them even more power. Once the masculine perspective was woven into the language, it became part of the knowledge base that further solidified male power and the imbalance.

Many experts also have different perspectives to explain this inequality. Wilber, for example, says that men did not create the double standard of men being stronger and women needing to be cared for and protected while they are caring for the children, nature did. He states that testosterone has two and only two functions. It makes men want to "f*** it or kill it," therefore men dominate simply because they can.[5]

In *Why Men Rule*, Steven Goldberg[6] states that men have 10 times more testosterone than women do, which not only makes them stronger, it also makes them more aggressive and assertive. It makes them want to dominate and be heroic. Goldberg studied every possible factor that has put men in the alpha position. He finds that the truth of why men rule lies in the interplay between human behavior and the nature of society. Societies are set up hierarchically. Every society, no matter where it is or what it values, will nevertheless value some things more than others. According to Goldberg, hierarchy is integral to the nature of society. In fact, he says, show me a culture without a hierarchy and my hypotheses will have to be changed.

Testosterone is part of the neuroendocrinological system of males, which serves to make them "more strongly motivated to exhibit whatever behavior is necessary to achieve position, status or dominance." He predicts "that in every society it will be males who, far more strongly and more often than females, exhibit whatever behavior—fighting, kissing babies for votes, or whatever is necessary for hierarchical attainment." Again, it appears that even the nature of a society is influenced by males.

Nature created males and females differently. Nature may even be responsible for creating societies that are structured hierarchically and for providing testosterone that seeks dominance and status in that society. For many reasons, a double standard has been created in our world culture that values the masculine qualities more than the feminine. Nowhere in nature is such an imbalance present.

Sex, Gender, and Equality

The issues of sex, gender, and equality are varied, interwoven, and extremely complex. First of all, there is often confusion between sex and gender. Sex typically refers only to the physiology of male and female, while gender refers to the cultural roles of men and women. Added to the confusion is that there are also masculine and feminine qualities associated with male and female sexes and their gender roles.

Every culture proscribes gender roles for men and women that are fixed or malleable depending on the culture, and to some extent, gender roles reflect differences in sex. For example, males are typically taller, larger, and have more upper body strength than females. For this reason, heavy labor is more often done by males. While some females are capable of doing work that requires much strength, for years feminists have pointed out that it was only stereotyping that kept women away from such jobs. Further, because the feminine qualities have been so denigrated, males often shunned various roles and qualities simply because they were associated with the female. Males, for example, may be very capable of being loving and devoted parents. Because this role has been associated with females, however, many males have, until recently, refused to embrace such roles for no reason other than that they were associated with women.

The sex role over time nevertheless has become equated with the gender role, which in many cases was correct in literally reflecting sexual differences. There has, however, always been a continuum of exceptions, and for this reason, almost everything said about sex differences is a generalization to some extent. Even more generalizations are apparent when it comes to gender differences. Generalizations are always problematic because there are always exceptions. Generalizations, however, can also be extremely helpful when trying to determine the average or normal of anything that can be measured. Without generalization, we would not know the average height, weight, or intelligence of a man, woman, or child, for example, and would have no way to determine potential exceptions or problems. The understanding that there will always be exceptions to any generalization is implicit.

Feminism was wise to point out these generalizations and how limiting gender roles are for both sexes. The result is that today both males and females are far freer to explore interests and occupations that have typically been reserved for the other sex. In truth, it has been far easier for females to move into spheres once considered masculine than it has been for males to move into the feminine world. Feminism opened the door to a world that had long been closed to women. The halls of academia, once denied to them, were stormed by bright young females eager to level the playing field.

Feminism acted to correct gender stereotypes that held women back. In doing so, gender roles were often generalized to include sex roles and qualities. With the focus on difference gone, women could, hypothetically, do anything that men could do. Females were considered to be just like males, and in the eyes of many feminists, there simply was no difference—not only between men and women, but also between males and females. This premise, while helpful in so many ways, is also problematic.

Nature Makes Males and Females Different

First, according to the feminist hypothesis, women are just like men. While this may be true in relation to gender roles, it will never be true on the physiological level of sex. Males and females are different, and this difference is essential and represents the primary condition for life to develop. Without this difference, there would be no new life. It's that basic. Further, our sexual orientation is the primary way in which we know ourselves. With rare exceptions, males are not females and females are not males. Sex is the biological given. We are born into the world as either males or females.

It is not just that males and females have different external genitalia; there are hormonal and structural differences as well. Males produce sperm and females produce eggs. The differences are biological and exist regardless of culture. While our definitions of ourselves as men or women may change, our maleness or femaleness is a given.

The human organism is hardwired with certain major sexual differences, and this difference forces us to contemplate the logical implications of how and why we evolved in certain ways.

For example, the male produces millions of sperm per month; a female produces one ovum. The egg to sperm ratio—one egg a month to 3.6 billion sperm a month—may account for evolutionarily acquired behavior, rather than cultural influences. The sex act may or may not be important to the male, it is a far more precious and important event to the woman because it is the female who will carry and primarily care for any resulting child. This means to the woman that the sex act has the possibility of changing her life forever. Both sexes appear to have a subconscious awareness of these differences that were hardwired long before we were born.

According to Dr. Louann Brizendine, in her book, *The Female Brain*,[7] sex differences start in the womb. Interestingly, all embryos begin as female. At eight weeks, small testicles begin to put out testosterone that literally marinates the brain of an embryo destined to become a male. The result is that the sexual pursuit area of the brain in a male is twice as large as that of a female. This is one reason that makes mature males naturally more sexual and aggressive.

Further, males and females have different hormones that figure largely in shaping one's behavior. Psychiatrists today believe that hormones affect about 50 percent of behavior and that we must take hormonal aspects into account because they have such a major impact on mental health. Brizendine states that the more we learn, the more we realize the impact of the sex differences. It is hormones that cause males to think more about sex and act more aggressively.

"We are, despite our modern advances and sophistication, animals whose genes and hormones continue to drive our behavior at the most basic levels," states Bridget Law.[8]

Men's hormones and mating behavior respond to women's cues. Both men and women, however, have little conscious awareness of how much they are influenced by hormones that affect their behavior. It used to be said that women were more attracted to hypermasculine men when they were ovulating. Today, we know that this effect is negated if women take birth control—and most women today take birth control. This reason alone may be responsible for the fact that very few women today are attracted to the hypersexed male.

Males are cued into female hormones and get more possessive and loving when women are ovulating, most likely to stave off competition. Smell is powerful. Testosterone levels drop when males enter committed relationships and have children. It is almost as if nature attempts to ensure the protection of the next generation in this way. In fact, the most effective way to reduce testosterone—short of castration—is for a man to have a child. The male sexual predator who abuses his own child or the male who kills the mother of his unborn child must apparently have such high levels of testosterone that they can be driven to override the strong social taboo of incest and millions of years of evolution. High levels of testosterone can be so powerful that it can reduce men to the most primitive animal states. The fact that sex and aggression are closely linked in the male brain as well as an overabundance of testosterone appear to be among the main reasons for sexual abuse.

The hormones in a woman's tears alone can produce a drop in testosterone. The hormones associated with her menstrual cycle appear to drive sexual attraction more than we have realized. Despite our advancements, we are animals whose genes and hormones drive our behavior at the most basic levels.

Females are far more articulate at a young age and are wired to seek social harmony. Females, who are shaped by estrogen, are more attuned to and interested in the nuances of emotion and have a greater ability to remember emotional detail. Young girls have a wider range of feelings and are more interested than boys in looking at faces and using terms of endearment. Girls talk more about people while boys talk more about things. Females value communication and relationships, and are more intuitive, creative, and integrative. These findings have recently been confirmed by newer research, which reveals that women literally store their memories in a part of their brain that synthesizes emotion as well as the actual facts, while males store their memories in a part of their brains that is separate from emotion.

Nature Influences Nurture

To further compound the issue, biological differences are often naturally translated into cultural differences. Male genitals are external; female genitals are internal. It appears that physiology alone has much to do with psychology. External genitalia, says Wilber,[9] serves to make men more externally oriented. Nothing really enters his body and there is no invasive threat involved. His territory has an external component to it. A man can leave—it's all external to him. The woman, on the other hand, has to let another being actually enter her very body—her territory—which serves to make her orientation more internal.

Some theorists believe that men, who are far more sexual than women, began to resent that they could not have sex whenever they wanted. In the wilds, men could have their way any time, with any female they wanted, and some theorists hypothesize that men are still genetically wired to seek that kind of free access. As any number of sitcoms today reveal, many men still resent that they have to enter into a cooperative agreement before they can do the very thing they are thinking about all the time. They resent having to play such games with women. But while he wants to play for 10 (or maybe only 2) minutes, she was aware, especially prior to birth control, that she may be playing for keeps.

Even if a female actually *wanted* to have large amounts of sex, experts argue, she had to learn that she must restrain herself. Early on, women who understood the connection between sex and pregnancy also had to learn to say no because of the risks to both mother and child during pregnancy and childbirth. As human beings evolved over the past 40,000 years, their intelligence increased dramatically. The brain literally developed and the human head grew to accommodate the growing brain, which in turn made birth far more difficult. Balance again stepped into the evolution story as nature gradually, over many generations, increased the pelvis size of women to accommodate the larger head. Human females, however, still have the most difficult time of any species giving birth and almost always require assistance, which may have provided an impetus for humankind's evolution as an even more social animal.

The Impact of Nurture

Sex, gender, and the masculine and feminine qualities have been viewed through different lenses at different times. How we know what we know about these three concepts appears, at any given time, to swing between the two poles of nature and nurture. Within most of our lifetimes, there was a shift in the 1970s and 1980s toward the nurture hypothesis that almost negated any influence of nature. Much of the confusion appears to have come from a landmark study that influenced our thinking on gender for decades. If the long-suffering subject of the study hadn't killed him (or her) self and turned the current beliefs about the strong influence of nurture upside down, we might still be thinking that our sex is as changeable as our clothes.

Can a Boy Become a Girl?

When twin boys, born in the 1970s, were circumcised and the penis of one of the boys was severely damaged severely, doctors had a simple solution: the penis should be removed and the child should simply be raised as a girl. Given the thinking prevalent at the time, this was considered to be the best and most viable option. Since, at the time, the experts believed that gender identity was as easily moldable as the physical sex attributes, the simplistic solution was that the child would have the surgery and take hormones at a later time. The child was expected to adjust well to being a girl. Ironically, and based mostly on the *assumption* that the child was doing well, the doctor did little follow-up on the child's progress after puberty.

The procedure was reported to be a glowing success. The results were pop-ularized, reported in every media, and people came to believe that the dif-ferences between males and females were for the most part conditioned by nurture and how the child was raised. Years later, psychologists discovered that the boy had never adjusted to being a girl. He had, in fact, fought it at every step, was miserably unhappy not really knowing who he was, and at-tempted suicide. After several attempts, the subject, who later became well known through television and a book about his life, finally succeeded in ending his life in 2006.[10]

This case, however, had already strongly colored what we thought about sex and gender. For years, we believed that sex and gender could be easily changed. This position worked well for feminism and enabled us to con-tinue to think that the actual sex of a person really didn't matter. The theory was that the way children were raised and the gender roles they learned would take over. Countless well-meaning parents, during this time, bought gender-neutral toys for their children, only to feel that they had somehow failed because their daughters still turned teddy bears into dolls and their sons fashioned their Legos into guns and shot teddy.

Only recently have we begun to really look back and question every-thing about this study that so erroneously shaped our thinking along these lines. We learned years later that many professionals in the field, even at the time, questioned the findings of the doctor. The doctor, how-ever, refused to publish any definitive results. In hindsight, his colleagues now realize that he lied about how the subject was really adjusting. As a "girl," the subject urinated standing up and refused to wear the dresses his mother was advised to force on him. The boy raised as a girl never adjusted, and his death provided strong evidence that the pure nurture hypothesis doesn't work.

The Bottom Lines of Today

For many reasons, sex and gender, and the interactions between the two, as well as the shifts between nature and nurture that color our understanding of males and females and men and women at any given time, are still con-fusing. Two major and interrelated factors appear to be impacting us today.

The first is the politically correct atmosphere that was born out of de-construction, feminism, and the recent importance of the nurture hypoth-esis. We are living at a time when any discussion around difference is still considered taboo to some extent. The nurture hypothesis, however, was strongly embraced and confirmed by a feminism that had so much to gain by reducing the impact of sex differences.

Feminism, in its attempt to convince us that no real differences existed between men and women, was forced into a corner, however, where they could not really articulate anything about women's strengths in particular because according to their hypothesis, women were just like men. Nor could they reconstruct what they deconstructed. This meant that the old male standards that deemed women as less perfect than men remained intact and unchallenged. If women were like men then the standards for women were the same as the male standards. This failure to acknowledge difference escalated to such an extent that women themselves embraced a virulent attack on the feminine qualities, just as men had done for thousands of years. Even worse, these staunch positions often served to turn woman against woman.

The great opposition to the concept of difference is just one indication of how far we still have to go toward equality. Many males still refuse to consider women as equals, and the idea that the concept of difference might actually reveal females' strengths and superiority is completely unthinkable to them. The concept of difference appears to imply to both sexes that females are still of a somewhat lesser status.

The differences between the sexes is a given that we seemed to have almost forgotten in our politically correct world. On the surface, we are all collectively ignoring any implications of difference. Our research, however, especially neurological and physiologically-based findings, has continued, and new differences between the sexes are being discovered daily. We rarely fully comprehend the impact of these differences, however, because the findings are always very carefully couched in politically correct ways that make the differences appear equally different.

The other factor, intertwined with the desire to avoid any real talk about difference, is the strong influence of the male-based stories that have remained unchanged. Though the world has changed dramatically in the last 2,000 years, the stories have not, and they continue to influence the issues of sex, gender, and difference. In fact, as we shall see, it is the very difference between males and females that continue to keep them so firmly in place.

The Deep Implications of Difference

The stories begin with the beginning of consciousness. Humans are the only species that has evolved its consciousness to the extent that it came to comprehend that one's life will ultimately end. Once humans began to know that death was inevitable, they had to find ways to make sense of this most primary of all facts.

Grasping that each of us will one day cease to exist, according to many experts, seemed to impact men far more than it did women. Females have always lived their lives with a sense of immanence and harmony of purpose, they are more connected to nature, and they give birth and seem naturally to know what their purpose is. Men, on the other hand, until very recently have lived very peripherally to that which is most meaningful in life. They don't give birth and historically were disconnected from the time of insemination to the actual birth nine months later—if at all.

Just as women had long ago intuited the connection between sex and birth, surely the smartest men, at some point, figured out what women had known for years—there was a connection between the sex act, pregnancy, and new life. Prior to that, males had probably not realized that sex had something to do with pregnancy and, thanks to an innate and hardwired wham-bam mentality, failed to intuit that there was a one-to-one connection of an individual man and a single sex act to a single individual child. Women were forced to make this connection—for them pregnancy often meant death and for much of history, childbirth was the leading cause of death for women.

When the connection between the sex act and paternity finally became clear to men, it brought with it the promise of a kind of immortality: he may die, but his—his very own—children would continue to live, and in this way a part of him would go on. Knowledge of fatherhood gave men a new purpose and a meaning to sex beyond just another gratification.

With this new understanding came the necessity for men to keep track of the women they slept with, and further, to try to get the rest of the men to do the same. Long before DNA testing, men must have realized that they all had to cooperate if this system of immortality via offspring was to work. Most importantly, he had to ensure that the woman with whom he had sex did not have sex with other men. It was the only way for each man to know that his children were actually his. He came to realize, too, that he had to keep track of his own offspring, and in doing so, humans became the first species in which males manifested a strong desire to care for and love their own children. He invented monogamy when he realized that he had to care for, provide for, and often control the mother of his child.

This restructuring of society and the tendency for males to regard their females as possessions initially appeared to work to the genetic advantage of both males and females. A female had greater assurance that one male would provide for her while she was pregnant, birthing, and nursing. This protection greatly increased the chances that she and her child would survive, because if he knew the child was his, he would be far more inclined to stay around to help protect and raise the child. For each man, it was the only way to ensure that his own children would benefit by his care and be the recipients of his advantages and possessions when he died. He couldn't take it with him, but he could leave it to his surviving offspring.

These three factors—birth, death, and paternity—are all closely related to sex and have been a primary shaping factor in every culture. According to Leonard Shlain, men had to learn new interpersonal and social skills when they asked themselves nearly every two minutes, "What do I have to do to get her to have sex with me?" For the first time, suggests Shlain, human females needed a way to tell if a man would be a good partner. They could no longer just go by physical looks. Females realized that the most advantageous couplings were those that were more than just another one night stand. He might have to be around for a long time. Females had to be able to tell if he had good character. And, this came about through being able to communicate. Similarly, for the first time, men needed a good way to convince the female to have sex with him. According to Shlain, language probably evolved so that males and females could negotiate sex and convey intentions. Given that males, because of their greater strength, could simply have had their way with women whenever they liked, Shlain's hypothesis is not only kind, but also suggests why some males, probably the less virile ones, chose to develop some social skills.[11]

Along with understanding the connection between sex and his immortality, at least through his genes and future children, the male also began to comprehend that his mate might be the only one who could guarantee his lineage. His resentment probably deepened when he understood that he had to play according to her rules. And this initial balance, struck over generations, was lost little by little by women. Other factors also became associated with sex and gender. Females know when they become women. But knowing when a boy becomes a man is a problem because men have no significant marker in time. There was more of a need, therefore, to define just when a boy actually became a man. Men created rituals to help the young males, while the young girls' place of importance was secure. Further, men could not deny that their very existence was dependent on a female—that, were it not for a female, they would not be alive.

Now we come full circle with the need for the male story. Because men do not give birth, he had to invent stories that placed him in the primary role. Because of the testosterone-fueled need to be in control and on top, he not only had to create stories of his greatness, he had to ensure that her status was diminished. His need for the central role was encoded in language and knowledge was skewed to reflect this limited perspective.

The world, however, has changed. We are no longer natural, but are, in fact, by definition the most domesticated species on earth; we don't live in the wilds where protection is primary, and very few of us would want to. Women can protect themselves for the most part, and if protection is needed at all today, it is usually protection from males.

Everything has changed and one would think that the stories would have changed with the times. The stories, however, have a built-in agenda to ensure that the status quo remains intact. Historically those who ventured to promote stories with opposing views were often silenced or killed. The stories, however, do not reflect real life, and for this reason, they make all males and all females a little bit crazy. The only way to fix the problem, however, is to identify the real and correct bottom lines. If we start with a premise that is incorrect or limited, such as the male is more perfect, the solution will similarly be incorrect and limited.

And, just when Goldberg has convinced us that male domination is inevitable because of the nature of testosterone and society, he also chooses to explore even deeper epistemological bottom lines. He writes at the end of his book that happiness, an ultimate for both males and females, is not dependent only on high societal status. Emotions, which are the correlates of our neurophysiology, are what actually motivate our actions and prescribe the limits of our sexual and social roles as well as our happiness. In this realm, says Goldberg, "The central role will forever belong to women; they set the rhythm of things. Nature has bestowed on women the biological abilities and the psycho-physiological propensities that enable the species to sustain itself. Men must forever stand at the periphery, questing after the surrogate powers, creativity and meaning that nature has seen fit to make innate functions of *their* (women's) physiology. . . . At the bottom line of it all, man's job is to protect women, and woman's job is to protect her infant; in nature all else is luxury."[12]

His words have a ring of truth that cuts through all the imbalanced stories and politically correct confusion and registers on the soul level as a place to begin to shape a more authentic story that better reflects real life.

But how to begin when women both know and do not know that this is true?

Chapter 4

Women Know and Do Not Know

Yin	Yang
Cooperation	Control
Peace	Aggression
Know and do not know	Think they know
Waking up	
Unlearning	
Waiting	

Women today have been placed in the strange and uncomfortable position where they both know and do not know who they really are. They certainly don't recognize themselves as the center of life despite the fact that they are. How could they know themselves as the true females they are when the very essence of the feminine has been absent, denigrated, and distorted, first by men, more recently by women in an attempt to fit into the male world, and finally by today's culture that deems it incorrect to talk about difference? We women truly have very little concept of how remarkable we are.

It has often been said that women feel guilty, and most probably this guilt is based, for countless centuries and countless reasons, on the absence of any correct information. Women, today, however, have changed faster than the culture and there is still little or no support for this new reality. Guilt is the result of women having been put in the classic double-bind between two mutually exclusive demands. She lives in society and her relationship to the world is critical for her to accurately assess her place in this world. The world, however, reflects incorrect information and mixed messages about who she really is. She also lives in a world that she knows is male-based and certainly doesn't want to be angry at men in general. She has grown and changed while being confronted with conflicting information and at the same time has little power to change the status quo.

Countless women have awakened today. While this is currently happening everywhere in the world it is especially true in relationships. Like bulbs that have remained dormant for too long, something almost like an evolutionary imperative has caused them to push through the hard soil that has kept them contained and controlled for so long and start to grow. This new growth may have come as a small still voice or a sensing that there could be more to life. It may have been the result of the women's movement or it just may be that now is the time. And, like the early spring plant that must grow, it often found its environment to be cold and uninviting.

In many ways, realized, when I thought back to those earlier times that I, too, had tried not to grow. I didn't want my life to change. It was the 1970s, we had three young children and were settling in to suburban life. I had been happy, or thought I was, until the evening when the mixer talked to me, and after realizing that my brilliant idea of a small lobotomy wouldn't work, I had just tried to stop the new thoughts and questions. I really tried, but, as I look back, I realize that the strength of this new call could not be denied. I thought about the confusing issue that presented itself to me from every angle. Was it me? Was it him? Was I wrong to think it? Could I trust my thoughts? Endless thoughts. . . . and, apparently these new thoughts were germinating on an unconscious level also because I would wake up thinking about them.

Finally, this push toward growth was on my mind so much, that like the plant that finally pushes through the soil, it started making its way out of my mouth with Dave. One day, I just said, out of the blue and in no context whatsoever, "I'm smarter than you." I had practiced saying it so many times in my head that I was as surprised as he was when I actually said it out loud. He just laughed and said, "That's right, Sherry. You're really smart." Once I'd announced to Dave that I was smarter than he was, I couldn't seem to stop saying it. The words just came unbidden out of my mouth. And after months of hearing me say those four words, Dave finally confronted me, "What are you trying to do here, Sherry?"

"I don't know," I said, "I just think that I, and a lot of other women, know a lot of things that men don't know." I had started to pay attention and appreciate my own inner voice.

"OK, so what's your point?" Dave replied.

I wasn't sure what my point was. This was all new to me. It was more of a feeling rather than something I could articulate. Looking back now, I realize that in that "still small voice," I was experiencing an awakening similar to what Mary Belenky refers to in *Women's Ways of Knowing*.[1] While I could not express myself fully with words, I was *feeling* something. I was feeling the need for something *more*, and this wanting more was confusing.

I certainly did not want a divorce, which at the time was the only other option. I wanted more, but I didn't want a divorce and I didn't know what was in between those two options. I knew the only other solution was for me to change, but I felt I already had changed and accommodated and tried to understand. As I started to get clearer on what I needed, I realized I wanted more from him.

Apparently, this new solution came from my unconscious because I started waking up with the idea that Dave had to change and was filled with guilt. *Shit,* I would think every morning when I woke up thinking that he had to change. *Something must be wrong with me. I am one of those women we read about in psychology books that has some kind of female syndrome.*

I used to love the first thoughts that appeared in my mind as I was waking up. I had come to trust these thoughts to the point that I felt I could synthesize a problem while I slept and wake up with the answer. Sometimes, I would open my eyes in the morning just knowing something new that enhanced my life. Now, however, my first thoughts every morning were that my husband had to change. Having learned to trust myself and my thoughts and intentions, I was disgusted to realize that I could even think such thoughts. It was bad enough that I was no longer blissfully happy. It seemed like a new moral low, however, to blame it on Dave. I was further disgusted with myself when I realized that my new thoughts also flew in the face of the grand maxim of the very psychology I had studied and learned—"You can only change yourself, not the other person."

I was certain that people were going to discover that I had numerous disorders listed in the *Diagnostic and Statistical Manual.*[2] I tried harder to keep these new thoughts to myself, but almost every morning, the first four words in my head were, "He has to change."

I tried to talk with my friends, inquiring carefully if they ever felt they wanted more from their husbands. Typically, I was met with confused stares. I didn't realize back then that I was ahead of the curve, and relationships were the one area where women still weren't honest with each other. If problems existed in a relationship, we didn't know about it until after the fact. Consequently, back then, none of us were really free to express our concern or even support. I remember being shocked when one woman, who lived in our neighborhood and sometimes carpooled to nursery school with me, was suddenly gone from our small community. I heard weeks later that she had endured being physically abused for years by her husband, a man who was a faculty member like Dave. She fled with her children while her husband was at work.

I thought about these situations, involving men, women, and relationships all the time. Finally, I talked to my new friend, Lynn, a wise woman who was older than my own mother and always seemed able to understand. I started slowly, "I know you like me and you have helped me so much—to trust myself as a woman and mother and wife in just the few short months that we have really started talking." I hesitated before continuing. "But I have to tell you that you don't know the real me. Something is wrong with me," I confessed. "I wake up with the same ugly thought every day—that Dave needs to change. I think I have a syndrome or something. I know that in psychology it is true that you can only change yourself, not the other person. It is like the queen mother of maxims, the bottom line truth in psychology. There's probably an entry in the DSM III that describes me, like the 'Can Never Be Pleased Syndrome' or 'Bitchy Wife Psychological Deficit Disorder.' There is something wrong with me! I hate that I think these things. But, what I hate even more is that I can no longer trust my inner guidance that you helped me develop. I really hate that," I said miserably. She let me talk and mostly just listened.

After weeks of listening to me complain about how messed up I was, she finally responded. "It's not wrong," Lynn said, gently. "Yes, it is!" I replied, a little too loud, my emotions catching in my throat. "You're just saying that because for some reason, you really care about me. But these thoughts can't possibly be right. No one should think things like this. Something is wrong with me," I responded more quietly, trying to regain control.

"It's not wrong," she said again quietly. I rolled my eyes. She did not seem to be hearing me.

"OK. Then tell me why it's not wrong," I said, again, a little too sharply.

"Because, my dear Sherry, you don't want him to change for you, you want him to change for *himself*," she replied simply. I blinked. I took a deep breath and blinked again as I let her words settle inside me.

"You don't want it for yourself, you want it for him"—those words flowed over my mind like soothing, warm, honey-colored light, and I *knew*, at the level of my soul that she was right. I started sobbing as the truth of her words washed over me and my soul responded to the feeling of 'rightness' in her words. They penetrated my heart and lodged there, in the way an authentic truth does when you hear it spoken. I cried, too, because I knew in my heart that I really wasn't some cold bitch who could not be pleased. I cried because I recognized at that moment that some deep source of knowing had been trying and trying to get me to listen to what it wanted to tell me. With Lynn's help, I finally had. And I cried because, perhaps most importantly, I knew, in a stronger and renewed way, that I could trust my most precious way of knowing, my inner guidance.

I am sure that my journey is similar to the path of millions of other women today who have awakened or tried to wake up to the call of their inner knowing. There was no physical abuse in my relationship with Dave. There really was no emotional abuse either. I just wanted more. A thousand times I argued these issues with myself. I told myself again and again that my life was good enough. I had already changed myself to accommodate him as much as I possibly could. I had asked myself too many times why I had to want more and why could I not just be content?

I knew on some deep level in accepting Lynne's wisdom to trust my inner guidance and not blame myself, that I was letting go of an old belief system that has kept women away from their truest knowing for too long. It was both uncomfortable and freeing at the same time. I felt like I was taking off tight hats that had been on the heads of all women for millennia. Like a dormant plant, I had tried to cling to the safety of sameness and security as long as I could. It's uncomfortable to be the person who thinks outside the box or is the early bloomer. I didn't know back then that each of us hears a call that beckons us to follow. I wouldn't learn about this spiritual roadmap until years later. I did not have a framework large enough to contain my thoughts and never even realized that I was at the beginning of a journey.

As the result of my newfound trust, I started asserting myself more. At first, he didn't like it at all and shut me out even more. I learned to wait— and wait. I also began to sense, as time went by, that I was on the right track with my ideas. Everything I was learning and experiencing, over the next months and years, seemed to confirm what I was thinking. I sensed intuitively that the problem between Dave and me was much larger than the two of us. It almost seemed universal. I started to become aware that many women seemed to want the same thing I did—*more* from her partner. My reading started to confirm the same thing—women wanted more and men really didn't know what to do about it. It was the 1970s, the women's movement was in full force and divorces were on the rise.

As the years went by, many of the couples I knew seemed to be frustrated. Women had started talking about their problems more openly. I sensed that Dave and the other men I talked with needed to be more in touch with themselves. I checked in with my own sense of self constantly because I knew I was walking a thin line. If I had felt that what I was asking for was in any way selfish, I never could have maintained the hypothesis that I was developing. All the soul searching enabled me to trust my intentions even more. I felt, at the same time, that I was getting a clearer picture of who males and females *really* were. I was also learning things about myself as a female that I had never before been aware of. I felt that I was pushing on the boundaries of what women have always known on some level, and also did not know. It just felt right.

I began to sense in my relationship with Dave that I had to take a firmer stand and draw some lines. I not only had to mean it, I had to know consciously what I was doing. He had to know it consciously, too. I also realized, since there was no guarantee that things were going to work out, that I had to be sure of what I was doing. I knew that if I pushed things too far or too fast, he could very easily say "Screw you, Sherry. I'm not going to take this crap anymore." I recognized that I had to be prepared for that option, and for that reason, I had to know in the depths of myself that I could go on with him or without him. I knew I had to be able to follow through. In other words, I knew that I had to be prepared to leave.

A kind of problem-solving seemed to enter my mind and replace my emotions. I just knew somehow that if I stayed in the same emotional place, things would stay the same. I knew I had to become almost an observer and figure out what needed to be done. I started to think of our relationship as being at different places along a continuum. For example, if I felt that our relationship hadn't really improved, then we were at step A—which was that I wanted him to spend more time with the children. Since he didn't regularly do this, his greater involvement with the children would be new— like step B. So I would wait until a good time when we could talk without the children hearing us and I would bring it up—carefully and gently. The last thing I wanted was to nag him. I also didn't want to have to bring it up again and again. I wanted him to do something about it that represented a new and solid change that became part of him.

So, when talking to him, I drew a line. I talked in a firmer voice and told him that I didn't want to keep bugging him about this anymore. I wanted him to either start spending more quality time with the children or tell me why he wouldn't. I told him that I wanted to disengage from that place where I bring it up and he reluctantly does it once or twice, only to return to his old behaviors a week later. I wanted him to know exactly why I was doing what I was doing. In the past, I knew that a part of him was just waiting for me to return to my old self and for things to return to normal. I also knew that wasn't going to happen. Finally, he, too, began to realize that we had entered a whole new place.

The whole process began unfolding in ways that even I could not have anticipated, and I was surprised how much the process taught me. I not only felt stronger, I began trusting the process that was unfolding within me implicitly.

It seemed to work. He was actually starting to be more involved with the children. I loved it; they loved it. I tried to get him to talk about the fact that surely he enjoyed it too, and he would agree. I would think, "Ahh, finally, I think everything is going to be OK." Initially, I naively thought that if he would just make that one change, things would be good. He had moved to B and we both moved to a new, more contented place.

I would wake up weeks later, however, sensing C! This shocked me and really made me question what I was trying to do. Was I just a witch who continually kept finding fault with him, or was this another tight hat and I should trust this new insight as one more step in a process that was unfolding in me? In this case, C might be something like helping more around the house. In truth, the steps will always be relative to your own perceived unique situations. He was actually pretty good with doing what I asked. Unlike other husbands I knew, who saw anything related to the house as her job, he did do what I asked. Even my friends were like, "Geez, Sherry. You really are a bitch. Dave does more than our husbands." Step C, however, had started to include why I had to bring it up in the first place. Even though I thanked him and let him know that I appreciated what he did, I still couldn't help wondering why hadn't he thought of it on his own.

And before I knew it, I would wake up wanting D (Geez, how many damn hats were there?!), which was wondering why I had to thank him for things that he should be doing anyway. What needed doing was so obvious. Instead of just doing it myself, or asking and then thanking him when he helped me, I started wondering why he just wasn't more "present" and could just sense what needed to be done—and then just do it. I wanted everything to stop being my job and I wanted his intentions to be more involved.

The new line drawn in the sand with D seemed to have even more heft to it. It seemed to require more discussion because I was now asking for something more global and required him to think of things on his own. I was aware that this was pushing it. I often looked at my own behavior and concluded, on my own, that I was being a royal bitch. I think many women get to this point and decide to drop the whole thing. It just gets too uncomfortable for both of them to move into deeper issues.

I was having to stretch to find the courage to say things that I would never have said before. I had no practice and no role models. I had to trust my soul that what I was doing was the right thing for both of us. I kept Lynn's words, that "I didn't want it for myself, I wanted it for him," very much in my mind. I would suggest D and wait. Every once in a while, I would be delighted to discover that he had indeed done something on his own initiative. Ah, peace. Now I could relax.

On the morning I would wake up with E, even I would get pissed off at myself. "Damn," I thought. "Does this never end?" I could picture our life, if we even stayed together, as being endless rounds of me seeing something that he didn't see and getting mad at him for not seeing it and feeling I had to tell him and him getting mad. On the other hand, it did seem, as I looked back at all the changes he had made, that my promptings were ultimately correct and had needed to be said. And further, I felt that I was almost researching myself as the subject and watching an unfolding process in which new thoughts just seemed to come unbidden. I wondered if this process would have a stopping point or if I would just keep going into untamed madness. I wondered if my mind's process was an example of a collective female process and if I was taking the process further than most women because of Lynn's affirmation. I paid careful attention to how I felt stronger and expanded as a female with each step, as well as how my sense of love for Dave seemed to deepen and change. I continued to follow the internal promptings, which led me to a place of deep appreciation of feminine wisdom. Dave, too, came to respect this process, as you shall see.

Countless women have awakened over the past 40 years or more years. Most of them, however, were not lucky enough to have a wise mentor, like Lynn, to confirm their process like I did, and often sought divorce as their only option. Regardless of whether they stayed or left, women during those years did indeed wake up, typically in the absence of any real support.

Books that were popular for women at the time inadvertently confused us. They seemed to be based on a premise that now that we women had liberated ourselves, we were ready for the cold hard facts of how we better shape up. *Women Who Love Too Much*,[3] *Ten Stupid Things Women Do to Mess Up Their Lives*,[4] and *Smart Women, Foolish Choices*,[5] all seemed to be berating women who, now on the other side of the women's movement, should know better. The premature assumption seemed to be that as a result of the women's movement, all women had immediately acquired instant self-esteem. Even Gloria Steinem finally recognized this problem years later, and in 1992 wrote *Revolution from Within*,[6] because she "continued to encounter women with too little self-esteem to take advantage of the hard won, if still incomplete opportunities" that the women's movement had provided. Even today, one female author's response to women in the Huffington Post essay, *Why You're Not Married*,[7] is that they are shallow, bitchy, selfish sluts who lie.

Other books that tried to address the equality issue often confused both men and women even more in their failure to address the real bottom lines of the issue. In *A Fire in the Belly*,[8] Sam Keen's bottom line was that we should blame the still-present inequality on culture—hardly a solution when many of us were well aware by that time that males had created the culture. Ken Wilber said we should blame Nature for the double standard.[9] Addressing the feminist critique that males imposed patriarchy on females, he said that it was Nature's fault, not men's, that women gave birth and needed to be protected and that males had millions of sperm that needed to be spread around.

The 40 years since feminism began have been a time of both real and superficial social changes. The real reason why women in the 1990s, and even today, still have so little self-esteem is because the bottom lines of how we know what we know about women really never changed. As Steinem said, self-esteem must start at the core of one's being. Ironically, even if a woman has great sense of self-esteem, it is rarely reflected back to her from her partner, workplace, or culture.

At New Choices, I tried to become for the women what Lynnie had been for me. I tried to help them, redefine their lives and strengthen their core selves. I tried to put their problems in a larger context so that they could understand that the issues they faced were not just of their making. If they had not been good students, I taught them about right brain knowing. School, I said, was a left-brained arena that never accessed the best ways that more right-brained females learn, so I told them they should create right-brain oriented mind maps rather than left-brain outlines, and that taking notes would strengthen their kinesthetic knowing. If they had come from traumatic backgrounds, I helped them know that they were all the more heroic for their willingness to begin again.

While working at New Choices, and still in my doctoral program in Women's Studies and Transpersonal Psychology, a Women's Studies minor had started at our local college, and it was particularly interesting for me to get to see the real-life side of the theoretical issues we discussed in my program. Not surprisingly, many of the New Choices women, who went to college, often minored in Women's Studies, and because the college was only a few blocks away, our center often served as a resting place for the college women between classes. As they would recount their experiences in class, the women were often wild with excitement. "They told us in Women's Studies class today that we were victims," said Michelle, a perky blond. "So, I raised my hand and said 'I may have been a victim at one time in my life, but I am not a victim now and I don't think you should tell women they are victims!'" she said heatedly. "The teacher wanted to convince us that we were still victims because of the culture. We were actually yelling at each other. I told her that viewing oneself as a victim is a state of mind. Once you are strong inside, mentally, you cease to be a victim!"

"The discussion was really wild," confirmed Joyce, who had been in the same class. "We argued really well and made lots of great points. The younger students in class were just staring at us. I don't think they ever heard students challenge teachers like that. It was great! And I know we were right!"

"It is so much fun to argue really interesting points," said Michelle. "But this isn't just some theory. These are our lives they are talking about. I am so filled with adrenaline right now. I am pumped! I can't wait for the next time they try to tell us something we can't do!"

It was ironic because in many ways the New Choices women were indeed the real victims that the feminist theories were designed to help. They refused, however, to view themselves as victims, and it was fascinating to see all sides of the issue. On the one hand, I certainly recognized that women had been victimized by a male-based culture. On the other side, I realized that real women, some who had had the toughest of lives, could certainly regain their confidence, cease to be victimized, and most importantly, refuse to view themselves as victims. Women seemed to need very little to get to this empowered state of mind. I had needed Lynnie's words of wisdom to trust myself. Her words filtered through me to the women in the New Choices classes. They, in turn, trusted themselves enough to challenge theories that didn't fit them. They seemed to turn into "women of steel," and actually contributed to a book with the same name.

I also continued to see more deeply into the problems with relationships as the women woke up and the men in their lives did not. In the early years of New Choices, I thought that our program had just gotten a group of women who just happened to have the bad luck of being with the wrong partners. Ten years later, after hearing about the same defensive male behavior again and again from the women, I started to realize that most men seemed to be threatened when their partners took any steps to better themselves. I learned too at our state meetings with all the other New Choices directors, that the women in their programs were having the same experiences. The men felt threatened and obviously thought that they would no longer be able to control their wives and girlfriends. Occasionally, a good supportive partner or husband turned up who sent flowers on graduation day or lunch for all of us. It was rare, but allowed us to know that good men still existed.

The women who attended the program over the years also seemed to be changing. My life seemed to be filled with working with amazing women and trying to get to bottom lines about women, men, and their relationships. Many of the issues that the New Choices women had with the men in their lives were similar to the issues that Dave and I had dealt with. I wanted so much to understand the reasons why men seemed to be defensive and threatened. I began to see that the issues of males, females, and relationships were all interrelated, and started understanding even more that these issues needed to be addressed at the deepest levels.

For example, many of the New Choices women who went to college majored in psychology. Like me, who had started college in the 1960s, along with countless other women since then, they were interested in people and wanted to help. As young undergraduates, we often learned theories that didn't really make sense, but we just thought it was because we didn't understand it well enough. We tried, for example, to comprehend that, as females, according to Freud, we had penis envy. Because we could never quite come to grips with that notion, our only option was to assume that we were probably doubly compounding our envy by repressing it. It seemed like every psychology class began with an overview of Freud, the Father of Psychology. As good little students, we learned it but never really understood its male orientation. In this case, while I am speaking only for myself, I have talked with hundreds of other women who felt the same. In my case, I kept going to school. When I got my master's in counseling, we studied Freud in almost every class. When I continued on to a post master's degree in school psychology, I took a required three-credit class solely on Freudian psychology. I have to admit I was a little excited. I thought, finally, once and for all, I would understand Freud. The essence of his psychology kept eluding me, and like any good student, I was quite sure that back then, although I got A's in my courses, my brain was still somehow limited in my inability to understand his genius. The teacher of this class was personable, interesting, and in-depth. I remember when he talked about the anal phase and the pleasure of bowel movements, I caught just a glimmer of real comprehension, thinking, "uh, well . . . uh, maybe, uh. . . . No, I don't think so." It just never really made sense to me.

It wasn't until years later in my doctoral program that I learned about Freud in a way that finally enabled me to understand. Freud's clients, says Jeffrey Masson, were, for the most part, upper middle class females who were nervous, weepy, and often hysterical; in fact, the term used at the time to describe them was "hysteria." Most told similar stories about being sexually abused by their fathers, brothers, uncles, or other men, and, initially, Freud believed them. He wrote *Aetiology of Hysteria*[10] in which he concluded that the sexual abuse of women by male relatives or friends during Victorian times was epidemic and unchecked.

The field of psychology was becoming popular and growing rapidly as it entered the early 20th century, and the psychological association at that time was organizing. Freud presented his findings, that many of his young clients had been or were being sexually abused, to this newly forming group of male professionals. No one at that time, however, was willing to have their dirty little secret become common knowledge. The learned men acted quickly to force Freud to change his theory.

So Freud recanted, and recast his findings into a theory far better suited for those repressive times. In order to keep the sexual abuse hidden, Freud interpreted the accounts of abuse given by his young female patients, at the hands of the males in their lives, as simply untrue, and instead construed these accounts as wish fulfillment on their part. He said the abuse they described never really happened but was instead something that they, in their hysterical states, only imagined.

In order to justify this theory that women fantasize about such things, he had to maintain that the females *wanted* it to happen. Women had to want to be controlled, possessed, and dominated sexually. Females secretly desired, said Freud, to be ravaged sexually.

And why would women want to be ravished and controlled sexually? Women, he said, were always sadly aware that they were lacking a penis. Envying but not possessing the most wonderful of all bodily extensions themselves, women sought the next best thing—possession by a penis. Women desired to be ravaged by the very thing they wanted and did not have. They, of course, also fantasized about it because they had the kind of weaker personality that wanted to be controlled. Ah, finally I could really understand Freudian theory.

Arguably, this theory is a hypothesis, but given what we know about sexual abuse today, which perspective seems far closer to the truth? Countless statistics still reveal that a third of all women are sexually abused, usually by a male member of their family. We also know that this sexual abuse did not just start in the last forty years since they started tracking it statistically. That young women were being sexually abused and the male culture, desiring to keep this hidden, invented a theory that blamed women for their own neuroses seemed to me to have a far clearer ring of truth. Further, females today know which theory to believe because chances are one in three that they themselves were sexually abused. Like every counselor, I had heard recounts of sexual abuse again and again from the female clients I worked with. It became just one more reason why I could no longer embrace traditional psychology.

In truth, the re-visioning of history and theories that took place over the last 40 years of deconstruction helped not only females, but benefitted many groups who had been marginalized before then Ironically, Susan Faludi[11] revealed in *Stiffed,* that the repressive culture founded on white male values didn't even work for most white males either. While the deconstruction and unlearning helped women and men immensely, it is important to recognize that this unlearning has been done in absence of any real reconstruction.

The feminine Yin principle continues to be the marginalized and questionable counterpart of the Yang quality that is valued. In every case, with each Yin–Yang concept, the masculine concept is, 100 percent of the time, more valued, understood, and accepted. Even today, the response of women, when asked how they feel about the feminine principle or women in general, is often negative. They still seem to associate women with the feminine archetypal stories: Eve, Pandora, Medea, who killed her children, the witch who lives in the woods or the female lion who is more vicious than her mate. Right below the surface is a well-spring of negativity that is associated with the feminine principle that we all carry.

The Archetypal Depths

Most discussions around gender still reveal that both sexes, despite evidence to the contrary, believe that women are just as aggressive as men. This misinformation bubbles up from the deeper levels of a collective consciousness that has been shaped and informed by mythological stories. Not surprisingly, these old stories were, even then, similarly biased against women. Many still easily recall the old archetypal tales about Pandora and Medusa, which in truth were created by men and projected onto women, in the same ways they have been more recently.

Because we don't really know what the real feminine qualities are, most of us will fall back on what we have learned. Not surprisingly, it is often women who believe that females can be even more vicious than men, and this appears to be especially true in the business environment today, which is still a male-dominated milieu. Often described as "dog eat dog" and "every man for himself," females in male-based environments are required to play and act rough like men if they want to keep their jobs, where the double standard of the male viewed as assertive and the female viewed as a bitch is still alive and well. Because we have no real comprehension or appreciation of the feminine principles, nor have we reconstructed any new understanding about the female, it appears that our minds are still filled with old, archetypal models that almost appear to be the default setting for our thought processes when it comes to the feminine. *Gender War, Gender Peace,*[12] for example, uses the concept of archetypes to justify the belief that females are and always have been as aggressive as males. Because archetypes define women throughout history, we are inclined to think that because the concepts of women as evil or wicked have existed for millennia, that they somehow reveal a truer picture of women. Even though it belies the statistics that 97 percent of those who are incarcerated are males, and despite the research that reveals that women typically only kill to defend themselves, we still somehow think that the negative picture of women reflects a deeper truth.

Explore bottom lines and we discover that the need to cast females in a negative light has existed since the first written words, revealing, not the truth, but the patriarchal lens that was alive and well even then.

There are countless accounts of the story of Medea. First of all, Medea was never a real person, but rather a play written by Euripides. Rather than ask why Medea killed her children, a better question is why Euripides chose to write a play in which Medea killed her children. The answers are many and range from the mundane reason that the ancient audiences were getting tired of the same old myth about Jason, and Medea who helped him, to the more deeper, more complex recognition that Medea was never a real woman, but a compilation of earlier goddesses and wise women whose images were being displaced by a male portrayal of the ultimate female wickedness. In the play, she is portrayed as a mother who kills her children to exact revenge on a cheating husband.

Medea is a good example of how a story can morph over time to meet male needs. Medea and other feminine archetypes, whether portrayed as early mortals or a group of goddesses, were originally associated with the continuum of life—birth, death, and regeneration. Over time, these powers were recast into stories of Sirens, Harpies, and other figures whose functions were more aligned with death than life. The feminine association with life-giving was usurped and reshaped by emerging patriarchal stories. Medea and most other powerful female characters were demoted from goddesses in mythology into witches or monsters, and despite the fact that no such person ever existed, even today Medea represents an archetypal image of what a woman can do if she gets mad enough.

The Gorgon Medusa is another similar story. The stories in Neolithic cultures in 700 to 400 BC reflected the seasonal activities of planting and harvesting, which were considered sacred and part of the cycle of life. This Sacred Source, portrayed as female, was a metaphor for life giving birth to itself and absorbing itself in death. The same goddesses of death also presided naturally over the regeneration of life.

According to researchers, there was for a period of time, a blend of the more feminine and egalitarian myths and the more male-based, androcratic social structure, that embraced both warfare and sky gods with the sacred earth-based goddesses. During this time, the word "hero" actually referred to Hera, the great goddess, who was later cast in the role of the wife of Zeus. The concept of the hero at that time, suggested a new male role, that of son and protector, of women. The rise of the heroic consciousness that sought to conquer death could not tolerate reminders of the natural mortality that had long been associated with the feminine. Over time, the feminine took on horrific female forms. The new hero then became one who killed these earth-born and female demons.

In the story, Medusa, with her snake-like hair, could turn men to stone. In truth, she was originally a variation of the Great Mother, the earth spirit and nature goddess. Older than Zeus, Medusa was originally associated with the Triple Moon Goddess. Even the Triple Moon Goddess was a later composite of Hecate, the white mask of the full moon, whose powers date from the abyss of time. She was the Titaness who moved freely between realms of life and death. Her rituals were used to maintain spiritual boundaries, viewed then as the place between death and new beginnings. The Triple Goddess represents time—past, present, and future—and the circular continuity of mythic time. The Gorgon over time became associated with the bird and the earthbound snake, which emerged from Medusa's head.

In the myth, Perseus kills Medusa. He is helped by Athena, a new male-formed goddess who emerges fully born and armed for battle from the head of Zeus. Thus, Athena became the first daughter of the patriarchy, a new standard of mental and rational activity, unpolluted by her mother's womb. In the Eumenides, Athena states, "There is no mother who bore me for her child. I praise the Man in all things. Wholeheartedly am I, strongly for the Father." The emergence of Athena, not surprisingly, coincided with the loss of women's rights in Athenian society.

The stories of Medea and the Gorgon Medusa essentially represent the death of female wisdom. Images and myths of the great cosmic mother, in all her aspects, have been found all over the world. Once associated with the cycle of life, most goddesses over time came to be linked only with the death and destruction aspect of the cycle.

Today, there are few psychological scholars who even bring the concept of the feminine into consideration. Carl Jung is one of the few who talks about the feminine aspects of consciousness and suggests that we can balance the masculine and feminine in our own brains. A careful reading of some of Jung's deep archetypal works, however, appears to suggest that even he had very little concept of a real woman in his writing. As he describes the process in which a man must embrace his anima, the creative feminine aspect of himself, he uses the template of the alchemical process. The king, standing on the sun, and the queen, standing on the moon, join left hands. Since the joining of left hands is contrary to convention, Jung believes that this suggests something sinister and even incestuous. The female, according to Jung, is viewed in the context of a mother–son or sister-brother relationship. He references the feminine only as an abstraction, a muse or right brain or a product of transference—not a real female. Jung states that "Marriage with the anima (the feminine part of a man) is the psychological equivalent of absolute identity between conscious and unconscious. But since such a condition is possible only in the complete absence of psychological self-knowledge, it must be more or less primitive, i.e., the man's relationships to the woman is essentially an anima projection." And, with all the historical and incorrect negativity surrounding the feminine qualities and archetypes, chances are that even the anima can never be understood in its purest sense.

How Can We Know the Feminine?

Because there has been no real reconstruction of what the feminine is, we continue to shy away from any discussion around difference. Even books like *The Female Brain*[13] that attempt to address difference are heavily questioned and scrutinized by traditional thinkers, the press and other researchers. To this day, research that attempts to confirm the differences between males and females appears to be unsure about what to do with the results.

"People are afraid that studies like ours will turn the clock back," said Paul Irwing, whose most recent research in 2012 found that males and females are so different that they are "almost different species."[14] Janet Shibley Hyde, professor of psychology and women's studies at the University of Wisconsin, Madison, whose earlier studies had shown that males and females were more alike than different, retorted in a typical feminist response, "If men and women have wildly different personalities, then how can we (women) do the same job men can, and deserve equal pay for equal work?" she asked. "A married couple have marital difficulties, and they go to the therapist, who says 'he's from Mars, you're from Venus, you'll never be able to communicate. It's hopeless.' If you have a gender similarities point of view, you just need to work on communicating."

It appears that our knowledge base is still so indoctrinated with the male perspective that we cannot even conceive that viewing males and females as different could actually reveal a positive, hopeful, and new perspective of women. Women apparently still feel that if they are viewed as different, they will be victimized by being stereotyped and forced back into old roles again.

Separate the Sexes When Considering Any Issue

Women have been deemed by men as the second sex and have always just been included with men when we generalized about the human race. We combine the statistics of the sexes in such a way that we are all part of the family of man or mankind, and, not surprisingly, a very dismal picture of the human race is revealed. Our history is filled with violence and we are forced to view ourselves as an aggressive species. This question about the fundamental nature of human beings is profoundly important. Are we an aggressive or cooperative species? The answer makes all the difference in terms of how we view ourselves. The answer also appears to depend on whether or not we are coming from a male or female perspective. Because until recently all knowledge reflected the male perspective, it is not surprising that we thought of ourselves as aggressive and male-like. Look at the other half of the human species—the history of women—and a completely different picture of humanness is revealed. A picture of humans as a cooperative and peaceful species emerges. Further, viewing the human species from a feminine perspective is far more in line with and reflective of the newest research about humans as well as the newly emerging quantum perspective.

According to Tom Shadyac's documentary video *I AM*,[15] there is a sense of cooperation even in animals. He found communal decision making in schools of fish or flocks of birds that all change direction at the same time. Careful observation reveals that it is often when the 51st member of the species gives an initial indication, such as a group of gazelles that are grazing and all suddenly run to the water hole even when no predator is detected. When slightly more than half of the group look toward the water, the group moves together as a whole.

It is most interesting, however, to realize that if we simply look at all these variables from the perspective of each sex separately, the picture that emerges about woman and her history is very different from that of man. Separating the sexes reveals a story that is so different that a visitor to earth would think, as Irwing suggests, that they were learning about two totally different species. Women don't kill. In fact, research reveals that the closer a woman gets to the proximity of a weapon, even when her own life is threatened, the less likely she is to use it. Females typically do not enjoy warfare, boxing, and pummeling each other senseless. Fighting to see who has the most power is not nearly as interesting to far less aggressive females.

Males have a completely different pain body than females. Although he does not suggest separating the sexes, Eckhart Tolle[16] began this inquiry into the concept of pain bodies when he was forced to ask himself why human beings would pay money and spend time watching other human beings kill and maim each other. Why? He proposes that males have bodies that collectively are attracted to pain. These pain bodies are essences, most probably fueled by testosterone, that become hungry and need to be fed. What other possible reason could human beings have to watch in delight as other humans are injured, maimed, and killed? Watching violence appears to appease the male pain body. Women have very different pain bodies. As a species, females have been sexually abused, physically hurt, and mentally controlled. Most females have no desire to feed their pain bodies in the same way men do.

The concept that we are an aggressive species therefore is true for only half the species at most. If you separate the statistics by sex, you find that it is males not females who kill. Males commit a startling 98 percent of all murders, rapes, molestations, tortures, and other atrocities against other human beings. The remaining 2 percent belong to women, who were, for the most part, defending themselves or their children.

The history of women reveals a gentle, cooperative, peace-loving species. It is no wonder that males do not want to separate the sexes when it comes to such statistics. It puts males in the spotlight where the real reason for humankind's ills are all too visible and identifiable, and the answer to fixing it is too obvious. While changing our culture and epistemological basis may seem like an idea that is far too simplistic and idealistic, it is nevertheless an achievable, desirable, and important goal.

Of course, not all men kill nor enjoy feeding their pain bodies. Most men are protectors of women. The concept that we are an aggressive species therefore is as untrue for good males as it is for women. This generalization needs to be fixed in order to better reflect reality. If the good males were to join with the females, it would appear that we could change things overnight. If we identify the real source of aggression, the solution for aggression would be revealed almost immediately. We could begin to think of ourselves differently, and our definitions of mankind would instantly become far more positive and hopeful if we include women and good men in the statistical stew. The fact that most of the human race *isn't* inclined to be highly aggressive could literally change the way we feel about ourselves and create a more positive self-fulfilling prophecy.

The fact that, currently, we cannot even imagine what possible good could come from viewing males and females differently reveals the present extent of the continuing inequality.

This new ideological perspective would then reveal new questions that have never before even been considered. If the female half of the population were in charge or even valued equally, would we have war? If women had equal access to managing and impacting the world, would we still torture each other and tolerate rampant humiliation-based pornography and rape? My belief is that we would not. With so much violence in the power-based world, why would we, as a species, *not* want to recognize that less aggression and kind, compassionate qualities might be our only hope for the future?

Women's Greatest Learning Is Often Unlearning

There is so much misinformation around the concept of the feminine that one of the first things women should do is to unlearn most of what they learned about themselves and their roles. Only then will they be free to begin to access and trust their deep intuitive knowing of what they think is correct.

While there are countless reasons why women's wisdom is still unknown, perhaps the most damaging has been her separation from the natural and magnificent aspects of her own body. There is actually a rich history of information that was once associated with the female body. Thousands of years ago, when the feminine was revered, there was no distinction between creator and created. Women knew who they were. Females brought forth new life and were honored and revered in the same way as nature that brought forth abundant food. Early cultures were involved with the blood mysteries. Blood was recognized as the essence of fertility and new life and was celebrated as divine. For women who grew up with the idea that menstrual blood is unclean and considered their periods to be a curse, it is hard to believe that menstrual blood was revered and symbolically equated with fertility.

In the original trinity, which was feminine, blood mysteries played a part at all three stages of a woman's life. A female leaves childhood and becomes a maiden when she has her first period. It was believed that this was a day of celebration and honor for the young woman who would herself one day be a mother. With pregnancy, periods stop. The blood becomes the essence of a new life and is held within to nourish it. The young woman gives birth and now becomes a mother who is busy tending her children. If she is not pregnant, blood will continue to flow during these years. In the same way that her energy flows out into the world at this time, her blood flows from her body. She becomes a crone when her menses ceases. The blood, the essence of creativity, no longer flows outward, but rather stays within her body to nurture her soul and provide the opportunity to become wise as she finally has time to sit and reflect. She becomes the wise woman passing on her wisdom to new young mothers. As a grandmother, her help and wisdom has been credited with helping the evolution of the species.

Women often know instinctually what their bodies can do. They instinctually feel connected to a feminine principle larger than themselves—even though they have no words for these experiences. In this sense, the divine feminine is not lost, but resides in the collective conscious and unconscious of all women.

The female is the living embodiment of the cyclical nature of life. Shlain believes that it was women who discovered and developed the concept of time by making the connection to the cycles of the moon and their menses.[17] Once this connection was made, people could finally understand the cyclical nature of life and continuity. They could grasp that something planted in the fall would begin to grow in the spring. This concept was perhaps one of the most important understandings necessary for human evolution and the participation in life's cycles. Because this understanding is so primary, Shlain suggests that our species should be called gyne-sapiens, not homo sapiens, in recognition of the sex that first made the connection.

The next logical step was to understand the connection with planting the seed in sex and gestation. Most probably there were countless generations of women who understood the connection between sex and pregnancy before males ever had a clue. There were also thousands of years when women were the natural choice as helpers and midwives for women giving birth and are well aware of what happened to those wise, intuitive women. Once males entered the picture and took over the birthing process, it became a clinical procedure and any of the natural and spiritual connections around birthing were lost.

Countless women, nevertheless, do indeed report having experiences, feelings, or sensings of a connection to something greater during pregnancy, labor, and delivery. Even without a context, women both know and do not know, and report having archetypal experiences where they became one with every woman who has ever given birth. They experienced becoming one with all women who have endured pain and who, though attended by family or medical professionals, were ultimately alone in this effort. They had experiences in which they identified with every mother and every child— the child who is becoming a woman and a woman who is giving birth to a child. Unlike male rituals where death and transformation are acted out, women literally experience these archetypal moments of life during birth.

Labor is an intense experience. There is an inherent risk of death, and the woman is literally transformed mentally, spiritually, and physically. Nursing too is a spiritual act. Women literally feed their young from their blood that becomes the milk that the infant receives. Nursing is also symbiotic. Feeding the baby not only nourishes it with the best possible nutrition, but also brings the woman relief and serenity.

Countless women have had experiences around birth and nursing that barely register consciously because they have no mental framework for them. They both know and do not know and often dismiss these experiences because they don't know what they are. And, for this reason, women can literally miss the richness of their own lives. What better personifies the act of nursing, suggests Jean Shinoda Bolen,[18] than the words, "Take. Eat. This is my body. Drink. This is my blood."? For many women, however, nursing their infant is the first time the depth of this truth which has been associated with the masculine, is stirred.

Despite the fact that every aspect of her ability to bring forth and nurture new life has been usurped by male stories, women often reconstruct this deep knowing, bit by bit, simply by talking with each other about their shared experiences. My friends and I realized how universal these experiences around birth were while we were away for a girls' weekend. We had just learned about archetypal experiences and our conversation quickly started to center around birth experiences. Carol started, "It was early morning, around 5:00 A.M. It was early spring. The birds were back and I could hear them. The sun was just coming up—and I was sitting nursing Sara," Carol paused, remembering. "And suddenly I was one with every mother who had ever given birth and nursed her child. Suddenly and inexplicably, I was connected to something greater than myself and for years, I didn't understand how to describe it. I mean there aren't even words. I think at the time I thought it was some post-birth hormonal thing."

"That reminds me of my experience right after birth," Sandy said. "It was my third pregnancy and I was supposed to be induced the next day. I went into labor the night before. The hospital was about 45 minutes away and I barely got there in time. Fortunately, the birth was a piece of cake because they didn't have time to do anything—no meds or anything. It was easy, the baby was a girl and I was thrilled. A couple of minutes after she was born, however, I started to sense that I was being filled with a powerful and uncomfortable energy. This was like energy I never felt before. It was like blue-white and so intense that I was arching my body practically off the table. I felt that I could not contain it and was hyperventilating. The medical staff must have felt that I was out of control because they sedated me. I finally came to and had no idea what had happened. It was 17 years before I ever really understood what really happened and for those years, if I thought about it, I always felt sort of guilty that I couldn't control myself.

Years later, however, I was reading about kundalini—spiritual energy that exists in the universe and can enter a human body. In other cultures, they are very aware of this energy and devotees meditate 20 hours a day for years just to have a kundalini experience, where spiritual energy literally enters your body and breaks through your chakras and blockages and frees one to have a spiritual experience. It is often powerful energy, and when I read about it, I wonder if that is what happened to me," Sandy said. "Then it occurred to me and I knew in my soul that that is what happened. I had just given birth, in other words, I had just been involved in the highest act of creation. I was one, at that moment, with every woman who had ever given birth. I was participating in creation! Of course it was a kundalini experience."

She stopped for a while and said quietly, "The sad thing is that I think it happens to women much more than any of us realize. We miss our own peak experiences, or experiences of enlightenment or whatever you want to call them—and we miss our own experiences of the feminine, too!"

Her eyes grew shiny and she took a deep breath, "That experience should have been something that I appreciated and savored spiritually, but for years I just felt guilty about it."

We sat quietly for a while, looking at the fire and just breathing together.

"Talk about feeling guilty," said Connie, breaking the pensive tone and starting to laugh. "I had an experience around birth that I have never talked about before. I always thought that I had imagined it, but it wasn't until just this year that I read about women who actually climax during the birth process."

"You didn't!" We all sort of said in unison.

"Well, actually I didn't, but I was pretty damn close. There I am with my legs in the stirrups and a bunch of people in the room and the doctor with his face in my crotch and I am pushing, right?"

We were all hanging on her words.

"And, I swear, it starts feeling pretty damn good with all that pushing and all the intensity and suddenly, my mind starts thinking, 'Sweet Jesus, not here! Not now!' So, it didn't actually happen—but it very easily could have. I know I stopped it. Talk about feeling guilty! I had never in my life thought about birth that way. Then when I heard about it, and heard a female doctor explain why that was very possible—same area, same stimulation, same possibility . . . I knew exactly what that was."

After we stopped laughing, we raised our glasses to all the women who had come before us.

Think how differently women would feel about themselves if just the epistemology around birth were changed. Women would understand and appreciate themselves in a far richer way. They would embrace the magnificence of their central role.

We live in the most amazing time—a time when a new paradigm of understanding allows us to look back, self-reflexively, to where we have been. We are aware of our history and how knowledge developed. We are finally discovering that so much of what we have believed is just not true. Not only is it not true; often, the exact opposite is a closer reflection of reality and truth. We now have the option of a new and fresh way of looking at life that is also closer to the truth. This ability is not divisive, but rather, corrective. It is the over-valued male perspective that destroyed the cohesive balance. We have the ability to see with far more clarity and discover things most of our predecessors never saw before.

The imbalance is making both males and females half crazy. In a recent poll it was found that a woman's greatest fear of a man is that he will kill her. A man's greatest fear of a woman is that she will laugh at him. We seem to have gone very far from nature and balance and the lens of life. When the greatest threat to an unborn child is its father, something is very wrong. Some men often seem to have a difficult time of keeping their two main roles—that of killing and protecting—separate.

Recognition of the imbalance, however, is just the first step. One soon realizes that if the feminine has been repressed and relegated to "other" for thousands of years, then it would be very wrong to simply assume that we know what feminine really is. Most importantly, it is wrong to cling to old epistemologies simply because that is the way it has been.

While the imbalance has skewed reality for both males and females, it has been particularly difficult for women, who are more tuned in. She often knows things she shouldn't know. She typically knows more than her husband and her boss, and often has to pretend that she doesn't know. She goes to college and learns a body of knowledge that she will in many cases have to unlearn as she comes more and more in touch with her authentic self. So much of her life is playing a game of knowing and pretending not to know. She has to learn to hide her strengths.

It is so easy to blame women either consciously or unconsciously. Males often do it as a way of life and very often women too blame other women. Blaming women is second nature in this male-based world and it is bad enough when men do it. Once women begin to think the issues through, they begin to see the inequality. Refusing to blame women is like taking off another tight hat. Once we do, we discover that we are in a better position to appraise the world and all its so-called facts, research, and experts. Make no mistake, women have been blamed since the beginning of time. Today's blaming hasn't stopped, it is just more subtle. For example, a recent article revealed that the sexes waste time at work in different ways. Men think about nothing, while women generate too many options. One has to read the article carefully to recognize that the differences between thinking of nothing and generating too many solutions are certainly not of equal value. Ironically, months later, an article revealed that 31 percent of men admitted to masturbating while at work. So, that next thought you had after reading that men think about nothing was correct. It is actually interesting and fascinating to look in-depth at any research that dares to address the difference issue today. We will never be able to judge both males and females fairly until true equality exists.

Women Know

Although true equality may still be many years away, women would be wrong to wait. Start now, to trust that you are a part of this primordial feminine essence. The feminine, however, is more than a powerful primordial force in the universe. It is connectivity, relationality, wholeness, intuition, all the things that have been relegated to other for thousands of years. It is that which has been sensed and intuited during those moments of enlightenment when we go beyond our five senses and become aware of the wholeness that exists. Know that because feminine knowing is more than a concept, it cannot and did not go away because we have repressed and ignored it. The feminine wisdom has been waiting for us. And like any great primordial essence that has been ignored, it is now, just as predicted, entering quietly through the back door.

Women have changed. The culture has changed. The one thing, however, that did not yet change is the epistemology—and women are now poised to change that. They have taken all the necessary steps—they got the vote, they went to school, they read all the self-help books, they expect equality. So, as true as it is to say that women do not know, it is equally true to say that women *do know*. They know themselves as women, and they know who they are. How could it be otherwise? Whether or not they have ever had children, they know their bodies and their more permeable boundaries. They naturally respond from a feminine sense, despite the fact that they are often ridiculed for being too emotional or sensitive. They are more intuitive and often just know things without being able to explain how they know it. They are relational and talk often with their friends. Emotional support is extended back and forth when needed within this circle of friendship. Many women today realize that they don't have to lower their standards and act like males just because they are now free to do so. They understand that strength for a female is different than strength for a male. She knows more than she ever did before, and seems to be waiting in a space that is yet to be defined—and these new definitions can only come from women.

Chapter 5

Women Are More Rational

Yin	Yang
Self-in-relation	Self as separate
Connected	Separate
Oxytocin	Testosterone
Right brain	Left brain

The groundbreaking book *Emotional Intelligence*[1] was published and became a best seller in 1995. This book can serve as a great example of how we know what we know. Less than 20 years ago, we collectively believed that there was only one way to be intelligent—cognitively and rationally. Our concept of intelligence was understood only within a masculine context, because we had no idea that emotions were part of intelligence. Emotional intelligence, like right-brained knowing and so many other feminine qualities, was considered as something baser less real. Emotional intelligence, however, says author Daniel Goleman, can matter as much or more than our intelligence quotients. For the past 80 years, our understanding of intelligence focused on the IQ, which researchers now agree, accounts for only about 20 percent of our success in life.

Throughout our lives, we were told that the only correct thinking was logical and rational. Emotions were thought of as somehow bad or negative in a strange undefined way. They were considered to be the opposite of clear thinking and, for this reason, were certainly associated with women. Goleman's book tells us that emotions are necessary components of clear thinking and essential to our decision-making process. Even while using a pro/con list to help us with decision making, we are ranking them according to emotional valences. Not only is emotional intelligence as important as rationality, it is a meta-ability. EQ determines how we use all the other mental functions we have.

To have intelligent emotions, we have to first know what our emotions are. It is surprising when we realize that not long ago we had so little idea of what emotions and emotional intelligence were that we had to start at such a basic level.

Through self-awareness, we can recognize feelings as they occur. We also have to be able to manage our feelings so that our emotions are appropriate—not overreacting or underreacting to situations. We need to be able to soothe ourselves and motivate ourselves to short-term and long-term goals. Recognizing our own emotions helps us to recognize emotions in others. Handling relationships with any degree of skill would, of course, require that we first know how we feel.

Goleman calls the ability to manage our feelings with self-awareness the "observing self." Being aware of how and what we feel, yet at the same time, being able to control what we feel and how we react is the observing self at work.

Numerous studies now reveal that women are far better at synthesizing their emotions with their thinking. Because of the male biases in research, even today it is not surprising that studies still attempt to disconfirm the importance of EQ. Nevertheless, Goleman stated almost 15 years after the book came out that women have the edge when it comes to emotional intelligence.[2] Haier stated in 2005 that "female brains are more efficient."[3]

Different Emotional Worlds

From the time they are young, girls have far more experience with articulating their feelings. Their emotional lives appear to be far richer. Parents, especially mothers, talk more to their daughters about emotions, and females are literally exposed to more emotional information. Because they are better at language development, it is easier for girls to put their feelings into words. Girls develop the words that act as tools to talk about their emotions sooner than boys.

Boys grow up being largely unconscious of emotions, both in themselves and others, and are far less sophisticated in the arena of emotional life. Boys, instead, take pride in their independence and autonomy. Most boys view themselves as separate individuals as opposed to girls who see themselves as part of a web of interconnectedness, and are threatened when their web is disrupted. Boys are threatened by things that challenge their independence. Further, these differences don't really change when they grow into men and women. Men continue to minimize emotions, especially those that have to do with vulnerability, guilt, hurt, and fear. Men continue to be more comfortable talking about external things, mainly because that is their area of comfort and they are more left-brain dominant.

Women tend to be more balanced between right- and left-brain processing. They are more intuitive and better communicators. Women have deeper limbic systems, making them better at expressing emotions and connecting with others, qualities that are actually more highly evolved.

Hormones, too, contribute to the vast differences. Oxytocin makes females want to nurture the connections with others. Women work naturally toward developing emotional relationships and helping these relationships survive. Women know intuitively that the key to relationships is communication. Sharing feelings and talking it out is perhaps the most essential ingredient for a woman in a relationship.

That women are more emotional is not new. What is new, however, is the context for emotional behavior. Once considered negative or somehow lacking, we now recognize that the old context was simply part of a larger pattern developed and supported by men that relegated the whole emotional realm to a lesser status because they were uncomfortable with it.

Further, many males and females still think that if their partner yells, screams, cries, or emotes all over the place, that he or she is in touch with their emotions. As articulated so well in *Emotional Intelligence,* true emotionality is balanced with reason and rarely includes emotional outbursts.

Few studies as of yet actually say that women are the *more* rational sex. The current climate of political correctness alone would deem such information as unnecessary or invalid. If true rational thought must include and integrate the affective and emotional realm, however, then according to the newest information we have, women are the more rational sex. Women have been considered more right-brained and men have been considered more left-brained. The left brain is associated with rational, logical, cognitive thought processes. Not so long ago, it was common knowledge that women just weren't suited for important roles that required rational, concise thought. I can remember years ago when we *all* joked about what would happen if a woman were president, and Lord, help us if she were having her period or had PMS. She would push the button that would set off the bomb for sure.

Time and female success, however, have revealed how misguided those jokes were. It is the aggression and testosterone-fueled males that we really have to worry about. Women not only have brains that are more integrated, but as they became educated and were encouraged to use the left sides of their brain, they have excelled and in many cases, outperformed males. Entering academia, they did not as earlier predicted, stop having their periods, produce sickly children, or keep the culture and species from evolving.

We used to believe that raising children required little or no skill. For this reason alone, it is not surprising that we believed that women and their small, inferior, emotional brains were well suited for this job. Now we know that raising children is the most difficult, intellectually challenging and valuable job there is. Considering that our culture has always valued the work environment over the home environment, it is no surprise that a woman's new sense of pride and power is more related to her paid work than to her personal life.

Women seem to thrive at complex and challenging jobs. Substantive complexity is "the degree to which the work, in its very substance, requires thought and independent judgment." Research has found that there is a reinforcing interplay between the complexity of work and the worker's intellectual flexibility. Women, in particular, become more flexible thinkers as the work becomes more complex. This flexibility then extends to other areas of their lives, and they become even more self-directed. In a major study of factors that influence the mental health it was determined that mental health in women was related to how much mastery and how much pleasure they got from life.

For women, the combination of work and intimate relationships was deemed most important. Paid work was the best predictor of mastery, while a positive experience with her husband and children was the best predictor of pleasure. The single best key to general well-being was a challenging job. Women who scored the highest overall were mothers who were employed and married. We are discovering that women seem to flourish in multiple roles and find it stressful to have too little to do.

The Stages of Knowing

The changes in women's roles appear to reflect the different levels of knowing proposed by Belenky in *Women's Ways of Knowing*,[4] which charts the stages women go through in terms of their own knowing. The first stage, not surprisingly, is silence. Because women often weren't permitted to speak, they learned by listening. Of course, this appears to have changed drastically since the days of Father Knows Best. Few women are silent today.

The second stage, subjective knowledge, can be equated to the 1960s when women discovered their own voices. Often described as the "still small voice," this stage represents a collective shift toward recognizing and knowing oneself as one's own inner authority. This occurred when women came together in consciousness-raising groups. The quest for self began, and the personal opinions of women began to be viewed as valid, or even more valid, than the opinions of outer authorities. The self-concept of women began to change, further recognizing and expanding a woman's ability for intellectual work and understanding. Women began to watch and listen to their own thoughts.

Most women today function at the stage of procedural knowledge—the voice of reason. Women realized there was knowledge out there to be learned and went out and learned it. This stage includes the conscious, systematic analysis of information. Women learned, especially in the 1970s and 1980s, that the knowledge out there typically did not include them. This was also the waking up period when women realized that there was more than one way to look at information.

The collective of women learned to discuss intellectual ideas and quickly discovered that these ideas were heavily biased. Procedural knowledge can be thought of as learning how to learn, which can be acquired as either separate or connected knowing. Separate knowing is the ability to learn without really being connected in a personal and passionate way. You can get a PhD and become knowledgeable in a subject that you are not really emotionally connected to. Some women adopted this more impersonal, male-like way of acquiring knowledge. They are smart and objective. They learned to think like men and to view information with impersonal reason.

Most women adopted a connected sense of procedural knowing that was more comfortable and better suited for their more feminine-based learning styles. For them truth was personal. These women learn empathically, and value data and relationships that they *feel* are directly applicable to their lives. They are passionate about what they know.

The highest form of feminine knowing is constructed knowing—a level where she literally begins to construct her own knowledge. Having mastered how to learn and acquired all the knowledge that is associated with a certain subject, she is now ready to go beyond it. At this level, all the voices within a woman become integrated, and, with her greater access to her creative right brain, she goes beyond the givens to create new concepts. She has unlearned information that no longer resonates and begins creating a new system. The question for these women is *What is real?* They have gone beyond anger because they have gone beyond feeling victimized. At this level, they know that they are free to reconstruct new knowledge and recognize that to understand knowledge is to invent it. This way of knowing is moving outside the givens and into true creativity.

Constructing Our Own Knowledge

Most knowledge is constructed and the knower is an intimate part of that which is known. This understanding greatly expands the possibilities of our epistemologies. Constructed knowledge is of extreme importance for women today for several reasons. First, all male-based knowledge thus far is limited to the extent that it was and is the product mainly of the left brain. It lacks the synthesis and balance of the right brain and the sense of completion of the whole brain. This is particularly true as it relates to philosophy, psychology, and theology. Each field is diminished in that it has been restricted to one side of our knowing. The literal and linear male brain has, for the most part, created knowledge but not wisdom. The more balanced female brain has always been associated with a whole-brained wisdom. As females, we are now called on to expand the knowledge in each of these fields, recognizing that this endeavor is something that only those with a whole-brain approach can do. In truth, many good males and females have explored and created more whole brained approaches that are still considered questionable by traditionalists because they reflect a more feminine perspective. It is time for women to deconstruct the limited and traditional knowledge base and begin to reconstruct a more viable and comprehensive perspective.

We now recognize that true objectivity, the holy grail of the masculine perspective, doesn't really exist, but rather depends on who is asking the question and how the answers are reached. Recognizing this, when women begin to construct their own knowledge, they also become passionate knowers who are deeply involved with what they know. This is the level where passionate knowing resides. At this level, women learn to use themselves as instruments of understanding. Real and authentic talk lives here. Women at this level resist premature judgments on moral issues. There is a commitment to action while at the same time there is a resistance to judgment. Women here are beginning to reconstruct their own truths and recognize that it has to be done carefully.

Women as Decision Makers

Decision making is typically considered to be part of rational thinking, but it is also closely related to morality, for moral reasoning is often based on making some kind of decision—to help, to care, to act or not act, and so on. Not surprisingly, women have always been considered poor at making decisions. The ideal decision maker was the male who just readily arrived at closure. "Yes—Do it." "No—Don't do it." The ability to make an instant decision and thus get the issue off the table or out of your mind was viewed as the pinnacle of quick, adept, rational thinking of the male, and further, was always compared to the woman who thought long and hard, and even after doing so, was still not completely clear about the rightness of her decision. According to traditional research, women seem unable to make a decision without considering the needs of others. When confronted with a decision a woman will ponder every side and consider how the decision will affect others in her life. Few women make decisions based solely on their own needs.

Women, of course, have internalized and believed the research that reported they were not good decision makers. I remember talking to my friend, Marsha, who reflected a process that typically includes and reflects a woman's decision-making process. "If I had a decision to make, I would want to talk about it to Ron. I would want to look at each side of it and talk about it with him until we came to some closure that worked for the whole family. After about two minutes of me telling him the problem, he would say something like, 'You want to do it—whatever *it* was (spend the money, go some place, go back to school)—just do it.' I would say, 'It's not that easy. If I go to school, then. . . .' He would just get frustrated and say, 'Then don't do it!' I could never understand why we just couldn't talk about it. I used to blame myself because I couldn't decide as easily as he could. Now that I understand that my way of approaching the problem may be just as correct as his, I find myself thinking 'What's wrong with him?' He's the one that literally cannot sit and talk about important things that are going to affect him or me or the family."

Like most women, Marsha assesses her decisions based on her intention to include others. This is why she needs to talk things through. Her sense of self is intimately related to her decision. Because she is connected to herself—and others—she must make sure that she is not making decisions that serve only her needs. Women who feel best about themselves as decision makers have developed a new perspective that takes their own needs, along with the needs of others, into account.

Decision making happens on both the personal, day-to-day, micro level and the macro level that impacts our futures, others, and our environments. On this larger level, we are presented daily with the end results of decisions that failed to consider variables like the impact on the environment or the future of the next generations. In truth, every decision *should* be weighed carefully, discussed, and considered from all angles.

We Do Not Think in Isolation

It is almost impossible to talk about thinking and cognition without including how we feel. The right and left sides of the brain, representing these two areas, are connected by the corpus callosum that serves to integrate these two neurological functions. The corpus callosum in women is far larger than in men, which is part of the reason why females are the more whole-brained sex. It is only since the advent of neurological imaging that we learned that women have up to 33 percent more connecting fibers, enabling greater integration between the two hemispheres. This is why women are more aware of and can better express their feelings. It is also why women can multitask better, because brain lateralization enables a multitude of responses. One writer used the analogy of men having a little two-lane, rural road between their hemispheres, while women have a colossal superhighway. This is the reason women have always been blamed for bringing up the past when arguing with her partner. She does this because she *remembers* how she felt in reaction to what he said. He doesn't bring it up, not because he is a nice guy, but rather because he doesn't remember! Males just have a much tougher time integrating thinking and feeling.

The difference in brain processing is present in young boys and girls and appears to continue through life. Women remember the emotion associated with the event, while men store their memories in an area of the brain that separates feelings from the actual details.

Women have been blamed for eons for bringing up emotionally charged events from the past. For years, it was believed that men get over things more easily while women carry a grudge for way too long. This is only true according to male-based standard. Why should the standard be based on the sex who has an inability to integrate feeling into their memories? In other words, it is easy to let things go if you don't even remember it because your brain does not associate feelings and memories. Conversely, if we use a female-based standard, which also happens to represent a superior standard, then females are just better at remembering events and how they felt. If it is hard to let that event go, it is probably because there was never any real closure.

Because she is able to integrate thinking with feeling much more easily and naturally, she of course includes others in her decision-making process. Her process isn't wrong, it's actually more complex but because males have been the standard, she has been deemed inferior. Women are well aware of how easy it would be to make a decision based solely on what they want. It's not like they don't know. They willingly take on decisions that are more difficult to make because they are aware that others will be affected. Females, therefore, are far better at more complex mental negotiations. They are able to manage far more sophisticated mental processes that include both their own needs as well as the needs of others. Including oneself along with others, or actually leaving oneself out of the process, can be a selfless act that reflects a highly developed level of morality. We should honor rather than blame women for possessing a natural ability to do this.

Today's woman includes herself in the decision-making process and finds decision making harder than ever. She wants to be responsible to others but also to herself. She includes herself because she realizes that no one, herself included, should be hurt. This is the principle that governs her moral code, and from which she assumes responsibility for her choices in moral dilemmas.

Responsibility and Care

Decision making cannot be separated from morality, as both are tied to a sense of responsibility. Women feel an obligation to exercise care and avoid hurting others. People who care for each other are viewed by women as the most responsible. People who hurt others are perceived as selfish and immoral. Because we live in a culture that values separateness over connection with others, women have taken care of men and men have tended to take that care for granted. Women are rarely credited for the skilled development of their relational abilities because these behaviors have just been considered to be natural and instinctual. We don't value women's ability to care and just assume that they aren't doing anything special because they are biologically programmed to care.

Even the care that women do provide has been judged in some way. It has often been considered as compulsivity. It's her fault that she feels she has to clean up the house after working all day. If she were less compulsive, she would learn what men know and just relax. How many times have we heard that women can't relax because they are just too obsessed with having things right? Fortunately, her superior abilities enable her to handle the many roles she has in life. It is typically women, despite the fact that they work full time, who pick up the children at school or day care, stop at the store, and get the dry cleaning. While this is changing, it is still true that two-thirds of all working women don't go right home and are twice as likely to detour for groceries or other necessary errands than the men in their lives. Men, on the other hand, are twice as likely to stop at a restaurant or bar.

Women also focus more on the *dynamics* of relationships and the ongoing *process* of change. She develops an understanding of the ever-growing, ever-changing nature of the interconnections between herself and others.

New research also reveals that when men are tense, they are literally unable to read facial expressions. Their emotions shut down. Now that we can localize brain function with brain imaging devices, we have learned that the regions in the brain used for social understanding become less coordinated in males, especially when they are looking at angry faces. No wonder men don't want to talk and would rather punch something instead. Feeling the need to defend himself, testosterone begins to flood his system and fighting back is often all he can think of. Their brains shut down and they become aggressive and are literally in survival mode. One can only wonder if perhaps this is the real reason why we have wars. Now that we have new information about how males can't think straight, we should re-examine what war really is. Chances are conflicts and wars may have been a response, not only to a real or imagined threat, but also to a male's inability to think clearly. This may have been okay when males from one small village invaded another small village, but it isn't okay today when the lives of millions are at stake. It now appears that it isn't female PMS that we have to worry about, it is the male inability to synthesize thinking and feelings.

Males and their testosterone have been associated with increased risk-taking behavior. Today, this risky behavior is also interpreted as irrational and overemotional. This is not surprising given men have fewer of the components needed for emotional intelligence. It is the female sex that is cool and levelheaded.

Women when looking at the face of someone experiencing emotion, are more inclined to put themselves in that person's place. This skill appears to be crucial for negotiating peace talks or any difficult situation. What would it be like if empathy and compassion, not aggression and self-protection, were sitting at the negotiating table? Which sex would be better to sit across from the leaders of two warring countries? Who would be better at delivering devastating health news to the patient and his or her terrified family members? Yet, it is men with limited abilities, historically and presently who hold the positions of power in these situations.

A Psychology that Recognizes the Feminine Qualities

When I discovered the Stone Center, during my doctoral studies, everything fell into place and I could finally put real theory to what I knew to be true in my heart. I immediately realized that the inequality in psychology started at the most basic of bottom levels lines. I finally realized why so many concepts in psychology seemed to be skewed when I learned that even the most basic concept of self has been defined in masculine terms. The ideal "self", according to males, who had generated most or all of the further traditional psychological knowledge, was defined as independent, separate, and autonomous. The most fully actualized female client was and still is in many cases, therefore, the perfect male!

Recognizing that psychological theories will flow from the basic premise of how the self is defined, it makes perfect sense that males defined "self" in terms of what they understood. The male experts who contributed to the body of knowledge on the self apparently wrote about what they knew—and, of course, it rarely included relationships. Relationships and relational behavior are, by definition, a secondary value in traditional psychology. The Stone Center, a Harvard-Wellesley cooperative comprised mainly of women, challenged this most basic of concepts in psychology.

Recognizing that every human being, from birth to death, lives in relationship to others, the Stone Center proposes a "self-in-relation" theory that better reflects this truth. We are all human beings in relation to each other. Yet, often, it is not until an alternative is suggested that we even begin to see the one-sidedness of our old ways of thinking. It is this bottom-line definition of self that significantly changes how we know what we know in relation to psychology. The premise that we are not separate selves, but rather selves-in-relation, makes all the difference in how we view ourselves and others. Rather than strive for an ideal of being separate and independent, we need to recognize the truth that all of us are shaped by relationships.

If we view ourselves as separate beings, independent of others, the way we live our lives will, by definition, place a high value on autonomy and independence. This singular view will generalize to other important aspects of human functioning, such as human development. When relating to others is viewed as minimally important, it becomes just another task along the way. The developmental model proposed by Erikson, is one of the concepts I had struggled with in my earlier schooling. In the self-as-separate model, creating and maintaining a relationship was just a blip in the overall development of life—equal to getting educated, finding a job, and taking one's place in society. Of course, given this model, women would always be viewed as lacking and needing more than they will ever get, because the concept of being separate is literally built into the understanding of how a healthy human being develops. Women, who always desired more in their relationships, could only be viewed as codependent in a self-as-separate model. If we view humans as relational, however, everything changes. Relationships are granted utmost importance at every stage of development. Relating is seen in its central role, and for this reason it would be studied and valued. Ways to enhance relationships would be of primary importance.

The Stone Center suggests, almost jokingly, that if the self was perceived as relational and we all viewed ourselves as selves-in-relation, women would be immediately viewed as the relational experts. Everyone would recognize that our humanness requires that we relate to others. We would recognize the truth of our existence, which is that from the moment we are born until the moment we die, we are in relationship with others, and that we remain in relationships with others throughout our lives. This new theory would apply not only to women but also to men. Some psychologists at the Stone Center have also jokingly suggested that in a world where the self-in-relation model was recognized and valued, maleness would be considered a detriment to full humanness, and all men would be required to get counseling to learn how to be relational.

According to the Stone Center, women in particular have much to unlearn about thinking that they should view themselves and others as separate because for them autonomy develops *within* the relationship. Since this doesn't regularly happen for men, it is no wonder that most males do not understand or embrace the self-in-relation model. Self-awareness for both men and women is developed *through* practice in relationships. The relationship is where empathy is learned. It is through empathy that we learn to see through the eyes of others, and we learn to explore the feelings through which we begin to know, not only ourselves, but others. In this way, we can see how our perceptions of the world are like or unlike those of others. If they are alike, we feel understood and even normal. Recognizing that our perceptions differ is what starts a self-exploration that will lead to greater self-understanding.

The self-in-relation theory, the only feminine-based psychology, finally reflects the unique ways women perceive and relate to the world. With this new theory, women are able to develop a better perspective on the problems that have been attributed to them. The fact that we have believed females need relationships too much, are codependent, or have something wrong with them because they are more relational by nature, is the fault of all the incorrect and limited male-based theories—not women. The Stone Center isn't actually new. It was started by Jean Baker Miller who articulated her theory in 1976 in *Toward a New Psychology of Women*.[5] The actual Stone Center began in the 1980s and continues to provide research and new ideas for feminine-based psychology. Of course, despite its continued success and the fact that numerous books and countless "Works-in-Progress" have been generated, few women today know anything about the Stone Center or its theories.

According to the Stone Center, young girls don't desire a penis any more than they might desire the athletic ability that can be found in either sex. Girls don't think that they are missing something, or that the appendage that boys seem to think is so wonderful has somehow fallen off their bodies. The greatest point of truth about the concept of penis envy is that it is a blatant, obvious, and actually very funny, almost wish-fulfilling, male projection. Further, the Stone Center has determined that young girls have little or no need to identify with their aggressive fathers.

During their formative years, girls are not latent as traditional psychology suggests. During the time when little boys are supposedly learning to be autonomous and industrious by playing and learning the rules of the game, little girls are developing highly polished relational skills while playing with and relating to each other. Recent studies, for example, reveal that girls are far less interested in bloody, violent, and competitive computer games in which limbs fly and blood spurts, not because they shy away from aggression, but because they find them boring.

Traditional psychology has led us to believe that during adolescence girls turn their energy and attention to others at the expense of their own self-esteem. The girls supposedly resolve the fact that they are different from males by becoming passive. More recent studies, however, indicate that girls no longer believe in the myth of the white knight who will take care of them. Even at an early age females today know that it is their responsibility to take care of themselves.

Girls historically got strong messages that their sexual stirrings were wrong. This message came from and continues to originate from a culture that is still uncomfortable with women's sexuality. Even today, however, girls who feel free to express themselves sexually are punished by a society where a double standard still exists. Young girls are still constricted by the mixed messages of a culture in transition, not to mention the fact that they risk becoming young mothers.

Some theorists still propose that the academic performance of girls drops as they enter adolescence. It used to be thought that this was the time when girls started becoming aware of boys and the fact that they had to change themselves in order to attract males. More recent research, however, reveals that if the performance of females falls off at all, it is probably because she is sensing, consciously or unconsciously, the imbalance that exists in the culture and the corresponding message that it sends to females. She finally becomes aware of the bias toward the male perspective. Today, however, the typical response of young females is to become even more academically oriented.

Boys, on the other hand, are still free to develop themselves and their sense of independence. Girls are doing this same thing in a different way. They are developing themselves as selves-in-relation, which means involving themselves in increasingly complex ways in increasingly complex relationships. Relationships are still informed by myths that encourage girls to suppress their unique ways of seeing and acting. The fact that girls do talk about relationships more often has been interpreted as dependency. According to the Stone Center, it's not about being dependent or independent, but rather about desiring to be in meaningful and nurturing relationships with others. Girls really want to comprehend and understand the feelings of others. They want the nature of the relationship to be one where the other person is also engaged in this way. This is where the problem lies because girls are typically in relation with boys who don't get it.

Females are typically in relation with males want to relate to others in ways that foster the development of others as well as their own development. They do this with willingness and pleasure. The problem is that females, and especially young females, keep trying to have meaningful relationships with a member of the sex that not only doesn't understand it, but further denigrates it or takes it for granted, and further primarily views the relationship as mainly physical. And this perception continues to be reinforced by a culture that, similarly, still doesn't understand it.

The Divided Brain

Getting clear on the differences between males and females, as well as brain research, is not easy. Neurological research depends on the current sophistication of its instruments. In addition, the brain is extremely complex, especially when looking at differences between the sexes. Further, research is always impacted by prevailing cultural perceptions regarding what is acceptable to say or not say. Ian McGilchrist, in *The Divided Brain*,[6] addresses the changes that have occurred in our understanding of the qualities that were popularly associated with the right brain and left brain in the 1960s and 1970s when it was believed that thought, reason, and logic were associated with the left brain and that feelings and intuition were associated with the right. Today, this simplistic idea makes neuroscientists crazy and it is another reason why we have ignored the differences between male and female brains. What is true is that *both* sides of the brain are responsible for intuition and thinking. Both sides of the brain are necessary for right-brained imagination and left-brained reasoning.

What is also true, however, is that the brain really is deeply divided in terms of functions that are necessary to live, and although these functions aren't as simple as we once believed, each hemisphere literally does have its own ways of relating to the world.

These hemispheric divisions are true for animals as well as people. Not only does each hemisphere have its own unique properties, the human brain is becoming more and more lateralized as evolution progresses. This brings up an interesting dilemma for the field of research, long considered the pinnacle of male objectivity. The problem is that research is relative to our technological advances, which then change our earlier understandings. For example, long before learned men had microscopes, they proposed that females were nothing more than mere incubators for the fully formed male essence that created a child. When the microscope was developed and they discovered the largest cell in the human body was the female egg, a significant change had to occur in how both males and females knew what they knew. Discovering that the female had an equal, if not greater, contribution to new life had to have led to some major back-peddling among religious and scientific scholars at the time and chances are that the church overemphasized the virgin birth concept to overcompensate. Discovering later that all embryos begin as female must have been another such moment in time. As technology increases our ability to understand neurological functioning, more and more holes are poking through the once well-fortified story about male superiority. Faith and science, as well as the primacy of males over females, are trying to coexist peacefully today, but the cracks are becoming evident. This also means that those trying to explore the issue around differences between males and females still only get the minimal information that has seeped through the cracks in the wall of political correctness and rarely the whole picture.

It means that women today are put in a position where they have to—and should begin to—construct their own knowledge and try to fill out the picture based on disparate pieces of information that are gleaned here and there. For example, if rationality is based on the ability to integrate thinking and feeling and we know that women have a greater capacity to do this, why is it not common knowledge that women are more rational? Why are we still laboring under the misconception that men are the more rational sex? The misinformation makes us crazy. No wonder women are the sex that have mastered the art of eye rolling. It has been the only response that was socially permissible.

The following is an example of information that has seeped through a crack. The reader can decide for themselves whether or not the information on the brain also speaks to the difference between males and females.

The best approach today, says McGilchrist, is not to ignore the differences between the hemispheres of the brain just because it is not as simple as we once thought. Ignoring difference, however, appears to be what is happening. The position of many brain researchers today is to strongly refuse to acknowledge any real difference between males and females. The functions of the right and left brain should be viewed only as different with neither hemisphere valued as greater or lesser than the other. And, from a perspective of balance, it is true that both functions are of equal importance.

Until recently, we simply did not have the sophistication to better understand the brain. The majority of our understanding has come with the advent of FMRIs and other instruments that allow us to understand the brain in much more viable ways. The timing for all this political correctness couldn't be better to ensure that all the traditional values remain intact.

The Left Brain—A Focus on the Known and a Need to Control

The left, or more male-based brain, has the ability to focus critically and narrowly on things it already knows. For example, the left brain of a bird must be able to discern a seed among countless pebbles. The left brain helps do this task which is essential for finding food and surviving. The left brain is able to grasp things and pin them down. In a similar way, the left brain of humans helps them manipulate the world and use it for their benefit. It knows the specifics of a task very well and is able to specify categories within what it already knows.

Because the left brain is far better at the knowledge of the parts, it prefers a concrete and machine-like world. It likes to have control over the world that it sees clearly and has a disposition for the mechanical. Not surprisingly, the male-oriented left brain also views the body in the same way—as an assemblage of parts.

It uses language and abstraction. It has a tendency to see the world up close; however, this close-in focus causes the left brain to lose sight of the bigger picture. Because it focuses on the known and the narrow view, it needs a simplified version of reality and appears to be unable to grasp the more subtle nature of things. Unable to see things in a larger context, it has a tendency to view the world as empty of meaning. With so much focus on control and what it can manipulate, it sees the world as lifeless.

It is eerily accurate how the tasks and function of the left brain also describe our present world. Since males alone, until recently, contributed to the knowledge base, they defined it according to what they understood. This limited perspective has become solidified as the basis of traditional knowledge and knowing. The left brain still views the world, the body, and the mind as something that can be broken down into parts and manipulated. Specialists in medicine, psychology, and psychiatry, so focused on just one part of the person, very often fail to see the bigger picture or context and the complexity that accompanies it. The left brain has ensured, in setting up the world in this way, that its inability to grasp the whole is never recognized. Its ability to verbalize and articulate has not only created a way of knowing that is based solely on a limited left-brain perspective, it has gone even further to articulate countless reasons why seeing the big picture is somehow misguided, inaccurate and less valid. Because it is forever focusing on the parts, it will never be able to grasp the meaning and interconnectedness of the whole. It can define only what it knows and it plods along, making attempt after attempt in theology, philosophy, and psychology, to find meaning in the absence of a larger context. It proposes important theories about the meaning of life that, without seeing the whole, are essentially lifeless—an eerily accurate description of the world we currently live in.

McGilchrist is careful not to generalize the information from the hemispheres to the sexes. Doing so could be viewed as shoddy scientific methodology and prevent further exploration of the next logical assumptions. Constructed knowledge, however, has the leeway to move beyond the givens, especially when we know the given traditional approaches are not only limited, but are also highly invested in defending it limitations.

The Right Brain—Sees the Bigger, More Comprehensive Picture

The right brain is vigilant and always on the look-out. The bird, for example, while he is looking for food, needs to rely on a part of his brain that is also scanning the environment for predators and other dangers. It is always looking for the new. The right brain, therefore, has a broad, open focus and sees the bigger picture. For this reason, it is able to see things in context. It sees the bigger picture. It understands intentions and dispositions, not just categories. It is always looking for things that are never fully graspable or known.

With its broader context and understanding, it views the body and the world as a whole living, breathing organism. It is able to read faces and discern intentions. It picks up on subtle cues and enables us to connect with the world. It is our right brain that enables us to approach others, socialize with them and understand them. Because it is always looking for the new, it has a heightened awareness of the world as ever changing and evolving. It views the individual in context, with thoughts and feelings and an everpresent tendency to create meaning. Because it sees the larger picture, it has an embodied sense of meaning. It "gets it." The right brain is newer in evolutionary development, just as the prefrontal cortex is newer still. It synthesizes the right- and left-brain functions and enables us to empathize.

Just as the left brain is a good descriptor of males and our old and out-dated traditions, similarly the right brain appears to provide an excellent description of real women and the nature of feminine qualities. She sees the big picture. She understands the more subtle and unknown aspects of life. She is able to intuit and discern the feelings, body language, and intentions of others. She knows how she feels. She gets it because she has far greater connections between her right and left hemispheres and naturally and easily makes connections between what she thinks and what she feels. Because of these greater connections, she has a more highly developed and advanced brain that enables her to be an expert of empathy, the most evolved of all human emotions.

At one time in history, says McGilchrist, we did a great job of respecting both parts of the differing qualities of the brain. The Romantics honored nature and the Enlightenment valued intuitive insights. Although aspects of the right brain have been valued in the past, this focus never included real women. The past 150 years, however, have seen a major focus on the left-brain qualities. This has happened for several reasons. First of all, the left brain has a built-in need to control and, for this reason, has become very good at convincing us of the primacy and importance of analysis, focus, and concreteness. Since words are more left-brained, the left brain has become very vocal and articulate on its own behalf. The right brain is not actually associated with words—so it really has no well-articulated voice to extol its own virtues. It is easy to imagine, however, that if we had lived in a world where for the last 150 years the right-brain qualities were valued, today we would indeed have far better ways to describe them. This same premise is becoming popular elsewhere now that we better understand it.

The new evolutionary theories provide some of the latest perspectives regarding the evolution of intelligence. *Darwin Machines and the Nature of Knowledge*[7] presents an important distinction between instincts and intelligence. Instincts are defined as "behavior without thinking." Instincts, like the left brain, require doing the same thing over and over, and are slow to change, often remaining the same over millions of years. Intelligence, "behavior with thinking," happens when the organism is required to respond to something new, like a major earth change or disaster. The old instinctual patterns no longer work in novel circumstances and new behavior must emerge to respond. Human learning is the ability to adapt to the new and changing situations. The intelligence of the right brain comes into being to respond when things are different or unpredictable. All adaptations to sudden changes are instances of human intelligence. Are we permitted, therefore, to suggest that the more right-brain females may well have been the sex that is truly responsible for the origin and evolution of human knowledge?

Einstein said that the intuitive right-brained mind is a sacred gift, the rational left-brained mind, its faithful servant. In our left-brain oriented world, we have forgotten the gift and ended up worshipping the servant, and this is happening more and more every day. Perhaps real wisdom is to recognize this and re-embrace the gift of the more right-brained feminine brain.

What is it like to be a female who knows but doesn't know? Finding theories, facts, and information that finally make sense, especially in today's politically correct milieu, is like finding water in a desert. Today's females, however, are also living at the most interesting time that there has ever been for women. We learned male-based theories and now have the pleasure of outgrowing them. We can look back and realize that all the crap we learned in high school and college and beyond, for many of us, was, to a large extent, just that. And *it is* a wonder we can think at all. We had a harder time of it than males with so much to unlearn. Ah, but for those of us alive today, it has been and will continue to be a glorious ride. We have the pleasure of finally beginning to realize that what we always sensed was true, really *is* true.

Arriving at a more balanced epistemology, however, is not easy for numerous reasons, and some explanation is required. First, all knowledge is male-based and any attempts toward creating balance must be done from within this highly skewed context that is strongly oriented to maintain itself and the status quo. McGilchrist's research on left and right hemispheres also appears to be perfect descriptions of males and females, but today it isn't politically correct to actually say that. Aware of the great need to reconstruct a viable epistemology for females, women are forced to look for any viable seeds of information among the countless politically correct pebbles, while at the same time recognizing that our right-brain vigilance senses danger. Any potential reconstruction positing the importance of right-brain or feminine-based qualities, knowledge, or information will indeed be attacked by the traditional left-brained world that is so invested in maintaining itself. Further, in this touchy context, words themselves take on heightened meaning. The word "rational," for example, is often equated with analytical. Within this given understanding of rational then, males may still be viewed as the more rational sex. The word "rational," however, can also be viewed differently. Goleman, for example, states, "The connections between the amygdale (and related limbic structures) and the neocortex are the hub of the battles or cooperative treaties struck between head and heart, thought and feeling. This circuitry explains why emotion is so crucial to effective thought, both in making wise decisions and in simply allowing us to think clearly." He goes on to state that "feelings are typically indispensible for rational decisions." He continues, "The emotions, then, matter for rationality. In the dance of feeling and thought the emotional faculty guides our moment to moment decisions, working hand in hand with the rational mind enabling—or disabling—thought itself." The same is true of decision making, which is associated with both rationality and morality, making it difficult to even know where to place it.

For many reasons, detractors are therefore invited to consider the premises presented here as a work of fiction, intelligence having fun, the construction of new viable knowledge, or all of the above. The suggestion here that in many ways the female is the superior sex is certainly as true or false as the pronouncements of earlier learned males who stated that "women are incapable of learning," or today's statement (literally) by a psychiatrist that "the infidelity of a presidential candidate can serve to make him a better president because he had to tell the wife he was leaving the 'incredibly painful truth.'"

Despite the referenced material the concept of SHE-Q, *SHE-Q* is first and foremost an initial attempt at reconstructing a more balanced and viable epistemology for females. It is presented in a whole-brained approach that includes the insight, foresight, and intuitive leaps necessary for constructing new thought, something that the left brain may just be incapable of comprehending.[8] From this Whole-brained place of creative, constructed knowledge, SHE-Q believes that far from being less rational, females are the more rational sex.

Chapter 6

Women Are More Moral

Yin	Yang
Morality of care	Morality of fair
Oxytocin	Testosterone
Looks at the whole	Looks at the parts

It isn't easy to separate rationality from morality for they are intimately connected. If morality is treating others with respect and compassion, one need only look at the sex of those who are incarcerated for violent crimes to get a tip of the iceberg indication of the actual morality of the sexes. The morality of women was for so long defined by men and according to male standards that we are only now beginning to understand not only the differences between men and women in this area but what morality really is.

Lawrence Kohlberg,[1] one of the earliest authorities on morality, stated that most women never get to the highest levels of morality. I was first introduced to the studies on morality and Kohlberg in my master's program in counseling. I remember this whole issue well, because I recall that it never occurred to me to question any of his conclusions. And it never occurred to me to question Kohlberg's findings until I learned about the work of Carol Gilligan.[2]

The Morality of Care

In the early 1980s, Carol Gilligan was working on her doctorate. Like me, she was particularly interested in morality and, unlike me, began to wonder why, according to Kohlberg, women were never able to achieve the higher levels of morality. The basis of the problem, she discovered, appeared to be located in the interpretation of women's development and their experience of relationships. Kohlberg had used a story that contained various ways to view a moral dilemma, and he had men respond to the dilemma and offer possible moral solutions from which he inferred levels of morality. Gilligan, similarly, designed a doctoral study that was aimed at having women describe in their own words why they had come to the conclusions they did regarding the moral dilemmas they were asked about. The responses of the women were typically based on their feelings. They said things like, "It felt right," or, "I came to that conclusion because it just *seemed right.*"

Her all-male doctoral committee looked at her work and deemed it "sloppy thinking." A doctoral dissertation could not be based on feelings. They considered her study inappropriate, and neither logical nor rational enough to be considered true doctoral work. Ultimately, Gilligan redesigned her study using children, and her dissertation was accepted.

Gilligan was, and still is, careful to say that the morality of women is not better than that of men; it is, however, different—surely a politically correct and wise decision then and even now. From her work, she concluded that men are more likely to make decisions based on a "morality of fair," an abstract concept of right and wrong that may or may not include themselves. Women are more likely to make decisions based on a "morality of care," which includes others.

Gilligan's conclusions are similar to those of the Stone Center. Indeed, they work and present together. According to Gilligan, in any society the feminine personality comes to define itself in relation and connection to other people. Perhaps this is one reason why theorists have long believed that girls have weaker ego boundaries and are thus more likely to be influenced by others. Further, boys quarrel more and seem to enjoy the legal debate over rules more than girls. Gilligan believes that girls emerge from childhood with a basis of empathy for others built into their understanding of self.

More recent research has confirmed that young girls have a more pragmatic view of rules and games and don't enjoy competitive games as much as boys. They prefer games where they take turns and where one's success does not necessarily mean another's failure. Further, girls will stop the game if it is threatening the friendship.[3]

Gilligan determined that the sex and gender roles learned in society are among the most important determinants of human behavior. Men, because of conditioning, put personal identity ahead of intimacy with others. For females, however, intimacy is a major part of their identity. Men's social orientation, therefore, is positional. In other words, their identity is based on their sense of position in society. Because this position is based on the denial of any feminine perspective, the last thing males feel they should do is display qualities that are associated with the female. Women's social orientation is more personally oriented. They see themselves as directly attached to their social position and are far more sensitive to the needs of others. Gilligan concluded then, that in this culture, women's moral weakness is inseparable from women's moral strength. The very traits that have traditionally defined the goodness of women—their care for and sensitivity to the needs of others—are those that mark them as deficient in traditional moral development.

Studies on morality have also identified people who are considered to be moral exemplars. Such people have been identified by their real-life actions, not by how they score on a morality test, like Kohlberg's. These are people who have inspired others to moral action or have risked their own self-interest in dangerous situations. Their actions were consistent with their own beliefs and ideals, and they showed a constant commitment to principles that reflected respected a high respect for humanity. When given tests to determine moral development, however, at least half of the moral exemplars, whether they were male or female, did not score above average on the test—seriously questioning the actual validity of Kohlberg's test.

This study and others reveal that Kohlberg's test and hypothesis does not really measure moral actions, but rather, measures moral thinking that may or may not be related to actions. For example, people at Kohlberg's highest levels might *say* they would act morally, but may not do it in real life. We see this incongruity again and again in religious and political leaders who preach one thing and do another. According to Kohlberg, it is the reasoning one reaches in response to the moral problem, not the conclusion that is important. Kohlberg, it appears, was measuring only the cognitive aspect, which is a necessary component but not fully sufficient in itself to define moral development.

Newer research on children reveals that preteen girls are actually ahead of boys in moral development. Girls move into the stage of self-awareness while boys are still at the stages of egocentricity and social conformity. Similarly, preteen girls and boys were interviewed using a new ethics-of-care interview that incorporates both real life and hypothetical dilemmas. The students were scored on five levels that included "goodness" and "caring for self and others." The girls scored higher and generated more personal real life dilemmas than the boys, whereas the boys were more likely to *talk* about moral conflicts involving people or ideas in the abstract. Girls also tended to be more concerned than boys about maintaining friendships and not hurting people. The boys were more likely to be concerned about themselves, and for most of them morality meant staying out of trouble.

Since Kohlberg, there have been numerous studies that point to differences in morality between males and females. We have recently learned that female brains grow and enlarge right after giving birth, leaving women smarter than they were before. While old knowledge suggested that women become childlike and less rational after giving birth, this new information makes perfect sense from an evolutionary perspective. Women give birth and are, from that moment, placed in one of the most difficult situations to deal with. They have to put the survival and needs of their infant in front of their own. It makes perfect sense that the new mother would become smarter and more capable. Males, throughout history, have been unreliable when it came to helping and protecting the mother and newborn. The mother has to protect the vulnerable child—often from its father. Research now suggests that the new baby becomes the equivalent of an enriched environment for the mother, who learns naturally to multitask and become more selfless and empathic.

Not surprisingly, the male-based bias in psychology expanded outward to color every aspect of human development. According to psychoanalyst Erik Erikson's traditional developmental stages, men don't have to develop the virtue of care (for others) until midlife when they finally begin to develop concern for guiding the next generation. Finding a partner and creating a family was viewed simply as a developmental task for men that occurred along the way as they were fully developing their independent selves.

Even the field of stress management that was so popular in the 1980s was colored by the self-as-separate orientation. People were supposed to focus on their breathing and relax various areas of their bodies—which was done alone in a quiet place. They discovered, however, that method didn't work very well for women, who were inclined to talk with her friends when stressed. This feminine-based response to stress, known as "tend and befriend", is typically found at the basis of women's friendships. Most women have an overriding concern for relationships with others. Feeling responsible to and for others is part of the female moral code. They define themselves in the context of human relationships, but also judge *themselves* in terms of their ability to care. Of course, within this very unmale-like context, almost every woman, especially in the 1980s, was also considered—and considered herself—to be codependent. She simply cared too much about the others in their lives. Both Gilligan and the Stone Center explained this codependence in a kinder light, recognizing that a female's definition of herself is less concerned with achieving a separate identity than with developing and maintaining relationships with other people. This sense of defining oneself as a separate or relational self appears to be a primary difference between men and women.

There are then currently two ways of understanding moral development and two modes of describing the relationship between self and other. While the difference is characterized by theme and not gender, it is the feminine perspective that is less known and valued. The early development of morality in males is based on the concept that separation is primary. The male-based morality of fair relies on logic, rules, and rights to find the solution to moral dilemmas. Rule-bound competition including sports often provides a mode of connection that establishes clear boundaries and limits aggression. Hurt is viewed as arising from aggression. With the emphasis on individualism and personal accomplishment, males grow up with little opportunity to practice relational skills. As a result, there is a lessened capacity for relationships and emotional expression.

For males, full moral development means coming to see the other as equal to the self, and later discovering that equality provides a way of making connections safe. Intimacy becomes a way for the male to see both sides and learn to include others in his picture.

In most cultures, women focus on relationships. Girl's play tends to occur in smaller, more intimate groups, which fosters the development of empathy as well as the sensitivity necessary for attuning to others. As a result, females define themselves in a context of relationship. When asked about success, even highly successful women mention relationships first, and often view academic and professional achievements as part of the definition. Moral development in females extends from an ethic of care and responsibility. Females begin by caring for themselves and extend this to caring for others. Being accepted by others may require self-sacrifice, which is not viewed as a limitation of action, but rather an act of care. Hurting another is considered selfish while care is seen as the fulfillment of moral responsibility. Given that women were raised to get married, have children, and be self-sacrificing, it is no wonder that we have viewed women as having problems with individuation and self-expression.

In the final stage of female moral development, women question whether it is selfish or responsible, moral or immoral, to include their own needs along with those of others. Over time, her moral judgment begins to shift from goodness to truth, and the moral question shifts from what is right to what is right for me. She recognizes her own failure to assert herself and also acknowledges her earlier lack of understanding that she should have been asserting herself. The act of assertion is then seen as an act of self-communication rather than an act of aggression. The disparity between selfishness and responsibility dissolves as she comes to understand that self and other are interdependent.

The impact of this cultural split in understanding morality has been harmful to both men and women and their relationships. Men worry about attachments, fear intimacy, and may grow up denying themselves the pleasure of authentic human interaction. Women may have the opposite problem and may recognize that self-sacrifice has hurt their development. For women, her ability to honor herself has also meant challenging a whole set of cultural beliefs. It is no wonder that women have felt powerless and compromised.

The abortion dilemma, for example, has been especially difficult for women because there is no resolution that does not hurt someone. Crises like this offer the opportunity for significant questioning of the self and personal growth. Recognizing, however, that it is females who have a more embodied sense of morality, it is shocking that males then and now continue to try to exercise control over her choices. Since the woman will carry the fetus, deliver, and most probably parent the child, the decision appears to lie only in her hands. The intrusion by males into this decision is not only wrong, it appears to be still based on the old outmoded assumption that males are the morally superior sex who must make this decision because less moral women make these decisions blithely and without considering every option, when not one shred of evidence supports that this is true.

As men and women mature, both begin to recognize the paradox of the two positions: We know ourselves as separate only when we are in relationships with others, *and* further, that we experience relationship only as we differentiate other from self. Given the truth inherent in both positions, it is also true that the feminine path not only leads to a less violent life, but also to a maturity that is realized through mutuality. There is value for everyone in this less well-known path as it defines a different, and possibly more advanced, approach to life.

An Embodied Sense of Morality

Women's sense of self revolves around the issues of responsibility for the care of and the inclusion of other people. It involves the appreciation of relationships and the intentions of the people in the relationship. Women have been viewed as deficient because they have consistently wanted to include others in their psychological connections. This becomes the primary way a woman defines herself. Women tend to define power as having the strength to care for and give to others—which is very different from the way men have defined power. Women seem to have almost a faith in interconnections. For them it feels like a necessity to build day-to-day emotional connections with others.

Women's ways of relating and of being in the world, however, have never been viewed as sources of growth, satisfaction, or empowerment. It is ironic and sad to think that because theories of human development have been based on the male perspective of the lone and independent self as the ideal, we have devalued the quality that is most human and important for all of us—the ability to relate to each other.

Empathy

We have known little about empathy until recently because it too has been considered "other"—the opposite of rationality and clear thinking. Because it has been relegated to a lesser status, it has been considered primitive and questionable. In traditional psychology, empathy was, until recently, considered as a regression of self, caused by a loss of ego boundaries. Because males created the epistemology and because they are the less empathic sex, empathy has generally been considered as a less-than-rational quality and therefore a somewhat undesirable state.

In truth, empathy is the highest and most advanced state of human mental functioning. It far surpasses the notion of a separate self that reaches a developmental milestone where it is finally ready to seek a connection with another. It is instead the highest human function and ability—that of the recognition of the other in oneself and at the same time, the recognition of oneself in the other—a *Namaste* or acknowledgement that the spark of divinity in me has the ability to recognize the same spark in you. It is a sensitivity to both the difference and the sameness in the other. Most importantly, it requires a surrender of personal feelings.

The Stone Center[4] has determined that empathy involves both cognitive and affective functioning and is a far more complex, developmentally advanced, and interactive process than we have previously understood. The affective aspect includes feelings of emotional closeness and the capacity to fully take in and contain the feelings of the other person. Further, there is an accompanying feeling of deep connectedness—an interpenetration of feelings between two people. There is also a physiological component to the affective aspect, where the empathizer picks up and mirrors the posture, eyes, muscle movement, and even visceral experience of the other person.

The cognitive aspect rests on one's sense of self and the capacity to act on the basis of that self. While there may be an interpenetration of affect and feeling, importantly the self remains *intact* and differentiated. Maintaining the separate self enables the empathizer to make good judgments. In therapy, for example, the self of the therapist has to remain intact. If not, the therapist would be acting out of countertransference, a condition where the therapist would pick up and identify with all the feelings of the client, and basically become ineffective. Women appear to be able to move in and out of the highly developed empathic state with ease.

Empathy is the inner experience of sharing in and comprehending the psychological state of another person. Rather than being a lower regressive state, where one loses one's sense of self, as was long believed, the Stone Center reveals that empathy requires a highly differentiated sense of self. Far from being an infantile state where one's weak boundaries are merged with another, empathy can only be accomplished if one has a sense of one's self that is strong enough to extend to another.

For empathy to work correctly there has to be just the right balance of the individual's own thinking and feeling aspects. There also has to be a perceived sense of balance between one person and the other person. Only after this balance is present can the distinction between self and other merge. If the boundaries of the self are too rigid, the person would be unable to pick up on the emotional state of the other person. Further, the perceiver would continue to see through their own lens and judge the behavior of the other only from their own perspective. Because he or she could not identify with the feelings of the other, it would be impossible to understand how the other could feel. The perceiver with rigid boundaries would unknowingly see the behavior of the other as something they didn't want to identify with, and any true understanding of the other person would be somehow distanced, intellectualized, or projected.

On the other hand, if the self-boundaries of the perceiver are too open or permeable, the connection with the other person would only be an extension of self of the perceiver. In both cases, the opportunity for the genuine understanding that is essential to human connections would be lost.

In the case of too rigid boundaries, it should come as no surprise that men have a far harder time surrendering their egos to make empathic connection possible. For most men, this feels like a passive loss of control. It is also no surprise that many of the men who contributed to the tenets of psychology most probably had rigid boundaries. They apparently never understood what women were feeling or why they were feeling that way.

Had they understood, this highly advanced skill that women readily possess would never have been judged so harshly.

Empathy is the key to intuiting the feelings of others. It enables us to pick up on nonverbal cues, such as gestures and facial expressions. Emotional truths are most often found in *how* something is said, since 90 percent of emotional messages are nonverbal. Our empathic ability lies in the brain, and perhaps it is the differences in the brains of males and females that make women much better at empathic understanding.

The Roots of Morality

The roots of morality are, not surprisingly, found in empathy. Morality is based on our ability to understand or empathize with potential victims. It is for this reason that the inquisitors at the witch trials were warned never to look into the eyes of the woman they were accusing. Supposedly, they believed that the devil could control the judger through the witches' eyes. In truth, we can rarely condemn others to torture or death if we look into their eyes. Empathy then is the guardian of justice, for it underlies many aspects of moral judgments and actions. The more empathy exists, the more positive the world we create. In fact, most psychopaths have reduced activity in the empathy-circuit regions of their brains.

Reading between the lines for the implications of all the research on rationality, morality, and empathy, it is simple to conclude that women are not lacking in any way when it comes to the moral domain. Many females are convinced that if women were in charge, there would be no war and atrocities. Women are aware that their own sex would think first of their own children who would be hurt by those wars. Without the masculine abstraction of patriotism that serves to dull one's empathy, women would react straight from the moral compass of their hearts, recognizing that war would kill not only their children but the children of all mothers with whom they can easily empathize.

Hormones and Morality

The female counterpart to male testosterone is oxytocin, which is so powerful that many researchers today have suggested that it can literally make people more social. Oxytocin is the hormone that bonds lovers to each other as well as the mother to her newborn. It has been called the cuddle or love hormone. One company in Florida now sells it in a cologne-like spray called Liquid Trust. Research has linked it to increased trust, social bonding, and even a predisposition to increase more charitable and even more confident behavior.

This hormone is so potent that researchers are hopeful that it can be used to treat social anxiety disorders as well as autism. It has the potential to help people relate to one another. It influences trust, bonding, and social understanding, and helps reduce anxiety. It has been called the "molecule of connection." Recognized as a social lubricant, it enables researchers to analyze social information through a more accurate lens. A person certainly has to have a sense of connection in order to be able to live and behave morally.

Paul Zak,[5] who has always been interested in morality, wondered if morality actually came "top down" from God, as most of us were taught to believe, or "bottom up" from within us. In his quest to understand the origin of moral behavior, he discovered oxytocin, which Zak believes is the molecule of morality.

It turns out that morality comes from within us and originates from oxytocin, which is found mainly in females. Oxytocin is responsible for trust, empathy, and other feelings that help build a stable society. Empathy not only helps us connect and makes us more moral, it also creates a feeling of happiness by getting to share in the joy of someone else and feel what the other person is feeling.

We have our own sense of morality within our own biologies. We don't need God to tell us how to be moral which is certainly a new understanding to the centuries old assumption that we are only moral if we are associated with traditional religion. Interestingly, Zak proposes that there are two aspects—a sort of Yin and Yang of morality. Yin-like oxytocin makes us want to connect with the other person while Yang-like testosterone makes us want to punish people who have behaved immorally. According to the newest research, a change in oxytocin can predict feelings of empathy. For this reason, oxytocin not only makes us want to connect, it also makes us moral. Zak actually measured the levels of this powerful substance at weddings and discovered, as predicted, that the highest levels of oxytocin were found in the bride. The second highest, however, were found, not in the groom, but in the bride's mother.

Oxytocin is mainly found in females. Males apparently only experience the benefits of oxytocin during sex. They also have a short-lived jump in oxytocin when interacting with females. Males have 10 times more testosterone than females and testosterone is actually a great inhibitor of oxytocin. Although researchers are not ready to come right out and say it, one need only connect a few easy dots to arrive at what appears to be a very logical and biologically based conclusion: Oxytocin is responsible for feelings of trust, connection, and empathy. Empathy is necessary for morality.

Women have more oxytocin, which creates more empathy, therefore, again, is even more evidence that women are the more moral sex.

Mirror Neurons

Mirror neurons have also been associated with morality and empathy. Mirror neurons are miniscule brain cells located behind the eye sockets in humans and other highly developed species such as apes, dolphins, and elephants, who also exhibit empathic behavior. These neurons comprise a part of our brain that does not distinguish between our self and another.[6] If we observe a behavior in others, the same neurons light up in our own brain, connecting us to that other person, revealing that indeed, we are not separate from each other. Mirror neurons connect intimate partners at an internal level. Each partner mirrors the other partner's actions and feelings of attraction, romance, love, lust, moods, erotic desire, memories, and intentions. And that's what humanity, intimacy, and love is all about. Females, not surprisingly, have a greater density of mirror neurons. In addition, their mirror neurons are more sensitive and more easily activated, enabling them to better detect the emotions and feelings of others. This is why women are more likely to recoil when they see others in pain. This ability to respond to what others are feeling is one of the most highly evolved aspects of humanity and is literally the essence of what makes us human. This empathic response in females, however, has often been considered a disadvantage to being a leader, who may have to inflict pain to achieve power. However, the fact that nonempathic human responses are required in leaders by our culture speaks far more critically of the culture than of women and should further, cause us to question the morality that is required to lead a culture.

Women Are the Relational Masters

Both nature and nurture appear to have shaped women into relational experts. With full access to all their Yin qualities, women have honed their relational and intimacy skills to a fine edge. They are not only emotionally intelligent; they know these truths even as they do not know them. They must first learn to value their own feminine qualities, an inherently spiritual process, then exorcise their guilt—one day at a time—one toxic thought at a time—to get to what is true for them.

According to *Emotional Intelligence*,[7] there are three interrelated aspects of emotional intelligence: hope, optimism, and empathy. Hope is more than something that makes you feel better when things don't go right. It is the will that enables you to reach your goals. With hope, you feel less defeated and depressed, and even less anxious overall. Studies have shown that people with hope are better fortified against emotional distress.

Optimism is like a meta-ability that enables you to expect that things will turn out all right. People high in optimism see failure as something that can be overcome. Rather than focus on a time when they failed, optimists are able to feel that they will do better the next time. Studies on optimism reveal that the way we talk to ourselves about our successes and failures is more important than the actual events. How we explain things to ourselves—our attributional style—reflects the degree of control we feel we have in our lives. The more control we feel we have, the more positive our attributional style and the better we feel about ourselves. Further, a sense of control is closely linked to self-esteem.

Numerous studies reveal that boys and girls grow up in different emotional worlds. Parents, especially mothers, talk more to their daughters about emotions. Girls are literally exposed to information that is more emotional from the time they are born. Because girls are better at language development, it is easier for girls to put their feelings into words. Girls develop the words that are tools to talk about feelings. Perhaps these many relational skills are why CNN reported that studies reveal that it is women who excel in a crisis.

It is often difficult for us even to think of relationality and connection as relevant and related to moral behavior. Female relational abilities and the way women relate to others and the world has never been fully explored, described, or included in any theory, knowledge, public policy, or cultural belief.

Our traditions have made it almost impossible to think of human intellect, power, and resources as existing within a context of caring for others. Understanding women's ways of knowing gives us a deeper appreciation of the most essential elements of human development as well as the realization of all those untapped human capacities that have remained dormant and unexplored for so long. In a world where power was defined as the ability to care for others and have faith in connections with people, everything would change.

Morality Is Relational

A woman's experiences of connectedness to others lead to a different and enlarged conception of self, morality, and relationships. This marks a new step in the evolution of our understanding of human development—the self is relational. It is caring, nurturing, and compassionate. The new concept of the self-in-relation involves an important shift in emphasis in how we know what we know from separate to relational. Relationship, in this new context, is seen as the new basic goal of development. Aspects of the self, such as creativity, autonomy, and assertiveness develop within this primary context. There is no need to disconnect from others in order to develop oneself.

In the self-in-relation model, empathy is the central organizing concept in women's relational experience. In fact, relationship is defined as mutual empathy, and the ability to be in relationship is dependent on the capacity for empathy.

A woman's sense of self is organized and developed through practice in relationships, where the goal is increasing development of mutually empathic relationships—often a difficult task with a non-relational male. Her self-esteem is often related to the degree of emotional sharing, openness, and shared sense of understanding that she senses in return. And very often it is true that although she has provided empathic and relational understanding to the relationship, her partner has often been incapable of returning these qualities—which then impacts her self esteem. Women, therefore, need to feel that they are good enough at understanding and caring for others. Accurate empathy involves a complex process of interactive validation of the differences between self and other, and further, the validation changes as the relationship changes, in a subtle and complex dance that women seem to understand so well.

The context of women in relationship with men evokes the same caring qualities that are seen between mother and child or therapist and client, areas that have been studied more often than the male–female relationship, which only now is being looked at carefully. Like a mother or therapist, a female often provides a holding environment for the male. In this nurturing space, the female responds to the male's reactions and accepts him. Her sense of care is constant and reliable, and her judgment is less critical of him. She is, initially, primarily concerned for his needs.

Many times, she has a better understanding of his inner psychic reality than he does himself and therefore may clarify what is confusing for him. Why should it surprise us then that women, who know the feeling realm, have a better understanding of men than men do of themselves? This greater understanding occurs far more frequently than we have been led to believe. It further should come as no surprise that men are not at all interested in exploring this issue further.

Cathy said recently, "I know that I knew Donnie better than he knew himself. I could anticipate what would upset him, and I would try to talk to him about it before it happened. For example, he would always get upset when he was around his father. He would say that I was creating a problem if I tried to talk to him before we were going to see his father, and would tell me he could handle it. And every time, after seeing his father, he would be so upset. Then he began to realize I was right, so instead of saying I was right and talking about it before he saw his father, he would just deny that he was upset. But he wasn't okay, he would just sulk around and within a few days of seeing his father, pick a fight with me or one of the kids."

Carol easily identified: "I could tell almost immediately when I saw him what kind of day Rich had at work. I would say something about it, like 'do you want to talk about it?' He would deny that anything was wrong, but he was different—like absent for the rest of the night. It used to really bug me that he would just carry that around, when I knew if we could just talk about it, he would feel better."

Accurate empathy involves a complex process of interactive validation of the differences between self and other. This interaction changes as the relationship changes, and new depth and competencies are added. This involves the capacity to see the other and make oneself known to the other. Women excel at understanding this subtle dance and love to see relationships become richer and deeper, while men often seem to be unaware that they are at the dance.

Women "Get It"

The biggest struggle for women has been how to be completely open and in relationship with others and still be able to meet their own needs. The female solution has never been to seal themselves off and take a 'me first' attitude. Nor has it been to betray their own deep source of wisdom now that they are rediscovering it. Instead, women struggle to find the unique balance that includes themselves and others. Because things are changing so much, this means that an even bigger struggle will soon be emerging for women who must come to realize that the man in her life may simply be incapable of providing the depth of understanding that she needs and expects.

For many women this whole process of trying to relate to someone who has little or no idea of what is going on has been too difficult. So many women have left relationships because they felt that they could not really be themselves. Fewer and fewer women today feel guilty for including their own needs, and often their only choice after trying and trying with their partners is to leave.

Women no longer automatically need or want to defer to men. Similarly, women are no longer willing to change their personalities to accommodate their husbands or lovers. It appears now that women's willingness to do these things was often the glue that held relationships together. When she is no longer willing, the relationship breaks down. Divorce rates for baby boomers are skyrocketing and are higher than any other group.[8] These were the women most at risk. Many of them were raised in the 1950s and 1960s and believed what they were taught as they grew up. With the women's movement, these women were also the ones who woke up at midlife. Less than a third stayed in a committed relationship. Of this group, many women were maintaining separate residences. These women had everything to gain by changing, and leaving often meant finding themselves. In doing so, they were sailing with postmenopausal zest. The feelings of well-being in older women have been improving with each generation. Women are thrilled to break out of the old restrictive stereotypical roles. Almost every woman over 50 was certain that she would never marry again. They were thriving and developing new stories with larger and more vital themes for themselves.

No matter what age, women are thriving. They are falling in love with themselves and are quite sure they will never return to the old outmoded ways.

Men have far more problems with divorce than women, says Gail Sheehy, in *New Passages*.[9] Most men will tell you it was their wives, not them, who wanted the divorce. Two-thirds of the time the divorce was initiated by women. Men have a harder time picking up the pieces once separated. They had depended on their wives for their primary social support and are much less connected emotionally to others. They are lonely and often try to marry more quickly. They are more depressed, and many report that their needs aren't being met. These men, who typically say that they were shocked when their wives asked for a divorce, were surprised because they were never really emotionally involved in the first place and were further shocked to find that their wives were unhappy. The typical relationship today is made up of a woman who has changed and will continue to change, and a man who has not changed and will continue to resist change.

A clear picture in terms of relationships is emerging—that of a train wreck. One train is filled with zesty women who are filled with new esteem and purpose. The other is filled with men who are depressed, don't get it, and don't want to change, coming toward each other, at full steam (well, the female train is at full steam) on the same track, near a place called relationship, looking as if they are going to collide. Not to worry, the women's train sees what is going to happen, switches tracks, and heads off up the mountain. They were not about to let that accident happen. They had gotten off track once before, realized they were on the wrong train, woke up, went to school, went to work, and bought a new train. Now they are blazing a new trail, straight up. No one can stop them. And what of the men's train? Will they get it together? Will they stay parked by Pleasantville? Will they catch up? Are they capable of being in a committed relationship?

Our knowing, historically, swings between the two poles of nature and nurture. Today, the new technology that allows us to study the body more accurately from within is currently impacted by the nature (biological) hypothesis. We are learning more about hormones and their effects on our behavior. What is emerging is a picture of the female as clearly superior.

Should we predict that more and more relationships will fail until women finally refuse to marry or cater to men? Female science fiction writers have worked with this scenario many times. The heroines in these stories have learned that, one way or another, they can have babies without ever having to marry the men. Even centuries ago, the women in Lysistrata figured out how important they were to men. They refused to sleep with them until the men agreed to stop fighting. That was one of the few powers women had long ago. Not so today when science fiction and real science are often the same and there are many ways to have a child without having a husband.

The women, the stories, and the concepts here are just the tip of the iceberg—the foretellers of what is to come. Women have come too far to return to old roles. More and more, we will see that women will be unwilling to enter into a relationship they feel will not work for them and their children. The old equation is no longer viable. Women have changed, relationships have changed, and therefore men are going to have to change. This is the bottom line.

There are, however, bottom lines in relation to larger social issues. Currently, the issues are still just questions. Why, if females are the more moral sex, are males still the moral arbiters, the sex elevated to high positions of morality, when this position is founded on nothing more than male pronouncements? Why is our culture still based on an abstract, male-defined, eye for an eye, limited and punishing sense of morality when clearly there are superior ways of relating to each other?

As we continue to discover more about the biological underpinnings of males, females, and morality, we are faced with an ever-increasing need to change our epistemology. Males may indeed be biologically wired to cheat.[10] Further, they may be unable to control themselves and may require socially sanctioned outlets. But they can no longer have it both ways. They can no longer bask in their glow as the self-proclaimed moral sex, who feels entitled to make pronouncements on women's morality and reproductive decisions, when women have finally confirmed what they always sensed was true—that males have been considered more moral only because they said so. Women today know that females, with their more embodied morality, oxytocin, empathy, mirror neurons and whole brains are the more moral sex.

Chapter 7

Women Are the More Creative Sex

Yin	Yang
Caring	Curing
Create from their corpus	Create corporations
XX chromosomes	XY chromosomes

A recent commercial on television declared, "It's the cradle of Life. It's the center of civilization. Over the ages and throughout the world, men have fought for it—died for it. One might say it is the most powerful thing on earth, Hail to the V!" It is a commercial for Summer's Eve, and it's kind of shocking and funny because most of us have never seen the feminine presented in such a positive way. We love it or hate it because it's so true.

The long-held and erroneous belief that men are the more creative sex, however, is certainly one reason why the Summer's Eve commercial both shocks and amuses us. The belief that women are the less creative sex appears to be the foundation from which all the other beliefs that deem women as less than perfect arise. The word "creativity" here actually refers to the sex that gives birth or creates life—and historically, through the lens of culture, it has not been women. This most natural and primary act has been skewed to such an extent that, while we are forced to recognize that it is indeed females who give birth, there is an overarching story about a more important male who gives life and is more creative. Her contribution has been minimized as much as possible.

It is well known that the sex of the divinity that is worshiped by a culture informs all other aspects of the culture. The sex of the divinity aspect determines the sex that is revered and is considered more perfect. The sex that is elevated then influences all other areas and determines how we learn and how we know what we know. According to Achterberg,[1] for example, the sex of the divinity that is revered becomes viewed by the culture as the sex capable of curing disease. Because of dualism and the overvaluing of Yang, not surprisingly, we then value curing over caring. Most probably, however, caring was and still is more closely aligned to the perception of the body is an organic, interconnected whole, and more whole-brained females probably understood this even thousands of years ago. The act of caring, also needed when a person is ill, is still viewed as less valuable. It is difficult to even imagine a culture where caring was considered far more important and valuable than curing. In most cultures, curing is at a premium and for this reason, until very recently, the doctors who cured were males. Because caring was granted little value, women were permitted to be nurses who cared for the patient and were paid correspondingly less.

Our history is full of witch hunts that sought out and condemned women for practicing the art of curing and healing on their own. As late as the 1980s, being a midwife was still considered an illegal practice in some states. Of course, this did not happen out of context. Because men were in charge, they then ensured that health care became a huge business and the medical association powerful.

Today, however, many women are becoming doctors, and little by little the field is changing. The medical profession is slowly conceding that some of the Yin aspects may be important. When the medical profession can no longer help patients with chronic pain, they are sent to learn meditation techniques as a last, but often helpful, resort. Complementary medicine is slowly becoming more and more popular despite strong resistance from traditional medicine. Even today, however, the fields of medicine and psychology are still strongly controlled by a left brain system that continues to view the ill person as an assemblage of parts and thus orders more meds and more tests.

It wasn't always this way. Women were revered as the sex that brought forth new life for millennia before patriarchy began. The lens of life was an accurate reflection of the way things really were. In other words, what we believed and knew to be true (the lens of culture) was a direct reflection of what was actually true (the lens of life.)

At that time, women were also associated with the deep and natural mysteries of life and death. Archeologists and artifacts reveal that the human race has had an interest and fascination with deep philosophical and spiritual mysteries since the earliest times.

Part of the mystery was an attempt to understand the cyclical nature of life. Jean Shinoda Bolen[2] states that it is through a woman's body that a deeper understanding of the feminine aspect of divinity comes. Very often it involved the trinity, which, in ancient times, because the feminine was revered, reflected the stages of a woman's life—maiden, mother, and crone—as one very good example of a great cycle that brought together both the humans on earth as well as the moon and heavenly bodies. It is believed that the trinity we know today as father, son, and holy ghost is most probably derived from the earlier feminine trinity and was changed when the godhead became male.

Those who were interested in studying the mysteries often began as initiates. Very often the initiate typically has a deep mystical experience that changes them in a profound way. They become aware of the mystery and beauty of life and no longer fear death. For women, the experience of pregnancy was often viewed as a similar initiation and women entered into their pregnancies with a deeply conscious appreciation of the whole process. While the experience is the same today, its magnificence is diminished somewhat because women no longer have the words and the same deep spiritual context for it.

Pregnancy and childbirth are actually a profound psychological and spiritual experience. So often today, however, we miss the sense of the mystical in hospitals where pregnancy is treated as a clinical process. During pregnancy, the woman's sense of self changes and becomes firmly located in her body. It continues to narrow as the due date approaches. The maiden aspect of the female literally dies and gives way to the mother aspect. Just as earlier cultures understood the connection between the fertility of the soul and the fertility of woman's body, the connection is only now beginning to be understood again. Pregnant women experience a quickening, in the same way that women in ancient times would go on a pilgrimage to quicken the divinity of their souls.

Bolen feels that if the same reverence for the feminine was still present, women would experience the quickening of pregnancy as a profound religious experience. A pregnant woman would recognize that she shares in the same essence of the Goddess or earth mother as Creator, who brings forth all life from her own body, and sensing her own divinity would occur simultaneously with the first stir of new life in her own body. The Virgin Mary is a remnant left of the Goddess days, says Bolen. The words applied to her apply to all women who give birth: "Blessed am I among women and blessed is the fruit of my womb."

Labor and delivery are similar to a dark night of the soul experience. A woman can only surrender to what is happening to her. Similarly, the baby who passes through the birth canal performs a heroic task. Campbell says we are all heroes in our births. Many women report that they have an archetypal, mystical, and spiritual experience during pregnancy, labor, and delivery. They become every woman—every woman who has ever given birth. They become all women who have endured pain and were ultimately alone in a process that only they could do. They identify with every mother and every child for they are both at the same time—the child who is becoming a woman and a woman who is giving birth to a child. Unlike male rituals where death and transformation are acted out, women literally experience these things. Labor is an experience in which there is an inherent risk of death, and the woman is literally transformed—mentally, spiritually, and physically.

Women often sense this connection to something greater than them-selves intuitively. They instinctually feel connected to a greater feminine principle even though they may have no words for these experiences. The feminine principle and essence is a part of our collective memory and we can remember the same feelings just as we can remember something that happened to us in our childhoods. Because of its profound nature, the sense of the divine feminine is not lost but resides in unconscious of all women whether or not they have ever had children.

For the longest time, we have believed that women were simple creatures who were mere derivatives of men. Again we find that the very opposite is true. Females are not the sex that enjoys feeling superior, but it is becoming very clear that everything that has ever been written, said, or believed about females being the weaker or less perfect sex is wrong.

Every human embryo begins life as female. It is only in the sixth week of gestation that the Y chromosome produces special antigens that serve to make those embryos destined to become male begin their differentiation.

Females have the X factor. Females have two X chromosomes, while men have one X chromosome and one Y chromosome. As it turns out, the X chro-mosome is imminently important in terms of health and strength. It is well known that women have a longer life span, by an average of five years. Ob-servation alone has shown time and again that it is women who are more stoic when it comes to pain. They are healthier and have stronger immuni-ties. There is now scientific evidence that reveals just how important two X chromosomes are. The X chromosome is larger than the Y and in general contains more genetic material, and further, these genes appear to bolster the immune function. Females are less likely to develop cancer and other immune-based diseases.

Women, therefore, do not come from Adam's rib; men come from Eve's chromosomes. In the past, science informed us that females were the prod-uct of the default hypothesis, which stated that females are just biologically deficient males. The truth is that in order for males to even develop, the gene that determines male development must neutralize the more primary female-determining gene.

Mitochondrial DNA in the female and the Y chromosome in the male are the only two parts of the human genome that avoid shuffling. The Y chromosome avoids shuffling and is passed down essentially unchanged from father to son, generation after generation. The mitochondrial DNA escapes shuffling through a different process. "When the sperm fuses with the egg, all the sperm's mitochondria are destroyed, leaving the fertilized egg equipped with only the mother's mitochondria. Because of this ar-rangement, mitochondria are bequeathed unchanged from mother to child and a man's mitochondria are not passed to his children."[3] Both sexes then have lineages and branches that can be traced back to the first chromosomal Adam and the first Mitochondrial Eve. "The Mitochondrial Eve," says Nicholas Wade,[4] appears to have lived considerably earlier than the Y chromosomal Adam—about 150,000 years—but that may reflect the difficulty of dating mitochondrial DNA, which gathers mutations more rapidly than does the Y chromosome." Thus, while currently we are not clear as to why, it appears that the essence of the feminine predates the essence of the masculine.

For this reason, until recently, it was hypothesized that the male and his Y chromosome might eventually become extinct. Not surprisingly, few of us ever heard about this research. This hypothesis was reached because when cells divide, the Y has no cell to recombine with and if it doesn't recombine, it doesn't regenerate. Fortunately, even newer studies determined that nature appears to have insured that the 3 percent of the genes that remain on the Y chromosome are so crucial that the Y chromosome, rather than continuing to be degraded, appears to have been stabilized. So, says Stephanie Pappas,[5] "for now, the future of men seems solid."

The female egg is the largest cell in the body. Further, mature eggs are different from every other cell in the body, engaging in incorporative and nurturing behavior. The baby's cells stay in the mother's body and brain, which may create the shift that happens during motherhood. The mother's cells also remain in the baby's body.

The ovum actively takes sperm inside and supports the replication of its genetic material. Furthermore, eggs can repair sperm that are defective, including those with chemically induced mutations in the genetic code. In other words, women appear to be programmed, even at the cellular level, to fix the wounds of men.

One of the strongest arguments for the primary nature of the feminine is mitochondrial DNA. This DNA comes solely from the egg and can be traced only through the maternal line. It is feminine and is not contaminated when the sperm and ovum mix because the egg incorporates the sperm's mitochondria. It is mitochondrial DNA that enables us to trace our earliest matrilineal roots back to the first woman, sometimes referred to as Mitochondrial Eve.

"The fact," says Borysenko,[6] "that there is an unbroken line of genetic information that has been passed down from woman to woman through the ages, genetic information without which no embryo would develop, is final refutation of the old thesis that women are unfinished men. Without Eve's clever mitochondria, and their ability to mend broken sperm and initiate embryogenesis, the entire race would vanish."

Thus, it appears very clearly that rather than being the less creative sex, women are the primary creative sex. The act of bringing forth new life is without question the highest act of human creativity. The fact that this information has to be reiterated, promoted, and argued for is primarily a reflection of the present imbalance. Further, the belief that a male and therefore all males are the primary creators has skewed and informed the foundation of a belief system from which all other premises of the female as less perfect arise, and religious beliefs still appear to inform every aspect of our lives. The greatest error here is the completeness of the removal of the female from the creative process in the belief system. On the other hand, in truth and in nature, although the new life will come through the female, the male contribution is without question included and recognized as equally essential and necessary—a truer reflection of the Yin, the Yang, and the Tao. Had some aspect of the contribution of Yin been included, rather than denigrated, the story would reflect a far truer essence.

So indoctrinated have we been with the rightness and primacy of the male perspective, it appears that the collective consciousness of both males and females will continue to place a higher priority on male values for years to come. The topic of religion is the most incendiary of all subjects. People have fought and will fight to death for their religious beliefs. Despite the fact that there is no one true version of the male-based story that is universally agreed on, it does not appear that it ever really serves in any way to help people question it or even think more deeply about it. Most people just readily assume that what they believe is true and what people in another country or in the church down the street believe is wrong. Thinking too deeply about religion or questioning one's spiritual beliefs is strongly discouraged and then replaced with the concept of faith, leading to a closed circular reasoning that goes something like—if you had enough faith, you wouldn't need to question and you only question because you don't have enough faith. The nature of faith however is never universally agreed on. It does appear, however, that in terms of traditional organized religions—not spirituality, but religions—there is one belief that is universally agreed on, and that is that the male is primary. It is traditional religion that appears to the primary reason for the inequality between males and females. If it were truly equal, inequality would not exist in religion and this problem would cease to exist. Because things probably will not change in our lifetimes, women today would be well advised to pay careful attention and discernment to what they believe about themselves, what they believe and why they believe it.

Women should trust first what they know, in their bodies, their psyches, and their souls to be true.

Women's knowing has rarely, if ever, been reflected back to them as real or valuable, yet women are beginning to value themselves. The newest research in many fields, however, is finally beginning to confirm the primacy and importance of feminine relational, physical, intellectual, and neurological abilities, and this trend—also being seen in medicine, philosophy, theology, and even physics—will only continue. The old stories that assert the primacy of the male were developed in the absence of microscopes, brain research, and knowledge of hormones and genetics. Despite the fact that they no not reflect real life, we continue to embrace them via faith. The old traditions and values, however, are being threatened and one should anticipate that these changes will not be welcomed or easily accepted by those who embrace the status quo. The more women come into their own, the more fiercely the established belief systems will fight to maintain control and the status quo. It should come as no surprise as women are finally coming into their own, that even in 2012, the federal budget almost failed to pass due to one very touchy issue—that of women's reproductive rights. Women would be wise to recognize that the bottom line that holds inequality in place is the male need for control.

The feminine is that which nature has ordained to comfort and repair. It does not sit comfortably in a female's nature to desire to be deemed the most creative, rational, moral, or perfect sex, despite the fact that this is true. Females have no need for one-upmanship. Women do, however, have a need for equality and we do have a need to right what has been wronged. In a quest for authentic balance and a reality that reflects what is true according to the lens of life, women understand that false beliefs and understandings must be corrected, so that we can all live life more authentically.

There is a bottom line to this very important, confusing, long-lasting question around creation and meaning, and it goes far deeper than masculine and feminine principles. The Tao includes both Yin and Yang. The Tao includes and transcends the duality of opposites. It is known by countless names—God, Wholeness, Emptiness, Allness and Nothingness, Love, the Beginning and the End, the Alpha and Omega, and Oneness, to name just a few. Most human beings have a belief in something greater than themselves or an organizing force in the universe. This concept is perhaps the most difficult of all to understand. It is one in which the deeper we go in our epistemological exploration, the more we are led, not to answers, but to more questions. For this reason, well-known theologians and philosophers have stated that the concept of divinity is difficult enough to comprehend and should never have been gendered. To get to the bottom of this complex problem, the very last thing we can do to understand it is to generalize from specifics, for almost every specific belief is relative to the person who believes it. There are so many variations relative to what people believe that we are forced to go to bottom lines to even begin to understand.

Schuon[7] suggests a model to bring some clarity to the issue. His model looks like an open fan, with the flat bottom on the horizon so that it looks like a sunrise. The rays that go out from the middle represent all the various religions. He refers to the point where all the spokes or rays come together at one single point on the horizon as *perennial wisdom*. In other words, all religious and spiritual beliefs have the same common core. The most basic truth at this core is that all human beings appear to have an innate ability to conceive of something that is greater than themselves. Individually, we are all free to determine whether the ability to conceive a divine essence or unifying principle comes from a god gene in our genetic code, a belief system, a specific part of our brain that when stimulated elicits transcendent experiences, or from the source itself that informs us. Each of us decides whether this hunger for something greater than ourselves comes from a primary divine essence or an infinite source of intelligence or, on the other hand is because human beings have a tendency to create meaning. Regardless of its origin, it appears to be part of our humanness and the seemingly finite nature of life. The ability to have an experience of enlightenment or peak experience appears to be universal in human nature. It is this magnificent aspect of our humanness that often comes uninvited and is hard to describe or explain. People who have had such experiences feel that they were connected to something greater than themselves.

They reveal that time and space was changed or altered. Often they feel overcome with gratitude and love. The main reason that people have such a difficult time understanding these universal moments of enlightenment is because these experiences have been usurped by religion and have been presented as occurring only for the most pious and spiritually worthy, and few, if any of us, would count ourselves as worthy. Each of us has been led to believe that these spiritual experiences have been reserved only for the most holy. As a result, when it happens to us, we typically miss what it really is, often thinking instead that it is some kind of mental illness or that we are going crazy. These experiences are often described as the *most real* and are felt to be more real than real life. And they are. What a shame to miss yourself and your most real experiences because you do not have a framework that can explain it.

When these experiences happen within a spiritual or religious context, it makes perfect sense to interpret them from within that framework. Thus, the religions of the Abrahamic traditions—Christianity, Judaism, and Islam—

attribute the experience as coming directly from God or Jesus. Muslims believe it is a gift from Allah. Each religion or spoke of the fan has a different way of conceiving of the transcendent. When we focus only on the spokes, it is difficult to see the common core and larger spiritual picture. One does not need religion to be spiritual or to have a spiritual experience. Because religious and spiritual beliefs are so important and primary to life, it is no surprise that people have a great need to feel that their religious belief is correct and the others are wrong. When millions of people share the same basic belief, it appears to become even more real. Religious beliefs become so important that they inform every aspect of our lives and have been one of the primary reasons for war and other atrocities.

When we focus on the spokes and any one of the countless variations within each spoke as the truth, we often miss the more basic and universal truths at the center. It is the center that holds a few simple truths—that every human being has a tendency to create meaning that includes something greater than ourselves, that love is of primary importance and that the perennial truths in the Tao are equally applicable to every person. And, further, these truths cannot be gendered and should never be used as a way to control.

Chapter 8

The Real Reason Relationships Fail

Yin	Yang
Subjective	Objective
Emotional manager	Doesn't "get it"

When Dave and I got married, we certainly had no idea that we were buying into long-lived, traditional descriptions that would define him as a husband and me as a wife, as well as our relationship with each other. We thought that by opting for a small, private ceremony over a big church wedding we had sidestepped a lot of what was expected traditionally and that we were free to create what worked for us. To some degree however, none of us, especially when we marry, are ever completely free of all the cultural dictates and expectations. Although I had never considered myself very conventional, when it came to being a wife, I really had no other model and was, in many ways, adopting more long-standing traditions than I ever realized.

The basis of marriage according to the myth of romantic love, which still informs most of us, if only on an other-than-conscious level, is based on the concept of the halved soul. The halved soul concept suggests that each of us, male and female, are only complete when we have each other. Women, historically, were supposed to be dependent on men. Their worth came and still comes from being needed and desired. They must give themselves to men in order to be complete. Women, according to the myth of romantic love, were also cast as disobedient and the source of temptation in the myths. Women's sense of self, therefore, has been shaped by sacrifice and guilt.

Men are also supposed to suffer while in love—but from a lack of wholeness that is caused by women. Men's confused longing was and still is often based on need, blame, and uncertainty. He must need her as she must need him. Because he needs her, he can blame her and she is the cause of any uncertainty he may have.

These misinterpretations grew out of the context of thousands of years of women having been deemed less than men, and, further, because women were considered to be the cause of most of the world's problems. Women today, finally growing beyond these myths, are in need of new definitions and myths. The very fact that so many women today want more from their relationships and yet feel guilty is indicative of the fact that the myth is indeed in transition.

Judith Pintar[1] explored the origins of Romantic Love and traced the rituals that we celebrate today back to the earliest myths. These myths were shaped in the context of patriarchy, which was already in place prior to the earliest written word. In a patriarchy, the male owns the land, the property, the material, and the wealth. How does he ensure that his stuff gets passed on to his own flesh and blood when it is his female partner who actually gives birth? And beyond the actual stuff, how does he ensure, in the sense of personal and spiritual immortality that his genes, and not someone else's, gets passed into the next generation?

The only way the patriarchy could be ensured, men discovered, was if the female's chastity was guaranteed. If she were free to sleep with someone else, then he could never be sure if the male child, his rightful heir, was really his. Marriage became the way to ensure that she would be only with him. Further, and, almost of secondary consequence, he was also supposed to be only with her. The man and the woman, through the marriage ritual, were to form a partnership, emotionally, spiritually, and sexually that would become the basis of a family into which children would enter.

Nowhere do myths operate more powerfully than in the arenas of love and marriage. The myth of romantic love tells us that there is a perfect person for each of us if only we can find them. Romantic love is based on the concept that we are incomplete without a member of the other sex. It teaches women that their worth comes from being needed and desired by a man. Moreover, the greater the man's emotional and sexual hunger, the truer his love. If this love is irrational or uncontrollable, it signals only the degree of passion of his love for her. It justifies why he had to beat her if she looked at or talked to another man. *She* made me wild with jealousy. I loved her so much that I had to do *something*. It's her fault. Romantic love is associated with longing—the longing for wholeness, love, perfection, and rescue. This longing is based, at its core, on a sense of separation and the lack of wholeness of each person.

In the story of Adam and Eve, two different versions of the creation of humanity are offered. In the lesser known Gnostic version, God created Adam and Eve at the same time, and as equals. Imagine how different each man and woman would be today if the Gnostic version had become the accepted and popular myth. Unfortunately, the more familiar Christian story has Eve being created from Adam's rib. Adam was created first in the image of God, which is the basis for why men have been considered more perfect. Woman was made from man, not the other way around. Woman was created for man, not man created for woman. In this more popular version, Eve is cast as secondary. Further, she must give herself back to Adam, so that he can be complete. Because she must give herself to him and he cannot be complete without her, women are viewed as responsible for men's feelings. The male is the standard, and female is other. This view has become a part of the way we think, and has come to be accepted as the natural order of things and informs the list of Yin and Yang qualities. We even accept these roles for men and women as divinely inspired.

If, as the romantic love myth claims, women are each only half of a whole soul, and if, as our society teaches that the female is the lesser half, then women must need a man to be complete. Women are therefore dependent on men in all ways, including their self worth. By logical extension, then, if any problems arise, women are the ones who must accept the blame and make amends. In essence, women accept feeling guilty as proof of womanhood.

The philosopher, Schopenhauer, wrote that the reason that women are by nature meant to obey, might be seen in the fact that every woman who is placed in the position of independence, immediately attaches herself to some man. She allows herself to be guided and ruled by him. Women need a lord and master.

The halved soul—a continuation of the split in the primordial opposites, such as light and dark, Mother Earth and Father Sky, the sun and the moon—may, in reality, suggest that the longing men and women have for each other is actually a metaphor for spiritual wholeness. What we *really* long for is a connection with the divine to feel complete. The myth of romantic love, however, has replaced this longing for the divine with a longing for each other in order to feel complete.

In the more familiar story, Eve is also responsible for the original sin of disobedience. As punishment for committing this act, she is made responsible for suffering. Eve, of course, is simply a stand-in for all women. The idea of original sin originated in the fourth century with St. Augustine, who viewed Adam's sin as sexual desire. This sexual desire, however, wasn't Adam's fault, but rather Eve's, because it was she who tempted him.

To maintain this shift in guilt, men were forced to accept that their sexuality was beyond their control. Eve, and, by extension, all women, were viewed as the source of temptation, and thus the source of evil.

Even today, in many places, women are still blamed for men's sexual violence against them. Because women are responsible for men's suffering, women's longing must, according to the myth, always be accompanied by self-sacrifice and guilt. Similarly, men, who are required to find a perfect woman and then possess her, are made to suffer a lack of wholeness by a loss, caused not by them, but by women. The result is that longing in men must be accompanied by need and blame.

There are, of course, other interpretations. The Gnostics, the more feminine version of Christianity mentioned earlier, viewed the story very differently: no sin, no guilt, no devil, and no disobedience. Eating the apple represented, instead, consciousness and the freedom that accompanies living consciously. According to this interpretation, Eve's job is to awaken life in Adam. It is not surprising that a patriarchal culture would change this interpretation.

Romantic love, at its basis, is not inherently loving, for the myth of the halved soul requires that a part of ones identity is projected onto another person. It further serves to objectify the other person. When women became the objects of men's spiritual longing, they lost their sense of personal identity. This projected identity has periodically taken one of two forms. Either women were considered to be evil temptresses, or they were put on a pedestal and revered as submissive and virginal. Good women, therefore, either needed to be weak, obedient, and unselfish, or they were at risk for being seen as evil or loose creatures. This virgin–whore split is still widely prevalent in society today. Further, inherent in the myth of romantic love is the idea that women long to be rescued. The knight in shining armor has to rescue the damsel from some sort of distress. The ideal woman in the throes of romantic love is encouraged to be helpless and powerless.

Romantic love teaches women that they want to be dominated by men and should, accordingly, strive to be submissive. In this conceptual environment, it is no wonder that Freud found it so easy to create a psychology of women who desire to be ravished by males, and who would suffer hysteria if granted independence. In both romantic love and Freudian psychology women are required to be obedient and modest—attributes that accompany submissiveness. Simone de Beauvoir says of the myth of Virgin Mary, that it is the first time in history that a mother kneels before her son and freely accepts her inferiority. The Koran is even more explicit in stating that a woman will find a place in paradise only if she enjoys the full approval of her husband at the moment of her death.

Pintar finds a strong underlying fear in the patterns of oppression and dominance of women. Romantic love did little to establish healthy relationships between men and women; in fact, it effectively separated them almost into two species and made each a mystery to the other; a mystery that we still grapple with today. According to Pintar, the mythical explanation of Genesis is a story of man's fear of women because, "were it not for this fear, no one would have thought of attributing evil, sin, and devilry to Eve. Woman, who was able through her power and sorcery and seductive beauty, to lead Adam into a trap, to make him drop in one fell blow from the high heavens to the menial earth, and to be the cause of his destruction, his downfall and his death; she must indeed be an awesome and fearful creature." One cannot help wondering which came first, the myth or the fear.

The best clue comes from examining the qualities men require in women, in order not to be afraid of them and ensure they could control them. They are the qualities of a child: virginity, submission, vulnerability, purity, and powerlessness. We can't imagine these qualities being applied to males. The myth is so powerful that even today, many men continue to view women in this way, and some women still have difficulty perceiving themselves beyond these restricted visions.

It's no wonder most relationships don't work. The myth of romantic love has, for millennia, given men the right to define the identity and sexuality of women. Many women today, however, seem no longer willing to allow biology or traditional roles to define them. They can no longer fit themselves into this outdated myth and are moving, much more readily than men, toward a new and redefined myth of a more mature love, which requires each male and female to know first themselves as whole and complete individuals. For a woman, her partner is not an extension nor an object, but another whole and complete individual. In mature love, women sense that individuals must have a sense of their own identity and integrity.

Not Two Separate Halves, Two Mature Wholes

The real problem at the basis of what couples fight about is that, despite all the changes that have occurred, the area of relationship is still heavily weighted toward masculine values and concepts. It is no wonder that couples can't agree and the divorce rate is soaring. The war between the sexes is, in reality, a battle between the old, defended traditional concepts in men's heads and the newly emerging, more authentic concepts in women's heads.

"Did I tell you about last summer, about when I was trying to talk to Bill?" Carol asked when all of us could finally meet for lunch once the children were in school. Not surprisingly, we were talking about relationships. "I was asking him how he felt—like emotional stuff. I know he doesn't want to talk about his feelings. And, I could tell he didn't like it, but I kept asking him questions and trying to talk to him. He got up in the middle of the conversation and left. He didn't say anything, so I thought he went to the bathroom or went to turn off the fan, or something. I waited for like 20 minutes and finally got up to look for him. He had gone to the living room and was sleeping! I went back to bed and just cracked up. It was too funny to be sad. It was ridiculous!"

"The next morning I said to him, 'What? What? Last night?'

"And all he said was 'I didn't want to talk about it.'"

Isn't it hysterical? I thought to myself. *We are all experiencing the same problem. We women have all changed but the men haven't.*

"Well, what I want to know," said Nancy, "is why. We didn't marry idiots, but it seems like I got smarter and he got dumber. Didn't you talk all the time before you were married? My husband used to think my ideas were wonderful and creative. I am beginning to think that his interest was just some kind of a courting ritual because he knew talking intimately is what I loved best about him. And, I think he really liked it, too. Now, almost any discussion that goes beyond the weather makes him nervous. Even when I ask him how he feels about easy stuff—like how he feels teaching, he just clams up. He used to try to stop my questions by making me feel stupid, but I'm not buying into that anymore. A lot of time, I feel that he really doesn't know how he feels, and recently I realized that if he doesn't know how he feels, how is he ever going to know how *I* feel?"

"I've pretty much given up," said Pam. "He thinks sex solves everything. He has no idea how he really feels. No wonder he doesn't know how the kids and I really feel."

"You know I don't talk about our counseling," said Cathy. "It just doesn't seem fair to Greg. Confidentiality and all, I owe it to him and he really is trying. But I'll tell you, they don't talk to counselors either. So it's not just us they don't talk to. Our counselor asks him stuff and he seems to have the hardest time answering her. And sometimes he says the dumbest. . . . Oh, you get my point." She didn't continue and no one expected her to.

Karen tried to change the subject. "It's no wonder we all feel this way. I was at my sister's last weekend. She had the *Men Are from Mars*[2] book, so I start reading it. There is this part where it says he's supposed to listen to me more, and I'm not supposed to make 'unsolicited comments.' I was driving home the next day and it hit me," she said, "an 'unsolicited comment' is anything he doesn't want to hear. And I thought 'Are you kidding me?'"

No, it's no joke, and it isn't entirely funny how much damage one little book can do.

Men Are from Mars, Women Are from Venus. Then What?

For many years, the *Men Are from Mars, Women Are from Venus* books were the bible of relationships. Author John Gray continues to write books with the same themes that apply to different age groups and situations. Until recently, he used to appear on television, give lectures, and do infomercials. His books were the most successful books ever on relationships. They were best sellers, and before Harry Potter, sold more books than any book other than the Bible. They were compelling and popular because Gray, at a time when it was not politically correct to talk about differences between men and women, had the nerve to say and capitalize on the fact that men and women were indeed different. Women knew intuitively, especially when it came to relationships, that men and women are very different. Saying that the sexes were different, during the time when feminists were telling women that they were just like men, appeared to be the hook that snagged women and made his books so popular. Once in, Gray managed to use this premise of difference against them, in the same way that, historically, difference has always been used against women. Men liked Gray's difference premise, too. It let them off the hook by saying that men really just aren't all that interested in relationships. The difference premise when applied to women, however, appears to have been skillfully designed to blame her and keep her feeling guilty.

The author states that it's women's fault that men are not relational, for men are like rubber bands, and if women would only leave them alone, men would return to intimacy. Women, he says, are also compulsive creatures who drive themselves and men crazy with their desire to get everything done. They need to remind men, nicely, of the jobs they are supposed to do. Most women, however, get "resentment flu" because they keep forgetting what great guys their husbands are. Further, women need to feel loved mainly because they can't handle their new independence.

Why bring up a book that nobody talks about any more? Because, if you are an adult, it probably impacted you in some way. It revealed that even after the so-called equality that resulted from the women's movement, women were and are still interested in improving their relationships—and can still be controlled by guilt. It showed further that men and women were hungry for information that spoke, not to their politically correct sameness, but to their differences. The two historical themes, women's need to be controlled and men's need to control, were finally, becoming obvious to any woman who has freed herself of the old concepts and collective female guilt. The subthemes of the book, however, were a conceptual disservice to both men and women. Men were reduced to their lowest common denominator and rendered incapable of thinking of anything but sex and protecting their egos. They were encouraged to retreat emotionally and listen rather than talk. In addition, women, according to Gray, keep doing things that make men crazy. What man wouldn't love the premises in Gray's books? But, interestingly, it was women who bought the books.

The fact that women bought these books in record numbers is an excellent example of where the collective of women was even 10 years ago. Women were willing to accept what an expert said about them for the small trade-offs that were required of men. Women may still buy these books out of desperation, but they no longer seem to buy what he says. The books typically frustrate them, but they usually can't say why. Women have told me about throwing and burning these books because they got so angry. Few, however, can actually articulate what it is that they find so frustrating. Part of the reason they are frustrated is because they do not yet have concepts to help them clearly define their frustration. Just like wanting more, they sense that something is wrong but can't quite articulate it.

It's Always Her Fault

Like most male experts before him, Gray continues to make it the women's fault that men aren't more relational. The reason men pull away, like rubber bands, for example, is that they need to get away from the woman's compulsivity about the relationship.

"When I read that part," said Carol, "I immediately thought, *well, of course, he'll come back—for sex,* but I didn't think that Gray would actually think that sex was intimacy, so I gave the book the benefit of the doubt and tried to wait Jim out at one point. I read the book and it assured me that if I would just leave Jim alone—back off from pressuring him about intimacy—he would just be more intimate. What a load of crap. I backed off for three months, and he didn't make one move toward intimacy. Sex—yes—but not intimacy. He seemed to take me for granted all the more. He forgot my birthday. I didn't say a word. Three weeks later, when we were talking about his mom's birthday, he realized he had forgotten mine, and he said, 'Sorry, babe.' He seemed to love it that I never said a word about anything. In fact, one time, he said, 'Gee, that book seems to be working.' He loved it that I didn't say anything, but he sure never got more loving or intimate. When I thought about it, it occurred to me that back when women never said anything because they weren't allowed to, then, according to Gray's premise, the men should have been all intimate because they were never pressured, right? Ha!"

"Greg says things to me that I don't want to hear, so how come Gray acts like men don't make unsolicited comments?" asked Nancy.

"And, why is it that when men forget how wonderful *we* are, *they* don't have resentment flu?" asked Carol.

Gray appears to base women's compulsive behavior, resentment flu, and unsolicited comments on the fact that women really aren't comfortable with their new independence.

He starts with erroneous assumptions that appear to be documented only by him since his book has no references at all, and then makes further sweeping generalizations aimed at women's self-esteem that are based on the original false assumptions. On what is he basing his assumption that women can't handle their new independence? Who said that women become compulsive when they forget they are loved? His books seem to be perfect examples of male projection.

In the ultimate misreading of women, he states that women only try to change men because they really need to change themselves. Here was the big sticking point for me. This premise, based on the "you can only change yourself, not the other person" just seemed to be a very easy way to ensure that it always her fault.

The premise ignores all the information about men needing to change and blames women doubly for sensing that men might have a problem. If she acts to help him because of what she senses, she is wrong to do so. She is further wrong because the problem is, in reality, hers.

"That sounds a lot like what I call the 'church loop,'" said Nancy. "There's no way out. If you have any questions about church or what you believe, the answer is that you just have to have more faith. If you had more faith, you wouldn't have questions. So, in the relationship, if you have any questions and think there should be changes, it's really your fault and you just have to change yourself."

"Or leave." Pam volunteered. "I can't believe that a couple years ago, when I first heard about this book, at my high school reunion, I actually sort of believed some of it. It's really interesting to see how I have grown out of it—or grown up or something."

"I think we all have, but I am sure that there are a lot of women who still think this is the way to fix their relationships."

It is interesting that Gray never justifies male behavior. Apparently, he can't. For example, he blames women for treating men like children, but never justifies or explains why men often act like children. Men, according to Gray, just aren't that interested in relationships, and it's the woman's fault if she tries to pressure him. He should be allowed to withdraw to his cave, and she should not bother him unless she wants to be "burned by his dragon." Men are encouraged, by Gray, to resist women, either actively or passively—the logical extension of the self-as-separate psychology.

If he's unhappy, it's her fault for not being supportive enough. If she's unhappy, he feels like a failure—and it's her fault for making him feel that way. According to Gray, men aren't motivated to listen to women, and don't have a clue that they are supposed to take turns in the conversation. He goes on to say that "Men get so focused on solving a problem that they don't respond."

"Men think they don't have to say anything else to a woman because they've already paid her the ultimate compliment by marrying her."

"Men should 'duck and dodge' in conversations."

He suggests that men can only listen if women are completely supportive. He never gives any hint that men are capable of going beyond listening. He also says that men are prone to argue even when they are the ones that have made the mistake. Despite all the mistakes men make, however, it's always, automatically, her fault—a perfect example of how women have been controlled.

Even when he presents a list of mistakes that both men and women make, Gray isn't fair. Women try to change men, attempt to improve and correct male behavior, and criticize them. Men get angry, don't listen, and minimize women's feelings. In every case, the things she does wrong are responses to the things he does wrong, yet the lists are presented as equal.

Women apparently read his books because they wanted to make their relationships work, and they probably tried his suggestions. While there is no question that Gray was a major influence on women and relationships, hopefully, with just a couple years distance, can now look at his books as a reflection of the repression in our own lifetimes and laugh-almost.

His books are a great example of how women know what they know. We believed him because he said he was a relationship expert. Even though his suggestions went against the grain of what women know to be true intuitively, we bought into it because we are so desperate to make our relationships work and because he was one of the few who talked about the differences between men and women. Unfortunately, he used the concept of difference to continue the negative stereotypes against women.

Interestingly, most of us thought Gray was gone from the scene but he showed up on the Internet recently in 2012 to respond to a flurry of interest around why men cheat. Sadly, he hasn't changed with the times. Men cheat, says Gray, for three basic reasons: even if his partner is beautiful, she may not be interesting. Her fault! They also cheat because she may not be providing enough sex. Her fault! And, even if they are having regular sex, she may not be having orgasms, which would release pheromones that would keep him attracted to her. Her fault! It is hard to believe that any female today would still believe his outmoded reasons for why men cheat.

Gray capitalized on difference and measured women against a male standard, where they fell short. Dr. Phil,[3] on the other hand, promotes equality and because our culture or knowledge base is not really equal, women get blamed again. Men and women, says Phil, are equal in every way. Therefore men and women are equal contributors to both the problems and the solutions in relationships. It's interesting how, in just a few short years, women went from being guilty of resentment flu and not loving themselves enough to being equally responsible for all the problems and solutions in the relationships.

This seems, in a way, to be a step forward for women. Men are now at least half responsible for their actions. Women, too, are now equally or half responsible for all the solutions in the relationship. This premise would be true if the culture was completely equal—but, of course, it's not. Dr. Phil's suggestions don't appear to be nearly so blatantly skewed as Gray's suggestions. Women today wouldn't tolerate it. This, however, makes the whole issue of relationships more subtle and difficult to understand and respond to. Dr. Phil seems like a good guy. He even clearly states at the end of his book, "Men just don't get it." Countless women have said this countless times in their lives. Many men have also said they don't get it. But what does this statement really mean? What is it that women get that men don't get? If so many women feel this way, it would seem that this issue is the most fundamental and primary issue worth exploring. If men don't get something and women do, shouldn't it be women who are writing about rescuing relationships? And, really how can things be equal between the sexes in a relationship if men just don't get it?

Saying that things today are equal often appears to be just a new and more subtle variation on inequality. For example, on *Oprah,* women were furious when Dr. Phil gave his advice to the couples who had recently had babies. The women stated that their primary focus after the birth of the baby was, not surprisingly, the baby. The men said that they resented the fact that their wives focused too much of their time and energy on the baby. The men no longer felt special. They felt that they had been displaced from the center of their wives' universe.

Phil's response was that the children will eventually grow up and leave but the partnership of the man and wife should last a lifetime. His advice to women was to pay attention to their husbands too. This same issue was explored in the HBO series, *Tell Me You Love Me*. The men wanted their wives back—the way they were, before the baby arrived. They felt that their wives, who were now mothers, were consumed with the care, responsibility, and love for their infant.

This issue only presents itself when true inequality is still the norm. In an ideal world where things are truly equal, this issue of a new baby would assume its proper perspective. First of all, the couple would decide—free of all ridiculous rules about contraception and reproduction—when it was time to bring a new life, that requires full time care, into the world. The mature response, from *both* parents, would be to focus on providing what is necessary for that new life to survive, thrive, and grow. Because she is the one who is most biologically wired to feed and nurture the child, and will by necessity be the one who responds to the child's needs for care around the clock, she should have full support to do that. His first and mature response should be to support *her* efforts. His job is to do whatever it is that makes this most important and full time task easier for her. Whining that he wants his wife back or that he feels left out is just exactly that: an immature response that we shouldn't even have to consider, think about, or rationalize.

In truth, this issue is far larger than merely an equality issue: it is a biological imperative. Trying to make a woman feel guilty that so much of her energy is directed to her infant while at the same time ensuring that her husband doesn't feel neglected is about as ridiculous as blaming her for not giving him sons, when it is his sperm that determines the sex of the child.

In general, women are just better than men at being the experts in the relationships. Men have problems in relationships because they are less skilled in being relational and, further, less skilled in generating solutions to relationship problems. Relationship books and therapies that view men and women as equal contributors to the problem and the solution fail to acknowledge her skill and his lack of ability.

Today, we all pretend that it is equal, and it is hard to see the inequality because it is so present and pervasive and accepted. For this reason, it is a little easier to see the inequality when it appears in the law, which is supposed to be, unlike subjective relationships, more clear and objective. However, even in the legal arena the laws remain biased toward males. Today, both men and women are judged innocent or guilty based on what is referred to as "the reasonable person standard." The word "person," not surprisingly, means male. In other words, all people are judged according to what a reasonable male would do—and therein lies the problem. The authors of *A Law of Her Own*[4] suggest that both men and women would fare better with laws that reflect a "reasonable female" standard. They believe that we would all benefit from developing increased empathy toward women's experiences. We should ask whether a particular experience respects women's well-being from a feminine, rather than a masculine, perspective. Using examples from the law is a good way to look at relationships. Legal situations where there is a female victim and a male perpetrator are worth closer scrutiny, since they cover issues that also occur in relationships—sexual harassment, rape, and even murder. Because both law and relationships are based on the male experience, both areas are presently skewed toward men and the male perspective. What is written about both relationships and legal matters conforms not only to societal expectations but further, continues to affect people's perception. And both scenarios fail women.

Women recognize that relationships are based on feelings and that a man must know how he feels before he can know how anyone else feels. Romantic Love is designed to keep both lovers on a superficial level. Women are just more mature about relationships. They have the emotional intelligence necessary and mature love requires emotional intelligence. *Emotional Intelligence,*[5] the book that first shed light on the importance and necessity of consciously integrating one's emotions into one's life, clearly states that women are the relational experts.

Basing his findings on the latest studies on both nature and nurture, morality, and developmental theory, author Daniel Goleman states, "All of this means that, in general, women come into a relationship groomed for the role of emotional manager, while men arrive with much less appreciation of the task for helping a relationship survive."

Millions of women have outgrown the concepts from *Men Are from Mars* and the halved soul—and are certainly struggling with leaving behind the fossilized indoctrinations of the old ways of thinking. They are starving for something that better reflects their new understanding. Many women are collectively banging their heads against the wall. They thought they had been smart and done the right thing. After dumping their first macho husbands, they had married sensitive new age guys, only to find out that all the wonderful relational skills these men had displayed prior to the marriage were usually nothing more than new and revised courting rituals.

It seems as if society has been set up to provide these skills to unskilled men. Movies, songs, and even billboards provide models for men on how to display the new intimacy skills women wanted. Women warmed to the new hints of relationality and assumed that's what they were getting. They thought that since they changed, the men had, too. And, to make it worse, women blamed themselves, for being dumb enough to have hooked up with the wrong man—again. Even recently, actress Demi Moore stated in a *Vanity Fair* article that she felt unlovable and wondered if she was capable of love—after her husband felt the need to spread his seed.

While some things, like women taking their husband's infidelity personally, have not changed, other things have changed very quickly. It appears that in the past 30 years, human males, like males of all species, have quickly adapted new strategies to attract the females. Women today are looking for relational skills in a mate. Just like the female bird, who sees the male attractively fanning his feathers for her benefit and thinks "Oooo, Nice genes," and the female gorilla, who observes the male pounding his chest and displaying his manhood and thinks "Mmmm, good protector," the human female, today, hears the male say, "I just love sitting and talking with you for hours, and I understand exactly what you are saying, and I've been thinking about our relationship . . ." and is smitten. It is just what she wants to hear. The problem is that it often doesn't last. Three months into the marriage or the relationship and most males have sunk back into the status quo.

We continue to struggle with the ramifications of inequality at the deepest levels. Inequality gets translated into myth and beliefs that fail to reflect reality. Occasionally, we find examples of what can happen before or after patriarchal values exert their influence.

In a small indigenous tribe, one of the few matrilineal cultures left today, it is the woman who woos the man. The men wait to be asked. Everyone in the tribe agrees that this is best because they all know that it is the women who are the experts, and that love comes first into the heart of the woman. The tribe wisely makes a distinction between sex and love. Only after love comes to the women, can it also come into the man. The female, they believe, will make much better and stable decisions concerning love. Women have the unquestioned authority in matters of the heart. Unfortunately, the matrilineal cultures are changing and joining the rest of the world that embraces the male standard. Divorces, which had been almost nonexistent in that culture, are now increasing as the men are becoming westernized; and as Christianity, which teaches the young that it is the man, not the woman, who is in charge of love enters the picture, the male standard is becoming solidified.

Myths are the stories we tell ourselves and myths about love are one of our most important stories. It all depends on how we explain it to ourselves. Robert Sternberg[6] realized that the psychological theories about love are often at odds with how people actually think about love. People think in terms of stories, and the old story no longer matches reality for women. If it doesn't work for women, then by extension, it won't work for men. The stories of each partner, says Sternberg, have to match to make love last. With so many conflicting stories and misinformation about love, it's no wonder that people so often divorce. Perhaps this impasse has always existed between the sexes. If it did, however, we never heard much about it before women came into their own. Relationships for women are primary. For men, relationships have often been secondary—like irritating background noise, or something they put up with, or something that took them away from their real focus—work, sports, or anything that didn't require real talk.

The process that questions the roles and standards that determine how we collectively live our lives usually evolves slowly—giving people a chance to adjust to new ideas. In part, this is accomplished through the use of myth and role models. Actor John Wayne, for example, provided a role that matched the collective understanding of men, and served as hero and model of a real man. Like John Wayne, men were supposed to be brave and strong. They went to war fully prepared to be heroes—and in the movies, they usually were. They protected women and children. They talked about their feelings so rarely that we believed that men didn't need to.

The Relational Lie

A perfect example of how women can be confused is the relational lie. Although it has rarely been acknowledged, women have always intuitively known that they have better relationship skills than men. The relational lie, however, puts men, who have very little understanding of, relationships, in charge of women and the relationship. Men with little relational ability then determine the standards that are acceptable. Thus, the degree of sharing, the quality of interaction, and the sense of closeness have all been decided by men who basically have no idea what relationships are about.

Given that their feminine knowing has rarely been valued and that this knowing has never been reflected back to them, women have actually done a remarkable job, throughout time, of intuiting this problem correctly. Their appraisals of relational problems *are* more accurate. Their suggestions for improving relationships *are* more effective. They have just never gotten the chance to say anything. Years ago, they weren't educated. Today, anything women say along these lines, risks being labeled as male-bashing.

Having had little practice with feelings other than anger, fear, and dread, men are typically relationally challenged, resorting to silence, blaming, stonewalling, anger, defensiveness, and even violence to solve any problem. Contrary to popular male-myth, a woman doesn't try to change the man in her life for her own good; she does it to improve their relationships and the quality of men's lives.

One by one, women are beginning to recognize the relational lie. As many men see women getting stronger and starting to catch on, they are often reacting in the only way they know—getting more defensive. Because both men and women are affected, each sex seems to be at different points of understanding. A woman, part of the relationship equation for example, who does not yet recognize that her husband doesn't really doesn't know how he feels, may find it almost impossible to believe that the very feelings that are so inherent in her are so elusive to him.

It is only a matter of time until both sides of the relational lie are exposed. The more we understand the relational skills of women, the greater insight we will have into the relational problems of men. Women have always been blamed for men's relational problems, are still impacted by the myth of romantic love, which accompanies the relational lie. The problem is compounded because few women make a distinction between their external and internal lives.

Relationships are the last bastion of male control and this is one of the main reasons relationships fail. Men have so much to unlearn in this sphere that it probably feels to many of them that they will never be able to have peace in a relationship. Men feel threatened and women feel guilty as both sexes try to navigate their way through a major myth shift. Until the real problem is identified clearly and worked through, however, there will never be true equality between the sexes, especially in the area that matters most to both of them—the relationship.

Relationships don't exist in some separate little sphere that can be fixed with 10 easy steps. There are at least three elements to any relationship—the man, the woman, and the relationship between the two of them. Each element has its own history, its own context, its own perceptions, and its own way of functioning. Each aspect—men, women, and the relationship—is anchored in its own epistemological framework of how we know what we know. And it's all changing.

Chapter 9

Male Relational Dread

Yang
Relational dread
Asleep emotionally
Reluctant revealers

"Did God make a mistake—like a tidal wave or earthquakes or floods—when he created women, or did he do it to men on purpose? I really want to know because if it is a mistake then maybe we can do something about it. Find a cure, a vaccine, or build up our immune systems. Twenty push-ups a day and you never have to be afflicted with women ever again!" railed Jack Nicholson as the devil in *Witches of Eastwick*. What a wonderful male-based epistemological framework and it has lasted for thousands of years, alive, well, and basically unchallenged until recently.

Of course, it couldn't be women who were allowed to say there was anything wrong with males on a personal level. Feminism had challenged the abstract male epistemology and theories, but their attacks were never directed to the personal and interpersonal, everyday levels of relating to each other. For that reason, my memory is unclear about how my knowing actually unfolded over those years. My learning seemed to occur in a process that took two steps forward and one step back. I had started to sense that there were real and even universal problems around relationships, but no actual research ever confirmed this. I had the sense that what Dave and I were experiencing on a personal level went far beyond our relationship, but I had no way of knowing if this was actually true or not.

The changes that had started several years earlier had certainly improved our relationship. We realized that communication was so important, and as the children got older and started being able to help with clean up and dishes after dinner, we settled into a routine of taking our coffee and sitting outside or in his office if the weather was bad, and just talking. We would often talk about the topics that Dave had covered the week before in a weekly study group. Lynn, her husband, and about a dozen other people meet at our house every Friday night, and Dave led a discussion on various philosophy books, often Jungian, that we choose to study.

Married to Dave, I had become familiar with discussions around abstract philosophical concepts, which, most of the time, truly alluded me. When I talked with Lynn, however, about these concepts during the week, she was somehow able to explain them to me in a more personal way that was easier to understand. This was long before I had ever learned about the differences in the ways that males and females think or the concept of separate and connected knowing. All I knew was that when I talked to Lynn everything Dave had discussed earlier finally made much more sense.

So when Dave and I talked each night over coffee, without really realizing what I was doing, I started moving the abstract philosophical discussions into a more personal realm. Because I had finally started to understand how deep philosophical concepts actually related to my own life and our relationship, I was excited and wanted to know what he thought about these same things. I sensed, however, that he was uncomfortable when the discussions got too personal. When I started to link the concepts to what was happening in our real lives, he often seemed confused or angry, and I literally did not understand his reaction.

"Why are you getting mad?" I would ask carefully.

"I'm not," he would say. "I'm just tired of all this talk."

"I don't understand," I would respond, "I love it that philosophy finally makes sense to me. I just want you to share *how* you understand it."

"I don't understand what you are asking me," he replied rather dismissively.

I continued cautiously, "I just want to understand how you connect what you teach to your personal life. I mean isn't that really what philosophy is all about? Isn't it meant to be applied to one's real life and sense of authenticity."

"Yeah, so what is your point?"

"Well, I just want to know how *you* feel about how what you teach relates to your real life . . ."

"What do you mean 'real life?'"

"Well, like, do you feel you are living an authentic life?"

Silence. Waiting.

"What do you mean authentic?"

"You teach philosophy. You know what authentic means."

Waiting . . .

"I mean . . . ," I would continue, after waiting for what seemed like ages, "when you spend more time with the children, does it make you feel like you are living more authentically? Does it feel like you are relating to your children in a more authentic way? Are you happy about this? How do you feel about it?"

"What do you mean, 'How do I feel?'"

I was surprised that the more personal questions about how he felt were almost always answered with another question: "What do you mean how do I feel?"

I would think to myself, "This really isn't a hard question. It is how my friends and I talk all the time." At first, I thought he was just putting me on or trying to make me mad. Everyone knows how they feel, I reasoned. I could not believe that he didn't know how he felt.

While I was surprised that Dave didn't seem to connect his feelings to his thinking, I thought for a long time that maybe that was just how he processed information or that philosophy required objectivity. I would get hints from my friends that they were sensing the same types of problems, but without any information to confirm this, there was no way that we could understand that this might actually be true.

For this reason, I remember very well the first time I ever read anything that suggested that males might indeed have a problem with feelings. I remember where I was and who I was with like it was yesterday.

My friends and I were sitting in a circle, actually reading aloud to each other. The article, written by Robert Bly in the late 1980s, was called "Male Naiveté and the Loss of the Kingdom."[1] Bly had started a mytho-poetic movement that attempted to connect men with their male ancestors and roots because he felt men had become "soft." He encouraged males to meet, read poetry, beat drums, and connect with other men. It actually became a rather popular movement that men either embraced or ridiculed. My friends and I were aware of the men's movement and, for the most part, thought it was a male response to women's consciousness raising groups. We thought it was more of a social thing—women met in living rooms and men met in the woods. We had no idea that men had started meeting because of a *real* problem, and my friends and I were mesmerized that an article that actually addressed this new issue had been written.

The article we were reading was a myth about a male who had failed to complete various tasks such as keeping the kettles boiling. Much of the mytho-poetic story didn't make sense to us, which was one reason we were taking turns. It was hard to understand what the mythic images were supposed to represent. For example, boiling the water was associated with shrewdness and power. The lost gold shavings in the story represented the loss of male power. Tucked into the myth, however, were ideas that we had never before heard or could even imagine being written. It was the first time that I had ever read anything by an expert that suggested that males might have some issues. Bly identified three problems that he felt defined today's males.

Naiveté

Naiveté, according to Bly, comes to men who avoid the dark side of their own motives. They discount their own anger and think there is more goodness in the world than there really is. This is particularly true of "New Age" men, said Bly, who are soft and avoid anger and refuse to fight. They go around, however, as if they are victors. Naiveté occurs because men have not been initiated, and this lack of initiation makes it impossible for the man in a relationship to keep a good container around himself. When he is fighting with a woman, he opens himself to attacks and allows his chest to be pierced with her arrows. He promises to be more thoughtful and less sexist. The naïve man talks too much and tells strangers his most intimate secrets. He values sincerity above all else and fails to respect his own genius. He loves wholeness even though he is not whole. He is a permissive parent who lacks authority.

Passivity

Because they have never actually been initiated, men are also passive. According to Bly, the whole male emotional process fails to become activated without initiation. In aborigine cultures, the older men rip the young boys from their mothers' arms. They take them away and initiate them into the male world, which activates their emotional body. The bodies of today's men are not activated and, thus, men can't hold their own boundaries.

Women's bodies, on the other hand, are activated, and their emotional and physical bodies appear to be more interconnected. Women notice that men's emotional bodies are not activated and often offer to help them make the connection. According to Bly, however, a woman cannot activate a man's emotional body. This is the task of the older men in the tribe.

If the man's emotional body has not been activated, then he will let women take the lead in many areas of relationship. He may not recognize certain emotions that he experiences and will be unable to talk about his feelings. He may not know how to fight fruitfully with a woman and develops weak boundaries. He will then live through years of relationship turmoil being passively enraged and secretly hostile. This kind of man lets others do his thinking in public arenas. In his private relationship, he lets his wife do his feelings for him. At parties, he is unexpressive and impassive while his wife is actively and excitedly talking. In private, his wife is angry at his passivity and expresses the anger that he cannot express. These men also let their wives do their loving.

Numbness

Both passivity and naiveté are related to numbness. To define numbness, Bly tells a story about how most boys feel. If the boy is afraid of the big scary world and he asks his mother to protect him, he knows he will eventually be at a loss to protect himself. To learn from her protection, he must learn to feel as a woman feels, and this will mean that something inside of him will die. Therefore, he rejects becoming like her and he becomes numb instead. This numbness is only in the heart region. His brain and pelvic area remain alive and passionate, but the heart space, in between, must go numb. The man, says Bly, recognizing that he feels numb, needs to sever the tie of protection he made with his mother and needs to connect with his father. Even at midlife, he requires the same protection he asked from his father at age two. Because he probably didn't get it, he must now get it from other men.

Naiveté, passivity, and numbness are all a kind of sleep. According to Bly, these changes in men, which began when industrialization and technology replaced the pioneer spirit, have intensified in the last 50 years as fewer men worked the soil or grew and hunted their own food. The modern boy-man is caught in limbo. He has lost the kingdom, the gold shavings, along with their vitality and meaning. Bly's solution was to set up "initiations" for men that would allow them to reclaim those elements of life.

Ten years later, the movie *Pleasantville,* another story about modern life, showed men coming home from work, hanging up their hats, and saying, "Honey, I'm home." Dinner was waiting, and everything was pleasant. Wives never challenged their husbands, so unpleasant discussions never come up. But Pleasantville changes as women start to get their own ideas about what is pleasant. The wives learn to say a new word—"No." Both Bly's fables and Pleasantville's story deal with our discomfort around the male inability to express his real feelings.

Prior to the 1980s, feelings were considered to be something that only women were involved with. Because they were associated with the feminine, the whole mode of relational skills, communication about feelings, and feelings themselves were granted little importance. Feelings have always been considered as baser, grosser, and less noble and perfect than thinking, and, until recently, we shared a collective and pleasant belief in the John Wayne myth. Like strong, silent John Wayne, the myth implied that men knew how they felt, but they didn't need to talk about it.

It appears that we were all working with two incorrect assumptions about men. First, we believed that men did not need to express their feelings, and second, we believed that men knew how they felt. Being granted wisdom without having to say much of anything was a wonderful thing for men, and it should come as no surprise that they don't want this cultural belief to change. To this day, there are still millions of families where the man, simply because he is the man, is not expected to speak. It is assumed that he knows how he feels without having to say so. If he does speak, his word, no matter how brilliant or stupid, is the final word.

Maybe It's Men's Turn to Be "It"

The decade of the 1990s saw a swing of the pendulum, however. Articles, books, movies, and television all reflected a change in how men were viewed. The war against women, identified by feminists in the 1970s, seemed to become a war against men, with the assumption that men were now fair game. The war, however, was more of an abstract anger against patriarchal values than any real understanding of the problems that males had on a personal level. Gray's *Men Are from Mars* had managed to hide the male inability to be relational by continuing to blame the female. It was a confusing time for both men and women when both sensed something was wrong, but no one really knew what it was. For most of history, men have simply assumed their own importance and primacy and now things were changing. With masculinity under assault, men were unsure how to defend the very thing that they regarded as most important—their manhood.

A survey of commercials in the 1990s showed that 100 percent of the time, men were at the receiving end of the joke or intention. The jerks in male–female relationships were always men. The one who got dumped, lost the contest, smelled bad, got put down, got rejected, or was the object of anger was always male.

The days of *Father Knows Best* were gone. In *Home Improvement*, Tim Allen portrayed a bumbling husband and father who tried to be macho but "just didn't get it." Similarly, *Men Behaving Badly* and *The Secret Lives of Men* portrayed men at their worst: interested only in sex, living in filth, childish, and immature. Dumb blonde jokes were replaced by stupid men jokes. (What do you call a man with half a brain? Gifted! What do you call an intelligent, sensitive man in America? A tourist.) Male-bashing bumper stickers, T-shirts, and cards were everywhere. One well-known greeting card company at that time included a free card in a popular women's magazine. The words on the front said, "Men always complain that we are smothering them." Inside: "I say we aren't holding the pillow down hard enough." It was signed "Louise"—an obvious pun from the popular movie "Thelma and Louise," who choose suicide over living in a male-based world. Apparently, marketing to women's anger and her strong desire to kill the opposite sex seemed like a great sales technique for card companies. And while it did seem like it was men's turn to be the target, it was presented mainly as a joke. We had to acknowledge the beginning shift in some way, so we all just tried to make it all funny.

American women no longer looked at men adoringly. In fact, women today appear not to mirror men at all, and the result is that men feel bashed, devastated, and unappreciated. If men are too forceful, they are considered macho. If they are too sensitive, they are considered soft. Many men no longer know what it means to be a man and find it difficult to be proud of their sex. Today, they are being hit with a double whammy. First, they feel exposed. The strong-silent cover that worked for so long is gone and has been replaced with confusion.

They also feel defensive. They are being forced to defend and justify behaviors that they never thought about before. Most men would like to think that their problem is just a simple reversal of who is "it." They are hoping that all of this will soon resolve itself in a good laugh and a concession. "It's OK—we made fun of you, now it's your turn to make fun of us. Ha Ha."

As with any new paradigm, which typically begins with humor, these ideas point to something much larger and deeper, something that is not going to disappear with a good laugh. New research is beginning to support the jokes, reveal the secret lives of men who behave badly, and show why Pleasantville needed to change. The jokes and movies like *Pleasantville* are ways of preparing the culture for what is to come. These early stirrings pointed to something that was and is still going to get much worse before it gets better. Nothing less than the death of the myth of masculinity is beginning.

What's under the Rock of Masculinity?

There were more than snips and snails and puppy-dog's tails under the rock-solid masculine myth that remained in place, unturned and unexplored until the 1980s and 1990s. The first things we saw when we began to look at masculinity were the glaring results of the imposition of strict gender roles on men. Having accepted the masculine standard for so long, the facts that were unearthed came as quite a shock to the culture. Since the mid-1980s, numerous books have been written, studies have been conducted, and research has been done exposing these male problems. Few of us, however, were aware of them. The main response from the male-based culture at the time appeared to have been, "Let's put this rock back. Let's bury these studies. Maybe no one will find out."

All of my friends and I had read *Passages*[2] by Gail Sheehy when it came out in 1976. It seemed the whole culture, especially we baby boomers who had lived through so many changes, loved to learn more about ourselves. Because of the changes, it was helpful to put our lives in perspective to those who were older and younger than ourselves. Sheehy helped define our generation as very different from those that had come before, and this seemed to be very true. Her next book, *New Passages,*[3] followed our generation, to which she also belongs, into midlife. Her findings confirmed what many of us had only intuited: the female baby boomers, despite doing double duty to catch up, were thriving. The men, on the other hand, were in big trouble. The problems in men that writers, such as Bly, had started to identify several years earlier were indeed revealing themselves everywhere.

Men, says Sheehy, have a much more difficult time facing aging. While women have the biological marker of menopause, men have a tougher time realizing that they are getting older. Most men dangerously suppress their emotional needs. While we have always assumed that the aging process was kinder to men, Sheehy found that most men have much more uncertainty about the whole process. She was so surprised by the many problems that seemed unique to men that she quickly followed up *New Passages* with yet another book. *Understanding Men's Passages*[4] delved more deeply into the male psyche. She discovered that it was difficult for men to even realize that they had to change. Many were depressed. Reprising Bly, men said they let their wives do their living and feeling for them. They sat back and watched their wives go back to school, create companies, and love their work. The wives, who had waited and waited for their husbands to develop into someone with whom they could have a meaningful relationship, had finally given up. They went off with their girlfriends and were having a wonderful time, going to school or starting their own businesses, while their husbands were asleep—either literally or symbolically.

Asleep Emotionally

Both heredity and the environment seem to have created situations where most men are unconscious or asleep emotionally. Bly seems spot-on with his appraisal. What he gleaned from looking at male myths is being confirmed more and more by psychologists today. It appears that men learn to define their masculinity by spurning anything feminine. As the male grows up, he falls into an unconscious quandary, trying to nurture what he lost as a boy and yet defensively rejecting it when he finds it. This cultural solution of the asleep male has been accepted and justified as the norm by both men and women for centuries. Studies revealed that men become violent toward their partners because they fear being abandoned and brutally try to control them. Feeling devalued and restricted led them to become abusive. Their emotions seemed to be related only to negative feelings, probably because the only emotion that had been considered acceptable for males to express was anger.

Psychologist Robert Pasick[5] also defined the deep sleep that many males experience. This sleep causes men to neglect their emotional, nurturing, and creative natures, and while these traits are needed especially in a family context, most men dull this energy by throwing themselves into work. Their deep sleep is comprised of social isolation, a mistrust of emotions, and much confusion about intimacy with women. Men often do not even recognize that anything is even wrong until the women in their lives threaten to leave. The deep sleep occurs on all three levels of social interaction. On the cultural level, men have been raised only to work. In the family and relational context, however, men were unaware of how to gauge their emotional closeness with family members. Having been taught to keep their emotions hidden, men, on a personal level, don't know how they feel and don't know what they need in their lives. Any sense of healthy balance for males had been thrown off long ago. Men grow out of touch with their bodies early on. Even if men did acknowledge their losses, they still didn't grieve or seek help, but, rather, ended up carrying around a lot of pain.

Not knowing how they feel makes it difficult to impossible for men to know how others feel. With no empathic understanding of others, men feel uncomfortable when the other person is hurting. Trying to hide their discomfort in dealing with emotions, men develop strategies, like getting angry or sarcastic, which only further hurts them and their families. Because of their defensiveness and lack of understanding, says Pasick, men really have no idea how to be in relationship with women. Because men never developed their inner resources, they often started to treat their wives as they did their mothers, demanded constant attention, and often became threatened and envious of their wives.

Research by Charles Tart,[6] a well-known psychologist, also confirmed, not surprisingly, that men are asleep emotionally, particularly in the context of relationships—the main area that men do not understand and where they do not shine. Men, he found, often existed in a kind of self-induced mindlessness. Their motivation was often *not* to know much about the relationship, and in order to keep this nonknowing intact, they erected psychological defenses that induce a kind of male consensual trance. And this consensual trance finally has a name.

Male Relational Dread

It is no wonder women didn't have words for the problems they were sensing in men; there were no words for it. Add to it the centuries-old assumption that male authority was not to be questioned, and you have some idea why this problem has never been articulated.

The Stone Center has identified a syndrome present in most men who have never learned to be comfortable with their feelings. It is called "male relational dread." It is interesting that most of us have never heard of it. It's not like a woman thought it up, for if she had, she would have been ridiculed. It was conceived of and written by a male. And, it is not as though it came from a small, unknown college and author. It came from The Stone Center at Harvard/Wellesley, the Queen Mother of academia. One would think most of us would have heard about male relational dread before now.

While there are many standout exceptions today, great numbers of men experience this dread. If you are one of the lucky women who is married to a man who does not have a masculinized ego or seems to be asleep emotionally, you can skip this part. MRD isn't really hard to identify. It starts when she asks how he feels and his body language changes. If he can, he'll end the conversation as soon as possible—ideally, by making it her fault. We never knew about male relational dread, because relationships and women's questions about feelings were never granted much importance—until now.

The importance of being in relationship with oneself and others is now far better understood, and women everywhere certainly identify the symptoms even if they don't have a name for it. "I finally have a name for it!" said Sophie. "I always knew something was wrong—now I have a name for it!" Some friends and I had been talking about relationships and I told her about The Stone Center work. Sophie literally jumped off the couch when she heard the words, "That's it! I finally have a name for it. I am going home right now and tell Curt he has male relational dread!" she said on her way out the door.

Both men and women attend the relationship groups that are held at The Stone Center. The men and women are separated initially and are asked to respond to questions. The women all share a common desire to know how the men feel. The men discover that they have one thing in common—a sense of dread. The groups of men and women take turns talking. When the men talk, the women all sit forward in their seats, literally leaning in toward the men as they wait for their answers. The men, reluctant to speak, hang back. Most say that they are afraid that something might happen.

Dread typically begins when a woman asks a man about his feelings. The question can be simple, but to the man, it feels like criticism. His typical response is a visceral reaction in his body. So, he pauses. The woman typically thinks he's just pausing. She thinks he's thinking about an answer to her question, but the pause is really his way to buy time. Because the answer to the question would be easy for her, she doesn't realize that he has such a strong reaction and doesn't understand his response. It never occurs to her that his dread is beginning. The typical man says that, at this point, things start to get fuzzy and uncomfortable. He begins to feel like he is put on the spot.

At issue here is the actual process of the relationship—the way the relationship flows and unfolds. To the male, when dread enters, it often feels as if the process and flow of the relationship just stops, and all his earlier negative learning around sharing feelings comes to the forefront. All the times that as a boy he was conditioned *not* to talk about his feelings seems to take him over.

According to The Stone Center, there are also experiential aspects to this dread: He feels that if the conversation continues, nothing good will come of it. He feels that the conversation will last forever and further that it will lead to disaster. There will really be no end to this, he senses. It will just go on and on. He feels that further talking will only be damaging to him. The dread appears to intensify in proportion to the closeness he feels to the woman. The more he cares about her, the more intense the dread. He begins to question himself and his relationship and feels like he can't get a firm grip on himself. He begins then to feel afraid that he will let her down.

Feeling trapped, he fears that he might get violent. This same testosterone-fueled reaction that could, in some circumstances protect her, may in others, inadvertently hurt her. The protective part of him may feel that he is doing her a favor by not going into it. Another part of him, however, feels like he is in second gear, pumped with adrenaline and ready to physically take someone on. The old "f*** it or kill it" response kicks into action.

This is most probably the reason why men literally hear her words, as kind as they may be, as bullets, darts, and arrows. Her words seem like an attack that triggers all of his sense of unworthiness. He is being asked to engage in something that he has had no practice or experience with. He feels threatened, which is the main reason he feels defensive. He feels like he has to defend himself from her words and questions.

According to Bergman, a man often feels a sense of incompetence when he is asked to relay his feelings. He thinks to himself that speaking about feelings is the one thing he has never been good at. Because he feels incompetent, he begins to feel ashamed. Ultimately, he feels paralyzed to act. He feels as though he should fix things, but at the same time, this is one thing that he has no idea how to fix. Often the bottom line if men stay engaged in relational dread long enough is that they begin to feel as if they have no answer to even deeper questions, such as who they really are or what their purpose in life is.

American men have been so wounded by this masculine version of culture that, in some ways, their plight is more brutal than women's oppression. They have been severed from their own feelings at the most primary level of life and left with a hollowness at their core that no right-of-passage, coming-of-age, or religious ritual can heal. Many men sense that there must be more to life than power, dominance, and competition. They just don't know what that *more* is or how to find it. The idea of seeking the answer through their own feminine aspects frightens and unnerves them.

While this is difficult for women to understand and live with, it is also heartbreaking that men must endure it. There is no solution within the present status quo. The solutions presented by some male experts, to retreat to their caves, bang on drums together, or try to connect with their fathers, who know even less about feelings than they do, will not heal this wound. The solution is *not* to avoid feelings just because they are painful. When the dread is repressed, it expresses itself elsewhere, and often in even more negative ways. It colors all future reactions. It infects the whole household. It stifles all future attempts at change and remains as the elephant in the living room of life. It may be true, as one male theorist suggested, that because it is not faced properly, it manifests in violence. As hard as it may be, the only way to get beyond male relational dread is to go through it.

Bergman is certainly not the only male therapist who sees the difficulty that men are having today. *Psychotherapy Networker,* one of the most popular journal magazines for therapists, devoted a whole issue to "The Secret World of Men" in 2010.[7] So many of the problems that males have currently can be traced back to the fact that today there is no longer any clear definition of what it means to be a male. Men are used to being in charge. They are used to hunting, building, lifting heavy things, and in the best cases, protecting women. Women today however, want men who are relational. The men don't know how to be relational—so they don't know who they are.

It appears that the only option for men is to go to therapy to try somehow to learn to be relational. This isn't a good solution because, unfortunately, they hate everything about the idea of therapy. They even hate the words "feelings," "emotions," and "sharing" that come up in conversation. If they show up at therapy at all, their typical response is that their wife told them they needed to be there.

They have no idea how to process their emotions, so they resist even wanting to talk about something that may be wrong. They hate feeling discomfort inside, and more than that, they hate talking about it aloud. They feel like they are in uncharted territory and are confused and anxious. Of course they experience dread.

The experts suggest that therapists should send a message of "good guys behaving badly" so that the men don't feel so isolated. They also suggest that male therapists share their own stories of when they did stupid things.

I was shocked to discover that research has been done and many books have been written on this very topic. Apparently, but not surprisingly, this whole topic never got much attention. Books such as *Crisis Time, The Wounded Male, Uneasy Manhood, The Male Ego, The End of Manhood, The Angry Man,* and *Wrestling with Love—How Men Struggle with Intimacy with Women, Children, Parents and Each Other,* to name just a few, give some idea of the problems that existed and continues to surface around men. All the books are variations on the same issues of how hard it is for males to be relational. These books aren't about brain surgery, obscure tribes, or something else that does not relate directly to our lives. They are about relationships and the problems men have with relating. I couldn't help but wonder why they weren't more popular and almost seem to have been buried. It would have been so helpful for women to have some clue about the real relationship problem. It was also interesting to realize that these books were all written by men. If a woman were to write on these same areas, her work would be viewed only as male-bashing.

Men and Intimacy

The McGill Report on Male Intimacy[8] was the largest study ever done on intimacy, surveying more than 5,000 men on every aspect of their emotional lives. It was based on a decade of research, and is well written, yet, again, few have ever heard about it.

Was this information just too threatening to the collective male psyche? Was this just one more thing to make sure that women didn't learn too much about men? Today, anyone can just go to the Internet and discover a wealth of material on any subject. In the 1980s and 1990s, however, most of us depended on books, magazines, or television for our information. Most of us also had our copies of *Men Are from Mars* that served only to maintain the status quo.

McGill defines intimacy as what makes us feel close to each other. Intimacy, then, is time spent together involving a variety of interests and a depth of interpersonal exchange. Intimacy requires a disclosure of personal information. Women expect depth from a man equal to their own personal investment, but rarely feel that this depth is reflected back to them. McGill found that men strike out on all aspects of intimacy. Their relationships are typically one-dimensional in that they continue to relate to others in the same ways as they did in the past. They prefer to limit intimate talks to their specific interests and appear to be unwilling to broaden these areas. They are most uncomfortable with the skills required to deepen intimacy.

Reluctant Revealers

Until recently, it was men who determined the degree of depth in a relationship. If women had wanted more, they certainly weren't permitted to ask for it. Today, women are asking, but it doesn't appear to be doing them much good. Even in the gravest of scenarios, such as the death of a child, women in the study had no idea how their husbands really felt. Men, says McGill, are reluctant to disclose their feelings because it makes them feel vulnerable. They are "reluctant revealers" whose wives watch them closely for any little clue as to how they feel. As I read the McGill report, I laughed remembering the time my friend Patti told me, "I used to feel like I should have a list of feelings. I could read the list of feelings to him and let him pick the ones that he felt applied: Do you feel Sad? Depressed? Angry? Confused? All of the above? What?"

Cautious Confirmers

Men are also "cautious confirmers," says McGill. They strive to remain in control of what they disclose. The closer women come to men's personal selves, the more they become "emotional evaders." Many men have played this game all of their lives with women who have tried to please them. Their behavior is like a riddle that says, "See if you can figure out what I'm feeling." For most men, the personal self is also the sexual self. For them, intimacy is sex, and further, they seem to believe that sex will solve any or all problems. Sex for men is equal to all public and private disclosures. It is both a measure of intimacy and a means to intimacy.

Long before I ever read McGill's book, my friends and I had talked about this very thing. Carol said, "If I tell him I want to talk, he thinks that means sex. We can talk, or rather, he will listen, either before or after—preferably after, but sex will be in there somewhere."

Trisha agreed, "I know. I like sex. Actually, I love sex. It's great! But, for me, it's not the whole world. It's just one part of the whole relationship. There's so much more to a relationship for me, but for Tim, if he's having sex, he thinks everything is peachy. It's like heaven to him, or nirvana or whatever the ultimate experience is. I mean it is really like heaven to him . . . well, I mean, think of those other cultures where men think they get 72 virgins in heaven. It's the same thing! I really think that sex is like heaven to men."

Because self-disclosure was found to be such a barrier to intimacy, McGill asked *why* men withhold themselves from their wives. The answers vary from "She already knows how I feel," to "She should just accept me the way I am," but the theme of discomfort with self-disclosure is always the same. Most men see self-disclosure as very risky in that it allows other people to know you. If people know you, they can have influence and control over you and men sense that this information could be used against them.

Rich, a 46-year-old executive, says, "If I tell my wife too much personal information, then she will know things about me that will allow her to have power over me. For example, if I tell her too much about my childhood, then she'll say that's why I can't relate to her better, or, that's why I'm not a better father. I don't want her analyzing me, and I really just don't want to hear it."

Men have managed to keep their problems invisible by blaming women—and until recently it has worked for them. "It's her fault. She just doesn't recognize my loving behavior. She thinks I have to act just like her," said Rich shortly after his divorce. "She acted like she was the judge of the 'right' way of being intimate." His friend, Carl, still struggling in a long-term relationship agreed, "It is like my wife sets the rules and decides what the rules are. She made it real easy for me not to be really involved with the kids. It was like she could just do it better, so why try?"

McGill found that men don't typically self-disclose with other men either. Men usually feel a pressure with other men that is best described by sociolinguist Deborah Tannen[9] as the "one up/one down" measurement. Like chimpanzees who strive for dominance in the tribe, men are always gauging their position with other men. As further reasons for their silence, men accept the stereotype of being strong, silent, and unemotional, and McGill says there is also an implicit and underlying homophobia in male defensiveness. The assumption is that whatever a real man is, any behavior that is not real male behavior is considered to be not male. Because of these strong stereotypes, few older men can serve as role models from whom younger men can learn to communicate emotionally.

The Mystery/Mastery Behavior of the Male

McGill appears to have had the same experience with men while doing his research as women have had in relationships. As women try to get men to express themselves, they hear mostly vague nonanswers that lead to further questions. Most men adopt mystery/mastery behavior, says McGill, because the mystery that comes as the result of not self-disclosing provides them with a sense of mastery.

Mystery/mastery behavior discourages the sharing of feelings, motivations, and goals with others. The truth is, however, that men's feelings also remain a mystery to themselves. By being a mystery to others, this kind of male keeps others from knowing him. Ironically, however, it also keeps him from ever knowing himself.

Our most important way of knowing ourselves comes from the feedback we get from others. As others give us feedback that confirms or denies our perception of ourselves, we learn about the accuracy of our own perceptions. When a man fails to share information about himself, he also gets to avoid facing his own incongruities and inadequacies, says McGill. Thus the man who doesn't self-disclose never has to be confronted with the inconsistencies of his own behavior. Mystery/mastery serves two purposes. It gives men the power they associate with success in life and it protects them from feedback that might reveal their inadequacies.

The issue that I had sensed years earlier was now becoming more and more clear to me. Because Dave and I talked constantly—or rather I often talked and he listened, Dave, too was beginning to understand.

Chapter 10

Confessions of a Male Chauvinist Pig

Yang
Confrontation
Response

The annual Women's Conference was a popular event that brought in thousands of women, and some men, to our small college town each March in the late 1980s and early 1990s. I was usually actively involved, but in 1991, I had taken a break because I was working full time and completing my doctorate. Dave took my place on the committee. It wasn't as unusual as it sounds. Many faculty males helped the women with the conference. Some even taught the seminars that were offered that day. I was shocked, however, when Dave came home from one of the early meetings and told me that he was going to give a talk on "Confessions of a Male Chauvinist Pig."

I was proud that he was going to be involved. I was even proud that he was brave enough to talk on such a touchy subject. At first, I thought he was going to make it a joke, but he assured me that it would be no joke.

I was surprised to realize that my first response was to feel protective of us and our relationship, which obviously had continued to improve. We had talked at length about all I was learning in my doctoral studies, much of which was about males and relationships. Now he was going to talk about it publicly and no one had ever done this before. I also felt protective of *him*. He was going to tell people about himself, where he had been and how he had changed. I found a part of myself wanting to maintain the old male standard, where men kept quiet and were accorded wisdom just because they were men. He was going to tell all and my part in it would be included too.

Hmmmm, I thought. The whole thing was scary and somewhat confusing, but it was also interesting. He let me read his speech before he presented it. Although we had talked many times about the process we had gone through, I was now reading a well thought out, well synthesized version of how he had felt about it.

I went to his workshop with a hundred other women and a few men who seemed fascinated by the title alone. Here is what he said in his words:

"Good afternoon, women and men of this audience. My name is David T. and I am a male chauvinist pig. With this admission, I am consciously relating to Alcoholics Anonymous, which involves a presentation by its members giving testimony or a confession, if you will, of his/her life. And, by consciously relating male chauvinism to Alcoholics Anonymous, I am asserting that like alcoholism, male chauvinism is a sickness, which is potentially destructive of personal and social relationships. In Alcoholics Anonymous there are no ex-alcoholics, but rather only alcoholics who consciously endeavor each day to resist the urge to drink. Likewise, I am not an ex–male chauvinist pig, but rather a male chauvinist pig who endeavors each day to resist the urge to practice male chauvinism.

"The program of Alcoholics Anonymous[1] articulates 12 steps that have been extremely effective in the rehabilitation of alcoholics. For the purposes of my comments this afternoon, I would like to reduce the twelve steps to three: (1) admitting that a fundamental problem exists; (2) seeking a resolution of the problem by understanding that this is fundamentally *my* problem and doing whatever is necessary to transcend the problem, which involves an appeal to some power and/or person outside yourself for direction and guidance; (3) endeavoring to achieve integration by self-analysis and intimate relationships with those who are important in one's life, and by living a life of spirituality and transcendence.

"Before I get into my 'Confessions of a Male Chauvinist Pig' as such, let me explain my understanding of male chauvinism. Male chauvinism is fundamentally the attitude that the relationship between males and females is based on the principle of hierarchy, that is, males are the dominant, the powerful, the authoritarian, the independent, the positive, whereas females are the passive, the weak, the subservient, the dependent, and the negative. This hierarchy is called the patriarchal system.

"The practice of patriarchy is based on one fundamental perspective accepted since primeval times: male superiority exists by virtue of divine and/or natural right. Coupled with this is the male's belief that he is superior by virtue of his physical strength, his intellect, his education, his profession, or his economic status in the social order. The system of patriarchy is so ingrained in our historical/social order that whenever females challenge the system, males react with diverse responses: (1) an uncomprehending puzzled stare; (2) the patronizing comment that she probably isn't getting a good lay or that she is probably 'ragging it'; (3) ignoring the comment or criticism; (4) a gentle rejoinder that the comment/criticism is without merit; (5) attacking with verbal abuse; and (6) attacking with physical abuse. Males thus express their patriarchy from benign indifference to naked brutality, from gentle persuasion to raw power. Underlying the male's comments and action in their relationship with females is the belief that males indeed are the sons of gods and the true inheritors of the earth.

"The obvious victims of the patriarchal system are the female of the species, and, in the process of being victimized, she suppresses and often loses her sense of personal integrity and self-esteem. What is not as obvious is that the male of the species is also a victim of the system of patriarchy. In order to maintain the top position in the hierarchy, he is not permitted to manifest any characteristic that may be interpreted as 'weakness,' or as acquiescing to the needs of the female. To do so would mean losing control as the dominant force. He is permitted to show emotions of joy, elation, anger, frustration, fear, and to weep in specific situations such as victories and defeats in wars and battles, in games, and during momentous occasions in his life such as births, marriages, and death.

"However, he is not permitted to 'feel.' Feelings are that nebulous twilight zone between the cognitive and the emotive, difficult to define and hence to articulate, yet necessary and essential in the context of relationships. In order for a relationship to transcend the realm of acquaintance and to achieve intimacy, there must be the bonding that comes with sharing feelings. But, in order for feelings to manifest themselves in a relationship, there must be *equality* and not *hierarchy*. Thus, when the man and the woman bond on the level of feelings, they are basically saying to each other: 'I accept you as my equal; I give to you your personal integrity and self-esteem; and whether we have problems or not, come, let us sit down and reason together.'

"The contemporary American male is caught in a double-bind: on the one hand, he has been raised in a patriarchal system, and he implicitly deals with this as a given condition of his existence. On the other hand, he hears the demands of relationship based on feelings. Given the system, he cannot understand what feelings are about, but the insistent noises about feelings make him miserable. If he does tap into his feelings, he senses that he is not exercising his superiority, that he is losing control and is no longer the dominant force in the relationship, and this makes him miserable. Thus, either way, he is miserable, and above all, he finds himself 'stuck.'

"One final word on these prefatory remarks: chauvinism and feminism are not gender issues as such, that is, a chauvinist is not necessarily a male and a feminist is not necessarily a female. Chauvinism and feminism are fundamentally states of consciousness. Thus, a chauvinist is a person, male or female, who basically accepts a hierarchical structure on the patriarchal or matriarchal models. Furthermore, today we are aware that sexual harassment cuts both ways—men exercising their roles of dominance to elicit sexual favors from their female subordinates, and women, in their newly gained roles of dominance, to elicit sexual favors from their male subordinates.

"A feminist, on the other hand, is a male or female, who basically accepts equality as the mode of operation in their relationships to each other. And please let us be careful how we use this word *equality*. I do not mean by this that any person is just as good as any other person. What is meant is that a feminist does not presume that a hierarchical relationship exists between persons solely on the basis of sex. A hierarchical relationship obviously exists between two individuals on the basis of their respective strengths and weaknesses.

"I am now ready to get into my 'Confessions of a Male Chauvinist Pig.' As you listen to my comments, I want you to keep several questions is mind: (1) What conditions created the sense of Dave's male chauvinism? (2) What are some significant consequences of Dave's male chauvinism? (3) What situation made Dave aware that his male chauvinism is a sickness and not a divine or natural right? (4) What are the consequences of Dave's recognition that male chauvinism is a sickness? (5) And the most important and perhaps the most presumptuous question for me to ask you, what are some comments, ideas, suggestions that you have gleaned from this presentation that may help you in your relationship?

"My 'Confessions of a Male Chauvinist Pig' is a brief look into my personal history, from the time I was born until the present time, with the key focus being on what I call the 'confrontational period' (1975–1980). Thus events prior to 1975, I will call the pre-confrontational period, and events after 1980, I will call the post-confrontational period.

Pre-Confrontational Period

Family

"I am of Japanese ancestry, born in Honolulu, Hawaii. My father comes from a long line of samurai warriors whose genealogy can be traced back to the 13th century. Both of my parents were raised in Japan, and Japan was, and still is, based on a strict patriarchal system. Permit me to give a couple of examples of this system: (1) At the time that my parents were married, property rights transferred exclusively to males. My mother had only sisters. So one of the conditions for my father marrying my mother was that he give up his family name and take my mother's family name. (2) The second example involves my mom, who is now deceased and who was a beautiful, gentle, and loving person. But she believed in the patriarchal system. On our visits to Hawaii, she resented my doing the dishes or hanging laundry on the clothesline or doing anything that could be construed as 'woman's work.' On one occasion, my mom and I had a rather humorous confrontation. I indicated that I was going to do the dishes after dinner. She strongly protested and when I got up to do the dishes, she physically stopped me. She said that doing the dishes was 'woman's work.' I said, 'That's okay, I don't mind doing woman's work.' She then proceeded to give me a lecture. She said, 'I don't care what you do in your house, but you are now in my house, and in my house, men are number one and men do not do woman's work.' The whole conversation was in Japanese, and I started to laugh and so did my sister. My wife, who did not understand any of this, asked me what was going on and when I explained the gist of the 'goings-on' with a degree of relish, her eyes glazed over, and I believe she was endeavoring to stifle a negative behavioral reaction.

Religion

"I attended the University of Hawaii and two significant events took place relative to my male chauvinism. The first significant event was that I became involved with conservative Christianity which takes the teachings of the Bible seriously. Fundamental to the biblical perspective is a patriarchal system. God is father. It is Adam who is created first and Eve is created out of the side of Adam, which is further interpreted to mean that she is to be at his side, his helpmate. The consequence of the fall is that Eve must now bear children in suffering and Adam is to rule over her.

"The covenant between God and his people is specifically articulated in the relationship between God and the patriarchs: Abraham, Isaac, and Jacob. With the people in bondage in Egypt, God calls upon Moses to be the deliverer of his people. When the children of Israel are ready to enter the Promised Land, God calls upon Joshua to lead his people. When they are in the throes of becoming a nation, God calls upon Samuel to anoint Saul to be king, followed by David and Solomon. Women become prominent in the biblical discussion more often than not to the extent that they cause the chosen men to deviate from the course of their mission. Thus, we have Samson and Delilah; David and Bathsheba; Solomon and his legendary harem; Ahab and Jezebel. While there were prophetesses as well as prophets, it is the proclamation of the prophets that have been preserved for posterity.

"In the context of Hebrew theology, man is said to have been created in the image of God. You may think that this is generic man, which includes both male and female, but in practice, it is the male who is created in the image of God. In the life of the temple and the synagogues, only males were permitted to study the scriptures and to take an active part of the ritual life of Judaism. Women were permitted to observe the proceedings and were able to participate in the blessings of God only via some male member of the family—a father, a brother, a husband.

"In the New Testament, Jesus acts contrary to the practices of the patriarchy. However, in one of the tragic ironies of biblical interpretation, the Lord of the Church is glorified as the champion of patriarchy. Thus, Paul articulates an analogy: As Christ is head of the church, so is the husband the head of the wife. Thus, wives are called to be subservient to their husbands. While women played a prominent role in the development of the early church during the time of Paul's ministry, they quickly faded from the scene and men emerged as the dominant figures in the rise of the institutional church. We have the emergence of the Church Fathers who laid the groundwork for Christian Theology and institutional practices that continue to be prominent, especially in the Roman Catholic Church.

"Mary is honored, not because she championed the cause of women, but because she manifests the idea of femininity in the patriarchal perspective. She is the receptor of the impregnation of the Holy Spirit, the bearer of the Son of God, the long-suffering mother who ministers to her son with resignation, acceptance, and equanimity at the time of his crucifixion. Thus, Mary is declared to be the Mediatrix, the Mother of God, the Queen of Heaven because of self-effacement, of her subservience to the will of God, the will of the Jewish authorities, and the will of Rome—all of which are manifestations of the patriarchal system.

Philosophy

"The second significant event during this period of my life was my decision to major in philosophy as preparation for enrolling in seminary. Philosophy is likewise grounded in a patriarchal system. On occasion, the sense of this system is explicit as in Aristotle's *Politics*.[2] He draws a distinction between citizens and slaves. Among citizens are males and females. Adult male citizens exercise rationality. Young male citizens are such that their rationality is not yet in operation and thence must be trained until the time their rationality is exercised. Female citizens have reason but it is basically inoperative. Thus, it is imperative that women take their direction from rational individuals, that is, adult males.

"On other occasions, the sense of the patriarchal system is implicit because it is simply assumed that rationality is a given function of males and not females. The history of philosophy, both East and West, is a parade of male philosophers. The presumption is that philosophy is fundamentally a male activity. In the history of philosophy, I am aware of only two philosophers who have postulated the possibility of total equality between men and women. The first was Plato in his visionary creation called *The Republic*,[3] in which his principal concern was to articulate a definition of justice. In order to clarify his definition, he constructed a social order in which the 'gold and silver souled' men and women were totally equal. Plato, however, never intended this social order to be a viable and operational scheme. The other philosopher was John Stuart Mill,[4] who in the 19th century championed the cause of women's rights.

"After completing my bachelor's degree, I attended seminary, during which time the patriarchal perspective was reinforced because, after all, it was the biblical perspective. The seminary, however, did endeavor to have us exercise our patriarchy in a benign and a loving manner, given the fact that God is love, Jesus is love, and the Christian community is based on love.

"Work toward a master's degree in philosophy followed my seminary days and I began research for my thesis on Soren Kierkegaard, a 19th-century post-Hegelian philosopher/theologian. One of Kierkegaard's major works is called *Fear and Trembling*,[5] ostensibly an analysis and interpretation of Abraham's sacrifice of his son Isaac, but in reality an attempt to justify sacrificing his love for Regina, unto whom he was betrothed, for the sake of a higher calling—a call to the service of God. Thus in Kierkegaard's mind, he was placed in an either/or situation—either his love for Regina or his love for God. It did not seem to have occurred to Kierkegaard that he might accomplish his mission via his relationship to Regina, that is, his love and commitment to Regina might have been the catalyst toward a more profound sense of service to God.

"Upon completion of my master's degree, I attended Pennsylvania State University in order to work toward a doctorate in philosophy. It was an exciting time for me because of the comradeship I established with my fellow graduate students, who were all males, taught by professors of philosophy, who were all males. For my dissertation, I worked on theologian Paul Tillich's ontological system,[6] which was his endeavor to weave his interpretation of Christian theology and philosophy with his interpretation of the Hegelian system. I have always viewed Tillich as an enlightened patriarch, but recently I was reading Mary Daly's *Gyn/Ecology*,[7] which is a radical feminist critique of the patriarchal system. On page 94, she refers to Hannah Tillich's autobiography, *From Time to Time*.[8] Hannah was Paul Tillich's wife and she reports incidents of her husband's behavior, which reveals a less than enlightened patriarchal posture. That is to say, he was fascinated by the viewing of 'religious' pornography. Colleagues of Tillich endeavored to have Hannah delete these references to Paul's bizarre behavior, but she stood firm. I am personally glad to have read this, because another of the pantheon of my 'gods' has been toppled from its lofty position in the intellectual structures of my mind.

Marriage

"In the spring of 1962, I was looking for a teaching position in philosophy and wound up here at the university. I intended to stay here a couple of years and then eventually move out west. So much for intentions. In the summer of 1965, I fell in love with a female student. She was a sophomore in education, 12 years younger than me, bright and rather compliant in our relationship. We were married in May 1966. In the early years of our marriage, I encouraged her to continue her college education and helped her adjust to life as a faculty wife. Given the fact that she had some problems with her family, I also served as her counselor and mentor. She completed her degree work in 1968. We had our first child in February 1969, the second in January 1971, and our third in September 1973. She was now a mature woman, wonderful wife and mother, and her energies were directed toward maintaining the household, becoming a great cook—and could she bake! In between the arrival of babies, she was thinking about graduate school. We talked about it and I highly encouraged her to go ahead. So she started graduate work in psychology and is now working on her doctorate. I supported her 100 percent in her graduate school efforts and I became more involved in the care of the children and the household.

Confrontational Period

"Around 1975, the serpent entered into this Garden of Eden and began to whisper strange and radical thoughts to my wife, or so I thought. And how did I know this? Because I began to notice restlessness on her part. In her restlessness, her comments became questioning, challenging, and critical. Initially, I simply rebuffed her and dismissed her comments. But the comments were persistent and became difficult to ignore. She said I was spending too much time watching sports on TV. She said I was spending too much time reading my philosophy and theology books. She said I was not spending time talking with her. She said I was not a good father to our children. She said that watching sports on TV and reading my books were really means of avoiding her and the children. She asked me whether watching TV was more important than her and the children. She asked me why I was reading books in philosophy. She asked me what was the meaning of *my* life. She said I was basically uninvolved with the kids and that when I talked, I was talking 'at' them. When I protested and told her that I was doing a good job in babysitting the kids, she said, yes, that I was a good babysitter, but that did not mean I was a good father. More often than not, I protested that her criticisms were inaccurate and that she was really a bitch.

"I began to sense that matters were getting serious because of the persistent nature of her criticisms. So, I endeavored to change my habits somewhat. I endeavored to lessen my preoccupation with sports on TV; I endeavored to be closer to the children; and I endeavored to spend more time talking with her. But, sooner or later, the criticisms would ensue again because inevitably I would lapse into my old patterns of behavior.

"During this whole situation, the worst times were late in the evening, just when I was about to go to sleep, she would say to me, 'Dave, we have to talk!' And I would cringe because I knew what was coming up. Her comments and criticisms became more intense, more penetrating, more personal. She would ask, 'How do you feel about this or that?' And I would indicate that I didn't have the faintest idea as to what the hell she was talking about. I would then proceed to tell her what I thought and what I knew about this and that. She would stop me and she would say, 'I don't want you to tell me about what you think or know about this and that, I want you to tell me how you feel.' And, when she demanded this, I was in a state of emptiness, because I had nothing to say. My pauses and silences would stretch out into minutes and finally she would ask if I was avoiding her with my silence. And I would say to her, 'I really don't have anything to say. I really don't know what to say.'

"And thus, for a period of approximately five years, I was caught in this labyrinth of unending chaos, constantly walking on eggshells and ever so carefully taking my steps so as not to awaken the dragon of criticism and dissent. And please bear in mind that while the comments and questions that my wife directed at me were very pointed, they were always couched with great care and the endeavor to be as sensitive and considerate as possible. I was so glad to be able to go to the university because it gave me a sense of respite from my travails and gave me a sense of control in my realm of activity, if only for a few hours. She began encouraging me to talk with someone, and I strongly protested my innocence and screamed at her that there was nothing wrong with me. Members of the audience, it is at this point you *know* that something is indeed wrong with me. And so my chaos continued until I finally hit bottom.

The Turning Point

"It was a Saturday morning. I was installing a vanity cabinet in the bathroom on the first floor. I was having a damnable time because of the limited and crowded floor space. I was letting forth some choice expletives, and my wife came down to find out what was the matter. I told her that I was having a very difficult time installing the cabinet. I stopped so I could talk with her and leaned against the wall. And at that moment, I started to cry, and very shortly it became an uncontrollable weeping. I was embarrassed as hell to be crying in front of her, so I ducked my head between my legs and in the midst of my sobbing, I told her that I didn't know what was happening, that I didn't know what she wanted from me, and that I was quite miserable with my life. She tried to embrace me, but I wouldn't let her. She consoled me with words to the effect that things would work out. Then she left me to my misery. When I finally gained my composure, I sought her out, apologized for my behavior, and asked a question which was to set in motion the rehabilitation of David T.! I asked her whom she would suggest as someone who could help me with my problem. She thought for a moment and suggested Lynn. I said that was a good suggestion. I then got on the phone, talked with Lynn and made an appointment to see her some time during the week.

"Now, this Lynn is a very interesting person, and talk about twists of fate! Lynn is married and has several children. Lynn never went to college, while John, her husband, is a college graduate. When their eldest son went off to college and decided to major in philosophy, Lynn herself became interested in the subject. It just so happened that at that point in time, I was teaching philosophy courses for adult learners at Branch Campus under the sponsorship of the Chamber of Commerce there. So Lynn and John took my various philosophy courses and we became good friends. This was before I was married. Then around 1965, their eldest son was killed in an auto accident, and in her endeavor to find some meaning and sense for herself, she started to read her son's philosophy books. After a while, a core of individuals from her town about a half hour away from here continued to show interest in philosophy, so I invited them to come to my home for studies. Little did I know that as a consequence of her taking these courses with me, Lynn was growing and developing and becoming a very wise woman. After my marriage, my wife was introduced to Lynn and John. After a while, my wife would have extensive talks with Lynn and for all practical purposes, Lynn became her mentor. Lynn encouraged her in her times of doubts, questions, and problems relative to her relationship with me. And now, here I was going to Lynn for a basic counseling session. So for a period of time, I was Lynn's teacher and mentor, then Lynn became my wife's mentor, and for a moment of my life, she was to become my mentor, to be followed by a period of time in which my wife became my mentor. So that old cliché is true once again—what goes around comes around.

"So I went off to see Lynn and we sat on her porch swing and we began to talk. We talked about a lot of things, but we mainly focused on what it was that my wife wanted from me and my life. Lynn came forth with a somewhat enigmatic, puzzling, but right-to-the-point response: 'Dave, she just wants you!' And good old philosophical Dave, good old theological Dave, good old PhD Dave asked Lynn, because he felt like a babe in these new woods, 'Gee, Lynn, what does that mean?' And good old gentle and wise Lynn did not laugh in my face, but said very seriously, 'Dave, she doesn't want your money, your reputation, your prestige, your position. She just wants you and she wants you to be you.'

Post-Confrontational Period

"Since that meeting with Lynn, I have been endeavoring to understand what 'me' is all about, and fortunately, I had my wife as my mentor who helped me to understand 'me.' A whole new dimension of my existence began to open up. I began to 'feel' things. It was strange because it opened up a sense of inner connectedness with other people, especially with my wife and children. It almost seemed as if I could 'intuit' their thoughts and attitudes. My wife and I would talk about these matters, and all those problematic issues and questions which bugged the hell out of me during the confrontational period now made good sense. Her comments that were puzzling to me were now crystal clear. I used to have a recurring dream in which I was outside a strange and mysterious building figuring out just how to get in because there were no doors or windows. In the midst of this situation, I had another dream in which I was inside the building and there was nothing mysterious at all. Of course, this dream was a metaphor of the 'outside' and 'inside' of my own existence. Further, that which I was 'feeling' became connected with my intellectual understanding of Western Philosophy, Christian Theology, and Oriental Philosophies. I was often saying to myself, 'That's what they are talking about.'

"This new process was not easy. There were lapses and my wife would get on my case again, but even my lapses were never a complete reversal to the previous state. I was now on a higher plane. When she criticized, I at least understood her criticisms and understood that her criticisms were justified. Sometimes I would feel like a trampled victim because of these persistent criticisms, but my wife reminded me that she was not intent on destroying me, but rather helping me to become the best human being it was possible for me to be. Over these years since 1980, I have bonded with my wife and she is aware that this has happened. I have bonded with each of my children, though they may not have been aware of it. I do know this much. I feel very comfortable in my relationship with our children, and I do believe that they are comfortable with me.

"This 'Confession of a Male Chauvinist Pig,' this unveiling of one pig's soul, has a moral, and it is this: You women who are involved with a significant other who is a male chauvinist pig need not continue to be victimized by a situation which is neither his nor your making. Stop waving the flag of femininity in your hopes that somehow he will see you as his role model for fairness and equity. He will not see you because for all practical purposes, you are invisible to him. Chauvinism is so ingrained in his consciousness that he perceives your deeds simply as a part of the nature and/or divine order of things.

"Women, take heart and courage and put on your battle armor and make war with the pig, not in order to destroy him, but to exorcise his demon which prevents him from becoming a loving, feeling, and authentic human being. Bear in mind, however, that when you make war, you must count the costs and the risks, for in war there are always casualties. The question you face is, is it worth it? Perhaps you are considering the fact that you have 'half a loaf,' and that perhaps this is better than nothing at all. Beware of such tempting and attractive compromises! For in the realm of personal integrity and self-esteem, there is no place for such a compromise! Once you become conscious of the fact that you have only 'half a loaf' relative to a meaningful relationship with your significant other, then you are compelled by your sense of self-worth to seek and demand the 'whole loaf.' It is evident that there are no guarantees that you will gain the whole loaf.

But it is also evident that you cannot gain the whole unless you risk and venture forth toward that goal.

"In the philosophy of Kundalini Yoga, when an individual truly becomes an authentic being, when through hard work and discipline he/she rises finally to the highest level of the Chakras, a third eye is said to appear in the center of the forehead—the eye of wisdom and truth. Some of you out there might say, 'Yes, Dave, I think I see something like that. Yes, you do have the third eye.' And I will say to you, 'Hey, look again and look closely. It is actually a bullet hole put there with the special gun which my significant other used to unscramble my mind.'

"Women, I say to you, that special gun is right there in your heart. Look for it, learn how to use it, and then use it. I have spoken about 'confrontation,' 'bullet holes,' and 'the special gun.' My significant other may disclaim that this is what actually happened, but please understand that they are the images from the perspective of a male chauvinist pig. However, one may wish to interpret the situation, the bottom line is indisputable. Her persistence set in motion a revolution, and all revolutions intend to shake and shatter the existing structure and foundations, in order to lay the groundwork for a new and a higher order of consciousness. In this, my significant other has truly succeeded, and for this, I am forever grateful to her!"

The Response

He looked at me when he said his closing words. It also felt as though everyone else was looking at me too. Some women cheered, a few were quiet—stunned almost, as if he had spoken too honestly, as if no one was supposed to talk on this level about this subject in public. But most women absolutely loved his talk. I was particularly interested in the few males who talked to Dave afterward. It made me feel better to see that the few who told Dave they liked his talk were the guys in town I considered the "good guys." They were men I felt certain would help around the house and with the children. The one male who talked with Dave at length was married to the only female lawyer, who was kind of a shining star among liberated women in our town. If her husband got it, then it must have been all right on some level.

Afterward, both of us had people, mostly women, coming up to us and telling us how much they liked his talk. I was relieved. It had gone all right. After he left, women were still congratulating me and telling me how great Dave was. They said their husbands would never give such a talk. Dave was special. I was special. We were special. I didn't want anyone to feel that

I didn't appreciate their kind and generous words, but this reaction was exactly what I hoped wouldn't happen. Although he had clearly spoken to all women as he granted them permission to go home and confront their husbands and partners, most reactions seemed to reflect that this was only about Dave and me. I knew that what I was doing and what he was talking about were so much bigger than the two of us. We were just an example of what any couple can do. It really isn't about him or me. It is something that any woman can do.

That night when we talked about the day, Dave asked what I thought about his talk.

"It was great."

"But?" he said. He was learning to read me.

I struggled with what to say. A part of me knew that I should be grateful he got it and was willing to talk openly about it. I knew I should keep quiet and tell him what a good talk it was. Another part of me, however, had to speak.

"In the middle of your talk when you say how I persistently criticized you . . . I never did that."

"I say later that you did it gently and kindly," he retorted.

"I know. But, Dave," I said quietly, "I never criticized you."

"Well, it felt like it at the time. Geez!"

"You make it sound like I just opened my mouth and said whatever was on my mind—without thinking of your feelings, without weighing my words, and that's not true. Everything I said was said kindly and carefully."

He looked at me for a long time. It was a moment—like so many moments that had gone before. He wanted to be mad and to feel his anger was justified. He wanted to be able to say, "You, bitch! Is there no end to your criticism? I just gave a talk on confessions of a male chauvinist pig and gave you all the credit for changing me—and now you're quibbling about certain words." But he didn't.

He just looked at me. He went beyond his first thoughts to a whole new place. And I think for the first time, he saw me.

He didn't say anything but just looked at me, a look that softened after a while into comprehension.

I knew what he was thinking without his saying a word. As much as he wanted to be able to think that my words were harsh, he knew they hadn't been. And with that knowing, he had to look at himself—a person who, despite the kindness of the words, had still railed against them. I knew and he knew that, in that instant, he saw himself for the first time. First, as the one who still wanted it to be the other person's fault, the one who felt safe if he could place blame, and then, as someone who had been wrapped in the soft cotton of carefully chosen words and treated with such gentle kindness.

He looked and blinked in recognition. He knew me. He said quietly, "OK. I hear you. I understand what you are saying . . . I get it." And I was expanded at his recognition.

My friends continued over the next months to ask me about the whole process. I tried to explain it, but it wasn't easy. "It's like being in touch with something that is much larger than me. It is like feeling connected to a much larger essence. A lot of the time, I really don't think I was doing it. I often wouldn't know what I was going to say or think or do. Something much larger than me told me what to say, how long to wait, how to say it. I trusted it—most of the time". It seemed to come from the place that I touched into as I continued to take off the tight hats that I encountered.

"Does this make sense?" I would ask, realizing that it was just so hard to explain how I felt and what I was trying to do. It was much more than just learning something new.

"Well, kind of," they would say. "Can you teach us how to do it? Can't you put it into 10 easy steps?"

As much as I wanted to be able to explain it, I still found it difficult. By the time Dave gave his first talk, I had been teaching classes on the feminine archetypes and goddesses, which was as close as I could come to trying to finding bottom lines for what I was learning.

And while that material was wonderful, the essence I sensed was even more than that. I started to realize that women literally had to unlearn so much of what they thought was true before they could begin learning what was actually true.

Chapter 11

Learning How
to Be a Man

Yang
Disconnected
Defensive

So, how do males become so filled with dread by the time they are adults? Why is it that big strapping males would rather go to war than go to counseling? Why is it that no matter how nicely she talks, most men hear her words as attacks with weapons? I had been shocked when Dave had used the analogy of a bullet in his head that had been delivered by me as his wake-up call that led to the opening of his third eye. Without knowing it, Dave had described our difficult talks in the same way that the men in Bergman's work had described the words of their wives—as bullets, darts, and arrows. Similarly, several years earlier, Bly had referred to men who received her words as slings and arrows. There appeared to be almost a universal defensive male reaction to women's words. Not surprisingly, these reactions begin in boyhood.

The cultural dictates—and the male myth—requires that, almost from infancy, males are taught to disconnect. The Stone Center at Wellesley College, where much of the most important work on gender has been done, is careful to say that the boy is not just disconnecting from his mother, a major theme in traditional psychology. He is, instead, disconnecting from the whole process of being in relationship. He is taught to disconnect from the very process of growth that is fostered through relationship.

The Stone Center theory articulates the process imposed on males in most cultures:

> In learning to turn away, boys never learn how to be relational. This sets up a pattern that continues throughout life.

Because they turn away, boys get little practice paying attention to their own feelings or the feelings of others.

Not being good at the relational mode, boys tend to avoid it even more.

Learning to avoid it, boys learn to devalue it.

Having learned to devalue the relational mode, they develop a tendency to deny that it exists in their lives.

Because they don't believe it exists in their lives, they begin to see themselves as "different."

Difference, then, becomes a declaration and definition of maleness. "I know that I am a male and not a female because I don't involve myself in all that mushy feeling stuff like girls do."

Difference implies comparison. "If I am different from you, then I have to know whether this difference makes me better or worse than you." This need to classify difference as inferior or superior then becomes a large part of how males define themselves. It becomes built into their language and ways of thought. The classic "one up/one down" thinking is an example of this comparison/difference thinking.

Because boys learn to compare, they learn not to identify. Their focus is on "self" achievement. This often means that the more competence they have in the world, the less competence they feel they have in relationships.

The less competent they feel in relationships, the more they avoid placing any value on the whole relational mode.

Many men, therefore, seem to be in a hurry to be "somewhere else" and become "something else." The Stone Center researchers note that it's almost as if they need to become "something else" in order to be valued.

This can lead men to become actively afraid of conflict on the emotional level, which is typically where most marital fights occur.

The most important thing to remember is that most men never really outgrow the discomfort with their emotions and everything about being relational.

Add to this mixture the psychosexual element. As a boy, he thinks about sex all the time. To him, it's a game, just like those he has played with boys. Now that he has discovered a game that seems like it would be new and wonderful, he wants to play it with her. But she won't play—and all her rules and barriers confuse him. Once he hits puberty, testosterone floods his system with levels 20 to 40 times what they had been, raising the bar on his sexual tension to almost unbearable heights.

The biggest irony of all time may be the very fact that boys and girls grow up to be men and women who never actually realize that males are so tuned out of the relational mode because they identify it as feminine. Women have no idea that men don't know how they feel. Men, on the other hand, appear to have some nagging feeling that something is missing and develop a certain, almost unconscious, defensive stance to make sure that no one, including himself, ever knows this. Both men and women enter relationships without ever really knowing these facts. No wonder we have so many problems around relationships.

In his role as husband, men often start feeling restricted to only one female. His whole biological imperative tells him to spread his seed as far and wide as he can—and he feels locked in with one female for the rest of his life. As the saying goes, a woman looks to one man to have all her needs fulfilled and a man looks to every woman to have his one need fulfilled. We see this every day in tabloids and television shows that try to dissect the lives of well-known people and celebrities. They ask, with regard to philandering stars, "Why, when he is married to one of the most beautiful women in the world (insert the name of almost any beautiful and well known female name here—Princess Diana, Jerry Hall, Jennifer Aniston, Maria Shriver, Hillary Clinton, etc.) is he still dissatisfied and feeling trapped?" The beauty, brains, or goodness of females doesn't seem to have much to do with keeping him monogamous.

While Gray, with his limited perspective that just blames the woman, it appears that men stray, either because of a biological imperative, or just because they can.

The male doesn't like to restrict or have to negotiate his most pleasurable pursuit and begins to resent her. Most males sense on some level that they are continually failing to live up to the expectations of their partners. An added complication is that their partner is the one who guarantees their biological legacy. Many men want their wives to be only with them, yet at the same time, they want to be with many other women. This makes them feel guilty about their sexual behavior. The male version of "resentment flu" then gets translated into passive-aggressive behavior and learned helplessness.

According to a new book by Eric Anderson,[1] monogamy, the bastion of patriarchy, initiated by males to ensure that women did not sleep with other men is failing men. He views monogamy as socially dictated sexual incarceration that leads men to contempt and anger. Males, whether impelled by biology to spread their seed, or just because they can, typically *want* to cheat. His point is that just because men want to cheat and do cheat, doesn't mean that they don't love their wives, and for this reason, society shouldn't judge them. This is an interesting attempt on the part of males to have it both ways, in today's world where every roll of belly fat or even a bad hair day on anyone who has even the most minimal public persona will show up on TV or the Internet that night. In other words, it's a lot harder for males to cheat today—and, even though they thought up monogamy, they don't like it.

To be fair, there are countless "good" men, especially today, who are married and have never cheated. Historically, however, if they thought they could get away with it, many married men did indeed cheat. However, now that women are coming into their own, apparently the society that is judging the cheaters is starting to reflect a female perspective. Obviously, the society that Anderson is referring to is female because it's still way too easy to imagine males, upon hearing about some well-known male who has cheated, having a slight smile cross their faces, elbowing their buddies and thinking, "sweet!" Whether society is male or female, cheating is still a lot harder today. Anderson's new twist on this ancient problem, however, is to stress that the men still love their wives and want to maintain their emotional connections to family. Women, of course, would be very wise to question the degree and extent of these supposed emotional connections that the men have with their wives in the first place. The assumption sounds a little like something out of the 1950s. His book is apparently geared toward men, because it is hard to imagine a female actually buying what he is saying.

The pattern that begins early in a boy's childhood stays with him all of his life unless something changes. Maybe we should set up a world where a relationship is not based on one man and one woman staying together for life. It appears that society is moving toward this. More and more women, especially if they have been married for a long time, don't really seem to care if their husbands cheat. Many are no longer in love and just don't really care if they are married or not.[2] The truth is, however, that society and families are still set up on the premise of monogamy, and it is men who set it up this way.

Real Men *Do* Cry

William Pollack, author of *Real Boys,*[3] says there is so much pressure on a boy to act like a male, or in a way that is not considered female, that by the time a boy is five years old, he has learned not to register emotion on his face. The boys are given messages from the time they are toddlers to act like little men, not to cry and to be strong.

But in truth, the stronger a man is, says Pollack, the more he is able to cry. As General Norman Schwarzkopf Jr. has stated, a man who is so unfamiliar with his feelings that he can't or won't cry is a man to be afraid of. And yet, the male myth would have us believe it is the weak man who cries. We have for so long believed that male strength is associated with the lack of feelings that it is hard for us to conceive that we have had it all wrong for so long. The male myth says that real men use brute strength, defend what they need to, and have no need for feelings.

Most mothers understand implicitly what Pollack is saying and have tried to keep their sons in touch with their feelings, only to often be undermined by the boy's father. The fathers, who are uncomfortable with their own feelings, are of course not going to be comfortable with a son who expresses feelings. The son who tries to get close to his father often discovers that his father doesn't know how to respond. In fact, sons have indeed tried to get close to their fathers only to be rebuffed as sissies—not because what they were asking for was wrong, but because the fathers didn't know how to do it and felt uncomfortable.

The reality television series *Trading Spouses* aired a segment where the visiting mom encouraged the father to hug his sons for the first time. In a stunning display of honesty, the father asked the new mom to help him encourage his *own* father to hug him. Often men, who try to dismiss affection by saying they weren't raised to be touchy-feely, will, in the next breath, without realizing what they are saying, mention that their fathers were tough on them.

"I remember at my high school graduation," said our neighbor, Gary. "I'd had a little to drink, not much really, but enough to make me open enough to say something that I had wanted to say for about a year. I put my arm around my dad and I told him that I loved him. I thought this would be all right because he'd been drinking, too. He just stiffened when he felt my arm on my shoulder. I told him anyway. He just looked at me and told me I was drunk. He told me to straighten up. I've never tried to tell him I love him since then. He died three years ago, and I never did tell him."

Women know what kind of men they want to be married to. They try to raise their sons to be the kind of men who will become good husbands and fathers. Women know intuitively that, if their sons are in touch with their feelings, they will be stronger, gentler, and kinder as adult men. Most women have not been permitted, however, to allow their sons to be raised this way and are typically cut off by husbands, fathers, uncles, and men in their lives who belittle their attempts to shape their sons into more whole people.

The whole culture seems to have conspired to make sure that boys continue to be raised with the male myth. Even the woman who knows that her son should be allowed to cry and remain in touch with his feelings may discourage him, sensing that it may lead to ridicule from his peers and the world at large. If just one generation of boys changed, it would become easier for all future generations of boys. It will also, however, make it harder for older men. Fathers could make a huge difference for themselves and their sons if they were willing to learn about feelings along with their sons.

Why should we begin to raise our boys to be in touch with their feelings? According to Pollack, it is the boys who can't cry tears who end up crying bullets. We are shocked when we hear about violence in schools and struggle to understand what makes boys kill their classmates and teachers. Some experts suggest the reason may be that children are bombarded with images of violence in video games, movies, and television. Others point to the fact that most sixth graders will tell you that their biggest problem is being bullied. The bullies are also in need of help, and according to experts, the best remedy to stop bullying is meaningful relationships.

Today there are 10 times as many boys with Attention Deficit Disorder as girls and the rate of ADD has risen dramatically in the last 10 years. Pollack believes that at least 50 percent of the boys with ADD can't focus their attention simply because they don't *get* enough attention. Perhaps, says Pollack, these boys are trying to connect with their parents but sense that this isn't permitted. Perhaps, part of their definition of being male is the sense that they aren't supposed to get the same kind of attention girls get.

The Stone Center theorists hypothesize that more boys have ADHD as a response to being confronted with and initiated into patriarchal, male-based values earlier than girls. Girls, according to the center, are initiated into these values around the age of 12 or 13 when the young girl begins to understand that male values reign. Her response, until recently, has been a change or drop in academic performance. The impact on a boy begins much earlier and is thus much more deep-seated.

Listen Up

We see warning signs in boys, but dismiss them by thinking, "Boys will be boys." Meanwhile, depression among boys has reached epidemic proportions. Young males, says Pollack, are trying to tell us something. He urges parents not to leave boys alone, but rather continue to be engaged with them until their true feelings come out. Parents are encouraged to give boys their undivided attention, in a safe and solitary space, and to encourage them to express all of their emotions. Often anger is expressed first, but parents are encouraged to look for the pain behind the anger.

It is much easier to talk about this problem in relation to our sons than it is to see the same problem in grown men—even when the roots of the problem have the same origin. Adult men are far less willing to admit that there is a problem. And the conventional wisdom that one cannot fix problems that one refuses to see is further compounded by this: many men refuse to even look, preferring instead to put their fingers over their ears and sing "la la la" at the top of their lungs. Is this why so many women think men are really just little boys? Is this why men are physically abusive to women? According to the Stone Center, most men use analogies of violence and weaponry even when they recall or imagine an emotional exchange between themselves and the women in their lives, just as Dave had interpreted my words as bullets in his talk. Similarly, when confronted with their own feelings, men are afraid that they may become violent.

When Norah Vincent went undercover for 18 months disguised as a man, she attended a men-only retreat where she discovered that the men were simmering with rage toward women. Some fantasized about chopping their wives into pieces. In her book, *Self-Made Man*,[4] she recounts how she hung out with men, joined a bowling league and even a monastery. She went to strip clubs and joined a men-only therapy group—à la Robert Bly[5]—that met in the woods to vent their feelings. She learned that the ability to understand emotions was beaten out of many men at an early age. They are so separated from how they really feel that they don't even have language for emotions. She found major differences in the way men and women connect with each other, experience sexuality, and even buy a car. She discovered that men have a desperate need for intimacy and no ability to give it. She learned that men are suffering. They need sympathy and love—and also need to be with other men. Men, she found, are just as emotionally vulnerable as we have believed women were.

The problem appears to be almost universal. Recently, some psychologists suggested, albeit somewhat jokingly, that there is so much research supporting the male lack of emotionality, inability to feel and be relational, that perhaps this deficit should be recognized, identified, named, and included along with other problems and personality disorders in the DSM (*Diagnostic and Statistical Manual*)[6] used by psychologists and psychiatrists to define and label psychological problems. Their suggestion is inspired by the realization that societies, like individuals, can only deal with a problem they allow themselves to see. Paul Levy[7] has named and identified the problem that occurs, when this lack of ability to feel and relate to others is taken to its extreme. It is found in people who create an existence that is separate from the field around them. For this reason, they have no ability for self-reflection. While he does not specifically call it a disease of men, it appears that it is only the behavior of males that is described by Levy. Malignant egophrenia, or ME, is a psychospiritual disease, found particularly in those who focus only on a need for power and control and is seen therefore in men seeking high political positions.

To some extent, as McGill[8] suggested, men benefit if they are *not* engaged relationally. When they aren't tuned in, they have less regret and guilt, and don't have to take responsibility for their relationships. This skewed perception toward the male perspective has for years made it her fault that she brings up the past too much or wants to discuss the relationship by trying to engage him too much, when in reality men don't bring up the past because they don't remember it and they don't engage because they are too uncomfortable. This male bias has based our entire understanding of relationships on the emotional deficits of men and, further, elevated it as the accepted standard. Today's men no longer get credit for being the kinder sex because they don't bring up a past they can't remember anyway. Men, however, have paid a great price to maintain this inequality. Because boys learn to disconnect from their primary relationship, they never learn the benefit of staying connected during conflict. Most men grow up deathly afraid of conflict around emotional issues. They know this is the one arena in which they cannot win. And they tend to see all disputes as being about winning, rather than about resolving or compromising.

Bergman[9] even suggests that perhaps men start wars and fights because they don't know how to manage conflict on an emotional level. As boys, they learned only to compete and compare. Add this to the fact that males think about sex—a lot—and Ken Wilber's hypothesis of "f*** it or kill it" rings even more true. The old scenario about a woman president pushing the button that sets off the bomb because she has PMS seems to pale in comparison to what might happen with men, with their testosterone and early training. It would be interesting to know how many men who blew something up, shot someone, or committed an act of violence had been told "No" by their partner the night before.

What's a Boy to Do?

The typical male has been raised to believe that to be like his mother, or any other woman, is shameful—and as a result, he can't connect with her. Some male theorists, such as Bly, therefore, suggest that he should connect with his father, but as discussed earlier this is also not a good idea—for many reasons. First is the absent father syndrome. Many fathers just aren't there. They followed the biological imperative to "go forth and multiply" and then they kept going. Secondly, when fathers are physically present, they're typically not in touch with their feelings enough to be emotionally present. How could they be? They've had an even stronger cultural conditioning and indoctrination than their sons did. The father has learned not to listen and not respond. The son, therefore, would be asking his father to teach him something about which the father knows little or nothing. Because the father is unfamiliar with that turf, he would be even more inclined to devalue the whole area of emotions. Many fathers can only teach their sons about further disconnection.

For years, men's emotional distance was hidden by making it the women's fault. Women were the punishing and dominating mothers who made boys want to flee from their feelings. Women pushed and nagged their husbands until they no longer wanted to be relational. Even Robert Bly, one of the first men to speak openly about his own emotional wounds, falls into the mother-blaming trap. Bly, who always felt disconnected from his own father, writes that when he went to visit his father during the last days of his life, his father was confined to a bed in a separate room. As the son, Bly had always found himself talking outside his father's room with his mother because she was easier to talk with. Examining this behavior, he concluded that he and his mother had unconsciously conspired to keep his father out of the emotional loop. He's right to see that his father is out of the emotional loop, but why blame his mother or himself? It makes far more sense to recognize that his father, like so many fathers, was probably always emotionally distant, and that he and his mother learned early on how uncomfortable it was to try to include him. To continue to blame mothers or sensitive sons for the lack of relational skills in the men they love simply continues to mask the real problem.

What Do Men Think About?

Every woman knows the answer to what men think about—sex. Countless statistics confirm this, despite the fact that the actual truth varies. Some research says that men think about sex every 16 seconds, or every 2 minutes, or every 5 minutes. Whatever the truth, it appears that men think about sex—a lot. And, surely, they think about other things. Bergman suggests that the disconnection men experience from the time they are young often leads to less interest in knowing about their own interior experiences and inner life. As the boy loses touch with his own internal state, he also loses his desire to know about the internal states of others. His curiosity about relationships and how they work becomes deadened. After a while, he devalues such knowledge and eventually denies that such feelings and experience even exist. So, maybe this is why men appear to think most about computers, tools, sports, an sports, cars and that fascinating external appendage that they are so fond of.

Few men talk to other men about their feelings. They have to contend with perceived hierarchy, competitiveness, and the power-over perception in other men. Many men, therefore, marry and have children without ever really learning to connect emotionally with anyone. Women find this almost impossible to believe, for they naturally maintain many active emotional connections that have a sense of continuity. Throughout their lives, says Bergman, men are left with a dim sense of wanting to connect, but they rarely actually experience a deep and real sense of "self-with-other." Poet David Whyte[10] says the same thing in a different way. Most men, he writes, are like stealth bombers and spend their emotional lives flying beneath the radar of life, trying to avoid any meaningful interactions.

Toxic Male Emotions Affect the Whole Family

Because men live outside the loop of connection, the following scenario is typical. Dad has a rough day at the office, he comes home in a bad mood. He yells at his wife, she gets in a bad mood, the kids fight, and before they go to bed, also in a bad mood, one of them kicks the dog, so even the *dog* is in the mood to bite someone.

We have accepted this kind of behavior since the days when we believed that Dad went out to work in the big, bad, stressful world, while the little woman stayed home with nothing to do but watch soap operas and eat bonbons. Today, of course, both parents go to stress-filled work, and both come home to stress, where he relaxes and she begins her second, often even more stressful shift.[11] The scenario is still the same, however. Dad's bad mood still infects the whole family.

Numerous studies have found that it is still the male and his negative emotions that, like a common cold, infect the whole family. Past research looked for and always found that it was the women's fault. Whatever the problems of society and the family, it was her fault. Today, we are more tuned in to the political correctness of findings in research and try not to blame either sex. "It wasn't our intention to be sexist," said one researcher, "but very objective, (and) what we found is that the chain reaction was most often triggered by the male parent, even when the mother was also working outside the home." The studies found that the male parent's mood is so influential that anyone looking at it can predict the mood of the whole family. Even being merely grouchy can have a toxic, chain reaction effect. All the studies found that it was the father who precipitated negativity. The mothers, even though they too worked outside the home—or even those who were severely ill—did a better job of protecting family members from the fallout of their own emotions and stress.

Family psychology researcher David Almeida,[12] one of the researchers who focused on nuclear families, said that he never set out to prove that fathers initiated most of the stress and admitted to being "startled when the research concluded that 'dear old dad' is most often the chief protagonist." The studies concluded that fathers need more work on their emotional intelligence.

We have also reversed our perceptions on divorce. When women started divorcing in record numbers in the 1970s, research supported the concept that children were resilient and seemed to adjust well to divorce. Since then, further research has shown that divorce can have a major impact on children causing them to act out in various negative ways.[13]

Nature and Nurture Are Interrelated

Both nature and nurture appear to work together to create the male psyche. Other than studies with identical twins that have been separated, it is almost impossible to separate the effects of nature from nurture, or heredity from environment. Both factors appear to contribute to the difficulty males have with relationships. Now that we have more sophisticated ways of studying the brain, we are discovering that, to some extent, there are biological reasons for why males have such a difficult time with relationships.

Clamming up during an argument appears to be tied to a dip in activity in the empathy regions of the brain. Researchers found that men under stress who were shown pictures of angry faces had reduced activity in the parts of the brain that handle understanding the feelings of others. The brains of women, on the other hand, had the opposite response: heightened activity in the brain regions responsible for empathy and processing other people's facial expressions. It appears that experiencing acute stress interacts in brain regions in opposite ways for males and under extreme stress, men's brains responded much less to certain facial expressions, namely those of fear and anger, than women's brains did. "Under stress, men tend to withdraw socially while women seek emotional support."[14] These are the first findings that show, when under stress, females are much better at the most basic of social transactions—the ability to read the facial expressions of others.

There are many reasons why it has come down to this. Men are hardwired and acculturated differently, and even as infants, males have a harder time with intimate contact, and find it harder to regulate arousal and may become overstimulated by direct eye contact.

Things Are Changing

The deconstruction of traditional values continues on a daily basis whether we are conscious of it or not. Postmodernism is now declaring the death of patriarchy. Patriarchy, however, does not equal masculinity, and many good males have adapted to these changes. You see them with their children at the park, actively involved in childrearing, gently nurturing an infant, cooking, cleaning, and keeping the house running. Many readily embrace the once-female domain of baths and bedtime stories. They are in the de-livery rooms, wide-eyed with awe, thankful that their wives are willing to go through the birth process. They may wear a kind of deer-caught-in-the-headlights expression, but they're doing it. These are the good guys who have dropped, or never had, the masculinized ego that told men they were superior just because they were male.

Cultural anthropology enables us to understand how we have evolved and that we are still in the process of evolving. The smartest and best, those who will survive and prosper, are those who adapt well to changes. Despite the fact that we have believed in survival of the fittest and thus that the strong male survived on his own, the truth is that real survival was actu-ally based on cooperation. Those who prospered realized that it was to the benefit of all to share food and help each other. The most intelligent of these smart adapters are those who changed, not because they were forced to but because they saw the need for change. They saw the external changes and understood what internal changes were required. Typically, these first adapters have been female; however, many good males, especially today, have similarly and easily accepted the new norms.

Because women have changed and because males and females are in rela-tion to each other, all men, whether they like it or not, are going to have to change. But how? Few will do it consciously and without being forced. For the most part, many of the men who changed, did so because their wives or girlfriends gently suggested or strongly demanded that they become equally involved.

It's hard to gauge the shifting baselines here. Much of the problem often seems to be among older men, who were acculturated at a different time and may or may not ever get it. We also see young men who do seem to get it. At the same time, however, we learn that the abuse of teenage girls by their boyfriends is escalating dramatically. We also know that the sexual double standard is still alive and well, even among young children. And, further, women of every age still claim that it's impossible to find a guy who really gets it. It is hard to get a clear picture.

There really are the good guys out there who are great fathers and husbands, and who value the personhood, autonomy, and integrity of both men and women. Then there are all the men in the middle—men who appear to be willing and able to learn and change, once they reconsider their attitudes toward gender roles. There are also the diehards—men who will not change and will always see the problem as the other person's fault. The diehards may not be able to really change, but they can learn to adjust their behavior. The diehards are men who have strong masculinized egos and/or testosterone levels that are out of control, but even they can learn to adapt and adjust.

And who is to judge which category a man falls into? The women in their lives, of course. Ask her. No one else will get it enough to be able to understand it.

Whether the male problem is due to nurture or nature or a combination of both, the first and most important step of identifying the problem is now being explored and defined. We have lived with incorrect assumptions for too long. Culture has changed and continues to change so fast that we simply can no longer tolerate behavior that is too sexualized, aggressive, or masculinized. These traits have created the majority of problems in our culture, and now that we have identified the problem, we can work toward solutions. Culturally learned male behaviors can be unlearned, and there are also solutions for nature or biologically based issues.

Chapter 12

Why Men Are Clueless in Relationships

Yang
Clueless
Simple creatures

Things had changed dramatically for us over the two years since Dave had given his talk at the Returning Adult conference. The biggest change was that Dave finally seemed to really get it. And the more he seemed to get it, the more he seemed to understand himself. As his perception shifted, he could see more and more clearly what I had been trying to do and why I was doing it. The more he understood, the more he grasped the bigger picture of the relationship and could now understand why I had persisted. He no longer viewed what I did as bitching, but rather as what I had to say as a result of my love for him.

He came to me one evening, while I was sitting on our bed, surrounded by books for my doctoral work and told me he had to talk to me. He seemed a little uncomfortable as he began. He cleared his throat and said, "I have to tell you something. I get it. I get it. I finally understand what you were trying to do. I can see now how I fought you at every step. I just didn't realize. I didn't know . . . ," he said, choking up. "I just have to tell you that I am so deeply grateful for you. I am so grateful to you for hanging in there with me, Sherry. I get it. I just want to say thank you."

Tears came to my eyes. I was so deeply grateful to him for telling me this. Had it been later, had our three teenagers not been roaming the house, we surely would have ended up in bed. In a way, however, his rational tone and the fact that we just stayed there talking made even more of an impact.

I felt like I got it, too. I felt that I finally understood the deepest levels of love for the first time. I was aware of many things all at the same time. I knew we had turned a corner. I knew that any problem that would come up after that could just be easily corrected. I was also aware that I was at this new and deeper level of complete trust and love for him now because he had been heroic enough to trust me. I understood how each of us was in relation to the other. My sense of self was now very different because of his sense of self. If he had continued to fight me, we may or may not have stayed together. I knew, however, that I certainly would not have been able to trust myself to the same degree. I realized that I was stronger *because* of him, and that his actions and responses to me had permitted me to grow. At the same time, he was stronger *because* of me. His openness to me and my actions had allowed him to grow. It seemed so clear, in that moment, that this was exactly what real love should be.

We both took a deep breath at the same time and just looked at each other with new eyes. I felt enlarged and expanded—one with every woman who had ever loved a man deeply.

Days later, he told me that he had been asked to give another talk at the annual Women's Conference, and his topic would again be about relationships, men, and women. He was now as interested as I was with this whole topic. In fact, he often talked to his students and his friends about his new perceptions. He talked mostly with women, who seemed to be much more open to what he had to say than men.

As he talked to women about their relationships, he began to see, just as I had, the problems that women had with men. Every day he would come home amazed with new stories of the problems that women were coping with. He would flat out tell them, in a way that I couldn't (or wouldn't), that they shouldn't put up with it and that they should stand up to their men. He was fascinated to learn, as I had, that so many women had problems in their relationships.

When a woman told me about her problems with her partner, I always took more of a counselor stance, empathizing and offering suggestions. I was trained in psychology, and I never would have felt comfortable saying "You should just dump his ass" like Dave did. Consequently, women loved to talk to him. It seemed like it was easier for a man to point out the problems with men than a woman. If I had said the same things he had, I think I would have been considered by most men and even some women, as a radical bitch.

Over the past year, he had really come to empathize with women. Like me, he had gotten to know many of the New Choices women, who were now at college, and was often shocked when he heard the stories of what they had been through—especially with their husbands. He was more than happy, therefore, to give another talk. Like me, he wanted to help women understand the problem. This time he talked about why men are clueless. The following is what he said at the Women's Conference in the fall of 1994.

Why Men Are Often Clueless in Relationships with Women: The Quest for Connectedness with One's Significant Woman

A. The Problem

The dialectical process between a man and a woman usually involves the following: the physical and the cognitive (discourse) aspects. These are what are usually involved when we utter the cliché—"boy meets girl, boy falls in love with girl, boy marries girl" and vice versa. The physical aspect incorporates physical attraction to each other, touching, caressing, petting, and sex as such. The cognitive (discourse) aspect may range from "Hi, my name is . . ." to a clear articulation of one's religio-philosophical belief system. Somewhere in between will be an indication of "I love you," "I can't live without you," "let's get married," "my (our) plans for the future are . . ."

The situation seems to be fine for several years into the relationship, until the man becomes conscious of the fact that his woman begins to make certain comments or raises certain questions that he finds distressing: you spend too much time with the guys; you don't spend enough time with me; watching sports is more important to you than me and the kids; you need to spend more time with the kids; I wish you would talk with me; I wish you would let me know how you feel about us; I don't want to hear about what you know and think. . . . I want you to tell me how you feel. Or, some of these statements may be presented as questions: Why don't you spend more time with me? Can you tell me how you feel? Don't you think you should spend more time with me and the kids? Can you help me with the housework?

Now the man in this situation may understand some of the comments and questions and may choose to respond to them in some positive manner. However he may choose to respond, he is beginning to sense that she is not happy with the situation, and he is clueless as to what she wants. I am here talking about a man who at least understands that he is clueless. The majority of men, however, are clueless about the fact that they are clueless. In other words, most men are not aware that a fundamental problem exists in the relationship. They will usually attribute the comments/questions as due to pre-PMS, PMS, or post-PMS. Or he may scream at her and storm out. He perceives whatever is happening now is her fault.

B. Answers to the Problem

The question is: Why are men often clueless in relationships with women? I have two interrelated answers to the question:

a. The first is a suggestion by Peter Berger in *The Sacred Canopy: Elements of a Sociological Theory of Religion*.[1] While this book is about the sociology of religion, there are some issues he mentions that are pertinent to our discussion. On page 45, he talks about the plausibility structure: "Worlds are socially constructed and socially maintained. Their continuing reality, both objective (as common, taken-for-granted facticity) and subjective (as facticity imposing itself on individual consciousness), depends upon specific social processes, namely those processes that ongoingly reconstruct and maintain those particular worlds in question. Conversely, the interruption of these social processes threatens the (objective and subjective) reality of the worlds in question. Thus, each world requires a social 'base' for its continuing existence as a world that is real to actual human beings. This 'base' may be called its plausibility structure."

What is a plausibility structure for men? For insights, I quote a brief article in our local newspaper, on Wednesday, October 12, 1994: "Newton, Mass. (AP)—If you hear a woman saying, 'Here boy. Here, boy. . . . That's a good boy,' and she is talking to her husband or boyfriend, maybe she's been listening to 'Mayflower Madam' Sydney Biddle Barrows. Most men, she said, 'are just like dogs. They react incredibly to praise. You can never encourage them too much.' The 42-year-old Barrows, who once ran two $200-an-hour escort services, made her comments last week to a women-only, paying audience of about 100. She said men need lots of attention, someone who will listen to them uncritically, tell them they're wonderful and bring them sexual excitement as well as intellectual fulfillment. 'Give them your undivided attention,' Barrows said. 'Just sit and watch them talk. Don't interrupt. If you ask questions, do it in a neutral tone. And don't give unsolicited advice.' (I thought, when I heard him say this, that she surely must have read *Men Are from Mars*.) Barrows, who was arrested 10 years ago Monday, pleaded guilty to prostitution and was fined $5,000.00."[2]

The following statements can be articulated on the basis of what Maame Barrows said:

1. Women are to praise men a lot.
2. Women are to give men a lot of attention.
3. Women are to listen to men uncritically.
4. Women are to tell men that they are wonderful.
5. Women are to bring men sexual excitement and intellectual fulfillent.
6. Women are to give men undivided attention.
7. Women are just to sit and watch men talk.
8. Women are not to interrupt when men are talking.
9. Women are to ask men questions in a neutral tone.
10. Women are not to give men unsolicited advice.

Where in the social order does this plausibility structure emerge for men? First of all, from historically dominant patriarchal constructs, which undergird much of the contemporary world-historical situation and its ramifications for the social behavior of individuals and secondly, from their peer relationships. Males in relationship with fellow males, consciously and unconsciously, reinforce existing patterns of behavior that are conducive to themselves as males.

Thus, the first answer to the question as to why men are often clueless in relationships with women is that her questions and comments are *contrary* and often contradictory to the plausibility structures of males.

b. The second answer comes from Eastern thought's interpretation of the human individual. Whereas in the West we talk of the body and the soul, as respectively the base for emotions and thinking, Eastern thought articulates basically three aspects of the human individual: the body, the soul, and the spirit. Eastern thought reckons with the limits of the body (emotions) and the soul (the cognitive), and the need to transcend both in order to attain a sense of oneness with the infinite spirit, via the pathway of intuition. Faith in the Western sense is not the same as intuition inasmuch as faith is a commitment to given cognitive content that cannot be proven either rationally or empirically. Intuition, on the other hand, is a sense of immediate awareness and oneness with the infinite spirit and with each other. Women seem to cultivate this dimension of human existence more readily than men, perhaps because the patriarchal constructs of our society owns both the mind and the body. It is the dimension that is often referred to as "feelings." Feelings are not the same as emotions. Emotions often are physiological responses to situations, such as anger, crying, exultation, and so on. We can, however, evoke the dimension of feeling in periods when there is no sense of emotions. Thus, in the privacy of a conversation, we can ask, "how do you feel about that?" The question calls for a cognitive articulation but the base of it is neither the mind nor the body. Men, whose plausibility structure is basically thinking and emoting in the interests of the male constructs, are clueless when called on to express their feelings on x issue. Usually, he can tell you what he thinks about the issue or he may react emotionally with anger or dismay and shout, yell, or scream at you. The second answer to the question as to why men are clueless in relationships with women is that women call for a response from a base that *transcends* his plausibility structure.

C. Responses to the Problem

There are several responses to the cluelessness of men:

1. A woman can scream, yell back at the male in her life, and accuse him of being dumb, dense, stupid, a jerk, or an a**hole. Since whatever she is com-

menting on and questioning are perfectly evident to her, she infers that it should be perfectly evident to him. And since he sits or stands there stupid-like, she infers that he must be spiteful and mean or just plain stupid. We need to keep in mind at this juncture that we are not involved in an interaction or interrelation within a common plausibility structure but actually the collision of two contradictory plausibility structures. This response does not resolve the issue of male cluelessness. This response simply reinforces for the male that the woman in his life is a cantankerous bitch, and for the woman, that the man in her life is an insensitive a**hole.

2. The second response is that of complicity. The jacket discussion of Rosalind Coward's *Our Treacherous Hearts: Why Women Let Men Get Their Way*[3] states the following: "So much appears to have improved for women. In theory, they have equal pay and opportunity; working mothers are no longer stigmatized; women are moving into the highest levels of politics. Yet in many fundamental ways, little has changed. It is still mainly women who take care of dependents, interrupting or downgrading careers to do so. Women continue to relinquish privilege and power to their male partners, and seem happy, at least at first, to make sacrifices for their children. Are women really victims of a backlash against their newfound freedoms? Did feminism underestimate the satisfaction women get from mothering? Or is there evidence of a deeper complicity through which women keep themselves from breaking with traditional roles? *Our Treacherous Hearts* looks at women's collusion with male domination. Drawing from revealing interviews on women's feelings about men, children and work, Rosalind Coward explores why working women still do the majority of housework and childcare and are grateful for even small contributions by men, and why women leave good jobs to be at home and then find that their supposedly idyllic time at home isn't as simple as they expected. As startling as it is compelling, *Our Treacherous Hearts* is an honest appraisal of what's really happening in contemporary women's lives and psyches."

    In her concluding chapter entitled: "Conclusion: The Complicity of Women," she says on pages 194–95: "Living an illusion is uncomfortable, and often women hover on the point of exposing the illusions of their lives. But most back off, preferring the illusions to the difficulty of *personal* change (italics, mine). And this is ultimately what I mean by complicity. Complicity is about not telling the truth—to other women or to ourselves—and not confronting men about the areas of our lives that don't fit the illusions. This complicity means that women don't pass on information and knowledge about their condition, and disparage those who try to do so. Complicity is about continuing to delude yourself about yourself and not being able to sort out what comes from outside and what from within. It means that instead of recognizing who they really are, women continue to project on to men and children what they haven't dealt with properly in themselves. It means they continue with miserable obsessions about what men can do to make them happier, and what children can achieve to make them feel better about themselves. Those without money cannot cushion themselves by buying time away from children and making their working lives easier. Without choice, there is less reason to mystify. But the less affluent do not have power in the public domain. The voices heard there are the voices of women who are fed lies and try to believe them."

She discusses two interviews with women, and with the latter, she says: "Here, in a nutshell, is the complicity of the 1990s. The family has internal and impossible tensions—in this case a successful husband who doesn't help in the house and is having an affair. The woman sees herself sinking in it. She uses work as a 'solution' to her own personal disintegration and a private school as a 'solution' to the anxiety and guilt she suffers as a working mother. She feels better. But she has failed to confront her husband: his success means more to her than negotiating a change within the house. And secondly, she has passed the problem along, buying into a system where she tries to quarantine herself from the aspects of her worries. She thinks that sending her children to private school will buy her some respite from one of her worries—which it probably won't—but in doing this she inevitably spoils the chances of an improvement in social provision for all women."

Fortunately, her conclusion does not end on a note of despair, but on somewhat of an unsatisfactory note. She presents some suggestions for us as we move into the third possible response. She says, "It remains important for women to find out who they are and to take responsibilities for their feelings without abandoning their obligations to those around them. This applies to women who work and to women who give up paid work. And it is crucial for women to refuse to be coerced by a society like ours, which needs women to assume 'feminine' positions so that it can maintain some moral fabric. . . . Women need the freedom to understand themselves, their individual strengths and needs, and what they can best contribute to others."

What is not satisfactory about her discussion is her resolution to the problem. She says, "I hope if this book contributes anything, it will help release women from the burdens of other people's prescriptions. But, above all, I hope it will encourage social, not individual, solutions. Because if women try to lighten the burdens imposed by society as individuals, it is other women who will pay the price." What I disagree with is her statement: "I hope it will encourage social, not individual, solutions." And I disagree because it is precisely her individual situation that gives rise to anger, frustration, despair, and complicity. It is at the individual level, in her involvement with the clueless man in her life, which is at the heart of the problem. Furthermore, a social solution is somewhat abstract and will not touch that man whose plausible structure continues to operate on the basis of the suggestions articulated by the Mayflower Madam.

3. The third response is the endeavor to bring about a resolution to male cluelessness, not by yelling and screaming, not by complicity, and not by social

solutions. It is, rather, to focus on the plausibility structure of males, and the key is a statement that Berger made in his clarification of plausibility structures. He said, "Conversely, the interruption of these social processes threatens the (objective and subjective) reality of the worlds in question." But, before a woman interrupts the male's plausibility structure, she needs to assess her own plausibility structure: Do I want change such that I am to become superior to him? Do I want change for personal and selfish reasons? Do I want change so that I can show him and others that I can bust his balls? If these are her expectations, then she is as clueless as he is, and what you have is the interrelationship of two clueless individuals.

However, if she wants change such that it enhances their relationship with each other, so that they can function as one, and truly be a nuclear family in which there is tremendous energy and heat, where there is the interplay of attraction and repulsion among the particles within the core, playing and bouncing off each other, but always directed within the dynamics of the inner core—then, indeed, she has just cause for the desire for his change. And, if this is truly her vision of her relation to her clueless man, then she must cultivate the internal, intuitive aspect of her life. As Eastern philosophical thought points out—you must turn within—within is the answer, within is the truth, within is the source of strength, courage, and the divine.

What must she do? With this vision, she must become his mentor, his teacher. She must treat him as a young pupil because he is called on to enter into frontiers and regions where very few men have gone before. She must ask him about his expectations of himself, of her, of the family. She must ask him how he feels about this and that. She must create that shift from thinking and emotion to that of feeling. More often than not, he will be clueless as to what she is saying and/or asking. He will resist and fight her. But she must be of courage, strength, and patience. She must share her vision repeatedly with him as she gently interrupts the expectations of his plausibility structure. Only when he begins to see her vision and begins to own that vision for himself will he be in a position to exchange one plausibility structure for another. And how long will all this take? Who can say? But she can hope, can she not, that at some given moment, in the twinkling of an eye, in that moment of his and her deepest despair, in that moment of magic, he will see what she sees. This is the moment that Hinduism calls *moksha* (liberation), what Buddhism calls nirvana (enlightenment), what Christianity calls the grace of God and forgiveness.

D. Concluding Comments

I wish to conclude this presentation on two notes: (1) Plato's Allegory of the Cave, which is found in Book VII of the *Republic* (Bloom translation)[4];

and (2) some reflections of a personal note. In the allegory, Plato portrays individuals who are prisoners in an underground cavern their whole lives and do not know other than what they know within the cavern. "Now consider," Socrates says, "what their release and healing from bonds and folly would be like if something of this sort were by nature to happen to them. Take a man who is released and suddenly compelled to stand up, to turn his neck around, to walk and look up toward the light; and who, moreover, in doing all this, is in pain and, because he is dazzled, is unable to make out those things whose shadows he saw before. What do you suppose he'd say if someone were to tell him that before he saw silly nothings, while now, because he is somewhat nearer to what is and more turned toward being, he sees more correctly; and, in particular, showing him each of the things that pass by, were to compel the man to answer his questions about what they are? Don't you suppose he'd be at a loss and believe that what was seen before is truer than what is now shown? And, if he compelled him to look at the light itself, would his eyes hurt and would he flee, turning away to those things that he is able to make out and hold them to be really clearer than what is being shown? And if, someone dragged him away from there by force along the rough, steep, upward way and didn't let him go before he had dragged him out into the light of the sun, wouldn't he be distressed and annoyed at being so dragged? And when he came to the light, wouldn't he have his eyes full of its beam and be unable to see even one of the things now said to be true? Then, finally, I suppose he would be able to make out the sun—not its appearance in water or some alien place, but the sun itself by itself in its own region—and see what it's like.

And after that he would already be in a position to conclude about it that this is the source of the seasons and the years, and is the steward of all things in the visible place, and is in a certain way the cause of all those things he and his companions had been seeing. What then? When he recalled his first home and the wisdom there, and his fellow prisoners in that time, don't you suppose he would consider himself happy for the change and pity the others?"

The Allegory of the Cavev is not, for me, just a discourse in the *Republic*. It is what happened in my life. That mysterious stranger who took off my shackles and made me climb that steep road up to the sunlight was my wife. I was fighting and resisting all the way, but eventually I saw the light. And if I saw the light, then I see no reason why other clueless men cannot likewise come to share in that vision. My wife persisted, she was my mentor, my teacher, and now, forever, my friend."

This time when we discussed Dave's talk, we seemed very much to be on the same page. It was so comfortable and enjoyable to be able to talk to him just like I talked with my friends.

He told me something that night that I will never forget. He told me that, although he had a PhD in philosophy and had been a popular teacher for many years, he really never understood much of what they talked about in philosophy.

He was well acquainted with the Allegory of the Cave. He had taught it many times, but he said that until I had pushed him and he finally understood what I was talking about, he had never really understood it. It was not until he had his own experience that he realized what it was like to be rid of the shackles and look at the light. Now it was all so clear to him—and he thanked me again.

This time because our children were older and therefore out on a Saturday night, we did end up in bed. Later, in the soft afterglow, when we talked, he said, "I think most women know what the light is—just because they are women. And women should do what you did for me—and they shouldn't stop until he gets it."

Men Can Change

Men don't seem to understand a female's mysterious ability to grow, give birth to, feed, and nurture a baby. Only recently have men been permitted to witness the birth of their children. Many men still long for the old way of letting her do her thing and presenting them with a healthy, cleaned up, new baby while they are outside smoking a cigar.

Women typically think that counseling is the answer to help men get in touch with their feelings. Most men, however, feel more comfortable preparing to meet the enemy than to sit and talk honestly about their feelings. Men have been acculturated to arm themselves and fight. They haven't been taught anything about entering the zone of feelings.

Women who have never been told they have any other option now feel that enlisting a mental health professional is probably the only answer. Women know that men won't hear it from them, but may listen if someone else says it. But even if men were to go to counseling, the deepest issues will probably never be addressed. The therapy will go as far as the therapist's understanding, and that is only if both he and she are willing to listen. Couples counseling is difficult. A recent issue of *Psychotherapy Networker,* called "Who's Afraid of Couples Counseling—Stretching Your Comfort Zone,"[5] was devoted to this touchy subject. It stated that the imbalanced cultural bottom lines make it difficult and it may or may not work.

The Big Impossible

Both nature and nurture have a hand in creating this problem for males. The culture has been set up so that men never had to talk about their feelings, and the nature of testosterone and limited connections between their right and left brains, as well as a male-based psychological perspective, have all combined to ensure that this deficiency in males was never noticed. Women, however, are part of the culture too, and as they are changing, we can expect things to change for men. It appears that on some deep level men always knew about this problem because they have always tried so hard to hide it. It actually has a name, but even male relational dread is just a symptom of an even greater and more bottom-line fear that most men have. Gail Sheehy[6] refers to it as "The Big Impossible"—the elusive quest for true manhood that men seek but seem never to find. This seems to lie at the heart of the question that Olivia Dukakis keeps asking in *Moonstruck*: "Why do men chase women?" Finally, in the movie, it is answered so that it makes sense to her: "Because they fear death."

We know that the people who fear death the most are those who feel that they have never really lived. When we feel we have embraced life authentically, given back and left a legacy for the world, the sting of death seems to be greatly diminished. Women just seem to know who they are and why they are here. The feminine quality, despite all it has been through, seems to have a solidity to it. As Goldberg[7] states, women are central to life.

Masculinity is not something that is given to a man, but rather something he earns, says cultural anthropologist David Gilmore.[8] In every culture, on every continent, "attaining the status of 'real man' is an uncertain and precarious endeavor." Boys do not just become men; they are made into men by meeting the standards prescribed by the culture. "A man is made a man" by fighting bravely, fathering many children, providing well for his family, proving that he is a good lover, or doing whatever the culture declares as success. In every culture, "effete men, the men-who-are-not-men, are held up scornfully to inspire conformity to the glorious ideal."

Because we are so acculturated to it, this whole process of filling men with the male myth is almost invisible to us.

Interestingly, girls are never required to perform such rituals. They start their menstrual cycle, heralding their ability to bring forth children. This natural ritual is just another variation of nature. The necessity of ritual belongs to the male. Chances are that the value men feel is associated with the work they do. In the past, they were required to use brute strength to protect the tribe, build structures, hunt, and defend women. Today, however, we are just beginning to see how damaging this need to prove themselves has been to men and women—and relationships. Men, especially those who are not totally invested in the masculinized ego, sense on some level that they need to change. This fact is usually lost on women, initially, who need only to look at the rest of the male world and see men who appear to be doing very well. Even if a woman gets a clue that the man in her life should change, this recognition is obscured by the fact that, on the surface, he seems to easily be able to move on to the next woman, who, at least for a while, will perceive him to be a prince among men. Women rarely get a clear enough picture to comprehend that men don't know how to change. The majority of women are inclined to think that their husband is not relational because of some problem he had with his own individual family, especially his mother who was too controlling, too passive, too demanding, or too something.

Few women understand that, *regardless* of his upbringing, this problem is almost universal in men.

Most men are not open to change—and because they aren't, any suggestion to this end will typically be interpreted as criticism. They are often unreceptive to *anything* a woman has to say, no matter how nicely she says it. Women and relationships, however, are not going to revert back to the old days. Women have come too far to go back. It is men who must change, and, unfortunately, the more they fight it, the worse it will be for them. No wonder men see the option of just leaving so appealing.

Today, women feel that they have everything to gain by changing. They view this unlearning of repressive cultural values as the key to their new self-awareness. Men, on the other hand, feel that they have everything to lose by changing. Unlearning cultural roles is threatening. The whole scenario puts men in a difficult position today, and there appears to be no way around it but to go through it. The problem, while solvable, seems to be rooted in both nature and nurture.

Nature and Nurture Contribute

Males are by nature embodied with testosterone, a hormone that was at one time necessary for survival in the wilds. Few males have to kill prey to feed the tribe or fight other males who are trying to conquer them. Of course, it helps drive males to want to procreate. Even females, however, with 10 times less testosterone, also enjoy sex, so it seems hard to imagine that most men wouldn't still want sex even though they had less testosterone. It appears that it is the overabundance of testosterone that creates aggression, sexual abuse, and so many other problems in the world, and most acts of violence can be traced back to elevated levels of testosterone. One cannot help but wonder that if levels of testosterone were regulated, that there would also be less crime, violence, and need to control. Research on hormones reveals that oxytocin will heighten prosocial behavior and foster peace in a culture. If this is what we want for our culture, we should then value the oxytocin found more readily in females, and control testosterone, which acts to inhibit oxytocin.

Even though both nature and nurture contribute to the male problem, the nurture side offers a far kinder, gentler solution for men. In other words, if men are nonrelational by nature, then chances of their changing are much slimmer. If, on the other hand, they *learned* their outmoded behaviors from culture, they can unlearn them. It appears that much of the male code and machismo are indeed learned and confirmed by many mothers who are highly aware of the sweet innocence of their young sons. They know that their sons and daughters are born with the potential for their feelings being intact. Women can now serve as role models for men. The fact that women have managed to outgrow their narrow definitions can similarly show men that life doesn't have to be defined by patriarchal definitions.

There are many reasons beyond relationships for men to want to drop the learned male-coded behavior. Boys who reflect heavy male-based behaviors are at risk of becoming more explosive and aggressive. Record numbers of children are being diagnosed today with bipolar manic depression. More young males are being diagnosed with attention deficit hyperactivity disorder (ADHD) and oppositional defiant personality (ODD), and the numbers are escalating rapidly. Susan Faludi[9] states that when a child is in the midst of violent, aggressive, meltdown behavior, he has lost the equivalent of 30 IQ points, which means we can't discipline these boys in the same way we can discipline other children. Similarly, when men are involved in male relational dread, they too are probably facing a 30-point drop in IQ and an equal drop in emotional intelligence. Bergman[10] states that the universal male denial of feelings may explain why even traditional psychology fails to capture the depth of male experience. The male therapists, themselves often don't get it. False pride, the emotional counterpart of testosterone and strong cultural conditioning, currently render revealing a male vulnerability or weakness as unacceptable and further compounds the problem.

To some extent, men have benefited by not being engaged relationally. When they aren't tuned in, men get to have less regret and guilt and don't have to take responsibility for the relationship. New research reveals that males apologize less because they think they have less to apologize for.[11] The dominance tendency, too, has put men on top—not a bad place to be.

But men have paid a great price to maintain this position. Not really knowing how they feel is a price that may be difficult to discern by both men and women. It is hard for men to know what they have missed because they haven't had it. They have spent lifetimes constructing knowledge and theories in the absence of true and deep understanding of relationships. And this has worked, on some low level, until we began to realize the importance and sheer joy of simply knowing how one really feels.

What makes this whole process even more difficult for men is that they are in relationships with women who are in the midst of their own process of developing a clearer vision of men. Part of how women come into their own self-awareness is in their relationship to men. Men and masculine qualities have been the standard, the goal to achieve and the way to be. So deep has this enculturation been for both sexes that women often literally cannot believe it when they see the real emperor without his clothes.

It is widely believed that women are the nurturers of society and men are the protectors. Masculinity then is often equated with an external orientation. Power and control still have more value than more internal values such as creativity, nurturing, compassion, or honesty with one's self. Most men seem to have little idea of what they really want, especially in the second half of life. And until they know what they want, they will never know how to get it.

Men need new definitions of mature masculinity. Rather than seeing every woman as a potential conquest, a greater focus on less tangible qualities, such as being a good father or partner, would increase their true happiness. Mature masculinity equals true self-confidence, the kind that is not diminished by peer pressure or questions of "what I *ought* to be." All wise people know that the search for oneself will always go beyond definitions of power.

Keen[12] agrees that males have been trained out of their feelings from the time they are young. Many are now realizing that they too have been victims of the system. Some are asking themselves why they feel so lonely if they are the ones who have all the power and control in the world. They are looking at the power women have and realizing that they don't feel that same power inside. According to Keen, men must prove themselves to WOMAN—the woman in their heads, the female archetype that is made up of their mothers, teachers, sisters, and wives. Men measure their self worth by whether they are receiving a woman's praise. WOMAN looms largely in men's heads for many reasons. Often, other older males were absent from the home. As boys, they were told to sit down and be quiet by female teachers. They have received negative messages from women. As adolescents, they couldn't help but notice that the girls were much more sophisticated than they were.

A woman in one of Keen's seminars told him that she felt the only place left for a male to have any feeling was in his c***, hence, men develop enormous expectations around sex. They need to learn that their bodies extend far beyond their penises. Sex with a partner would become much more real and meaningful—a sensual exchange; a communion, even.

When pressed, men often admit that their best friend is their wife. This is rarely true for women, who typically have numerous wonderful female friends. One of the reasons men may lack friends is that, as Goldberg states, it is men's nature that makes them want to rule. He also states, however, that men are in no way imprisoned by their nature-based, biological givens. There is far more to men than their physical natures. He concludes his book by attempting to understand male and female natures from a higher perspective. "Liberation," says Goldberg, "is an experience of personal salvation that implies power over oneself. It is far more than the attainment of social and economic freedom. Those who have found a well of pure meaning have no need to drown everyone in it. The (celibate) priest does not frantically ignore physiological evidence by arguing that the 'sex drive' is merely an arbitrary social value or that we could expect many people to choose celibacy; he acknowledges the power of this 'drive' while himself answers a more compelling call."[13] As human beings, we are always free to learn new and better ways to live our lives. We first, however, must be open to the fact that there are better ways to live.

Wilber,[14] too, states that even though men are saddled with the hormonal effects of testosterone, they can become more sensitive and relational. They can learn to recognize the effect of testosterone for what it is, and even learn to shrug it off. Wilber wonders why a man would want to be merely his body? His answer is that today it is an imperative to go beyond testosterone. Men, however, have to be educated to do so. They have new roles to learn and many reasons why they should be learned. He feels we have to cut men some slack as they grope toward this strange new territory.

Men Are Simple Creatures

Bill Maher and the males on his show, *Politically Incorrect*, often joke that they don't understand what women don't get about them. Men aren't that complex, they agree. Men are dumber and less complicated than women think, and are not nearly as tuned into the relationship stuff as women are. Maher reasoned that it should be much easier for the more complex woman to understand the more simple man. Their advice to women was to lower their expectations. "Men are more primitive creatures. We want to touch female bodies. We're simply like that." The males even said that women should teach men about love and intimacy. In the next breath, however, they blamed women for trying to change them.

"Of course," said Nancy, who was watching the show with me, "the main reason women don't understand that men are the simpler sex is because they are still in charge of everything. They still control most of the money, political power, and religion. They made all the knowledge to enhance and reflect them. And yet we are blamed because we don't understand that men are the simpler sex. It's good thing that women are smart enough to figure this all out."

There is, however, a deeper and truer reason why women have such difficulty believing men are dumb and simple. It is because women love men. We care about them. Women want men to be good role models for their sons and daughters and will even act to protect men from looking too dumb. One would think males would appreciate that.

Chapter 13

Her Advanced Knowing Matches New Perspectives

Yin	Yang
Heart	Head
Transpersonal	Traditional
Right brain	Left brain
Prefrontal	Neocortex
Seed	Husk

To their credit, when they are honest and unguarded, men have told us—often again and again—that they are simple creatures who don't really get it. Countless males have told countless females that they don't know what she is talking about or asking for, and we just haven't believed them. On some deep level, this imbalance has made us all crazy.

Elizabeth Cady Stanton, the brain behind the first women's movement in the 19th century, was a brilliant thinker. Even in the 1860s, she identified the bottom-line problem to women's oppression as the Bible that formed the cornerstone of male-based religion that continues to hold the imbalance in place. One hundred and fifty years later, we have a far greater understanding about how women differ from men in terms of their spirituality.

Author Patrick Arnold[1] states, "In its most basic sense, the masculine is defined by its opposition to, separation from, and contrast with the feminine." Qualities Arnold claims as radically masculine include: love of freedom, pride, competitiveness, humor, aggressiveness, courage, vulnerability, responsibility, "fighting for what you believe in," detachment, and hunger for holiness. "In contrast to feminine spirituality, which is inward and interior and rooted in Mother Earth, male spirituality is outwardly oriented and spatial."

Women are the naturally and intuitively spiritual sex. It should not be surprising to learn that women's spirituality often differs from that of men. Divinity is viewed by most women as a natural part of life and implies relationship in its very essence.

The authors of *The Feminine Face of God*[2] found that the spirituality that women experience is different from that of men in many ways. Women experience spirituality in a more internal and connected way. It feels like a natural process and is deeply connected to nature. Most women who participated in the study viewed divinity as less of a final perfection or product, and more like a process. Our whole modern culture has been product-oriented even in religion.

When spirituality is thought of as a process, there is no hierarchy to transcend, no ladders, no *thing* to achieve.

Men, who have as much as 20 times more testosterone in their systems, view things like sex in a linear way—leading to orgasm as the final product. Women have a variety of responses, says Kastleman and "experience sex in terms of sensing, knowing and feeling what the poet calls 'the song of life singing through them.'" He continues, "This may indeed be what sex was meant to be—an experience that touches the essence of who we are in ways not unlike spiritual revelation."[3]

For many women, sex and spirituality are experienced as a reunion of soul and body. Many women feel that as they learned to trust this unfolding process, they were, at the same time, learning to trust themselves internally. Women also learned how to wait, and learned further, that waiting takes trust.

The women in the study *The Feminine Face of God* agreed that regardless what had happened to them, they were able to learn to believe in themselves again. Often, a major disruption or ordeal in their lives was central to their spiritual unfolding. They experienced long-hidden emotions, fears of isolation, and even self-betrayals, yet all of these ordeals came to be cherished by the women who realized that the trials were their greatest teachers. The ordeal often became the very thing that helped the women find the deep source of wisdom within themselves. A fundamental characteristic was their ability to use times of adversity as opportunities for spiritual awakening and deepening. Women who had been abused in childhood felt that they were like dormant bulbs. They had not only survived the harshness, but had bloomed more beautifully as a result.

Most of the women could recall the beginnings of true spirituality in childhood. "I knew very early that the nature of reality was different from the story anybody had given me . . . from that moment on I was aware of a continuing presence within me, a presence I called 'my interior friend,'" explains Bernadette in the book. Another woman stated, "You could spend your physical energy, but I knew this other (spiritual) energy could never be depleted." Women could often trace back the beginnings of their innate spirituality to when they were young girls around age eight or nine.

Many women recalled acting innately spiritual without ever letting others know. "I remember often conducting funerals, little rituals which were very meaningful to me at the time, for little animals—even goldfish. The boys in our neighborhood thought it was funny to shoot birds with their BB guns or slingshots. They would laugh at us as we pleaded with them not to do it. After they left, we girls would try to find the birds that they had killed. We were often surprisingly lucky at finding them. We had many funerals with tears in our eyes and righteous indignation in our hearts as we buried our feathered friends."

Although the women completed the journeys, they often left their old and familiar states of mind. Initially, they moved to a place of not knowing. Most felt that every woman reaches this threshold at least once in her life.[4]

Marion Woodman,[5] a Jungian analyst and writer of many books for and about women, states that women's spirituality was often forced to go underground, revealing that she experienced a split away from her own innate spirituality that did not heal for 30 years.

Women, however, are able to rediscover their connections with the sacred, often after a descent into despair, rage, and helplessness. These feelings, they say, helped the next layer of buried feelings to emerge. They then learned to let go of these feelings and enter new possibilities. In order to do this, they had to learn not to be too harsh on themselves and to trust the process, which seemed to allow the unfolding to occur. Many sensed that there was nothing they could trust—no outer authority—except the process itself. Trusting this process, when they had nothing to trust except their inner instinct of truth, led many women to a heightened sense of spiritual and intuitive discernment.

Nature often became a spiritual guide for women as they noticed that they began to feel healed when they were among trees and water. They rediscovered the healing connection to Mother Earth. For many women, true prayer was, and still is, simply being outside and close to nature. Women know intuitively that nature and the female body are interrelated. Her body has a cyclical nature that synchronizes with those of the moon and the growth and harvest of nature. Life itself is about repetition. We breathe in and out. The sun rises and falls. New concepts emerge as women outgrow their old understandings. Spirituality becomes a cycle for women that cycles higher each time it goes around.

Women are the ones who care for and nurture the earth. Women often recognize their divinity at the same time they recognize their connection with Mother Earth. The relational consciousness of women seeks to transcend the hierarchy of the masculine and heal the split between spirit and matter—ourselves and Mother Earth. Women often realize through direct experience that they are made of the same stuff of the earth. Their cyclical natures enable them to reclaim parts of themselves that have been lost or disowned. Perhaps most importantly, the women realized that spirituality and religion are not the same.

The confusion comes when we do not make a distinction between religion and spirituality. Religion is an organized system of beliefs that are too often male-oriented. Spirituality, on the other hand, is an innate quality present in every human being. It does not belong to any one religion. Nor does it belong to any one gender.

In truth, the most basic and mystical aspects of religion are designed to speak to the Self (capital S), not the ego. It does not matter if this Self is male or female. This path should not be clouded with control or violence. It should be concerned with life and all that is alive.

All religions began with a mystical experience of the divine. Most probably, this occurred to women just as often as it occurred to men. The Gnostics, for example, believed that both men and women could share equally in this experience, and for this reason were voted out in 300 AD by Constantine when he consolidated works that would become part of the Bible as we know it today. Only the experiences of males were included. These breakthroughs, while leading to the same nondual experience, may have been experienced differently by males and females at the time. Women take the nondual experience of enlightenment for granted. It is part of who they are. Men, if they experience it all, experience it as a breakthrough.

Bernadette Roberts in *The Spiral Path*[6] states, "As solely representative of the masculine consciousness, what this history suggests is that we may not yet have the complete story of the human psyche in its encounter with divine." She goes on to say, "Thus one reason for the absence of women in our religious histories is this history's involvement in the more superficial levels of religion. Women, unfortunately, have been raised to believe the male dictates while at the same time integrating the ideas that women are lesser beings. The differences in religious beliefs exist only at the lower levels. On the highest level of understanding, true spirituality is something that is more elevated and inclusive. For this reason, religion has been used as the reason or excuse used by a domineering and authoritative ego. Women, because of their natures, appear to more readily comprehend the more transcendent, non-egoic, and mystical depths that are the true essence of authentic religion."

The patriarchal versions of religion are limited and incomplete for many reasons, the most obvious being the absence of any feminine contributions. Further, in many ways it appears to discourage questioning that might lead to spiritual self-realization, preferring instead to encourage group worship. It is not surprising that males created an understanding that, except for breakthrough experiences, is basically limited to their more superficial comprehension.

Bhai Sahib states in *The Spiral Path* that, "Women are taken up through the path of love, for love is a feminine mystery. . . . Women do not need many spiritual practices, but need only to renounce." According to Roberts, "We are not accusing men of suppressing a side of truth or revelation they do not know is there, or a side they may be incapable of grasping. On the contrary, we hold that the revelation of the divine to the feminine psyche may not be wholly understandable to the masculine consciousness, for which reason it has been largely ignored, not taken seriously, or simply brought into conformity with the masculine psyche."[7] It is certain that, some males have experienced deep, authentic spirituality. It is also clear, however, that many men are simply incapable of understanding a sense of divinity and a natural level of spirituality that women regularly experience. For this reason, unlike men, women do not need to create spiritual practice as separate from their daily lives, but rather should learn to appreciate the spiritual tendencies that occur naturally in their own lives.

The ironic thing is that in squelching the feminine voice of the divine, men have inadvertently limited their own experience and understanding of authentic spirituality. Divinity, by definition, cannot be true if its essence and understanding is limited to only one gender. It cannot be the Tao, the complete whole, if it excludes Yin and is based only on Yang. Our whole world would be different if the Yin aspects were equally present.

Further, Yang has often been associated with the head and with the left-brained cognitive and mental aspects of spirituality. Yin is more closely associated with the knowing of the heart. The compassion and empathy associated with the heart have always been more elusive and harder to comprehend because it is more associated with feeling than thinking. The latest research, however, reveals that the heart is far more powerful than the head. Both head and heart are electromagnetic generators that influence all aspects of our consciousness. The heart, however, is 5,000 times more powerful than the brain.

The same concept is true for the personal consciousness. Spirituality appears to be a natural part of female consciousness. It is embodied, not some separate act or abstract thing or state of mind that happens only in a religious context. Of course, males too, in their own way can touch into the Universal Source. And, many good men understand that religion, spirituality, and divinity cannot and should not be gendered.

Glenda Lee Hoffman presents an interesting perspective on the Bible in *The Secret Dowry of Eve.*[8] She sees the differences between the right and left brain as metaphors used, ironically, in the story of creation, and sheds new light on Genesis by recasting it in terms of brain development. In her interpretation, Eve preceded Adam. Adam's job is to *name* the animals. This naming, suggestive of alphabet literacy and Shlain's similar hypothesis, as well as descriptive of the left brain,[9] is external. Adam is to speak to the world around him and give it name. Eve represents consciousness awakening, and having wakened, her job is to awaken Adam. This, says Hoffman, is really what evolution is all about. Eve birthed our species and gave us insight.

We have four parts to our brain, says Hoffman. The reptilian brain was the first to develop and is the most basic. It is good for foraging, fighting, and mating and is based on routines and continuity. The reptilian brain is basically masculine.

The limbic brain is associated with attentiveness and feelings of conviction. The mother–child bond exists in the basically feminine limbic brain.

The neocortex literally means new brain and is equated with intelligence, rationality, and reason. It is what is measured on IQ tests and deals with certainties. It is where verbal ability and language are acquired. It is limited, however, in its ability to look inward and see the other parts of the brain at work. It needs a helpmate to see the points of view of others and sometimes itself. It can be equated with procedural knowing—understanding the information but not really connected to it emotionally. Not surprisingly, it is basically associated with the masculine.

The prefrontal cortex, the newest addition to the brain, evolutionarily, finally provides the brain with the ability to look inward. It is able to anticipate the consequences of its actions. It has a foresight, which is the intelligence used when searching for meaning and insight. This is the place of intuition and wisdom for personal and social transformation. The prefrontal cortex can process and make plans with its vast neurological potential that can analyze actions and anticipate consequences for one's own behavior and those of others. This newest part of our brain may literally involve light. The prefrontal lobes are equated with the feminine and allow for insight, self-awareness, and foresight.

According to Hoffman, Eve eating of the tree of knowledge of good and evil is actually a way of representing consciousness. Interestingly, many theorists have equated Eve with consciousness. In doing so, Eve discovers insight, the inner light that reveals to ourselves why we do what we do—self-awareness. She eats the fruit and sees that it represents wholeness. She understands that we cannot access only one side of our brain, for if we do, we will become rigid, less flexible, and see things from only one perspective. We will lack insight and self-awareness, focusing only on the interests of the left-brain. We will fail to recognize the importance of art, image, heart, symbol, the feminine, and every concept associated with the right brain.

Eve, in the story, represents disruption. Like the right brain, she disrupts the static and rigid left brain. In many ways, the story of Adam and Eve is like so many stories of women hoping to awaken men. Beauty brings humanity to the Beast. The princess kisses the frog. The female wants to wake up the male. Women, females, and the feminine principle possess knowledge and insight. With this knowledge, she realizes that if men and women are to go on together, he must also have insight if they are to understand each other.

The female brain is actually more highly developed. It is wired for expression, not aggression. Many males idle in the most ancient reptilian brain, which may be why men think about sex so much and are more prone to physical rather than verbal action.

The female brain has a gift for words. Girls talk sooner as babies and have fewer learning disabilities. Women have a bilateral neurological advantage. Their hemispheres process together dually. They notice more and navigate differently than men. Women's vision and hearing are more sensitive and their memory is sharper. The female brain is more intuitive and ages more slowly. At every age, women's memories outperform those of men.

The story of Genesis begins with the creation of light on the first day. While light has its own laws, the same laws are true for inner light, or insight. In terms of brain processing, the visual act of seeing is the most important and light activates the process of seeing. One of the most important functions of the brain is pattern recognition. This is literally what learning is—the ability to recognize and integrate new patterns. Once the new pattern has been recognized, our learning increases exponentially. Believing what we have learned without ever questioning indicates a lack of insight. Part of pattern recognition is also to understand the subtle interplay between the opposites. For example, both light and dark, wet rain and dry sun, are necessary for every living thing to thrive. Not just the opposites, but also the interplay of the way they relate to each other is essential. Females, says Hoffman, are just better at recognizing these subtle insights.

Our brains are still in a period of evolution right now. And females, the ones who carry the next generation, are the instruments of evolution. Female bodies have had to evolve and adjust, again and again over time to ensure the survival of the species. Just as women lived through the dangerous evolutionary period when the heads of their babies were larger than the ability of their pelvis to expand, women's brains are now evolving beyond all the known conceptual information. The next step for women therefore is to begin to construct their own new knowledge. And just as that was a time of physical danger for women, this time too, is dangerous. As the carriers of this new information, women need to stand together in a world that may not be ready to listen to what they know.

According to Hoffman, seeds are the containers of all new life. Women and the feminine are the seeds. They need no instructions to generate their own innate potential. Their natures are cyclical. Men and the masculine are the husk that protects the seed.

When women stop searching for truth outside themselves, a remarkable thing happens. They begin to feel a sense of interconnectedness to all life. They get in touch with their receptivity. They begin to act from a different place, for they become aware that choice is now conscious. From this conscious sense of choice, they become aware of their own true intention to embody the sacred in everyday life. They begin to recognize that the place to find the divine within is in the here and now of life. They recognize that true spirituality doesn't have to be hard or forced, but rather is as natural and nurturing as sleep. It is an awakening to our true nature just as it is. We don't have to tell an acorn how to grow into an oak tree. In the same way, women don't have to be taught to respond to a crying child or a person who is suffering. Their hearts open naturally. It is women's nature to align themselves with their innate spirituality. Women sense intuitively when they are in communion with their source.

The process leads to ever increasing authenticity. Many women get to a place where they can no longer tolerate falseness. They look behind the words for true actions. They want and need a genuine and valid connection to that which is meaningful, and often they discover that the main thing they can trust is themselves.

The qualities of the feminine are the same qualities that often comprise an experience of enlightenment. These experiences are what men have gone out in search of for centuries. It is what men need to feel whole—the thing they have repressed since the beginning.

The whole world of what we know has been set up so that both men and women never truly know themselves. None of this is her fault. Women have been, and still are, forced to go along with his limited understandings. They have been put into an impossible position of not being allowed to speak about this and at the same time not wanting to be angry. Most women are afraid that if they allow themselves to look at the problem full on, as it really is, it will be an impossible and unfixable dilemma.

Women are relational and want relationships with men. The problem is that they want relationships with whole men. Women have grown into their own expectations and it is becoming harder and harder to find men who can be equal partners. Much of the confusion around this whole area of relationships comes from the continuing error that puts men in charge. On the personal level, it infects our relationships. It keeps women silenced and men miserable. On the global level, we have to stop killing each other and infecting each other with outmoded perceptions.

In looking over the past, one thing that stands out is the fear that men have of women, which appears to underlie the need for the continued persecution and denigration of women.

The inner light of the prefrontal cortex has to be fully activated for the brain to be complete. Right now, it is women, not men, who appear to possess the insight and intuition and ability to plan for the future. The hero(ine)'s journey here is to actively undertake the process of neural generation. The brain cannot complete itself. Each person needs to activate their own neurological development. This activation is initiated by desire—the desire to change and the need to look inward with the intention of seeing the truth, and once again, males are called on to lose their masculinized ego. Neural integration is the intention of our souls, personally and collectively. "Adam needs to be rescued. He needs the inner world to be fully alive in order to claim his authentic humanity," says Hoffman. We are meant to transcend the past and envision a new future.

And the future is here now. We have known for 80 years that the way we have understood the universe and reality is incorrect. Newtonian physics told us that we are all separate from each other and our earth. True objectivity was considered an ideal. Despite the fact that this model does not accurately reflect reality, we still learn it. The new quantum perspective reveals that everything in the universe is connected to every other thing. We are not separate from each other. Just as the Stone Center suggested, we are all selves-in-relation to each other. This new global perspective shifts the worldview from a masculine oriented "we are separate" to a feminine "we are interconnected." Understanding this changes everything.

The quantum concepts are not new, yet we continue to focus on separation and matter despite the fact that we know mind is primary and matter is secondary. When mind is primary, then intention is of utmost importance. This means that if you believe that we have to arm ourselves to be safe, then you are right. If you believe that we can live without violence, you are also right. The second option is always there and always possible. Like a TV channel, millions of bits of information are bombarding us every second. We naturally filter out most of it. What we filter out and what we let in, in other words, which channel we choose, depends on what we believe.

Belief is the body's strongest medicine. A placebo effect, based on belief, can literally create changes in the body and even target specific organs. Researchers estimate that fully one-third of all healing has to do with the placebo effect.[10] When we change our mood from aggravation to joy, there are at least 1,400 biochemical changes that take place in our bodies. Our biologies are controlled by our minds.

We are all part of a zero-point energy field and are in constant contact with this field all the time. In the same way that a group of birds all change direction instantaneously, we could all embrace a new and better way to be in this world instantly. Each of us is an information system that is interacting with a larger system. We are currently embracing an information system that is in crisis. It embraces a model of war—war on cancer, war on drugs, and war on each other. It is a male model that no longer resonates with our implicit wholeness.

We are more connected to each other than we have realized. We are more powerful than we have known. Our natural state is coherence. Men who do not know how they feel, whose emotions are not fully connected to their thinking, cannot possibly be in coherence. Women and their whole body-mind energies are naturally more able to experience this inner state.

We still, however, live in a world that appears to be divided into opposites, and one of the most important patterns that we have to master is that of integrating these pairs of opposites. Each aspect of the whole is necessary for full integration and balance for the lives of individuals and also the earth.

There is no true objectivity because we know that the very act of observation changes reality. Interestingly, mystics have always told us this. It appears that women, with their more embodied sense of presence and connectedness, are far better aligned with this new reality. Like quantum physics, they understand that everything is connected.

In truth, psychology and spirituality never should have been separated because they are so intimately connected to each other. For example, if you believe that you were born in sin, that your husband has dominion over you, the devil is always tempting you, or you shouldn't use birth control, of course these beliefs will influence you psychologically. You will either adhere to your spiritual beliefs closely so that there is no discrepancy between what you believe and how you live; or you will, as in the case of the 98 percent of Catholic women who use birth control despite the dictates of their church, feel guilty.

Transpersonal psychology is the perspective that best combines the quantum perspective of the human mind and interconnectedness. Unlike traditional psychology, it readily embraces and includes information from the right brain, such as intuition, synchronicity, and spirituality. It is "the melding of the wisdom of the world's spiritual traditions with the learning of modern psychology," states Brant Cortwright, author of *Psychotherapy and Spirit*.[11] Both traditions ask the question, "Who am I?" Modern psychology answers this question with answers such as an ego, a self, or a psychological being. The spiritual traditions answer the same question as a "soul" or a spiritual being. "Transpersonal psychology is the attempt to put these two answers together. By creating a synthesis of these two profound approaches to human consciousness, the spiritual and the psychological, transpersonal psychology attempts to honor the learning of each."

"Trans" means above or beyond, as in a higher or transcendent experience of something greater than the self. It can also mean "across" as in transcultural, consciously including the beliefs of other cultures beyond just our understanding in the West. For example, in other cultures that view psychology and spirituality as inseparable, people who are interested in reaching the higher levels of consciousness regularly meditate for countless hours every day. They are hoping to have a spiritual emergence known as kundalini rising. Kundalini is the spiritual energy that exists in the universe. Bidden or unbidden, this energy can enter one's body and the person will be filled with energy that can feel very uncomfortable. In our culture, because we have separated spirituality from psychology, we label this energy as a panic attack and label and medicate the client.

"Trans" can also mean *beyond* the personal. The transpersonal perspective thus includes both the personal and what is beyond it. Transpersonal psychology reveals how the spiritual is expressed in and through the personal, as well as the transcendence of the self.

In the past, psychology was described as the study of the soul. As the field grew, it became what it is today—the study of the mind. Along the way, it often seemed that the real, potentially whole person had somehow gotten lost. As graduate students, we learned that if our client had a problem that was related to religion or spirituality, we were not to touch it, but rather send them to their priest or minister. The problem was that my clients, most of whom were female, seemed as unable as I was to see their issues in isolation from their source of meaning.

The transpersonal perspective is still little known even today. If students are introduced to it at all, it is only briefly. The field of psychology, when it shifted to the study of the mind in the early 20th century, attempted to make sense of some of the worst things in life. In the past 100 years, transpersonal and positive psychology has finally started to study the best things in life. New explorations into what makes life worth living have begun by finally looking into the higher aspects of human functioning. Martin Seligman,[12] who initiated groundbreaking work on optimism and positive emotions, recognized that how people explain things to themselves is of the utmost importance.

The new, more positive focus in psychology also reflects some of the encouraging and affirming changes happening in the larger culture. Rather than study what caused a person to become an alcoholic, for example, there is now a greater focus, in some of the more advanced spheres of psychology on the resilience of those who have recovered successfully. This shift in focus makes all the difference. Some fields of psychology are now beginning to look at courage, optimism, perseverance, and insight.

The general public, however, has little or no awareness of this field or perspective. It is so little known that transpersonal therapists, including myself, receive calls from clients who are wanting help as they go through gender reassignment. They think it means transsexual.

The transpersonal perspective represents a broader, more feminine and holistic perspective of life. Experts have told us that males are always wanting to be "somewhere else." It is not surprising then that the male experts created both psychological and spiritual perspectives where the true spirituality, true wholeness, full self-esteem, enlightenment, self-actualization, or any psychological or spiritual ultimate is always somewhere else—or sometime later, after we die, in heaven, not really achievable here and now. Real life is considered as somehow lesser than what happens later. Spirituality and psychology is often defined as a way to be good now so that we get the payoff later. In doing so, we miss the now and, further, miss ourselves in the now.

Women are more rooted in the now. Their main focus is on the now, the family, the present. Those who embrace the transpersonal perspective recognize that the essential nature of each of us is spiritual. While our being is both psychological and spiritual in nature, the transpersonal gives primacy to the spiritual source that supports the psychological structures of the self. Recognizing that consciousness is multidimensional, the transpersonal perspective has encouraged exploration and research into other psychological levels and states of consciousness. These nonordinary states of consciousness are found as often occurring in normal life—even if they aren't recognized by traditional psychology and religion. Ironically, every religious tradition was founded on a mystical and nonordinary experience. Stanislav Grof[13] reveals that according to the traditional psychological guidelines, the spiritual experiences of every mystic and spiritual leader who spawned a religious movement would today, according to psychological guidelines, be considered pathological. Traditional psychology is highly suspect of any nonordinary state of consciousness, focusing only on the rational, cognitive and conscious state.

In truth, however, most of us have had transcendent moments that feel as natural as breathing. These experiences often happens when we least expect it—we may be walking in nature, reading a great book, or looking in to the eyes of a newborn baby. It may last for just a minute but it seems like forever. We get a glimpse of something greater than ourselves and our everyday lives. There is often a rush of feeling as our consciousness is temporarily restructured, allowing us to feel in harmony with all life. The enlightenment experience is never *done* to someone; it grows naturally out of the individual.

It wasn't until the 1960s that we realized that people regularly have experiences of enlightenment. Like so many aspects of life, the church led us to believe that such experiences are rare, and happen only to those who are worthy and have engaged in grueling and disciplined meditation and prayer until finally they are rewarded with an experience that justifies all their hard work and God's favor. Such moments of transcendence are thought to be reserved only for saints and very wise men. Normal people never dreamed that they too could have such experiences.

The field of psychology, similarly, had no way to describe these experiences. Prior to the 1960s, people were considered to be controlled by their basic unconscious urges and drives, à la Freud. The only other alternative at the time was behaviorism's view of humans who responded only because they were conditioned either positively or negatively. It was not until Abraham Maslow introduced the idea of self-actualization that people began to change how they felt about themselves and these types of experiences. Before that, people had no idea how to even talk about their experiences.

Since then, we have not only learned more about these actual experiences, we have put them in a different framework of understanding. We now realize that experiences of enlightenment are the birthright of all human beings. Each of us is connected to something greater than ourselves, and sometimes we are lucky enough to see beyond our narrow, rational belief systems.

As human beings, we hunger for wholeness. We move toward seeking fulfillment through deepening our individual, social, and transcendent awareness. Seeking authentic spirituality is essential for human fulfillment, wholeness, and health, and people regularly have experiences that reflect a deeper source of wisdom and guidance within. Aligning their consciousness with their more authentic spiritual impulses often seems to happen naturally to people.

Walter Truett Anderson, in *The Next Enlightenment*, states that the enlightenment experience is a central and normal element of human life.[14] There is no need for any formal training in religion, spirituality, or meditation in order to achieve it. This is particularly important for people who are considering leaving organized religion to ponder. Many people have deep and meaningful experiences within that traditional context and connect the experience with the context. They are afraid that if they don't believe, pray, or go to church their lives will be devoid of these precious moments of enlightenment. Thus, it is vitally important for people to realize that these experiences are their birthright and will not stop because they change their beliefs. Most people, regardless of their belief systems, have had these experiences, which have become known as "Aha!" moments or peak experiences. Once this happens, everything else is seen from a different perspective.

People describe it as finally being freed from the illusion of separateness. They experience it as boundless love or feeling most fully alive. The experience feels like the most real thing they have ever experienced. In the past, a person who was a seeker often had few places to go other than the church. There are countless options today associated with openness and changes in consciousness. The experiences are real, and while they vary, there are, however, many common themes. The perceptions almost always involve the transcendence of the ego and feeling deeply connected to the flow of the universe.

The people who have these experiences, even though they are normal and sane, typically have no context from which to understand them, and often fear they are going crazy. They are afraid to talk even to therapists about these experiences, fearing that they will be labeled and medicated. Further, traditional psychology, with its perspective limited only to normal, waking consciousness, will almost certainly confirm the abnormality of such experiences. It is no surprise then that, from a traditional perspective, any client who has had a spiritual or mystical experience, risks be viewed pathologically. This perception is the very thing that keeps the client, who believes the expert, coming back and the therapist fully booked with patients. The whole field has become a multibillion-dollar institution geared to identifying, labeling, naming, categorizing, and medicating people. Counselors who entered the field because of a real desire to help, often find themselves in work environments that can serve to make *them* crazy. I have talked to so many therapists who know that their work environment is toxic to them and their clients. This sick system, however, is almost impossible to change—even though almost everyone agrees that it doesn't work.

I thought of the numerous women who had come into my office with all the symptoms of panic attack. They often said things like "I am just filled with energy." Or "I feel like I want to jump out of my skin." In our Western culture, we would immediately label this as a panic attack. Because of its broader perspective, the transpersonal recognizes people in other cultures, who understand that the world is spiritual and each individual as a part of the world is similarly spiritual. A spiritual emergence, however, may look and feel like a spiritual emergency. A transpersonal therapist understands, further, that not every spiritual emergency can be viewed as a spiritual emergence. It is shocking nevertheless how often symptoms that look like mental illness are in truth, spiritual emergence.

I was so thankful that I was aware of a broader transpersonal perspective. I would just ask my clients to tell what had been happening in their lives. There was very often a typical response. More than half of them would hesitate, look around, look uncomfortable, and kind of suck on their lips like they really didn't want to tell me. They often started the conversation by saying something like "You're going to think I'm crazy" or "You're not going to believe this, but . . . ," and then they would tell me about something out of the ordinary that had happened. For example, one said, "My grandmother, who has been dead for five years, comes and sits at the bottom of my bed." Another said, "I have never told anyone this, but I think I left my body and I was 'out there' looking down on it." Or, "You're going to think I am crazy, but I was looking at the sunset and . . ."

And these clients are so grateful and thankful that I didn't get a serious look and write something down like *needs meds immediately; is delusional* or some other DSMV label.

When you have a larger perspective that includes the full spectrum of human consciousness, you can tell more easily when people are or are not truly psychotic or delusional. It is also true that you can't make every mental aberration into spiritual emergence or emergency. Sometimes people really are sick—but sometimes they're not. Even a spiritual emergence can look like something in the DSM. I always wondered what would have happened to some of my clients had they seen someone who didn't have the larger perspective. If they weren't sick, they might have become sick just by believing the too small, left-brain, and limited categories we have for people who have nonordinary experiences.

Transpersonal psychology is based in the same systems theory that informs quantum physics. Systems theorists believe everything in the world exists in an interconnected and interdependent web of relationships. Thus, the earth and all living things naturally organize themselves. Similarly, every living thing renews and transcends itself.

People, therefore, have an innate and inherent ability not only to heal themselves but to become stronger as a result of the process that led to the healing. It is a meta-perspective in the same way that good emotional intelligence is a meta-ability. Looking at ourselves with hope, empathy, and optimism on a personal level works not only on the transpersonal level, but on all levels. The process is literally a progression. After we feel we are fine, we just naturally turn our thoughts to the larger collective of others. It is not until we view our selves as basically good that we can see others as good. It is not until we see ourselves as whole that we begin to see this perception can and should also apply to others. Transpersonal therefore is a perspective, a new way of looking at self and others. Mother Teresa was recognized as exemplary because she saw the divinity and potential for wholeness in every individual. Is this not the same gift that we as mental health professionals should extend to our clients?

Physicist and philosopher Fritjof Capra[15] states that the problems of the world are so closely interconnected that they can't be understood from a singular, limited, or fragmented perspective. According to Capra, problems are all different facets of one and the same crisis—a crisis of perception. We need a larger perspective from which we can view both the problems and the solutions if we are to bring about change. The transpersonal perspective therefore harmonizes with the newly emerging paradigm; it also matches with the newly emerging feminine perspective, to the point that they are one and the same and cannot be separated. The transpersonal perspective is the most viable and authentic search for meaning today.

The transpersonal perspective views human beings as having the ability to create meaning in any situation no matter how bad it seems. Often, our pain provides the impetus for our most meaningful inward journey. The transpersonal approach provides a framework that elevates each of us and provides a way to view our lives as a heroic journey. It includes both the good and the bad, the triumphs and the ordeals of life's journey. This little nugget of truth, this change of perspective. alone can make all the difference as to how we view our life's journey.

The Hero(ine)'s Journey

Women, especially, who have outgrown their own old selves, similarly, cannot go back to traditional beliefs and practices. They need a new map that better reflects their journey. And, there actually is a map of the journey of life. Joseph Campbell[16] spent years of his life immersing himself in the myths cultures create in relation to meaning. It is astonishing how the four stages of the her(oine)'s journey reflect the lives of people, especially women who are in the midst of a process.

HOME is like the safe, secure place you were before you woke up. Even if your literal home wasn't safe, HOME represents a metaphor for feeling like we fit in, for feeling comfortable. Your thoughts here are comfortable because they are similar to what others thought and it feels safe.

Many women who are moving toward a more authentic spirituality often hear a CALL that tells us, simply, that there can be more to life than what we are living. I think this is what happened to me years earlier when I heard the mixer talking to me. The CALL is really a fascinating time. The initiate—because that is what you are; the journey is initiating you—often feels very lonely and invisible. They speak and others seem not to hear them. The initiate, however, almost always finds a mentor who will help him through the journey. I remember when I heard the call. It was long before I ever knew the word "transpersonal," but nevertheless, my life had unfolded just like the universal pattern of the journey. I had started wanting more and Lynn had entered my life exactly when I needed her.

The CALL very often leads to the ORDEAL. The ORDEAL is the bad time, the illness, accident, divorce, or loss. As tough as it is to live through, we often realize, looking back, that the ordeal was also a time when we learned our greatest and most valuable lessons. We often emerge from the ORDEAL as wounded healers—with wisdom to help others, because we ourselves have been through the same thing. We are enlarged through the journey so that when we return HOME again, people may or may not be aware that we have changed. Often, and especially for women who have not literally left homes, as men typically do, the journey has occurred only in their minds or consciousness. The people who remained at home may or may not be open to hearing about our new understandings. They want us to be the same, but we are forever changed. And so, the journey may begin all over again. As I looked back over my journey with Dave, the model seemed to fit perfectly, just as it does for so many. Our life starts to feel a little too small, and like a crustacean, we shed our shell, and feel vulnerable as our new, more expanded sense of self—that will fit far better—is growing to a larger sense of self.

Chapter 14

SHE-Q—The Wisdom of Women

Yin
Natural wisdom
Caretakers
Changers of the world
Creative
Holistic
Intuition
Whole-brained
Insight

A New Intelligence of Feminine Wisdom Is Emerging

We have tested the IQ of people since the world wars when the government needed a way to assess the abilities of the thousands of men who were recruited to fight. An IQ test measures verbal and performance ability. Although IQ tests have some right-brained components, such as spatial ability, they are mainly geared toward assessing how well a person will do when learning left-brain knowledge. While an IQ test does a very good job of measuring potential academic abilities, there are many other human qualities that are not included, and it is often these absent qualities that make the difference between success and failure. A person, for example, could have a high IQ, but lack motivation. Others could have high intellectual ability but are never able to apply it. Something in our understanding of intelligence was missing.

In 1995, Goleman introduced the concept of EQ, the idea of emotional intelligence that brought together the qualities of both the right and left brains. To be truly intelligent, we have to use our whole brain, which includes self-confidence, intentions and attributions, self-control, and the ability to communicate. The ability to know and manage one's emotions, and integrate them with our thinking, is a major part of being intelligent.

Goleman does not say initially in his book, *Emotional Intelligence: Why It Can Matter More than IQ,*[1] that females are the more emotionally intelligent sex. His main focus, at the time, was on introducing a new concept. Almost 15 years later, this concept, like so many right brain–oriented concepts, is still heavily scrutinized, and applying it to gender would probably have ensured its demise. The latest research, however, confirms that women have far more connections between their right and left hemispheres, and possess many of the attributes associated with emotional intelligence. Goleman did state, more recently, that women "have the advantage" when it comes to emotional intelligence. Women are more in touch with their emotions and are better at managing these emotions as well as integrating their emotions with their more cognitive thoughts.

Now is the time to construct new knowledge in the area of intelligence, and a new more feminine-based way of knowing begs to be articulated. Currently, the concept of SHE-Q is a work in progress—based on available information that appears to be limited in a time when the avoidance of discussion around difference is the politically correct accepted standard norm. It is also based on constructed knowledge that has gone beyond the limited givens and premises and is thus gleaned from what one *senses* to be true from a more whole-brained perspective, or is implied from the research that has been confirmed.

SHE-Q

This new feminine-based intelligence goes beyond both IQ and EQ. It includes and transcends what we know thus far about what true intellectual excellence is. It is called SHE-Q because it refers mainly to the advanced neurological abilities found in women. Females are more whole-brained and, in addition, use more of their prefrontal cortex, the more highly evolved and recently developed part of the brain that includes intuition, foresight, and insight. In fact, it is this very ability that both allows and encourages women to go beyond the givens and construct these new concepts.

In the past, males constructed knowledge and measures to test this knowledge based on qualities that they understood. SHE-Q is a first attempt to define the intelligence of women that reflects female knowing, sensing, and cognition from a more whole-brained and female-oriented basis.

Despite the fact that women have been left out of knowledge construction until recently, they now excel in every field that men have created. The fact that females have succeeded in a world where knowledge is skewed toward a left-brained perspective appears to reveal that women obviously have the necessary prerequisites of IQ and EQ to outperform males. Females, however, also have an additional wisdom based on a combination of their unique hormones, their neurological connections, and their more embodied ability to internalize and synthesize knowledge. They are more intuitive, relational, empathic, and have self-awareness—qualities that have been described as being values or higher order functions. SHE-Q is an intelligence and wisdom that includes and transcends the given cognitive structures. It includes foresight, inspiration, and creativity, and blends body-based knowing that is felt and sensed intuitively with left-brained cognition and facts. It is knowledge that is embodied and rooted in a context of empathy, compassion, and an authentic sense of meaning. Oprah states that it is hard to make a mistake when you are in touch with who you really are. She feels it is like our own internal GPS that we can trust. One might liken SHE-Q to this internal GPS.[2]

SHE-Q is found mainly in women. Many good males, however, appear to have an abundance of SHE-Q. Further, some of the best statements and quotes about women that appear in this book have been articulated by males. The Dalai Lama recently said, "It is the western world women in general who can really save the world. We are in a critical moment in human history where we see systems breaking down; we see tremendous shift and change that is occurring. Most of all, we need women who do some of their work enough to realize that they have great capacity to be change agents, first in their family, in their workplace and in the world."[3] He calls for critical thinking followed by action, and it appears that SHE-Q, the new wisdom of the feminine, is what he is referring to.

It is important to recognize that women did not just acquire this knowledge in the last forty years since the women's movement opened the door for them to legitimately enter the male world of education and employment. This feminine way of knowing existed long before we learned how to measure cognitive and emotional intelligence. It has remained unacknowledged because our left-brained understanding and knowledge base could not comprehend it.

For this reason women today have to first unlearn so much of what they have believed to be true before they really begin to understand SHE-Q in its deepest sense. Because the knowledge base has been so skewed toward a masculine understanding, She-Q has similarly and consciously been skewed toward exposing the information around women that has been so incorrect, and is further consciously skewed toward an initial reconstruction of a more accurate understating and reflection of feminine-based knowledge. Recognizing that the traditional knowledge base as we know it reflects a left-brained and thus limited perspective is the main reason women sense intuitively that they have to go beyond it. Just as IQ and EQ are not tangible things in themselves, and are rather, based on what one knows or how one perceives, similarly SHE-Q is an orientation to one's life and the world we live in. Further, because true objectivity does not exist, all forms of measurements, including IQ, are based on premises and perceptions that, similarly, are influenced subjectively. This initial attempt toward the reconstruction of a wisdom that is more feminine-based is admittedly, equally, and necessarily biased and skewed toward the feminine perspective in attempt to create a more balanced epistemology over all.

SHE-Q includes the concept of the placebo effect. A placebo is basically a neutral pill that contains no pharmacological ingredients. People take the pill believing that it is designed to help them—and they do indeed improve. The important thing about the placebo effect is that it shifts the focus of the cure from external causation to internal—and this changes everything.[4] Internal location places the power to change and heal within our own consciousness. For women, this means that we no longer have to wait for anything else to happen. We don't have to wait until we are equally represented in boardrooms or politics or until we truly receive equal pay or respect to be considered the equal, or even superior, sex—it has already happened. Women simply have to believe that what they have always sensed to be true about their unique feminine strengths and qualities is indeed true. SHE-Q is the perspective that helps anchor this knowing in place.

SHE-Q Is the Natural Wisdom of Women

Women have an intelligence that is based on relationship and connection. SHE-Q is a highly developed relational ability based on cooperation, empathy, intuitive sensing, and listening. It is the result of stronger connections between the two hemispheres of the brain, thus linking thinking and feeling into a new higher synthesis that, prior to neurological imaging and research, we were unable to measure. It is related to oxytocin, the hormone so necessary for relating. SHE-Q is the ability to tune into the other person while at the same time maintaining one's own boundaries. It is a highly advanced skill that we have failed to recognize and identify.

Finally naming it helps us to better recognize it. SHE-Q has always been present in women; we just never valued it. It is not surprising that we misunderstood it. It's a little like looking at the picture of *The Last Supper.* We don't see a female sitting next to Christ because we don't expect to. In the same way, women have always possessed greater emotional and relational skill, but because we didn't value it, we didn't see it. We looked only to men for the skills we needed while SHE-Q has been there all the while—waiting until just the right time to emerge. The first thing women must do is acknowledge their wisdom. In doing so, we recognize almost immediately how far away we have been from comprehending this.

SHE-Q Helps Woman Recognize that Things Have Changed Dramatically

It has been at least 150 years since women first began to recognize and articulate the imbalance and started the first women's movement. Since then, they have gotten the vote and established a second women's movement. Women today are not only educated, they are outperforming men at every level of education. They are employed, have their own incomes, and are no longer dependent on men.

Within 40 short years, since women entered male-based academia in droves, they are beating men at their own game. The fact that women will soon be the primary sex in all areas of education should be enough to make both males and females take notice of our changing landscape. Fifty percent of women already feel that they are more successful than their husbands are.

In 2010, women became the majority in the workforce and many managers are women. There is a role reversal going on in business, reflecting the fact that changes in one area often result in changes in other areas. Our society no longer values physical strength. The sex that is hardwired to fight is not valued on Wall Street. Women's skills are more in demand. The economics of our new society appear to be better geared for the women who have the skills most valued today—social intelligence, open communication, focus, cooperation, and multitasking. Management styles now view creativity and collaboration as highly valued commodities. The new and innovative firms are hiring and promoting women.

In *The Richer Sex,* Lisa Mundy describes how the new female breadwinner is transforming sex, love, and family. Because 40 percent of women currently out-earn their husbands, Mundy also foresees what she calls "the big flip," where women are the new financial providers—and this alone will change everything. While some marriages may flourish under this new arrangement, countless men will feel threatened and defensive. As soon as their wives start making more money, many men, according to Munday, start denigrating them and telling them they are unattractive. When he brought home the money, she may have tolerated it, but no longer.[5]

This same ingenuity and entrepreneurial spirit appears to be true of women all over the world. In a well-known social experiment, males and females in third world cultures were each given a small amount of money. The males quickly spent their money drinking or gambling. The females pooled their money together and started small businesses that became profitable, and increased the income and quality of life for the family. Since the 1970s, it is women who have been seeking education, with 1978 being the peak year for women entering the workforce. And the fact that they are more empathic, better consensus builders, and better lateral thinkers is being valued more and more.

Women, like cream, are naturally rising to the top. Despite attempts to bury her achievements and abilities in ambiguous research and politically correct equality, she is still succeeding. Further, males are becoming the new underachievers.

There is a literal revolution going in colleges. More women graduate from college and obtain 60 percent of the master's degrees, and depending on the source of the statistics, half or more than half of all law and medical degrees.[6] One might think that men, similarly, would see the benefit of getting educated. Instead, they are failing to adapt and have a harder time committing to school. Boys seem to be failing at every level of education.

Girls actually learn better in traditional, male-designed, and structured environments than boys do. This trend of boys' underachievement continues through college. Fewer boys than girls even apply for college. Many of those who do are less academically qualified than the girls. For this reason, colleges often have tougher admitting standards for females than males.

Colleges claim that they need to have easier standards for males so that they can maintain a community of balanced gender ratios. Colleges sensed a coming gender gap more than 30 years ago, and for this reason, the new affirmative action at colleges is increasingly geared toward males. Attempting to avoid the dreaded 60 percent female and 40 percent male ratio at colleges, admissions offices explain away boys' deficits with phrases like "late bloomer," or "hasn't quite peaked." The picture that is emerging is that of overeducated females and undereducated males.

Young women today are more career-driven than men and include high-paying careers as one of their life priorities, says Claire Gordon. Women appear to be more money focused than ever. In 2011, 50 percent more women than men graduated from college.[7]

Further, males have few support groups. Marriages fall apart and 40 percent of children grow up without fathers. The bachelor party, however, is over for the single male. Family changes over the years have been bad for men and children, but not necessarily for women. Research reveals that women bounce back more successfully after a divorce, with 20 percent of women seeing actual gains in income. The happiest women today have a fulfilling life, many friends, and a sense of passion and purpose outside their relationships, whether they are married or not.

Additional changes are happening in many other areas. For the first time ever, females are the preferred sex for women who attempt to choose the sex of their children. Just 25 years ago, at least half of all women said they really wanted a son. By 2003, only 15 percent preferred sons. Today's mothers now have a clear preference for girls for whom they see a bright future. Women want daughters because they like who they are. Girls are less trouble, do better in school, and are more inclined to remain in relationships with their mothers. Importantly, women have achieved all of this without any epistemology that supported their own true natures, values, or more whole-brained ways of knowing. Imagine what women can do as things change. Now is the time to begin redefining ourselves.

SHE-Q Enables Women to Know that They Are No Longer Victims of Difference, and Can Embrace and Appreciate Their Differences in a Positive Light

Men would be wise to avoid discussions around difference today because the truth is that biologically women are the primary and superior sex. First of all, there are more women than men in the world, and they live longer. All embryos begin as female. Males would not be here if not for a female who gave birth to him. The only thing that supports his being the superior sex are books, incorrect theories and hypotheses, written by males that have created an erroneous assumption as true. It is time for women to take off their tight hats, stop feeling victimized and begin to appreciate their differences. They are the compassionate, caring, intuitive, and empathic sex. Why would we want to deny such attributes just because males have deemed them lesser status. We should value and trust our more emotionally intelligent selves that encompasses both thinking and feeling.

As women rise to the top, they may be righteously angry, but will never denigrate men in the ways men have done to women. It simply is not in a woman's nature. Declaring then that females are the primary sex is neither one-upping nor male-bashing. It is simply righting a long-standing wrong. Males have benefitted greatly from women's kinder natures. They can no longer have it both ways—receiving emotional support and at the same time downgrading it.

Goldberg[8] states that there are some feminists who try to have it both ways. They want to deny the importance of the physiological basis of the behavior of the sexes, yet blame the world's woes on the characteristics of its male leaders. The irony is that the very nature of a woman's life-sustaining abilities is also the same reason why women will never have the disposition or obsessive need for power. Women know that it is she who matters. If she doesn't know this, she should, for this knowing is rooted in her very essence.

Females are central to life, says Goldberg, bestowed with the capacity, unlike males, to bring forth new life. The job of males is to protect the new life and the mother who nurtures it. According to Goldberg, "While there are more brilliant men than brilliant women and more powerful men than powerful women, there are more good women than men. Women are not dependent on male brilliance for their deepest source of strength, but men are dependent on female strength." He continues, "Few women have been ruined by men; female endurance survives. Many men, however, have been destroyed by women who did not understand or did not care to understand, male fragility."

Fortunately for men, women *do* understand. Even after millennia of being ridiculed, they are still kind and caring. They understand intuitively that men need their reassurance. Imagine what it would be like if men could actually say how very appreciative they are of women. Imagine if they acknowledged how important her wisdom is to them.

Women are certainly not less moral, less rational, or less creative than men. In every case, females are, without question, the superior sex. It is only later that Nature, again female, provides the necessary ingredients for males to become males. If divinity has to be assigned a sex, she is without question a female. Why would any woman *want* to deny the biological basis of the enormous powers inherent in who she is? This is true of females with their more integrated body-mind, cyclical natures and permeable boundaries, whether or not they have ever actually given birth. The only reason we don't value the life-giving force in women is because of a male agenda to make sure women stayed unaware of their wisdom. To continue to negate the primacy of the female would be to continue to adopt a male standard, and further to continue to see ourselves as females who can be controlled by men.

"The experience of men," Goldberg continues, "is that there are few women who can outfight them and few who can out argue them, but when a woman uses her feminine means, she can command a loyalty that no amount of dominance behavior ever could. The experience of women is that the violence men often seek out is terrifying and overpowering, but that by using the feminine means that nature gave her, a woman can deal with the most powerful man as an equal."

Further, says Goldberg, "Women have more important things to do. Men are aware of this and that is why in this and every other society they look to women for gentleness, kindness and love, for refuge from a world of pain and force, for safety from their own excesses. In every society, a basic male motivation is the feeling that the women and children must be protected. But a woman cannot have it both ways; if she wishes to sacrifice all this, what she will get in return is the right to meet men on male terms. She will lose." Goldberg wrote those words in 1993, in response to a feminism that denied feminine qualities. His message to women was that embracing their inherent strengths and qualities was the only way they could win. At that time, for many reasons, it appears that the world was just not ready for both women *and* their unique qualities. The power of the male tradition was so strong that women had no other choice than to say they were like men. Twenty years and many changes later, the world is ready and this time she will not lose.

SHE-Q Helps Women Recognize that While They Have Been and Will Continue to Be Playing a Male Game with Male Rules, They Can Begin to Change It

Recognize that the strong male traditions will not die easily. Whether conscious or unconscious, there will be countless attempts by the status quo to discredit all activities that are right-brained and/or feminine in nature. Recognize that the left brain has a vested interest in sustaining itself and will by its very nature fail to grasp the larger picture. Women can begin to trust themselves and come forward at work and at home, as well as socially and politically, to demand that the feminine perspective be considered as equally as the masculine. Obviously, this will not be easy to do—and the difficulty serves as a further example of the basic inequality that is being addressed here. In 2012, five males met on a political committee to discuss women's reproductive rights. When women complained and asked to be a part of the discussion, they were told that the issue was administrative, not personal. Sandra Fluke, a law student at Georgetown, who had asked to be included was called a "slut" and a prostitute by Rush Limbaugh, who said that she was a woman who wanted to have lots of sex and make the government pay for her birth control. The powerful traditional standards appear to sense on some level that things are changing. That the issue was women's reproductive rights is, first and foremost, an obvious need for men to control women. It is no wonder that the war on women will only escalate before it gets better.

Until recently, a person's religious beliefs were considered private and not subject to debate or discussion. However, when a politician's beliefs mean that he or she will deny scientific evidence or lead us into a battle with the devil, people are beginning to recognize that it is necessary to focus on what the real bottom line content of these religious beliefs will actually mean for the policies of those who might be leading our country. Richard Dawkins suggested that just as we wouldn't go to a doctor who believes in a stork who brings babies, similarly, we have a right to explore what the beliefs held by politicians actually mean to those who may or may not vote for them.

The masculinized ego resents that it is women who give birth. They created a male god that usurped this act to allay facing this shadow so they could maintain control. Now that women are beginning to take control of their own reproductive processes, men, predictably, are trying to control this. I refer to the masculinized ego here because countless good males defended and even publicly apologized to Fluke. Perhaps this obvious and extreme need to control by some outmoded males will serve to make this whole issue more visible. A candidate, for example, who votes to limit women's reproductive rights should be perceived as diminishing himself, not women, and should be viewed as a red flag that immediately goes up in women's heads. Males only get away with trying to control women's rights because people vote for them. Stop. Women can demand equality by voting for good males and females who support initiatives that help foster equality. Jimmy Carter states, "The truth is that male religious leaders have had—and still have—an option to interpret holy teachings either to exalt or subjugate women. They have, for their own selfish ends, overwhelmingly chosen the latter. Their continuing choice provides the foundation or justification for much of the perverse persecution and abuse of women throughout the world."[9]

Since most working women are also the primary caregivers, it is now time to demand the same job-sharing and excellent childcare opportunities that are readily available in other first world countries. Refuse, flatly refuse, to support any religious or political positions that are based on control or attempts to limit females. Stop feeling victimized and fearful because positions like that of Roe V. Wade could be overturned. Voters put that person in a position to make those decisions. No votes and they are gone. A viral poster recently suggested that if some people wish to be exempted from paying for birth control because they are morally opposed to it, then those of us who oppose war should similarly be exempted from paying taxes that support the war. Obviously, women can think for themselves. Given that 98 percent of all Catholic women use birth control, it is obvious that women determine for themselves what they believe and how much doctrine they will accept. Further, that men set themselves up as the moral arbiters on decisions around abortion—when it is females who are obviously the more moral sex, who include the welfare of all others in their decision making, and who will carry and raise the child—is so ironic that it is almost funny and more than anything, reflects the male need to control women.

Drexler states, "If you want to take the Garden of Eden literally, fine. But the command to 'be fruitful and multiply' has a little different implication when you're the only two people in the world—as opposed to the seven billion people walking the earth, and the additional billion that will join us over the next two decades—most of them in places that can't support what they have now. . . . We all, of course, must be free to embrace our respective faiths. But when the interpretation of faith is used conveniently and selectively to create policy—people suffer."[10]

Women have a difficult enough time navigating this shifting terrain without the interference of men. Perhaps the hardest thing for women to do is question their long-held spiritual beliefs. Because spirituality and religion are closely tied to family and tradition, changes in this area often seem insurmountable. While continuing to embrace belief systems that perpetuate outmoded values that no longer work for her and her family may be easier on the surface levels, women who are strong enough to reexamine and reinvent these deepest and most personal beliefs, often feel that they and their daughters gained far more than they ever lost.

We also have to help our younger sisters understand that real women are not victims. In fact, they have an unmatchable power. Too often today, we hear about young girls being as aggressive as boys in a perverted sense of equality. As long as male values remain as primary, females look to these values as definitions of equality and view more aggression as acceptable. It is bad enough when males do it. There are already girls, who not surprisingly, don't have a clear understanding of the strength of the feminine sex, acting in ways that were at one time reserved only for boys. Is this the kind of world we want—where, in the name of equality, girls become just as physically and sexually aggressive as boys?

Young girls need a feminine model to steer them through the developmental years. *Girl Land*,[11] a recent book designed to help girls and their parents navigate this dangerous time, states, "The mass media in which so many girls are immersed today does not mean them well; it is driven by a set of priorities devoted largely to the exploitation of girls and young women." It also talks about the trend among teenage girls of providing oral sex, often to boys they don't really know. Surely, girls need a better way to express their sexual power. Further, according to Andrew Weil,[12] there is an epidemic of depression and anxiety today. Clearly, we need a new model.

SHE-Q Encourages Women to Refuse to Tolerate Male Dominance, Aggression and Need to Control

Until we stop accepting male-based values, we will continue to live in an aggressive and controlling world, run by men, where our most precious commodity, our children, and hence, our future, risk being raped and brutalized. David Cameron, prime minister of Great Britain, recently said, "Violence against women is an iceberg under the surface of society. Every day millions of women live in fear. . . . It is despicable that in the 21st century so many medieval practices and attitudes remain."[13] The question of what women can do and how they can change this is not new. *Lysistrata* is a story, written more than a thousand years ago, about the solution that the women came up with to deal with the constant aggression of their men. All the women in the town were fed up with the constant fighting and decided that as long as the men continued to fight, they would refuse to have sex with them. The men stopped fighting right away. We used to believe that as awful as war was, it at least served to benefit the economy. Even this isn't true. According to a recent study, Max Rosenthal[14] reveals that war creates a bubble that provides short-term gains while creating massive long-term problems, higher debt, and inflation.

Perhaps the best solution for reducing aggression among humans comes from a species that isn't even human. How sad and ironic that we have to learn how to control aggression and stop violence among males, something we humans have yet to learn, from chimpanzees. Bonobos are the closest species to our own, sharing 97 percent of DNA with humans. In many ways, however, they are far more advanced as a culture, and can serve as a great example for us. The female Bonobo chimpanzees live with males in a social setting. They are aware that males are far more aggressive than females and that this aggression creates problems in their society. They are an excellent example of *natural* female behavior because, while they show us how to handle the aggression of males in general, they have not been indoctrinated by our patriarchal values. They didn't attend a church where they learned that females were considered less perfect, and no one ever told them that males were supposed to be in charge, so they didn't have to learn or unlearn subordinate cultural roles. Without this indoctrination, they rely on their instincts and respond naturally. They know how males are and simply refuse to tolerate it when males get aggressive and try to be in control. They know that it hurts their culture, their social structure, and possibly members of their group, so they act to stop it immediately.

The Bonobo females cooperate naturally with each other, while the males do not. For this reason, the highest ranking and most aggressive male can always be stopped when the females gang up on him. The females form coalitions, beginning in adolescence, to ensure that they and their offspring get the best food and feel safe. If a Bonobo male becomes aggressive, it is understood that his own mother will be the first to try to stop him. If she can't do it alone, the other females will immediately come to her aid and make him stop. It appears that this forced suppression of aggression in males then generalizes to other areas of their behavior. Male Bonobos are the only species that will sit back and watch as the females from their tribe have sex with males from another tribe—almost unheard of in the animal kingdom. The females do this not because, as Freud suggested, they are "polymorphously perverse" and oversexed. They do it to reduce aggression. They know that their own sons could be maimed or killed by the intruders and apparently know what the marauders like even more than fighting.

Female Bonobos form core groups that contain more females than males. Females are closer to each other than they are to males and more likely to be at the center of the group, with the males on the periphery, which further helps to protect them against male aggression. They present a natural picture of a culture in the way Goldberg seems to suggest, with males again knowing their rightful place on the sidelines.

Bonobos show us that it is possible for a species to be committed to the moral aspects of what, ironically, we like to call "humanity." Female Bonobos are the exemplars of respect for each other—and for us. They teach us that it is possible to stop violence and aggression not only toward females and children, but also toward other males. The female Bonobos reveal that violence can be stopped by shifting the balance from a male dominated system of aggression and control to a female-based system of alliance and cooperation.

Imagine what women could do if they applied Bonobo wisdom to our world. If female Bonobos can form alliances, so can human women. And it will be women who initiate this change.

SHE-Q Helps Women Know that They Are the Caretakers of the Earth

Every decision made about the earth should be made in consideration for the next seven generations. We are at a crossroads. The doomsday clock, which measures how close we are to catastrophic destruction based on the current state of nuclear weaponry, climate change, and biosecurity, has been moved up another minute—and we are five minutes away from not being here. We need women, the sex that is more likely to make decisions based on how they impact others to be more involved.[15]

On a macro level, the human body can be likened to the earth, with males as its left brain and females as its right brain. It is the right brain and women, always vigilant for danger, that know something is wrong—with the world and with her body. At the same time, because the right brain sees the bigger picture, she recognizes that the left-brained males aren't going to do anything about it.

Research has shown that while girls and women bear the greatest brunt of poverty, they are also the ones who can bring the greatest long-lasting change to communities. As women are empowered, they create positive ripples that catalyze change within cultures.

Female bodies, like the earth, are far wiser than we know and can even comprehend. Scientists recently discovered the "Bruce Effect" in primates who are seeking reproductive access. The Gelada baboons live in small groups that are controlled by a dominant male who is replaced about every three years by a more dominant male. When this happens, 80 percent of the females who are pregnant miscarry. The new dominant male will kill most of the infants that have been fathered by other males. The female body somehow knows this and miscarries. It is suggested that the females who are able to miscarry are able to conserve energy that would have gone to an infant that was unlikely to survive.[16]

Despite her power to continually heal herself, Gaia, the body of our Earth Mother, is suffering. She is poisoned by oil spills. Her lungs are polluted because her bronchial trees have been cut down. Her skin is being fracked by a left brained perspective that is focused only on making more money from her blood. Fracking is disaster wrapped in a pretty male package. Countless books could be written on how awful, short-sighted, and insane this endeavor is. Acute impacts to health will occur. Air and water are being ruined in the name of money. We are trashing the earth and no one takes responsibility—and it is hard to imagine that women would be in favor of doing this. Money cannot bring back what has been and still is being taken away. Women don't have to spend all their time lobbying, but need support agencies and others who do.

We are doing things to the earth that are so insidious that it is almost incomprehensible to imagine that these things would be done only for money. What good is money if none of us can breathe the air or drink the water? We simply can no longer tolerate political candidates who continue to defensively deny climate change or the welfare of the earth. Conservative Rick Santorum, when asked to explain why he attacked Obama's "phony theology," said, "We're not here to serve the earth. That is not the objective. Man is the objective."[17] The conservative element is far more than just annoying, it serves to fragment America. It makes it impossible for leaders to compromise and work together.

We need viable solutions. According to Barbara Marx Hubbard,[18] our crisis can be viewed as a birth, and each of us does not have to do this alone. There are more than a million organizations today that are working for social and economic justice. We can withdraw our support from war mongering companies that try to convince us to use toxic chemicals and genetically engineered seeds. We can support new energy solutions, water resources and organic products. We can recognize that actions in one area impact other areas and a few actions can tip the scales. All of these organizations recognize that the changes must be nonviolent, for violence only serves to strengthen the need for control. We need genuine compassion. Compassion is not passive. It is sometimes fierce, and it says, "No."

A female-based society is more inclined to be egalitarian and based on a "power with" rather than a "power over" model. Females appear to embrace a partnership society that is more weblike rather than hierarchical. It is women and whole-brained men who are better at cooperation, diplomacy, and connecting with others who should be leading the world's countries.

Darwin[19] said sympathy is the strongest emotion in human nature. It is women who provide compassion and the soft place to land, who have always been the humanizing force in this world. Men can no longer have it both ways—both expecting and denigrating these most human of qualities.

SHE-Q Empowers Women to Refuse to Tolerate Sexual Abuse

Now that women are no longer accepting of being controlled, sexual assault has become the most rapidly growing crime today. One in three women is still sexually abused today. According to the APA, more than 700,000 women are sexually assaulted each year—mostly by men they know. Thousands of women in the military are sexually assaulted by their comrades, where it is estimated that 11,000 women are raped or assaulted each year. Men have to realize that this is a reality for women.

This abuse appears to be fueled by something far deeper than testosterone. This male shadow has been projected onto women since time began and will continue to influence men until it is viewed openly and honestly.

It is projected daily as physical, mental, and emotional abuse. It is projected because men are not women and at their cores have never come to grips with who they really are. It has been projected because the collective of men feels a need to be in control. A fanatical need to persecute seems to be at the heart of this male projection that has been and continues to be responsible for such denigration of the feminine qualities and women themselves throughout history.

Men have far less ability to repress sexual impulses when aroused. The neocortex, the part of the brain that looks ahead and plans for the future, can more easily be overridden in males by the baser instincts of the mammalian brain. In other words, male brains really are ruled by their penises when aroused. Why else would a fully grown man sexually abuse an infant girl? It is the most heinous of crimes and a betrayal of humanity's most basic moral code. In many ways sexual abuse is worse than murder. Goldberg states that while hormones are important, they can be overridden by answering a more compelling moral call. "It is these masculine and feminine feelings, the emotional manifestations of our biology's and the emotional prerequisites of political power that prescribe the limits of sexual roles and social possibility. It will help men to recognize that he can indeed change and that his own liberation demands that he define his own needs and emotional states from a context of wholeness."[20]

Somewhere deep in the collective conscious of women, however, there is an awareness of the shame that men carry. And even in this awareness, they still try to help men heal the wound that will not heal.

SHE-Q Connects Women to Women

The women who are currently intuiting the feminine in are like those people of earlier times who were considered geniuses. They picked up on something archetypal coming into the collective consciousness and expanded it with their own constructed thoughts. Similarly, all women begin to intuit the same concepts once they realize they are allowed to think such things. As they sense the new balance and wholeness in themselves, they, at the same time, recognize how imbalanced the culture and the world are. Rupert Sheldrake[21] studies various types of behaviors that we know exist, but can't explain. Pets, for example, seem to know exactly when their masters will arrive home. Humans, too, can *know* about things before they even happen. We just don't know how or why this type of knowing, often referred to as tacit knowing, works. Sheldrake recognizes that countless intuitive connections exist that we literally do not understand. He proposes the concept of morphogenetic fields, also known as the Hundredth Monkey phenomenon, to account for part of this knowing.

According to the theory of morphogenetic fields, when enough members of a certain species learn something new, this knowing will generalize to the rest of the species.

This idea is based on studying monkeys on a certain island that ate sweet potatoes. One of the smarter monkeys, after accidentally dropping her sweet potato in the water, realized that the water removed the sand and made the potato easier to eat. She then learned to wash her sweet potatoes before eating them. She showed other monkeys how to wash their sweet potatoes, and before long, all the monkeys on the island were doing the same. The interesting thing is that the scientists noted that monkeys on neighboring islands, who had no contact with the original monkeys, also, somehow began to wash their sweet potatoes.

Sheldrake proposes that when enough members of a species reach a tipping point or critical mass around certain information, others are able to learn it more easily and almost automatically. Women, it appears, have now reached a critical mass in their sensing and intuiting, making it easier for the whole system and certainly all other women to also sense whole new levels of information. Women all over the world are becoming whole and aware. Morphogenetic fields are important now—for as each individual woman changes and elevates her consciousness, it makes it easier for all other women to do the same.

SHE-Q, similarly, connects woman more consciously to the mitochondrial DNA roots that run only through the female line and their knowing through time. Women always sensed that, in many ways, they were superior to men. Even when they learned nothing that ever supported this idea, they still knew it.

Women have been blamed by men since the beginning of time. Let us not further contribute to this. It is shocking how often women make negative comments about their own sex. Let's think twice before we denigrate women in general. It goes without saying that we don't have to like every woman we meet, and, further, that there will always be women that we disagree with. We need to think twice, however, before we fall back on our default mode of blaming women.

SHE-Q Is Embodied Spirituality

Recognize that as females, you are where you need to be spiritually. Appreciate that you don't have to do anything except unlearn. Follow your instinct of truth. Trust your true embodied guidance and wisdom, and create rituals and practices that serve to strengthen this knowing. There are many entry points for feminine spirituality. Most women have at least one memory of feeling directly connected with the divine. Some have experienced a split-second revelation of knowing that instantly changed their lives. Others had a sense of illumination that built up gradually and finally culminated in many concepts coming together.

Recognize that nothing is lost if you venture away from more traditional beliefs and move toward a more authentic spirituality. Every person has experiences of enlightenment, "Aha!" moments, and peak experiences. Women who have moved beyond the context of their old traditional beliefs are often placed in the difficult situation of questioning whether their earlier spiritual experiences are now somehow less valid or real. Because these experiences are so precious and meaningful, this questioning period is natural, and she needs to be assured that her earlier experiences were and always will be real to her whether the context changes or not. Further, women who have had deep spiritual experiences worry that if they change the context of their belief system, they will also negate the possibility of continued experiences. Again, they need to recognize that, if anything, a more viable and authentic framework will likely serve to increase, not decrease, further experiences.

The feminine is the wellspring of all the higher aspects of humanity on both the personal microcosm of individual women and the macrocosm of females. Women have been the soft place to land, the gentle hands, the compassion, the understanding, and the nurturing that each soul requires.

Men created spiritual viewpoints based on their often limited views on spirituality. Many of these concepts do not apply to women, who already have a more embodied sense of knowing and an internal moral compass.

Women understand that religion and spirituality should be based on consciousness, not genitalia. Recognize that you are your own conduit to your source of wisdom, and refuse to have an intermediary between you and your source of divinity. Know that your morality comes from within you. Know that you will continue to have spiritual experiences even as your beliefs mature and you leave old traditional beliefs. Following your own path will lead you to right where you should be. The wisdom of SHE-Q is as close as your next breath.

SHE-Q Supports the Construction of Your New Knowledge

Now is the perfect time for women. We need female insight and foresight to fix the many things that are wrong and begin to construct new knowledge.

In the second half of the 20th century, the Grand Narratives that informed our knowing for 2,000 years were finally deconstructed. Now is the time for women to begin to reconstruct new stories that better reflect our knowing today. Think in new ways until you get to the point of being able to construct your own knowledge. It is the very nature of the right brain and whole brain with its larger and more flexible viewpoint to construct new knowledge that must come forward now. We cannot solve our problems with the same thinking that created them.

SHE-Q encourages females to embrace what they know to be true intuitively. Don't wait for research to confirm it, for it may not happen in your lifetime. Just because a male-based limited epistemology is in place now that ridicules information that is right-brained or intuitive in nature, does not make this information wrong. It simply reflects a limited perspective that cannot comprehend the more creative, subtle, or insightful information that comes from a whole-brained perspective. Decide to become your own arbiter of what is true or meaningful to you. Learn to trust it, develop new hypotheses, and talk with your friends. The feminine is a fertile field, ready to receive the seeds of new ideas that will further define it. Give voice, finally, to the qualities of the right brain. Hillary Clinton states that we now "live in an age where we can shape our destinies in ways never before imagined."[22] Women have the right to decide what they wear, how they worship, what their causes will be, and what is best for their bodies. America needs to set an example for the world.

Allow this new construction of knowledge to serve as a creative outlet for your frustration. As women become aware of the imbalance, they do feel angry and rightfully so. The frustration, however, is easier to bear if you feel you can do something about it—and waiting until patriarchal values die is not a good option. Simply refuse to continue working and thinking within a paradigm that we now know is limited and outmoded. Start talking with friends about it. Start writing. You can be more creative than you ever dreamed. This period of time is unlike any other for women. The world is not going to end in 2012, but this year does indeed mark a very significant time of change, supported by mythological and even planetary changes that herald this year as the beginning of the age of women.

The world knows itself through human consciousness. Each individual is literally an organ of self-knowledge for the world. We *are* human consciousness, not some unrelated part stuck onto the consciousness of the world. We are the evolutionary drivers—the ones who ensure the continual evolution and forward progress of consciousness. And, it is women, with their advanced frontal lobes, and good men who understand, who are leading the way.

What does this mean for the collective of women, today? It means that every woman who wakes up makes it easier for all other women to wake up. Every woman who says for the first time, "I will no longer take this," makes it easier for another woman to feel the same. Every woman who says, "I feel whole and complete in and of myself," makes it easier for other women to move to a similar mental space.

The confident young girls of today, with their unbound sense of freedom and self-esteem, will be the leaders of tomorrow. They can literally conceive of a world full of possibilities that is very different from girls just 20 years earlier. We all have to live on this small planet with each other. It is women, who care far less about dominance and aggression and are more skilled at diplomacy and compromise, who are now valued. Females have the natural skills to be the new leaders as a new sense of sisterhood is developing on both the collective and personal levels. SHE-Q enables each of us to literally move consciousness forward.

SHE-Q Encourages Women to Laugh

When you get overwhelmed by testosterone, remember Betty White's quote, "Why do they always tell you to grow a pair of balls? Balls are weak and sensitive. Why don't they tell you to grow a vagina? Those things really take a pounding!" Also remember that many women today are coming very close to a place where they feel that, "Men have feelings too but who gives a shit?"

In *The Witches of Eastwick,* the women learned that laughter quickly dispelled attempts to control them. We should now be laughing, not feeling victimized by these pathetic attempts at control.

My sister recently bought Dave a shirt for his birthday that says, "I only do what the voices in my wife's head tell her to tell me to do." It's funny. But think about it. There is also much wisdom in that humor. What a wonderful world it would be if men only did what the voices in their wives heads told them to do.

SHE-Q Encourages Women to Connect with Good Males

The Dalai Lama, surely one of the best males, has placed his faith in us. Countless good males have written the material in this book, and ironically some of the best information about women has been written by good males like Goldberg, Shlain, and Tarnas, to name a few. There are men who have also outgrown the limited epistemology and are attempting to fix the problem. Good men have often been the protectors, encouragers, and promoters of women. We need to recognize, appreciate, and support them.

SHE-Q Is a Necessary Corrective Measure for Women Are the Caretakers of the Soul of the World

The Dalai Lama says that the reason why love and compassion bring such joy to us and make us feel so good is because our nature cherishes these qualities above all else. The need for love is at the very basis of human existence. It comes from the profound interdependence we all share with one another.

The world has never been so interconnected. We have the Internet and the World Wide Web. Yet, at the same time, humanity has never been so fragmented, depressed, or disconnected. There is an awakening need for wholeness, and we are becoming unwilling to accept the discrepancy between our inner and outer worlds.

The feminine is the end soul, the embodied source. Once you find it in yourself, you begin to see it in others. You begin to see the sheer radiance of the soul. You see the tears of the tree that is cut down after being alive for 400 years. The feminine rhythm is the cycle of life, death, and rebirth. The life principle is always breaking down the old, letting the old die and bringing forth the new.

The soul is considered feminine. Women's consciousness goes far beyond themselves. It is related to everything else. Therefore, it is no wonder that as women get in touch with themselves, they also get in touch with the world.

Each of us is a microcosm of a larger macrocosm. In the largest sense, the hero's or heroine's journey undertaken by each of us is also the heroine's journey undertaken by the whole culture. Women realize on a spiritual, meta-personal, and even cosmic level that they must now put their knowledge into practice and into the world. We all recognize today that we cannot keep warring with each other and kill everyone on the planet. Our technology has far surpassed our moral or ethical understanding. Now that we have the ability to kill each other, we need the understanding of how very futile and stupid this ability really is. We know that we are connected to each other.

Can we not learn to live peacefully with each other? Women today are living at the best time in history to help this happen.

The feminine is all the things we have been looking for—connectedness, intuition, relationship, oneness, deep connections with the earth, feeling, being, empathy, and compassion. While feminine, these qualities are also exactly what the world needs now, for we have become so left-brained that it often seems that we have moved into absurdity. Balance is a birthright for each of us, and beliefs that are inherently imbalanced will only perpetuate the error. We need new knowledge, concepts, and perspectives to anchor in this new expanded viewpoint.

SHE-Q Encourages Women to Begin by Changing the World One Man at a Time

In the real life, day-to-day existence of men and women two things are true: men will not change easily and women have already changed. A woman may not be able to change the world by herself, but she can begin by changing the man in her life. The world has to be changed—so, where better to begin than with the one you love? Begin the first step toward balance in your relationship. Do you realize how quickly the world could change if each woman did this?

Being in a relationship is good for men. Married men live longer, have more sex, and are less likely to get cancer and PTSD. They are less likely to have heart problems, behave better, and drink less.[23] Being in a relationship is natural to women and is part of her spirituality. It surprises a woman when she realizes that he doesn't truly grasp her essence and intentions, and further shocks her when she recognizes that she knows the male in her life better than he appears to know himself. This realization certainly doesn't come all at once. She typically goes through numerous stages before she actually comes to this fully formed truth. Prior to this recognition, she blames herself for wanting or expecting too much. She retreats and tries to be more understanding. She tries denying what she senses to be true. She tries another way to keep the relationship intact and vital. She typically has tried every possible option before she finally realizes that what she felt in the first place was indeed right.

Chapter 15

Mentoring the Masculine

Yin
Wisdom and waiting
Wanting more and drawing lines
Foresight and insight
Empathy and intuition

It has been said that a woman marries a man hoping that he will change, but he doesn't; and a man marries a woman hoping she won't change, but she does—and therein lies the problem. Nowhere in the arena of the two sexes is the difference more pronounced than in relationships. Men and women are made to come together in relationships, yet this supposedly loving and cooperative venture, is the place where their differences are highlighted and magnified. The difference that initially seemed so attractive, such as "I love that he just seems to know without really saying it," soon becomes "Sweet Jesus, deliver me—that man has no idea of how he really feels."

By the time that she has even a clue that he is not comfortable with his feelings, she has already thought about this constantly and tried to figure it out. She initially assumes that he is closing himself off from her on purpose because of something she has done. So she has gone back to thinking about it before bringing it up again. And even with all of her thinking, it takes her ages, eons, light years before she realizes that he doesn't know how to do what she is asking for. Many women never figure this out. And even when they start getting a clue, women don't believe it, can't believe it. The funny thing is that men will often tell their partners straight out—that they don't know how they really feel, what to say, or what they are really thinking. The extent of the relational lie is such that even when he tells her, she just cannot understand what he is saying.

All the stereotypical behavior that defines men and women seems to change when it comes to relationships, and the qualities on the Yin and

Yang list seem to switch sides. She, who typically hates conflict and isn't very good at it, is more than ready to plunge right in. She, not always able to be as articulate as he was, now becomes a master of words and understanding.

Relating is where she feels most comfortable. This is her turf. This is where she plays because she knows how she feels and she knows how *he* feels. For this reason alone, it is particularly helpful to separate the behavior of the sexes. The differences are startling when it comes to relationships. This is where the tables turn. Nowhere are the differences greater—and this story is as old as man.

Mentoring is, unfortunately, not something that can be presented in 10 easy steps. Like all epistemology, it is based on deconstructing levels of understandings that often involve unlearning before women get to a more authentic understanding of who they really are. It often requires much growth on her part to really comprehend this ultimate feminine wisdom. Women have to redefine who they are to themselves and be aware of how they know what they know. They have to be aware of their relational abilities and strengths. They have to trust themselves and their intentions. They have to care about the man in their life. They have to know that they can go on with him or without him. They need to be ready to step into their own power and become wiser than they ever realized, which is the true SHE-Q. When all these variables are in place, they are then ready to begin to mentor.

In truth, mentoring, per se, is not difficult. It comes naturally to women and women have been mentoring or trying to mentor since the beginning of time. What is hard about mentoring is all the unlearning that women have to do to get back to this natural wisdom. Women know intuitively that each partner has to know themselves as individuals first—free of the gender roles prescribed by culture—to really be able to relate to each other. Having done this, women assume, usually erroneously, that their partners have done the same. Women recognize that relationships are based on feelings: If a person doesn't know how he or she feels, how can that person ever know how their partner feels? They know that relationships can be much more authentic and real. This is the "more" that women want, and men don't get. Indeed, this is what women have always wanted from men. Only now, however, can we recognize that women's intentions in relationships are, and always have been, far more honorable than the culture has been willing to acknowledge.

Understanding Mentoring

Now that women are wise, what do they do with this wisdom? Nature made her relational for a reason. Women like to share what they know. And who better to share it with than the person we are in a relationship with?

Until now, despite the fact that women have always possessed the ability to mentor and have tried to mentor men, the concept of a woman mentoring a man was and still is considered heresy. Wrong. Forbidden. Unheard of. Incomprehensible.

But the whole basis and point of this book has served only to get us to this point. Why continue to depress women by stressing the inequality if they can't do something about it?

We aren't wise women for ourselves alone. This willingness to share and these permeable boundaries and relational skills are embodied in women for a reason. We are designed to share our wisdom. We have arrived at this point in history and in the collective development of consciousness for reasons that may be hard to comprehend. When Lynn told me that I didn't want Dave to change for me but for himself, her words touched a depth of truth that I didn't know existed. This truth is present in the heart of to every woman.

Hoffman[1] suggested that women's brains are more developed—possessing the abilities of foresight, insight, and intuitive knowledge. Women are more rational and moral. They are more compassionate and caring. They are more empathic, understanding, and relational. Why? In the grand scheme of evolution, it is now time for these qualities on both the personal and collective levels.

Although the world is always changing, relationships may be the one sphere where little or nothing actually changes. Far less socially oriented, relationships appear to belong to the private sphere and are not often shared publicly. Very often, except for the two people in the relationship, no one really knows what actually happens.

Mentoring can best be understood as a new and different mode of consciousness. It is the highest form of feminine consciousness that includes and transcends all her natural skills, and also goes forward into completely new territory. In mentoring, the female becomes like the female mystic who, in going to a place of nonduality, imagines herself as strength, as a rock, as a peaceful and gentle warrior. The mentoring woman becomes strong. She takes charge because her strength is required now. At the same time, she retains all of her feminine qualities. Although she assumes the leadership role, she leads with compassion.

A woman becomes her truest self here—activating all the highest human qualities that are required. She is not just playing a male game of leadership where the rules are still informed by the masculine. She steps into her own style and trusts her own feminine qualities. A mentoring woman is the female at her most powerful. Her entire mind and body respond to what is needed. Both her adrenaline and oxytocin are activated. She stays calm, but she stays right in the middle of it. Often she is surprised by her lack of feelings and emotions and may misinterpret this lack of feeling as no longer caring. This is not the case, but is instead her deep feminine nature moving her into a problem-solving mode. While a part of her may want to lash out and fight, she knows that at this point it wouldn't be the right thing to do. She senses his discomfort, and at the same time may want to yell at him and say, "Grow up! Stop being so defensive! Trust me, know me, and know that I would never hurt you!" She is, however, able to remain silent and wait. She goes to a place in her mind that she has rarely or never been to. She recognizes that she has to look beyond the petty fights and hurtful words and see, really see, what she is working with and what she has to do. She knows now, and she knows that she knows. She is the archetypal wise woman. She is both willing and able to go to the highest or the lowest places, just as the shaman does. She has become wisdom.

She knows that neither she nor her partner can have someone else waiting on the sidelines. Mentoring is done to improve a relationship that is already intact and just needs improvement. If he has already started looking elsewhere, he will not be willing to summon the courage it will take to engage with her. He will see the other woman who is out there waiting as his best and easiest option.

The mentoring process is somewhat different for her. Because the concepts of SHE-Q and mentoring have never been described, women didn't know that they could use it. For this reason, women may make the mistake of leaving too soon. Many women state that they have done everything, tried everything they can think of before they left or realized that the relationship was over. Because women both know and do not know, it is hard to tell. I am certain that I am not the only female who ever experienced this place. I arrived here intuitively and learned to trust that I had been led here for a reason. For this reason, I can easily imagine that many other women have also experienced this new consciousness. On the other hand, many women do not know. Even if women feel whole and empowered within themselves, the idea of consciously expecting their partner to change and trusting themselves enough to know that they can help facilitate this change, may never have occurred to them. Further, few have the benefit of having a wise woman like Lynnie to confirm this wisdom.

For this reason, women often don't really start to mentor until they feel they have tried everything, and many women are indeed at this point today. Knowing she can go on without him is important because if she isn't sure that she really can leave or that she can do it on her own, she won't be able to follow through. She will lose her own willpower that senses the wisdom in what she is doing. She will be required to learn to speak honestly to him, to tell him things that she may never have said before. Often the process will become very emotional. Mentoring is done calmly and coolly. There is almost a sense of detachment from the emotionality because she recognizes that she must be the problem solver who observes him—his openness, defensiveness, willingness, and level of discomfort. She has to discern his receptivity after he has time to think about it. She has to learn to wait.

Many strong women are initially turned off by the idea of mentoring because they view it as just another example of women meeting men's emotional needs, and in many ways, this process is indeed helping males with their emotional needs. Mentoring is different, however, because women today are different. Many women have outgrown their partners and yet still want to preserve and enhance their relationships. Mentoring then is done out of conscious choice, not obligation. Further, when women were required to meet men's needs, they had little power of their own.

The bottom line, however, is that women have always tried to mentor men. It is almost like an innate desire to help that has always been present in women. It has always been a natural feminine response, a biological and psychological urge toward caring, similar to comforting a child who has been hurt. In mentoring, however, this natural outpouring of care is now done "consciously", so that both *the man and the woman* have a conscious appreciation of what she is doing. Women have never been permitted by the male establishment to mentor men. This is new to the collective psyches of both males and females.

She needs to recognize and honor that in following her inner urge to respond to need on his part, she is doing something that only she can do. In doing so, she learns to take off the tight hats that have kept this part of her so controlled. She will no longer have to second-guess herself and her intentions. Mentoring the masculine is the process where women *actively* and *consciously* help the men in their lives to outgrow their old masculine roles and get in touch with their feelings.

She begins by choosing the right time. Experience has taught her that it is important to create the right atmosphere for them to talk. She also knows to be kind and ease into the discussion. Nevertheless, regardless of how kind she is and how correct the moment, his initial reaction will most probably be to sense that dread is beginning. And chances are that he will do everything to avoid going through this process with her. She has to be strong and really trust herself and know that what she is doing is right for him.

She has a clear sense of what she is going to say and how she is going to ask before even beginning. She has thought about it long and hard and has waited until she can no longer wait. Finally, she senses that she must become active and become part of the change.

Even with her clear and kind introduction to the talk, he feels like he's been put on the spot and is unable to think clearly, and females can easily pick up on this discomfort. It is important, however, to realize that no matter what she does or how well she does it, he will still feel uncomfortable. His years of male cultural conditioning are, initially, stronger than all her skill and kindness.

She senses intuitively that he has a problem and knows that the best thing he could do is face it. She is well aware that his discomfort with true intimacy will always be in the way unless it is addressed. So, while she senses his discomfort, she knows it is for the best to begin to introduce him to the realm of relational sharing. She knows that this sharing is the one thing that can help ensure that they remain close. Unlike him, she does not see the discussion as leading to disaster but rather away from it. She knows that damage will only come as a result of *not* keeping communication open.

Most women are typically surprised by the extent of his dread. He and the culture have kept this well-hidden for so long that it is shocking when it is finally revealed. She often can't imagine why he is reacting so defensively and tries to understand why he would be so uncomfortable. The more she goes into the process, the more she begins to see that he has a problem. Initially, she will think that the problem is unique to him, and that he must have been very hurt in childhood. She cannot conceive that this problem applies to most men. As her compassion and empathy grasp how deep the problem is, she is further opened to help him. On a biological level, most probably there is a release of more oxytocin with her that allows for further empathic response. The process can become symbiotic—as she responds to him responding to her responding to him.

She is often unaware that he is feeling like he will let her down or that he feels ashamed—because of course, he probably will not be so honest. He will instead try to make it her fault. She has a hard time realizing that her words—so well chosen and so appropriate—are being interpreted by him as bullets, darts, and arrows. She can't comprehend why he feels the need to defend himself against her kind and loving words.

Despite men's discomfort, women must trust the rightness of their own intentions, and recognize that their request for more intimacy isn't selfish. As women begin to sense that this essential feminine knowing is spiritual in nature, they also realize that they are being guided by their souls. Only at this level can her soul see his soul and know that mentoring the masculine is soul work. It is a process where women, the relational experts, consciously help men, the relationally challenged, learn to be comfortable with intimacy—so that both can continue to grow together.

Make no mistake, many women today have encountered this discomfort and have proceeded on their own into this uncharted territory. Many women are so very well aware of the male problem that their greatest fear is that, even with her best help, he will not be able to do it and will be incapable of changing. And, even with this awareness, because she has a woman's heart and a female soul, she will continue to try.

Because most males are asleep emotionally, women rarely realize the extent of this fog until they start the process. Women know that any attempt at balance in the world must begin with their primary relationships. Granted, America cannot go from millennia of masculine thinking directly to equality, but women's intuitive overcorrection into the feminine to realign the balance of nature is one of the main reasons today that women say they want more.

Women can change the world—one male at a time—by doing what they know best how to do. Like women, men are products of both nature and nurture. Nature infuses men with testosterone, which is a natural inhibitor to relating. The culture has heavily reinforced this idea of males as non-relational. Mentoring is not designed to change the natural physical and biological differences in men that stand in the way of knowing himself. Mentoring addresses the masculinized ego and learned behaviors that have been strengthened by cultural dictates to keep males away from their feelings. In other words, mentoring addresses nurture, not nature. Other species don't have cultural overlays to contend with.

Why Mentoring?

Mentoring is necessary because he needs to change and probably will not change on his own. He won't go to counseling and even if he did, few therapists are aware of male relational dread and much of the new research that has been presented here. As Donnie Deutsch says on *Love Calling*, "The guy is not going to change unless you make it happen." Most importantly, you know him better than he knows himself.

Women have indeed been trying to mentor men throughout history. She has done this because it is a normal, natural, and intuitive response on her part to try to fix what she sees is wrong. She has always asked, "What ails thee?" But, of course, this questioning has always been within a context of needing to be very careful, of making him think it's his idea and knowing that he probably wouldn't listen to her anyway. She has always done this. It is a part of her nature and who she is. Now, women are finally given permission to knowingly, willingly, and consciously step into the role of mentor to men when it comes to the emotional realm. This concept, with few exceptions, is new in history. The *Divine Comedy*, for instance, is a rare exception where the male, Dante, must rely on the female, Beatrice, to ensure that he makes it into heaven.

Today, millions of women are sensing the same shared intuitions about what is necessary for relationships to flourish. They sense it as a desire for more from the man in their lives. And the "more" they are thinking about is rarely sex. Because there is so little good information or justification for why they should want more, most women blame themselves and feel guilty.

Women know that a relationship is a two-way interactional model in which it is as important to empower as it is to be empowered. A relationship requires flexibility and change. A relationship is both cognitive and emotional and includes inner awareness and responsiveness to others.

Women's experience of themselves is intimately bound to relationship, which is why it is hard to separate women from relating. Women have far more investment in relationships than men do. Their growth often occurs *within* the relationship. Unfortunately, many women have to outgrow their relationships today and go through much soul searching and blame before they find their true selves.

Women have more permeable boundaries, which may be why they value relationship more than anything else. Even their physical boundaries are more open. Women have monthly cycles, like the moon. They are penetrated and receive another during lovemaking. They carry another for nine months. When they are separated from the other, they feed it from their bodies. Whether a woman has ever had children or not, this remains true. This feminine permeability colors how women perceive reality, how they act, how they create, and what they value. Women appear to be hardwired to create opportunities for men to change.

Growth of self occurs when one comes to understand the experiences of the other. Women have bent over backward trying to understand men. The Stone Center, having devoted much research to relationships, states that men give women only enough information to keep them from going crazy.

We belong to one another and are sustained by each other. Joanna Macy[2] says that we are dynamic, ever-changing systems that influence each other so deeply that it is hard to determine where one leaves off and the other begins. Every living thing is connected in a dynamic web of life. This interconnectedness enhances us. When we feel our relatedness, we also feel the pain of the other. It has been hard for women, who are more naturally relational, to live in a world where separateness has been so highly valued.

We Change Each Other All the Time

The current psychological maxim "You can only change yourself, not the other person" has acted as an effective silencer to the many women who have changed and outgrown their relationships. We have been strongly influenced to think that if a woman has a problem with her partner, her only option was to change herself. That was, however, before we were aware of all the relational problems that men really do have. The dictate against trying to change a man is so strong that women who are unhappy in their relationships believe their only option is to leave. Our culture allows women to leave, but not to try to change him. The maxim ensures that the person who has changed has no right to expect that another person will also change. Perhaps we can't change our own parents, children, or bosses, but if divorce is the only option for women who have outgrown their men, then it is time to change the maxim. A more appropriate maxim for postmodern relationships is "I've changed. I've grown, come grow with me."

The degree of change that the woman wants is relative to the nature of her relationship. At some of the earlier levels of psychological functioning, women just wanted the man in their lives to stop abusing them physically or verbally. The fact that she has stayed in such a bad relationship reflects her own level of self-esteem. There are a multitude of books and a variety of helpful resources for abused women when they are ready to change their lives. Most women, however, would not tolerate abuse and little if anything has been written to help a woman who just wants "more" because this has been viewed as *her* problem.

In the old roles of relationship, women learned to put their family responsibilities before themselves. They learned to cater to the man's needs, put him first and let him feel that ideas were his, not hers. To keep disagreements to a minimum, they learned to argue mainly for the welfare of the children, not for themselves.

Women who have outgrown old roles are still, of course, in relationships. They still love the men they are with—but they also want them to change. These women have already worked through the guilt of thinking that they didn't have the right to hope that the man in their life would change. The problem is that they just don't know how or what to do.

Her Real Intentions

It appears that this problem will never be solved until we get to the bottom lines. For example, one major area of relationship therapy that continues to be overlooked are the actual intentions of the woman. The very fact that women have always been blamed for trying to change men is an obvious indication that, as a culture, we have never understood understood her real motives and true intentions. For example, if we had better understood empathy, this quality in women would have been appreciated, not misconstrued and misinterpreted. And for this reason, women often fail to see their *own* true intentions. One of the greatest gifts any individual can give to another is that of having one's true intentions reflected back in the highest and best way.

For these reasons, we must first look honestly at her real intentions and men's need to protect themselves from women who are trying to change them. Women try to change and mentor men because they know that men are suffering. They may not understand the differences in brain functioning between the sexes or his learned relational dread but they know that most males don't really know how they feel. Far closer to their feelings, women want men to experience the same ease. They understand, whether they have degrees in psychology or not, that if a person doesn't know how he feels, he will never be able to understand how another is feeling.

Further, until women acknowledge to themselves their true intentions, they will never really know themselves. They will miss the wellspring of wisdom that is within them and will fail to recognize their connections to the source within themselves. They will fail to recognize their connections to the wisdom in themselves. They will not see that their perceptions of what is needed in the relationship are not only born of love and care but are also very accurate.

The real reason women try to change men is far more honorable than the culture is ready to admit. We have already explored many of the reasons why. But the fact that women are ahead of the traditional culture is no reason to continue to deny something so remarkable and true in them. As women, we need to trust our sense of what needs to be done. It is time for a leap of consciousness. The old relational lie that led us to believe that the man knew best and was in charge is no longer viable. The more recent relational lie that holds that both sexes are equally responsible is, similarly, only a politically correct band-aid that masks his inabilities. Until we get to the bottom lines of these relational lies, both sexes will continue to be confused by one another. As Levy suggests, the masculinized ego or egophrenia cannot be countered with anger, which will only serve to escalate his defensiveness.[3] Genuine compassion is called for and fortunately, this is not difficult for women. In no way is she considered to be the female victim who must once again meet the emotional needs of the male.

Real Talk Is a Solution

Why is it that, according to all the research on relationships, it is women who don't mind engaging in marital discord? Is it because they enjoy fighting? Is it because they are aggressive? Do they like to make men angry? Do they fight with men because they know they will win? Of course, the answer to all the questions is No—but why do women even enter the fray? Most women hate marital discord as much or more than men do. They engage in the argument because they *know* that the only way to solve the problems is to talk it out. They know that if the problem is ignored, it won't go away. They know that if they wait for him to bring it up, hell might freeze over first. Thus, as much as they dislike arguing, they summon their strength and courage and do it.

Women similarly do not wait to ambush him during the fight. They do not see the fight as the place to get him when he is vulnerable. Women are typically very kind to the men they are disagreeing with. They know how much their words can damage him. Contrary to popular belief, women do not fight with men to get even. Women wait and wait, while men pause and pause, and shuffle uncomfortably in their seats. Women see the discomfort in men and while being as kind as possible, still at the same time, say what they need to say. Women engage in arguments with men as an act of love. It is because they care so for the men in their lives that they are willing to fight for what they feel they need. They want the relationship to stay as vital as possible. They are willing to fight a small battle for the greater, long-lasting health of the relationship. This is actually very high-level moral thinking. It would be far easier, in many ways, to just let the problems go. A great deal of discernment is required and to be willing to endure unpleasantness to ultimately improve the relationship is true morality.

Women know the relationship should be a flexible and changing process, where both people come to a deepening understanding of themselves and each other. The ability to change in a relationship depends on the capacities and willingness of all people involved to change and grow. The feeling of being emotionally real and connected in a relationship often necessitates risk, conflict, and the expression of the full range of affect. It includes gauging the levels of closeness and distance because this is what gives the relationship the energy to grow, and what gives each person the zest to grow mutually and authentically.

An evolving relationship is an experience that is both emotional and cognitive. Its aspects are both internal and external. It involves an ongoing, intrinsic, inner awareness and responsiveness to the continuous existence and changes in the other person—and the expectation that this is mutual. It involves the capacity to identify with something larger than the single self.

Not Manipulation, But Skill

Women have always been accused of manipulating men. For this reason, the word manipulation has rather negative connotations. In truth, it means *to handle with skill.* Women should recognize the skill with which they have related to men. It is only recently that women have been given any power whatsoever. What was a woman to do historically when they, who had little power, were in relationships with men, who had far more power? They had no recourse, other than to develop highly advanced abilities in this area. They learned to treat the one with the power in such a way that they could get what they needed for themselves and/or their children. Rather than blame women, we should study their abilities of negotiation and interactive skills.

Empathy Is Central to Relationships

Accurate empathy depends on emotional sensitivity. To be empathic one must be sensitive and responsive to all the cues of relationships. Ego boundaries must be flexible enough not to lose one's sense of self and yet merge temporarily with another person. The process of empathy is *central* to human relationships, yet it has been little understood. It is the discernment of the subtle, but crucial, interplay between people—between self and other.

Women are the carriers of the human experience of empathic relatedness, and of fostering growth and development of other people. Robert Bly says that because a man is passive, his wife ends up doing all his feeling for him. She is angry because of his passivity and while he can't express his anger, she can. He may even let her do his loving for him. Men are typically very actively involved in courting, but after several months, these rituals too become passive with nothing substantial to take its place.

Maggie Scarf says in *Intimate Partners*[4] that the woman desires intimacy and the man avoids or resists it—almost. "She pursues, but not fast enough to catch him, and he flees from intimacy but not quite far enough to break contact." She takes over the active role of pursuing, wanting more intimacy and closeness while he resists. She often does his loving and parenting as well. It is she who keeps in contact with the extended or even immediate family, plans the holidays, makes the phone calls, and remembers the birthdays.

Even in the recent past women have been blamed and then blamed themselves for putting the needs of others ahead of their own needs. Many women today are managing to do both and are creating a new morphogenetic field that enables other women to also go beyond this guilt. In psychological terms, these women recognize the necessity of going all the way to self-actualization. They recognize that to stop half way and continue to remain feeling guilty would be a disservice, not only to themselves, but also to others. An impetus toward health appears to step in and take over. Guilt is often the last thing to go, and when it does, the woman feels completely free. She then tells others that they don't have to feel guilty.

Morality, as we have traditionally understood it, includes the sense of the I in an abstract, not really personal way. We have learned from Gilligan, however, that true morality includes the "I that has had the experience.[5] In other words, we have to be able to identify and empathize with the other person before we can begin to really internalize the morality of the issue. This is the same line of reasoning used by Michael Moore in *Stupid White Men*,[6] in his "Prayer to Afflict the Comfortable." Moore prays that the bishops of the Catholic Church be smitten with ovaries and unwanted pregnancies. How else will they know what it's like? Woman's sense of self is included in an integral way in mentoring. She understands that the I that is her sense of self is also in an I–Thou relationship.

Women need to be given permission to mentor. They are the canaries in the mine, aware of the problems long before the men ever have a clue. Today, it appears that women have three options.

1. She can live without men. Divorce them, separate from them, or choose never to marry them. This option seems at least to allow women to be themselves.
2. She can live with men and keep quiet and adjust. Until recently this was her only option. It is surprising how many women reveal that for one reason or another, they always felt that they couldn't be themselves if they were in a relationship.
3. She can live with men and, at the same time, be herself. It is this third option that women seem to want but, for many, it appears to be the impossible dream. Why? Because to live with a man and still be herself, most women know that some changes would have to be made. And while it is true that she would be more than willing to make changes for him—the sticking point is whether or not he would be willing to make changes for her. The other reason often given is that he feels that he has to control her. Thus chances are, the only way she can live with him and still be herself is to mentor.

The Mentoring Process from a Male Perspective

If you are waiting for him to change on his own, chances are slim to none that it will ever happen. The acculturation of men away from their feelings has caused them to lose some of the energy in their psyches. Not being able to access feelings, which are one half of one's human birthright is almost like a loss of soul. Typically, the well-defended areas, like fortresses in his psyche, that say, "Stop!" "Don't go here," start to appear when she starts to probe. According to Jung, these areas are thresholds against the fearful embrace of the unconscious. On a more conscious level, it is protection against a level of intimacy that he fears. The female can act as a mediator. She knows to be careful and move carefully around his fortifications, for she understands that this is his stronghold. She doesn't need training in counseling to help her do this right. She is able to read the situation far more clearly than men or most professionals in psychology want to believe. Male relational dread feels like a defense against chaos. It is actually a defense against the powerful forces of the unconscious because his feelings have been relegated to this realm. These feelings have been there waiting and have been built on and fortified in his psyche for most of his life and in the collective male psyche for centuries.

It is hard to try to change on his own. He has been raised not to share himself or be truly open to counsel from others. He may feel that he is between a rock and a hard place—not wanting to go there with her, and at the same time, aware that his tension and frustration are increasing. The men who are closest to this understanding are aware that this tension lies within themselves—unlike men who do not get it and think that if he can only find a different partner, all of this will go away. The good men sense, on some deep level, that they will be more alive if they listen to and follow her. This is the man who realizes that his frustration can no longer find a conscious outlet and this can only happen in a man who is at least somewhat open to his own psychic process. He may long for integration. It is his longing for wholeness that literally beckons to him as he senses that a part of him is unfinished. Her words knock on the long-closed door of his deepest psyche, which has for so long remained unpenetrated.

There really is a very simple answer to his role in the process. Having witnessed countless men go through this process, the bottom line is actually very clear. If he wants to make it easier on himself, his first and best move is to lay down his relational dread and listen to her. To do this he really has to trust her—but shouldn't he trust her anyway? Rather than trying to control her by escalating the fight, ignoring her, or leaving, his wisest option is to listen to what she is saying, to what she has been saying all long. This option could literally save him years of misery. In the past his easiest option was to just move on to the next woman. As more and more women catch on, however, this option is quickly dwindling.

Of course, most men won't do this. They will go to any length to avoid going to the place where they have to really look at themselves. He will cling to what he thinks his maleness requires until he can't do it anymore. At this point, the couple will typically split up. He will think he's free and he will find someone else. If he finds another partner who is whole, however, the issue will invariably come up again. It really is that simple.

The Mentoring Process from Her Perspective

She has to know who she is after she has unlearned so much and relearned to embrace her authentic feminine. She has to be open to trust the process that will unfold for her. She is lovingly attempting to bring about the divine inner marriage in the male—to introduce him to the authentic part of himself that is feminine. In many ways, the process is similar to the experience of enlightenment.

While it has been suggested that some males may be incapable of understanding the higher spiritual concepts, the mentoring process "assumes" that he is indeed capable of becoming whole.

She has to be willing to go with her process once it has begun—a process that unfolds for both of them and is the sum total of her life as well as his. For this reason, it is hard to be more specific or to spell it out in easy steps. While she has to know in her gut that she will be able to go on without him, she is, at the same time, inviting him to go with her into an exciting new life.

Women often say that having tried and tried, they finally reach a point where they have no more energy to put into the relationship. The irony is that often this very point—when she is finally ready to leave, or does actually leave—is when *he* finally gets it. Many women are shocked to realize that he didn't take her seriously until she actually and literally left. Connie confided to me at one point, "Bruce and I had not been getting along for months. I kept telling him we had to talk and he wouldn't do it. And, of course, he wouldn't go to counseling. So I tried and tried to talk to him myself. He just wouldn't hear me. I got to where I would tell him to repeat back to me what I just said, and often he just hadn't heard anything. Finally, the kids and I went to stay with my mom for a while. I wasn't sure in my mind that I was actually leaving. I just felt I didn't have any other option, and just felt I had to get away. The next day he called me and told me he would do anything if I would come back. He was devastated. I could not believe that I literally had to leave for him to get it."

I told her that I had seen that happen so many times. "You know," she said, "when I went back, I didn't say anything to him that I hadn't already said. But, when I went back—and believe me, I did not go right back—then, for some reason, he was open to hear me."

"Did you talk to him at all while you were gone?" I asked. "Yes," she said, "but often we would meet someplace private where we could talk, or just drive somewhere. Often he would cry, so I would always take tissues." "Did you cry, too?" I queried. "You know, the funny thing was that I didn't. I seemed to go to a different place—like a problem solving place. A part of me knew that I had to be firm. I just kind of observed him. I was kind and loving and gentle, but a part of me knew that he had to 'get it' or it would just go back to the way it always had been. So I was always looking for signs that he really understood what I was talking about."

"How did you know he was getting it?" I asked. I was fascinated to see that there was almost a universal pattern to this process. "Hmm," she said. "It's hard to say specifically. I just started sensing that he got it. The defensive tone dropped out of his voice. When he asked me what I wanted, I started to be able to be really honest. He started asking me what he could do, instead of waiting for me to tell him—and then he would do it. It had nothing to do with flowers and candy—that's for sure. I didn't want any of that stuff. I knew that would just make it way too easy, especially for him, if he thought flowers would fix it. I wanted realness and talk and change. It took months of two steps forward, one step back, but I could tell he valued me and the kids in a different way."

"Did you think of it sort of like steps forward—like if he is at C and I want D, then he will have to show me D?" I asked, laughing. She cracked up at the analogy. "That is exactly how I thought of it! And, a lot of times I felt so guilty about that. But I just knew I had to keep asking for what I needed. I trusted how I felt and I somehow knew, like in my heart, that I wouldn't hurt him."

"What about the waiting?" I asked.

"Oh, my God, I had no idea I could be so patient," she said, laughing at how similar our experiences had been. "I would watch the clock sometimes just to have something to do. Oh, but, I also discovered a good thing to do. One time, he had broken his key chain, so I bought him a new one and gave it to him when we were meeting to talk. I could tell he liked having something to touch or play with. He put his keys on the new key chain, in different orders about five times, I swear. So, I would bring little things for him to do with his hands, things that weren't too distracting, like fixing one of the kids toys. It reminded me of William Pollack's suggestion to give boys something to play with when you are trying to talk to them," she laughed.

Women learn so much about patience, and love when they enter this process. Mentoring is actually embodied spirituality. A woman who chooses to do this with a partner will learn so much about herself as a person and as a soul, that whether or not she chooses to go on with or without him, she will have learned the deepest and most essential lessons of wholeness and spirituality.

Many women learn about the deepest love when they have a child. They learn to be self-less, patient, forgiving, and compassionate. Mentoring is similar to this process. It requires the same patience and compassion, but in even deeper ways. It calls on her to discover for herself the essence of mature love. *And, even if it doesn't work out, she has learned a wisdom that she could not have found anywhere else. Further, she can leave knowing that she has done everything possible.* Learning the process of mentoring will put a woman in a new place with herself and her relation to the Feminine Principle. It is the deep and spiritual sense of knowing you are whole. It is like feeling that you have finally stepped into your rightful place—that you are woman—that you are the center of life and everything else is peripheral.

Chapter 16

The New Hero

Yang
Waking up
Following the call
Dropping the dread
Returning home as a real hero

Countless women have completed their heroine's journey. Having everything to gain, they heard the call and responded. In addition to embracing the feeling and caring realms allowed to their sex, they mastered the cognitive and abstract realms and have taken their places to stand shoulder to shoulder on equal footing with men in the male world. In doing so, they have become the whole-brained sex. They learned from their ordeals and became stronger. They are at a newly defined home, waiting for the men to begin their journeys.

The Hero's Journey

If you are one of the good men who have followed a similar path, you should know that you are appreciated. You *are* the new hero. You are also the new role model for other males. Without knowing your story, it can be assumed that you, too, heard the call that there could be more to life—a better way to be in relationship than trying to control your partner. Obviously, you recognized that your ordeals were your greatest teachers. You too will benefit from a more balanced world.

There are many ways to explain the story of how we got here—at this place and time as a species. Why has the world been cast in masculine terms? How did the imbalance arise? Was it done consciously? Why has the history of humanity always been viewed as history and not her-story?

Women have the right to explain this story to themselves in a way that recognizes that, since the beginning, men have resented that she brings forth new life and consciously created a world that denigrated her in every way in an attempt to control her. This story has more than a ring of truth to it. But this story, true as it may be, provides few options for men to truly move forward in any positive way.

Richard Tarnas, therefore,[1] offers one of the kindest and most positive ways to make sense of our history in a way that while still true, provides a less angry context. "The man of the western tradition has been a questing masculine hero," he states, "who constantly seeks freedom and progress for himself. The evolution of the Western mind has been driven by a heroic impulse to forge an autonomous rational human self by separating it from the primordial unity with nature. The fundamental religious, scientific and philosophic perspectives of Western culture have all been affected by this decisive masculinity. All of these have served the cause of evolving the autonomous human will and intellect, the independent individual ego, the human being in its uniqueness, separateness and freedom."

But to do this, the masculine mind has repressed the feminine. The evolution of the Western mind has been founded on the repression of the feminine—on the repression of nature and the natural, of the repression of a unitary consciousness and any recognition of the soul of the world. It has been founded on the denial of imagination, emotions, instincts, body, nature, and woman. This separation calls forth a longing for a reunion with that which has been lost—especially as this masculine quest approaches its utmost one-sided extremes.

According to Tarnas, a great shift is taking place in the contemporary psyche. This shift represents a reconciliation or sacred marriage between the two great polarities.

The deepest passion of the Western mind has been to reunite with the ground of its being. We hunger for wholeness and balance. And this union of opposites can now occur on a new and different level. To achieve this reintegration of the repressed feminine, the masculine must undergo a sacrifice—an ego death. The Western, left-brained mind must be willing to open itself to a new reality that will include a new belief structure. This is where the real heroism is going to be. The average man would much prefer to go to war, get revenge, or even the score, for this is what the old hero did. The new hero is now required to listen, learn, and change. These skills will be new to him—and far more difficult. On the more personal level, he will initially respond in his old way of getting angry, making it her fault and doing whatever is necessary to stop her questions. He will try to maintain his comfort zone and has had, until now, nothing but support for these reactions. Everything until now has confirmed that this is what the hero does. Even the good males, who support and protect women, may still have no real idea how to be relational.

But a new, far more difficult heroism is now required. It calls men to leave the comfort of keeping the whole emotional realm external to himself. It calls for a new plausibility structure, a new way to look at himself, his partner, and his relation to the world. The new heroism might be the hardest thing that a man ever has to do.

As Tarnas suggests, this is not only true for individual males, there is now evolutionary demand for the masculine to overcome the one-sidedness that has led to its unconscious shadow. The masculine is now called on to enter into a fundamentally new relationship of mutuality with the feminine in all its forms. In the male mind, the feminine needs to be viewed as the source, the goal, and a real presence, not an objectified other.

According to Tarnas, it was necessary to repress the feminine to develop our thinking minds and rationality. We needed to move away from nature and ambiguity as we attempted to understand the world we live in. Shlain,[2] too, believes that we needed, at one time, to subdue nature in order to differentiate ourselves from it. Women, who have always been more closely related to nature, were the ones that were subdued. The masculine, however, has served its purpose and now a new journey awaits.

In truth, the hero's journey has never been about the gold and riches that one acquires as a result of the quest. While it may have been a good template for earlier, more-outer directed males, the call of every human being is an inner call. The riches refer to the real treasure that has always been internal—that of becoming more conscious internally. The treasure is discovering the riches of oneself. In *The Wizard of Oz*, Dorothy gets more than a brain, or courage, or a heart for her friends; she gets the wisdom of understanding how important these qualities are. The hero or heroine gains the opportunity to become more authentic.

Most men, when pressured, however, do indeed want to change. It is a human need to hunger for that which will make us whole. Not surprisingly, men have no idea how to begin.

Just as women's journey should have been recognized and valued for what it was, the male process, too, should be elevated and viewed as heroic. Males who are willing to set aside their need to control and open themselves to what women are saying should become the true male role models of today. In a very real sense, the woman's heroine's journey is often the very thing that precipitates the man's hero's journey. It is her invitation to him to grow as she has grown—so that they can continue to grow together. By confronting something larger out there, they are forced to confront something larger within, in order to complete the quest.

The transpersonal view of men and women today is the most positive and nonjudgmental perspective that exists. It recognizes that one sex has a problem and suggests a very viable solution, based not on anger or judgement, but an acknowledged need. A more internal orientation is essential to sensing that life has meaning.

Now is the time for the true male heroes to take this journey. This journey will lead, not to the feminization of men, as Bly has suggested, but to a more authentic humanness—first for him, and ultimately for both sexes. Currently, nature and nurture are so tightly intertwined for men that it is far more difficult to determine what uniquely male qualities will remain. Only the hero's journey can transform the big impossible into the possible.

Unlearning cultural roles is particularly frightening for men, yet experts agree that men can learn to become more comfortable with their feelings. Who better to help men on this journey than the women who love them? The happiest men are those who admire and love strong women. They are strong enough in themselves not to feel threatened, and for many men, their wives are their touchstones and guides.[3]

According to male experts, men need to learn that sex and love, or external stimulation and internal soul, are supposed to go together.[4] Instead of just joining bodies, men need to learn that true relationship is joining souls. Women, on the other hand, simply need to embrace the eternal essence of who they are. Men are more involved in "doing" values. Men are always going somewhere or wanting to be somewhere else, women understand being there. More men need to learn what women know.

The heroic act is not just the act of learning a new perspective, it is also the process of the hero becoming truer to himself, so that the whole society may become truer to itself.

The system, of which the hero is a part, becomes wiser, for personal human consciousness is the organ of self-knowledge for the whole system. Truth can no longer be separated from culture and history. Truth cannot be separated from moral considerations and its applications. It cannot be kept apart from the process of growth and self-transformation of the knower.

Hearing the Call

Pleasantville is gone and it's not coming back. The women have moved onto a new place where they are finally beginning to figure things out. They know that most men don't get it, and are asleep emotionally. They know that men have been taught not to share themselves or be relational and that they have been left out of the realm of real feelings. Experts today suggest that women should not back off, but rather continue to engage men. While this is a most threatening option for men, there seems to be no other way. We have discovered that men have a desperate need for intimacy as well as a desire to connect with something larger than themselves—just as women do.

In his book *Confessions of a Closed Male,* Kenneth Chance[5] says an extramarital affair turned his world upside down. He discovers that there are no quick fixes and realizes that he must work through the wreckage of his life that he has created at home and work. He is shown the cost of living in the illusion of the male myth, and discovers that males are closed to their feelings and are unable to share themselves intimately with the ones they love most. Like so many men, he literally had to bottom out to discover spiritual principles that enabled him to transform his life.

A very old and well-known myth seems to have anticipated this current male dilemma. The Fisher King is the most powerful person in his kingdom. He suffers, however, from "a wound that will not heal." His country lies in waste. Everyone in the kingdom is suffering. The King cannot heal because everyone has always told him only what he wanted to hear. No one in the kingdom wants to disrupt the way things are and they just go along with the way things always have been. No one wants to ask the very question that the King needs to hear—"What ails thee?" Women, however, have always asked men this question. They have forever asked, "What ails thee? What's wrong?" "How do you feel?" They ask because they sense that something is indeed wrong.[6]

Now, real men need to ask themselves "What ails me?" They need to hear themselves say the words out loud, so that they, too, can acknowledge that things are not alright. The King needs to develop the self-awareness to see for himself that he has knowledge, but no feeling.

It is interesting that he is suffering from a wound in the groin. Perhaps men feel that that is the area of the body most closely associated with the feminine. Someone once said that a man is softest when he is hard, so the location of the wound is not surprising. He cannot heal himself and his relationship to the feminine unless he begins to understand that women can offer so much more than just sex. Integrating knowledge with feelings creates clarity and wholeness.

Cut off from the feminine, nothing can grow. Having carried rationality, technology, and a need to control so far, we find that we can no longer proceed further without the corrective balance of the feminine. Many believe that this imbalance has gone far further than most of us are aware. Numerous documentaries suggest that the banks, large corporations and the energy industry, are merged and owned by a handful of the wealthiest families in the world, and are attempting to control everything necessary for life—seeds for food production, water and energy to name just a few.

These efforts, placing control in the hands of a very few, are the perfect example of the results of this imbalance. The solutions are, and must be, more feminine-based.

Similarly, our relationships have reached a point of barrenness and we find we cannot proceed. The masculinized ego must die, and men must leave their defensiveness. Both men and women must now recognize that the male wound will not heal without the feminine.

According to Tarnas, the Western mind has reached a conceptual turning point. The real new millennium is both internal and spiritual. Individual men and women are part of a larger masculine and feminine collective consciousness, which is, in turn, part of a collective human consciousness. It is time to move beyond outmoded gender roles, anger, dread, and victimization. The realization that the masculine must now undergo an ego death is not male-bashing, but rather a necessity, as the collective mind moves toward self-consciousness.

The crisis of modern man is an essentially masculine one. It is time for the masculine to overcome its own unconscious shadow—the feminine, the Yin qualities that have for so long been considered other. The masculine is now called on to enter into a fundamentally new relationship of mutuality with the feminine in all its forms. Keen[7] says that there is a shadow over men's psyches. The feminine, that has for so long been the shadow in the Western mind, must now be fully recognized and responded to for itself.

The women today, who still both know and do not know, are finally released from all blame. They have heard the call, embarked on the journey and under great odds, completed it magnificently.

Individual women are blazing the trail for the feminine principle, which, for many, still exists in the collective psyche as shadow. The collective conscious has not yet completed its journey, and is only now hearing the call. Collectively, we are still far from accepting this archetypal feminine principle comfortably and readily attribute negative qualities to it. Not until we have accepted the feminine as equally as the masculine, for a hundred years, or as long as it takes, will we ever be able to truly see the feminine principle in its truest essence. Further, as Andrew Harvey[8] suggests, only then will we be able to see the authentic nature of the masculine principle, for they are forever in relation to each other.

The confusion and conflict that is everywhere with the sexes reflect the fact that this evolutionary drama is now reaching its climactic stages. When the Copernican Revolution took place, we collectively took a giant leap in understanding that our tiny earth was not the center of the universe, but rather one small planet in a cosmic sea of countless planets and universes. At that time, there was far less ability to look back to where we had been collectively, so we could better see where we were going. Few people then could understand that the current changes were part of a larger emerging pattern.

Today, in a postmodern world that has deconstructed old truths, we have the necessary self-consciousness and self-reflection to act with more clarity. Women and men can literally see the new changes that are being ushered in.

Women have completed their journeys and returned Home wanting more. It is now time for men to respond to the Call. It is now he who needs to be convinced that he will gain self-awareness.

Einstein said that no problem can be solved with the same consciousness that created it. We can no longer adopt the same stance as the church during Copernicus's time, flatly refusing to accept new scientific findings. We have to help people change their consciousness. We have to recognize the need to integrate the masculine and the feminine. As Hoffman states, "There is no substitute for wholeness. None."[9]

One of the biggest problems women have is recognizing that the problem males have with the relational mode is universal. The relational lie has worked so well that few women recognize the universality of the male problem.

I remember my friend talking about her ex-husband. He had become defensive and insecure after they married. She knew his parents, and although she liked them, was convinced that when he was younger something terrible had happened to make him so defensive. Her heart literally broke to see him in so much pain and when they finally divorced, she remained convinced that his problem was unique to him. Years later, she started dating a man who taught at the same college. While they were dating, she kept assuring me, and herself, that if she got married again, she would know exactly what to look for. "I have already done this twice. I am intelligent. I know what I am looking for and I am never again going to settle for someone who can't share his feelings. I refuse to put up with another defensive man. Brent (the new man in her life) is finally someone I can really talk to. He knows how to share his feelings. I have checked him out from every possible angle."

After six months of examining him under a microscope of scrutiny, assuring herself that she had found one of the few relational men in the world, she married him.

Three months later as we talked over lunch, she said, "Kill me now. Just kill me. I swear to God he changed into every other man while we were still on our honeymoon. I just feel like banging my head against the wall. How could I not see it?" she asked herself aloud "You know, you told me that the problem was universal and I swear I just couldn't process it. I could not hear what you were saying."

This shadow is men's predisposition to feel a strong sense of guilt and insecurity in the presence of women and to resort to silence or violence when dealing with their inability to do anything about it. In repressing the feminine, we have not just repressed women, but half of all the potential human qualities. Men, of course, as human beings, also have access to all these qualities. The problem is that because these qualities have been deemed feminine, many men have never developed a real comfort level or openness to them.

We have carried male wisdom to its extreme. In the old paradigm, we believed that true objectivity existed. Because we thought that we could be truly objective, it colored our ways of looking at the world. Wilber refers to this old way of viewing the world as the monological gaze, which, for a while, allows us to feel that we are separate from the thing we are studying.[10] And, in looking at the thing objectively, we believe that we were capable of knowing it as it is. For example, we can open a person's head surgically and look directly at their brain. We can observe it and describe it, as part of the scientific method. We cannot, however, know what or why that brain thinks the way it does. Further, we realize that we can never know a person's *mind* unless we talk to them. Even then, we can't just talk *to* them. Both people must talk, and not only talk, but engage in two-way dialogue to understand each other.

Women have always sensed that they can only understand the other person through true dialogue. This is the reason women want to talk to men and want men to talk to them. Women know that the only way she will understand him is if they talk to each other. And the dialogue cannot just be talk. It must be talk that continues until it leads to understanding.

This talk, revealing one's real self, is the intimacy, according to McGill,[11] that is feared, because it requires self-disclosure. The irony is that without self-disclosure, which leads to self-awareness, a person can never really be sure that his own feelings, emotions, and priorities are accurate. In other words, no man can ever truly be powerful unless he knows himself. Intimacy also leads to a greater sense of connectedness, better mental and physical health, more effective action in the world and less sense of alienation and meaninglessness. Despite the many benefits of self-disclosure and self-awareness, McGill feels that most men will not change their ways. Men still feel that they have more power and control by withholding themselves. Men will only change if they see self-disclosure as empowering, and currently, because of the culture, it is still perceived as emasculating. The concept of power, therefore, must come to be viewed by men not as power over others, but rather as self-power. No wonder women are so confused by men. Most women cannot imagine having the opportunity to know themselves better and not taking it. They seem to actually like learning more about themselves. They seem to love thinking about insights gained in counseling or in talking with friends. It appears then that unlike men most women strive for greater self-awareness.

According to McGill, however, "I can't change" is an excuse. Self-disclosure is possible if men want to do it. McGill recounts numerous examples of men who have made major changes in their lifestyles, health practices, and religious beliefs. Men can indeed overcome the socialization that taught them the masculinized ego and change when they feel it is to their benefit.

McGill concludes that the common excuses men use to defend their lack of self-disclosure are groundless. He says the bottom line is that men are avoiding responsibility for their own behavior. When men were confronted with the need to take responsibility for their lack of intimacy, they agreed that they could be more intimate if they wanted to. With a sense of vague, unexplained reluctance, many said they just didn't want to. Responses such as, "I'm not really sure why I don't want to change," and, "I could if I wanted to. I'm just not ready," reveal a passive aggression that women have heard a million times. The real question, says McGill, is not "Why aren't men more loving?" but rather "Why don't men *want to become* more loving?"

Because the process is difficult, men must summon their courage to be truly heroic and drop their defensiveness around real talk. If he feels the dread or discomfort rising, he has to learn to rise above it. He has to put his need to be in control to the side and really listen to what she is asking. He has to learn to stop trying to make it her fault and stay open to her words and queries. The strength and courage that it takes to move from an angry, defensive place of "What do you want from me?" to a calm and open stance of "What do you want from me" is the new heroism of today's male. Moving into this new space allows males to realize that the feminine principle resides in them as well as women. In despising the feminine, men have hurt themselves far more than they realize. They have cut themselves off from half of their human qualities.

The new hero will not be involved in fighting battles with anyone or anything out there. If there is a battle, it will be with himself. Because it is with himself, it often begins first, with a descent into the darkness and chaos as he recognizes that he has failed to include his true self into what he knows. The journey always involves a descent before we can eventually integrate the higher levels of understanding.

Men often see this journey as having only two choices—denial or despair. Most men will choose to deny that there is anything wrong. The despair involves both dread and defensiveness. It is little wonder then that men are so fearful of taking this journey.

But the ordeal, the dark night of the soul, always contains within it the seeds for healing. Men have to be willing to feel and experience emotions, which at first may be overwhelming. This, however, is the beginning of emotional intelligence—the beginning of linking thinking to feeling. Men may cry for the first time, and of course, feel only embarrassment. They need, however, to recognize that experiencing emotions, other than anger, for the first time does not mean that they are going to remain emotional wrecks for the rest of their lives. They need to realize that this is only the first step in learning how to handle their emotions. Of course, it will all be very new and overwhelming to them but it is a necessary precondition for the hero. He is now in the perfect place to realize that everything that has happened to bring him to this point was necessary. In the dark night, the hero faces his limitations and asks necessary questions about his existence. He now faces the big impossible, for this question can never be answered in the absence of the feminine. Who is he really? Freud was famous for his question, "What do women really want?" The real question today is what do men really want?

Every journey has an ordeal—the bad thing that allows us to learn our greatest lessons. The hero can be transformed through the ordeal. The ordeal questions what he has believed. Like Dave, when he broke down while trying to install a vanity, he faces his limitations and learns to ask fundamental questions about his existence.

The resolution of returning home is not just the perfecting of his existing mental structure, but rather a surrender to something that is larger than his old self has previously believed. It is this surrender that enables the formation of new structures. Without a profound repentance that implies a profound change in self, the masculinized hero cannot complete his journey.

The same steps inherent in the journey can be applied to all institutions and belief systems that are based on limited, one-sided thinking. It applies to the scientific mind, the academic mind, and the hierarchical mind. In order to return home, we have to engage with what has been excluded.

The great challenge of our time is an evolutionary demand for the masculine to overcome its hubris and one-sidedness, to own its unconscious shadow and to enter into a fundamentally new relationship of mutuality with the feminine in all its forms.

The male shadow at its most active may very well be the malignant ego-phrenia, a psychological disease that has recently been referred to as the "bubble." Egophrenia results when the person creates a mental feedback loop that is closed to any input from the rest of the world around it. It sees only what it wants to see and is not open to alternative positions. Its main objective is to control.[12] The Catholic Church, for example, that refused to acknowledge countless reports of sexual abuse or the corporate leader who knowingly pollutes the earth just to make money or the husband who tries to control everything his partner does because he is the man, are all closed bubbles that consider nothing beyond their own self-interests. Levy suggests that egophrenia is like a collective psychosis that is the root of many of our current world crises. While it is typically men with masculinized egos who have egophrenia, women and good men who accept these power-driven values may also fall victim. This perception creates belief systems that make us all fearful. This unacknowledged and unowned male shadow, in ancient times, was called a "demon" that projected the evil out there to ensure it was never recognized within oneself. The shadow then ignores the role it plays in creating the demon. It makes all of us crazy. Even the mental health system doesn't recognize it, says Levy, because it is infected with it too, in that it continues to view the mental disease as residing inside the individual without considering the impact of the sick world on that individual. It creates a collective psychosis and is the root of the current world crisis.

Nothing in nature takes more than it needs. Only cancer takes more. Indigenous tribes understood that the accumulation of wealth beyond your needs was mental illness. Those who have studied this problem recommend nonviolent solutions. The first thing we can do is identify and define this as mental illness. With this recognition, the rest of us can refuse to participate. The real solution is the balance of the feminine. Men need to know that they can indeed change. Tilin,[13] who recognizes that men's brains have a high capacity to process emotions like fear and aggression, also believes, however, that time and training can take men past such competitive urges.

The Anima—The Feminine Aspect of a Male

Jung called the feminine aspect of a man's psyche the "anima" because it animates and gives life to his world. Despite the fact that his understanding of the feminine may not have readily applied to real women, Jung's work is the closest we can come today in providing a solution for men.

The feminine is the source of his creativity, his inspiration, his muse. It is the man's soul and the mistress of his inner world. The anima represents the mysterious and the depths of our nature, and is the carrier of meaning. Man's relationship to his own inner feminine has historically been regulated by strong customs and laws. For this reason, few men are aware of how important the feminine is to them—internally or externally.

According to Robert Johnson in *Understanding Masculine Psychology,*[14] a man's sense of value, joy, belongingness, and even happiness derive from his relationship to the feminine. For this reason, these qualities are often elusive and mysterious to him. While a man needs to be in touch with his masculine qualities to feel like a man, he also needs to feel connected to his feminine side to have a real sense of meaning about life.

Much of the definition of masculinity has been associated with rationality and detachment, which can easily serve to separate him from his true feelings. Women, of course, sense this detachment and are always trying to bring the realm of feeling to men.

Marie-Louise Von Franz, in *Alchemy: An Introduction to the Symbolism and the Psychology,* sheds additional light on the extent to which the male denial of his shadow and therefore his feminine anima has impacted our knowing. "The pronounced lack of a feminine personification of the unconscious has therefore been compensated by the radical materialism which has gradually taken hold of the Christian tradition. One could say that practically no religion began with such a highly one-sided spiritual accent and has landed in such an absolutely one-sided materialistic aspect. The swing from one to the other is one of the most striking phenomena we know of in the history of religion; it is due to the fact that from the beginning there was an unawareness, an imbalanced attitude towards the problem of the feminine goddess and therefore of matter, because the feminine Godhead in all religions is always projected into and linked up with the concept of matter." Because we live in a world created by males that is filled with their erroneous projections we are all forced to live in a "dangerous world estranged from its natural instinctive roots."[15]

Few males truly understand the female. Stephen Hawking, who wrote *A Brief History of Time,*[16] and who is one of the most brilliant men alive today, believes after a lifetime of study that he now understands the very nature of the universe. There is, however, one thing that he has yet to comprehend—he doesn't understand women. "They are a complete mystery," he says.

Johann Wolfgang Von Goethe, in his masterpiece *Faust,* ends the great drama with the words, "The Eternal Feminine leads us on."[17] According to Johnson, the feminine is that which colors a man's life. Without a clear connection to the feminine, a man feels somehow bankrupt. In many ways, because the feminine is life, he is without life. He will lack discrimination, and for this reason, may unintentionally wound the females—his mother, wife, or daughter—in his life.

Every male has a mother. Although there is a real mother, there is also an archetypal mother. In many of the old myths, the dragon that the hero was required to slay was in reality, his own mother. He had to develop a correct relationship with her before he could ever have a clear relationship with the fair maiden who would become his wife. His mother literally gave him life, fed, and cared for him. His continuing quest, however, is with the archetype, or concept, of the inner mother—the feminine. His inner battle with the feminine is really a struggle in himself to become clear with his own wholeness. At one point in his gestational development, he was not yet a male. "Every man," says Johnson, "wears a scar on the underside of his penis that is a reminder of the time when he was not yet a male." According to Johnson, there are many aspects of a man's relationship to his own feminine.

The mother archetype is, in part, the realm of Mother Nature—the whole physical universe without which we could not live. The job of the male is to transform the mother complex into the mother archetype. In doing so, the man discovers the Grail, which is consciousness. Jung cautions that the journey must be genuine. This is why religions, philosophies, and psychologies that have denied one half of human qualities in an attempt to maintain control have never quite worked, and always remained a little skewed, a little off center, never quite hitting the mark of authenticity.

On a psychological level, the unconscious and conscious are brought together. Often, this is described as a job for a therapist, who literally takes on the suffering of the patient by offering suggestion, advice, sympathy, and encouragement. It is a natural and instinctive process. Women, however, with their highly refined emotional skills are particularly well suited to help their partners with this process. The true hero faces this shadow, and only in doing so can he truly heal. As long as he thinks it is someone else's fault, he will never truly be free. Jung states that once he realizes that the enemy is his own heart, the conflict can begin to resolve.[18]

The feminine represents the experience of wholeness and true spirituality. It is no wonder then, given the historical fear and hatred of women, that our male-based religions are so one-sided, elitist, and dogmatic. Men keep adding more rules to their belief systems in hopes that the totality will add up to something significant. However, it is just more of the same rational, divisive dogma that will forever lack magic, mystery, and meaning.

No wonder males have projected their fears and hatred onto women. Without the feminine, he remains invalidated and vulnerable. In his quest to feel validated, he inadvertently scorns the very thing that will validate him. This perhaps is the greatest irony in our history. He is validated by the feminine—both his inner anima and the female(s) in his life. Without a proper orientation to the feminine, however, he will never truly understand how he feels.

All human beings have emotions. When misunderstood, these emotions become moods. "A man in a mood," says Johnson, "is a sundial in moonlight telling the wrong time."

The anima is a male's interior life and it can and should be acknowledged. If he doesn't understand it, he will project it outward onto a real female or as an attempt to control. Because he doesn't understand his own internal world, he similarly does not, and will never be able to, understand her her or the other projections in his life. Whether referred to as shadow, masculinized ego, egophrenia, or anima, the male must face, integrate, and make peace with this part of himself.

The end result in a man is that he has the experience of immortality. This immortality, of course, is not literal but rather the *experience of feeling* related to immortality. Men, once in touch with their feminine sides, can now access experiences of enlightenment—the feelings of timelessness, eternity, and immortality. This is the essence of alchemy and the process of transformation.

Jung calls this process of achieving balance "individuation"—the integration of the masculine and feminine parts of ourselves, the joining of the conscious and unconscious. Now the male can understand the experience of the mystics. Now he can go beyond the cognitive and abstract concepts to the intuitive and emotional knowing of the incomprehensible questions that arise as the result of inner unity. This inner knowing seems to resolve opposition and draws the sting from conflict.

He senses wholeness, consciousness, and higher self—terms that are used when attempting to define this state, which really has no words, but is in the truest sense *felt*. It is a state where contradictions are reconciled.

The ideas of the *hieros gamos,* or mystical union of the male and female, according to Jung, is an internal process that an individual goes through to become whole and individuated. Our world, says Jung, lacks a connection to the psyche, the soul.

It is no wonder because this connection for men is through the feminine, that it requires first facing the shadow of what has collectively been repressed. Later, as it begins to show up in dreams, images, and feelings, we must learn to connect with it and honor it. The feminine is painfully absent and this absence is felt, not only by both men and women, but the whole social order.

The imbalance creates two problems. Women have become individuated and are now aware of themselves. They have become whole-brained by immersing themselves naturally into the male-based world. Similarly, they are now aware of the imbalance, and with that awareness is a sense that something should be done. They are angry, and they recognize that living with such diffuse anger can create a heaviness within them. Further, there is a real sense that the problem is not unique to them. They have a keen recognition that this is not just a woman's problem that women should therefore fix. They know that they can't change the world alone, but they also know that there is something they can do. They know that men too must become aware of this imbalance in themselves and help change the culture at large.

Women know that men cannot heal without facing the shadow that they have created, and that men will never be whole without becoming comfortable with their own feminine aspects. They also know how hard this will be for men to do.

In purely psychological terms, women involved in mentoring are essentially asking men to enhance and expand their minds. Jung referred to the process of freeing unconscious material so that it becomes conscious as the "transcendent function." The mind, just like the body, is a self-regulating system that places information that one cannot or does not process into the unconscious. In his talk, Dave referred to this as his "plausibility structure." That which doesn't fit into a plausibility structure is put into the unconscious.

For many men, the ordeal often gets worse before it gets better. It is often described as passing through the valley of the shadow. He may feel torn between his old and newly emerging self for a while. This process, however, is the true alchemy. The old and new personalities will combine in time to produce a third transformed and integrated personality. Jung in his *Collected Works*[19] refers to work that had been done centuries earlier on alchemy. He recognized that alchemy was, at its basis, the universal quest for transformation, far more than the actual attempt to transform lead into gold. The process aims at a final unity.

Signs of synthesis can begin to show up in dreams. Dave, for example, was drawn to the analogy of the cave. He felt that he was no longer outside himself but rather a new and integrated person who now felt comfortable in his own skin. However the synthesis begins to emerge, Jung feels that the full synthesis is never really complete. The work of becoming fully individuated continues for a lifetime.

The original Jungian texts contain ancient, universal pictures and symbols. For example, the male stands on the sun and the female stands on the moon. They are holding hands. Once the male and the female have freed themselves of their shadows, they are able to stand side by side as equals. Each man and each woman is free to face the other with a full awareness of who they are. They are aware of what they can learn from the other and how they can help each other grow. This is the truest sense of the mystical union.

The new personality or self that emerges is a blend of both the animus or male energy in the female and the anima or female energy in the male. It appears many women today have already embraced their animus—and in doing so, became whole.

There is a new light that allows the new self to see the real meaning of the union. The result is the soul—which is the very essence of relationship. Its character is both personal and collective. According to Jung, the man's soul has a feminine character, and it is for this reason that he hungers so much for feminine qualities.

The new hero is now called on to become whole. He must unlearn all the false information that told him he was more perfect than his partner. In doing so, he loses his masculinized ego and becomes a more authentic human being. He is now ready to relate to his partner in a more meaningful and balanced relationship.

Chapter 17

A Balanced Future

Yin   Balance   Yang

We live in a world of pairs of opposites that together make a whole. Newtonian physics has told us that we are all separate from each other and our earth. The quantum perspective, however, now recognizes that this model of reality is not true. We are not separate from each other. Everything in the universe is connected to every other thing. Perhaps we experience the world as dualistic because this is what we have been taught, or perhaps it is just too difficult to perceive reality as it actually is. Mystics and enlightened states have always revealed that the quantum perspective is indeed true. The experience of oneness is often precious and fleeting, and even those who have been lucky enough to have an awareness of experience wholeness still live their day-to-day lives in a world that appears to be divided into opposites.

Our culture and our world is a collection of males and females, who have both similarities and differences. There are countless levels of integration—from the masculine and feminine qualities within an individual brain, to the recognition that there are two unique sexes on this earth, to an ultimate understanding of the dualistic nature of the world and life and how it can be integrated into wholeness. This is the central relationship of all systems of knowing. The Yin and Yang at every level should be recognized, honored, and integrated into the concept of the Tao, or wholeness.

Female/Yin	Male/Yang
Nonlinear	Linear
Connected	Separate
Eros (Love) Power with	Power over
Immanent	Transcendent
Process	Product
Web of relations	Hierarchy
Being	Doing
Reproductive value	Resource value
Caring	Curing

Why?	How?
Nurturing	Fixing
Invisible realm	Physical world
Flexible	Decisive
Collaboration	Competition
Mystery	Mastery
Wisdom	Knowledge
subjective	objective
Unity	Unique
Mythos	Logos
Self and others	Self-autonomous
Concern for all	Concern for self
Collective	Individual
yin	yang
big picture	narrow focus
creative/new	known/old
whole	parts
synthesis	analysis
present/future	past/present

We tend to structure our thoughts in terms of dualism. In expressing our feelings, perceptions, and sensings into words and definitions, we invariably limit our perceptions to match the limitations of language. Poetic language does indeed try to capture the higher essence of our experiences, but everyday language is too functional and too fast. The concept of the Tao, or wholeness, reflects the idea that in truth there are no complete opposites. Each always contains a part of the other. We sense the rightness of this symbol intuitively when we see it. It is the Tao that represents the All. It is a circle that is divided in half by a flowing curved line. Each has a part of the other within it. Each is complementary to the other. Each has qualities that are of equal value.

In *The Turning Point*, Capra[1] says that an objective description of nature is no longer valid. The Cartesian division between observer and observed is invalid when looking at atomic matter. We can no longer speak about nature without at the same time speaking about ourselves.

Each of us is a part of the whole called the universe. The matter that is in us is the same that is found in the stars and galaxies; the elements that comprise us were forged in the hearts of stars. This is what Carl Sagan meant when he said that we are "star stuff." And we share DNA with every living thing.

Physicist David Bohm,[2] similarly, states that things are not inherently divided, broken up, or disconnected. Yet, we continue to believe this, and carry this erroneous belief further into thinking that each part is essentially independent and self-existent. This is what leads to tribal consciousness or "us against them" thinking. If we believe the world is made up of fragments, then that is how our minds will operate. If we believe the world is interconnected, then that is how we will think. It is difficult to break free of this fragmented perception for our whole world often appears to be set up and viewed this way—starting with the fundamental distinction between creator and created.

Thinking in opposites introduces a framework in our minds; good and bad, right and wrong, true and false, friend and foe, self and other, us and them. The more complex the experience, however, the less valuable is the language to describe or understand it. The following passage from the Bible shows how difficult this is to understand. When his followers asked Jesus about entering the kingdom, he said to them: "When you make the two one, and when you make the inner as the outer, and the outer as the inner, and the above as the below, and when you make the male and female into a single one, so that the male will not be male and the female will not be female— then you shall enter the kingdom." A new poetic language has to evolve.

The feminine and the masculine are not things in themselves. They are not absolute, fixed, or predetermined, but, rather, are in a continual relationship to each other, and take their meaning from each other. This equality of value exists in nature and should be reflected in our culture. Currently, its emphasis on the masculine principle reflects a system that is out of balance and that will stay out of balance until it is addressed consciously.

Yin and Yang, in the ideal, come together to make the synthesis of the Tao—a sum that is greater than its parts. Each has its own strengths and weaknesses—different but equal. Lao-tzu spoke of the strength of the feminine, which like water could eventually wear down the strongest rock. The true balance of the Tao is based on an equal valuing of the masculine and the feminine principles—not just the feminine quality that has been so often stressed here. For this reason, the aforementioned list of Yin and Yang qualities are presented again, but with a greater sense of cooperation with each other. For example, as accurate as the self-in-relation theory may be, it is also true that each of us is also a unique and separate self. Caring is wonderful but curing is equally important. The product is as necessary as the process. We need knowledge as much as wisdom. This book has been oriented to a heightened sense of the importance of the feminine qualities only as a corrective measure to a knowledge base that has been so imbalanced with its overvaluing of the masculine.

And finally, we are able to address a long-standing concern of feminists—the fear that if women are connected too closely to their feminine attributes, they will be stuck back in the old roles as caretakers of the culture. This concept is fear-based, victim-based, and as unnecessary as the cups that declare that women are people too. Look carefully at any list of Yin and Yang qualities in this book and you will see that it is females today who have embraced and mastered both aspects of the Tao. It is women today who both cure and care, who have both knowledge and wisdom, who are both autonomous and relational, and who are closer to wholeness. It is males not females who must catch up to the new, more balanced status quo.

The feminine will lead the way. Because we cannot go directly from imbalance to balance, we must, like a scale, overcorrect into the feminine for a period of time. It appears that this is already occurring naturally. The only thing that needs changed is the basis of our epistemology.

According to ancient astral calculations, each age, representing approximately 2,000 years, is either predominately masculine or feminine. The Aquarian Age will usher in the feminine and for the next 2,000 years, we will immerse ourselves in it, know it, and live in it as naturally as we lived in the masculine Piscean Age. The power will shift from the masculine staff of power to the spirit of the feminine. It points to a reawakening of the divine feminine. This final glyph or prediction, according to the Mayan story of creation, is viewed as the turning point of the ages. All living beings have the same Mother Energy within themselves, the same font of consciousness. She will teach us everything.

Correct balance already exists in our natural world. Light flows into day, seasons into each other. Life continues. New life enters the world. Others leave. Our hope is that we maintain this sweet, fragile balance. In many other very real ways, however we are still imbalanced. It is the lack of balance that the Fisher King, whose lands lay in waste, senses. We need only look at the earth or listen to the news to know how out of balance we still are.

We respond intuitively to this imbalance. Joanna Macy and other deep ecologists suggest that our response to the plight of the earth is so frightening that we really cannot allow ourselves to face it and look at it straight on. We can't allow ourselves to process the full magnitude of what it means. We keep doing things that create imbalance and, until recently, the earth has continually tried to restore itself to balance. This corrective measure is not inexhaustible, however. At some point, our earth will no longer be able to correct.

Prince Philip, an avid organic gardener, writes and speaks about the thing he is most passionate about—restoring the balance between nature and people. He believes that as a species, we have become dangerously out of sync with the natural world. Learned men, in the past, have declared that we have to torture Nature for her secrets. We have taken and taken from Nature, without ever thinking of giving back. In losing our connectedness with Nature, we risk losing our souls. Prince Philip suggests that we should view what we take from Nature in terms of material capital and put a dollar value on the services and commodities that Nature has provided for us. In other words, if Nature has provided a forest that we cut down to make homes or burn for fuel, we should place a price on it. How much would it cost to buy wood for a 100 homes? How much would it cost to heat these homes for a winter? Once we have the costs, then we give back to Nature the equivalent in terms of care or nurturing, fertilizer, new plantings, or any other things that will help Nature thrive.

It is not hard to see the similarities and connections between how we have treated Nature and how we treat women. Females, too, are considered a natural capital who not only bring forth new life, but also bring love, compassion, nurturance, and softness to this planet. And like Nature, we have tortured her. Prince Philip's idea is excellent, yet it cannot stand in isolation without changing how we know what we know about Nature, the feminine, and women. The male and female relationship is similar to the plight of the earth. We have managed, for far too long, to live in imbalance by creating beliefs and stories that worked, mainly for males, for thousands of years.

We Need a New and Larger Story

We have only to look at the vast regions of space and the millions of galaxies to recognize that we have outgrown our two thousand year old story and need a larger more encompassing one. We have advanced too far to still believe that each of us has the only true understanding of a separate, personal divinity that cares only for us and the others who believe as we do, who wants our side to win, wants us to be happy, and wants us to triumph over others.

Research has shown that the very nature of the story one believes changes the neurological functions of the person who hears it. People who embrace more fundamental belief systems tend to have larger areas in their brains where they perceive threat and feel the need to defend themselves. Further, people in the Western world, who are educated and industrialized, have a far more egocentric view of the world than other cultures. Westerners rely far more on analytical, left-brained thinking than others in the world, focusing more on individual rights than those of the community as a whole. We used to believe that the concept of fairness, for example, was a universally understood human trait. Cross-cultural studies, however, reveal that this is not true. Westerners tend to be more personal and egocentric in their thoughts about universal fairness. It is not surprising then that our stories of divinity are so focused on preserving oneself at the expense of others. The personalized and self-centered stories that we believe in relation to spirituality and divinity are strikingly small when compared to the vastness of stories told in other cultures. Our very stories keep reinforcing our narrow and personal worldview of the West.

We need a new cosmology and way of conceiving the enormity and complexity of the universe and our place in it. We are connected to something that is so much more than we have imagined. All religions have a basis of mysticism that point to this same greater and universal truth.

Our focus should be on the core of deep similarities, not the spokes of individual differences in this ever-more connected world.

There can be a new spiritual context for tomorrow's world. We can start restoring balance and perhaps the best way to start is within each relationship. In personal relationships, women hunger for an I–thou relationship with their partners. At the same time, the I–thou relationship—the recognition that a spark of divinity in one person recognizes and honors the spark of divinity within the other—can only benefit the world. Imagine a world where each person honors the sacredness of the other.

The end of strict dualistic thinking is the recognition that each of us is intimately connected to each other. Connection is why we are here—even on a neurological level. Where better to start than with the relationship in our house that we have the most primary connection with. From here, hopefully, it will flow out into the world.

True and authentic spirituality is embodied in the mentoring process. She does this from love. He listens and learns because of love. This is not some kind of magical faith-based belief; it is the true embodiment of love. It is present, real, and embodied in the here and now. It shows in our faces and in how we live.

A new and enlightened story will bring together science and spirit, Asian mysticism and Western enlightenment, evolutionary theory and developmental psychology.

Teilhard De Chardin,[3] a Christian mystic, suggests that a new understanding of enlightenment that is practical, pragmatic, and relates to the here and now is needed to counter the old idea that heaven is somewhere else. It is here, and it is now. It is embodied—just as spirituality is in women. Regardless of their sex or spiritual tradition, all mystics have had a sense of going beyond duality. They intuitively sensed the balance of the quality of the other that was needed within themselves. Female mystics, for example, experienced themselves as hard rocks and strength. Male mystics have imagined themselves as soft breasts. There are images of both Jesus and Buddha with breasts that can nurture the world. Buddhism also has feminine influences and, interestingly, the more patriarchal the society, the more Buddha is portrayed as looking like a woman. Kwan Yin, the goddess of compassion in many Eastern myths, is often presented as both sexes. She begins as a god and transforms into a woman.

Thirteenth-century mystic Jnaneshwar says, "Without the God, There is no Goddess, And, without the Goddess, There is no God." This insight enables us to conceive of this progression and intuitively sense the need for balance.

Rabbi David Cooper[4] states that the idea of divinity in the Kaballah is beyond attributes and certainly beyond gender. The real concept of the divine is intended to be beyond the sum of all the names. The word "God" represents a paradoxical oneness that defies all relationship to the duality of time and space. Not surprisingly, the word itself is interpreted in a myriad of ways. Some conceive of God as a just and punishing male essence, while others imagine a more loving essence. Frank Lloyd Wright said, "I believe in God, I just spell it NATURE."[5] Our epistemology matters so much in how we perceive the world and ourselves. A gendered divinity has made the concepts of wholeness, divinity, and balance difficult for both men and women to understand. It has been especially hard for women to have been separated from a divinity that was not like them. As Cooper explains, the relationship of an individual with the concept of divinity is so personal that "in every aspect, creation and creator define each other without the possibility of dual existence. Attempting to separate creator and creation is like attempting to divide a circle into semicircles by drawing a line through the middle. As soon as we draw the line, the existence of one defines the other. They seem like two sides, but really are interdependent. We cannot draw only a yin circle without a yang, for neither can exist without the other."

Everything is evolving and in process. Evolution, say scientists, brings innovation—new ideas that could not have been predicted before. Change is the hallmark for the origin, development, and maintenance of all things in the universe.

Today, we have a much larger and more accurate lens of life. We know that history spans 14 billion years. Biologist and author Richard Dawkins states, "After sleeping through a hundred million centuries, we have finally opened our eyes on a sumptuous planet, sparkling with color—bountiful with life." We can either be enchanted or disenchanted—your degree of enchantment will depend on how you decide to be in the universe. Dawkins is neither a theist nor a believer in religion, yet he can conceive of our world in a rich and deeply spiritual way. For too long we have believed that without religion the world would be a tough cold place. Not true. Very often, we do not become truly enchanted until we leave our old ways of thinking.

Until recently, we have had very few words or concepts for our natural experiences of enlightenment. The new findings in science are so immense and powerful that even just the comprehension of the vastness of this awareness becomes an "Aha!" moment. Our minds and our knowing are literally being transformed as we liberate ourselves from the too small epistemological box we have been embedded in. We are aware, finally, that our minds play an active part in the literal construction of reality. And, further, that every step a single individual person takes helps advance the evolution of humanity as a whole.

The Masculine and the Feminine

Masculine and feminine qualities may best be understood as different modes of consciousness, or different ways of experiencing and expressing life at any one moment. They are available to any human being regardless of sex. The archetypal masculine has become associated with linear thinking, intellect, reason, and logos. The feminine has become associated with intuition, feeling, compassion, and eros. Each, however, needs the other to be whole.

Each person is connected to a larger collective consciousness.

Truly, the ideal for the future is not an overvaluing of the feminine. We have to fix that before we can even begin to understand what true balance looks like. Further, the most important thing is not even the concept of true balance, per se. The most important reason for balance is for future generations.

HOME

This is the final stage of the hero and heroine's journey. The heroine was at HOME. She heard the CALL that there could be more to life than what she was living. She responded to the call in stellar fashion, far exceeding every expectation in record time. She faced countless ORDEALS along the way. She dealt with them and learned and grew as a result. She is now returning HOME—whole and complete.

The hero is still at HOME. He hears the CALL. A few of the finest males have responded and are the true heroes of today. Most men, however, for countless reasons, stand poised at the threshold of adventure, fearful, reluctant, or angry. They want things to stay the same and have little or no idea how to proceed.

The new grand narratives and stories will begin to reflect the lens of life—of a future in balance and harmony—rather than the lens of a culture based on outmoded beliefs that are now distorted and obsolete. This synthesis leads to something fundamentally new. It brings an unexpected opening to a larger reality that cannot be grasped before it arrives, because the new reality is itself a creative act. The *hieros gamos,* the sacred marriage of the masculine and the feminine, will bring forth a third and larger new synthesis—the child, which at the same time is both real and symbolic. The divine child is every child, every person. The divine child is each of us. We should know this, and from this place of knowing look again at the messages we are sending to ourselves, our children, and the children seven generations from now.

A balanced world welcomes each child, who represents not only a welcome addition to the family, but also a living symbol of ongoing life and spiritual immortality. The offspring or child is most valued and most protected and nurtured in every species, for there is nothing of greater value. Nothing. In the new story, both parents nurture the child. Things return to their proper balance. Both adults put aside their sense of self for a greater purpose until the child matures and gains knowledge and ability.

Because the child is valued, all else flows correctly from this relationship. Life is our most precious commodity and, in our new story, we cannot imagine how we could send our children to be sacrificed for some greater abstract purpose because there is nothing greater. All else flows from life and love and happiness.

War becomes a thing of the past. We learned from those who had had experiences of enlightenment that we are all connected to every living thing. We now recognize that when we kill another, we kill ourselves. We learn that our consciousness has no bounds. We are learning more and more about why bad things happen. Some of it is due to natural causes and disasters and when those things happen, we help each other. We no longer create categories and labels for mental illness and, not surprisingly, fewer and fewer people become mentally ill.

We learn that many bad things came from incorrect or skewed information and beliefs. We do away with the too small stories that failed to unite us and served only to separate. We stop fighting with each other and demand that our story is right and theirs is wrong. We learn the importance of words on our knowing and learn to be ever so careful to tell global stories that reflect the truth of life and balance.

We begin to study inner space and we learn that our innermost selves desire to love and be loved, and to create, procreate, and cocreate with the life force of the universe.

We attempt to make this inner knowing the same as our outer knowing, to make our understanding of the below the same as the above. We embrace the lens of life and realize that spirituality is an embodied, inherent, and natural part of every human being.

And we look forward to peace for hundreds of generations.

Marion Woodman,[6] a Jungian analyst, describes perfectly the complementary relationship that exists between the qualities of the masculine and the feminine. What are these two energies in their natural relationship to each other? "Recently," she writes, "I watched the sunrise over the beautiful farm on which I was staying. At the same time, I saw the full moon riding the silver clouds in the dark sky. I heard the cock crowing, geese cackling, saw the cows and horses outlined in the darkness. 'How gentle night is!'" she thought. "How exquisitely it 'knits up the revell'd sleave of care.' Golden sunbeams were radiating on the horizon, even as the sliver moonbeams caressed the landscape. The two energies—feminine night and masculine day, complementary energies, both essential to life—were in love with each other."

Balance occurs when God and Goddess are complementary to each other—separate, but united. This is, symbolically, the divine marriage of heaven and earth, sun and moon, man and woman. There is an intellectual and soul level satisfaction with the harmony of the masculine and feminine polarities, for the union of the two creates the third and new level—the sacred marriage brings forth the divine child.

Shlain[7] sees the end of imbalance as occurring through the return of image. The return of image also harkens the return of the feminine. Interestingly, the two most indelible images of the 20th century are the cloud of the atomic bomb and the picture of our beautiful earth as seen from the moon. These two images present us with a choice. On the one hand is the masculine, the scientific, the killing invention that threatens to destroy us all. On the other hand is the feminine, Mother Earth, our home and nurturer. Those two images, side by side, tell us what we need to be afraid of and what we need to protect. No words are necessary.

Having arrived at this final point, I am left again to ponder the many levels of knowing. A part of me feels that it would be very wise to end a book with the words, "No words are necessary." Another part of me, however, recognizes that to end a book full of words with the idea that no words are necessary is almost like a Zen koan that I would have to ponder for some time or is maybe even a little absurd. Still another part of me realizes that I could have saved myself a lot of work—albeit delightful and insightful— and just put the two pictures in a very small book and let people figure it out for themselves. And still another part of myself—perhaps the truest part, because I am a real woman, smart and sassy, and not a female mystic or wise woman (yet!)—keeps recalling the words on Dave's shirt that says, "I only do what the voices in my wife's head tell her to tell me to do."

And, I think what a wonderful balanced world it would be if men really only did what the voices in their female partners' heads told them to do.

It would be balanced because women wouldn't tell men *everything* that is in their heads—only the things that men needed to know.

Notes

Chapter 1 A Band-Aid Equality

1. Gilligan, Carol, Jean Ward, Jill Mclean Taylor, and Betty Bardige. *Mapping the Moral Domain: A Contribution of Women's Thinking to Psychological Theory and Education*. Cambridge, MA: Harvard University Press, 1990.

2. Eisler, Riane. *The Chalice and the Blade, Our History, Our Future*. New York: HarperOne, 1988.

3. Greenspan, Miriam. *A New Approach to Women & Therapy*. Blue Ridge Summit, PA: Tab Books, 1993.

4. Chesler, Phyllis. *Women and Madness*. Hampshire: Palgrave Macmillan, 2005.

5. Steinem, Gloria. *Revolution from within: A Book of Self-Esteem*. New York: Little, Brown and Company, 1993.

6. Bartky, Sandra. *Femininity and Domination: Studies in the Phenomenology of Oppression*. New York: Chapman and Hall, Inc., 1990.

7. Paglia, Camille. *Sexual Personae: Art and Decadence from Nefertiti to Emily Dickinson*. New York: Random House, Inc., 1991.

8. Stanton, Elizabeth Cady. *The Woman's Bible*. New York: European Publishing Company, 1898.

9. Kern, Kathi. *Mrs. Stanton's Bible*. Ithaca, NY: Cornell University Press, 2001.

Chapter 2 A World Out of Balance

1. http://www.maricreativeresources.com.

2. Tuana, Nancy. *The Less Noble Sex*. Bloomington, IN: Indiana University Press, 1993.

3. Achterberg, Jeanne. *Woman as Healer*. Boston, MA: Shambhala Publications Inc., 1999.

4. Tuana, *The Less Noble Sex*.

5. Darwin, Charles. *On the Origin of Species*. London: John Murray Publishers, 1859.

6. Tuana, *The Less Noble Sex*.

7. Tuana, *The Less Noble Sex*.

8. Tuana, *The Less Noble Sex*.

9. Tuana, *The Less Noble Sex*.

10. Kohlberg in Gilligan, Carol, Jean Ward, Jill Mclean Taylor, and Betty Bardige. *Mapping the Moral Domain: A Contribution of Women's Thinking to Psychological Theory and Education.* Cambridge, MA: Harvard University Press, 1990.

Chapter 3 How Did We Get Here?

1. Wilber, Ken. *A Brief History of Everything.* Boston, MA: Shambhala Publications Inc., 2001.

2. Shlain, Leonard. *The Alphabet versus the Goddess: The Conflict between Word and Image.* New York: Penguin Group, 1998.

3. Aquinas, Thomas. *On Evil.* New York: Oxford University Press, 2003.

4. Kramer, Heninrich. *Malleus Maleficarum.* Germany: 1487

5. Wilber, *A Brief History of Everything.*

6. Goldberg, Steven. *Why Men Rule: A Theory of Male Dominance.* Peru, IL: Open Court Publishing, 1999.

7. Brizendine, Louann. *The Female Brain.* New York: Morgan Road Books, Random House, Inc, 2006.

8. Law, Bridget Murray. "Hormones & Desire," *American Psychological Association* 42, no. 3 (2011): 44, http://www.apa.org/monitor/2011/03/hormones.aspx.

9. Wilber, *A Brief History of Everything.*

10. Colapinto, John. *As Nature Made Him: The Boy Who Was Raised as a Girl.* New York: HarperCollins, 2000.

11. Shlain, Leonard. *Sex, Time, and Power: How Women's Sexuality Shaped Human Evolution.* New York: Viking Adult, 2003.

12. Goldberg, *Why Men Rule.*

Chapter 4 Women Know and Do Not Know

1. Belenky, Mary, Blythe Clincy, Nancy Goldberger, and Jill Tarule. *Women's Ways of Knowing: The Development of Self, Voice, and Mind.* New York: Basic Books, Perseus Book Groups, 1997.

2. American Psychiatric Association. *Diagnostic and Statistical Manual of Mental Disorders* Arlington, VA: American Psychiatric Association Publications, 2000.

3. Norwood, Robin. *Women Who Love Too Much.* New York: Pocket Books, Simon and Schuster, Inc, 1990.

4. Schlessinger, Laura. *Ten Stupid Things Women Do to Mess Up Their Lives.* New York: Harper Collins Publishers, 2002.

5. Kinder, Melvyn and Connell Cowen. *Smart Women, Foolish Choices.* New York: Crown Publishing Group, Random House Publishing, Inc., 1993.

6. Steinem, Gloria. *Revolution from within: A Book of Self-Esteem.* New York: Little, Brown and Company, 1993.

7. McMillan, Tracy. "Why You're Not Married," *Huffington Post,* February 13, 2011, http://www.huffingtonpost.com/tracy-mcmillan/why-youre-not-married_b_822088.html.

8. Keen, Sam. *Fire in the Belly: On Being a Man*. New York: Bantam Books, Bantam Doubleday Dell Publishing Group, 1991.

9. Wilber, Ken. *A Brief History of Everything*. Boston, MA: Shambhala Publications, Inc., 2001.

10. Masson, Jeffrey. *The Assault on Truth: Freud's Suppression of Seduction Theory*. New York: Ballantine Books, 2003.

11. Faludi, Susan. *Stiffed: The Betrayal of the American Man*. New York: Harper Perennial, 2000.

12. Kipnis, Aaron and Elizabeth Herron. *Gender War, Gender Peace: The Quest for Love and Justice between Women and Men*. New York: William Morrow and Company, 1993.

13. Brizendine, Louann. *The Female Brain*. New York: Morgan Road Books, Random House, Inc., 2007.

14. Irwing, Paul, Tom Booth, and Marco del Giudice. "The Distance between Mars and Venus: Measuring Global Sex Differences in Personality," *PLoS ONE*, 2012.

15. Shadyac, Tom. *I AM*. Flying Eye Productions, 2010, film strip, http://www.iamthedoc.com/.

16. Tolle, Eckhart. *A New Earth: Awakening to Your Life's Purpose*. Boston, MA: Dutton Adult, 2005.

17. Shlain, Leonard. *Sex, Time, and Power: How Women's Sexuality Shaped Human Evolution*. New York: Penguin Group, 2003.

18. Bolen, Jean Shinoda. *Crossing to Avalon: A Woman's Midlife Quest for the Sacred Feminine*. New York: HarperCollins, 1994.

Chapter 5 Women Are More Rational

1. Goleman, Daniel. *Emotional Intelligence: Why It Can Matter More than IQ*. New York: Bantam Books, Bantam Doubleday Dell Publishing Group, Inc., 2005.

2. Goleman, Daniel. "The Brain and Emotional Intelligence: Are Women More Emotionally Intelligent than Men?," *Psychology Today* (April 29, 2011), http://www.psychologytoday.com/blog/the-brain-and-emotional-intelligence/201104/are-women-more-emotionally-intelligent-men.

3. Haier, Richard. "His Brain, Her Brain," *US News and World Report*, February 27, 2005.

4. Belenky, Mary, Blythe Clincy, Nancy Goldberger, and Jill Tarule. *Women's Ways of Knowing: The Development of Self, Voice, and Mind*. New York: Basic Books, Perseus Books Group, 1997.

5. Baker Miller, Jean. *Toward a New Psychology of Women*. Boston, MA: Beacon Press, 1997.

6. McGilchrist, Ian. *The Divided Brain*. TED Talks, October 25, 2011.

7. Plotkin, H. C. *Darwin Machines and the Nature of Knowledge*. Cambridge, MA: Harvard University Press, 1997.

8. Pink, Daniel. *A Whole New Mind: Why Right-Brainers Will Rule the Future.* New York: Riverhead Trade, The Berkley Publishing Group, Penguin Group, 2006.

Chapter 6 Women Are More Moral

1. Gilligan, Carol, Jean Ward, Jill Mclean Taylor, and Betty Bardige. *Mapping the Moral Domain: A Contribution of Women's Thinking to Psychological Theory and Education.* Cambridge, MA: Harvard University Press, 1990.

2. Gilligan, et al. *Mapping the Moral Domain.*

3. McKenna, Eddie. "Competitive vs. Collaborative: Game Theory and Communication Games," University of Pennsylvania, http://ccat.sas.upenn.edu/plc/communication/biggie.htm (last modified September 24, 2000).

4. Jordan, Judith, Jean Baker Miller, Irene Stevens, Janet Surrey. *Women's Growth in Connection.* New York: The Guilford Press, 1992.

5. Zak, Paul. "Trust, Morality and Oxytocin," TED Talks Global, http://www.youtube.com (posted November 2, 2011).

6. Wiener, Eric. "Why Women Read More than Men," *NPR,* September 5, 2007.

7. Goleman, Daniel. *Emotional Intelligence: Why It Can Matter More than IQ.* New York: Bantam Books, Bantam Doubleday Dell Publishing Group, Inc., 2005.

8. Nacol, Mark. "Hey Baby Boomers: What Happened to Til Death Do Us Part?" http://www.nacollawfirmblog.com/family-law/boomer-divorce-family-law/hey-baby-boomers-what-happened-to-til-death-do-us-part (last modified November 2011).

9. Sheehy, Gail. *New Passages.* New York: Random House, 1995.

10. Anderson, Eric. *The Monogamy Gap: Men, Love, and the Reality of Cheating (Sexuality, Identity, and Society).* New York: Oxford University Press, 2012.

Chapter 7 Women Are the More Creative Sex

1. Achterberg, Jean. *Woman as Healer.* Boston, MA: Shambhala Publications Inc., 1990.

2. Bolen, Jean Shinoda. "The Call of the Goddess," *Magical Blend Magazine,* November 1994, 52–58.

3. Borysenko, Joan. *A Woman's Book of Life.* New York: Riverhead Books, 1996.

4. Wade, Nicholas. *Before the Dawn: Recovering the Lost History of Our Ancestors.* New York: Penguin Press, 2006.

5. Pappas, Stephanie. "Men Going Extinct? Scientists Say That's Unlikely, As Y Chromosome Not Degrading Rapidly," *Huffington Post: Live Science,* February 22, 2012.

6. Borysenko, Joan. *A Woman's Book of Life.* New York: Riverhead Books, The Berkley Publishing Group, Penguin Putnam Inc., 1998.

7. Schuon, Frithjof. *The Transcendent Unity of Religions.* New York: Harper & Row, 1975.

Chapter 8 The Real Reason Relationships Fail

1. Pintar, Judith. *The Halved Soul: Retelling the Myths of Romantic Love.* New York: Harper & Row, 1992.

2. Gray, John. *Men Are from Mars, Women Are from Venus.* New York: Harper & Row, 1992.

3. McGraw, Phillip. *Relationship Rescue: A Seven-Step Strategy for Reconnecting with Your Partner.* New York: Hyperion, 2000.

4. Forell, Caroline and Donna Matthews. *A Law of Her Own: The Reasonable Woman as a Measure of Man.* New York: New York University Press, 2000.

5. Goleman, Daniel. *Emotional Intelligence: Why It Can Matter More than IQ.* New York: Bantam Books, Bantam Doubleday Dell Publishing Group, Inc., 2005.

6. Sternberg, Robert. *Love Is a Story: A New Theory of Relationships.* New York: Oxford University Press, 1999.

Chapter 9 Male Relational Dread

1. Bly, Robert. "Male Naiveté and the Loss of the Kingdom," *Pilgrimage* 15, no. 5 (1989): 2–10.

2. Sheehy, Gayle. *Passages: Predictable Crises of Adult Life.* New York: Bantam Books, E. P. Dutton & Company, Inc., 1984.

3. Sheehy, Gayle. *New Passages: Mapping Your Life across Time.* New York: Random House, 1995

4. Sheehy, Gayle. *Understanding Men's Passages: Discovering the New Map of Men's Lives.* New York: Random House, 1998.

5. Pasick, Robert. *Awakening from the Deep Sleep: A Powerful Guide for Courageous Men.* New York: HarperCollins, 1992.

6. Tart, Charles. "The Dynamic of Waking Sleep," *The Journal of Transpersonal Psychology* 25, no. 2 (1993): 141–68.

7. "The Secret World of Men: What Therapists Need to Know," *Psychotherapy Networker,* May 2010.

8. McGill, Michael. *The McGill Report on Male Intimacy.* New York: Henry Holt & Co, 1985.

9. Tannen, Deborah. *You Just Don't Understand: Women and Men in Conversation.* New York: William Morrow, 1990.

Chapter 10 Confessions of a Male Chauvinist Pig

1. Anonymous. *Alcoholics Anonymous: The Big Book.* New York: Alcoholics Anonymous World Services, Inc., 2002.

2. Aristotle. *The Politics.* New York: Penguin Classics, 1981.

3. Plato. *The Republic of Plato.* Translated with notes and an interpretive essay by Allan Bloom. New York: Basic Books, Perseus Book Groups, 1968.

4. Mill, John Stuart. *The Basic Writings of John Stuart Mill: On Liberty, the Subjection of Women and Utilitarianism.* New York: Random House, Modern Library, 2002.

5. Kierkegaard, Soren. *Fear and Trembling.* Cambridge: Cambridge University Press, 1978.

6. Tillich, Paul. *Love, Power, and Justice: Ontological Analyses and Ethical Applications.* New York: Oxford University Press, 1954.

7. Daly, Mary. *Gyn/Ecology: The Metaethics of Radical Feminism.* Boston, MA: Beacon Press, 1978.

8. Tillich, Hannah. *From Time to Time.* New York: Stein & Day Pub, 1973.

Chapter 11 Learning How to Be a Man

1. Anderson, Eric. *The Monogamy Gap: Men, Love and the Reality of Cheating.* New York: Oxford University Press, 2012.

2. Honaman, Monique. "I Just Wish He Would Have an Affair!," *The Huffington Post,* March 8, 2012, http://www.huffingtonpost.com/monique-honaman/i-just-wish-he-would-have_b_1297919.html.

3. Pollack, William. *Real Boys: Rescuing Our Sons from the Myths of Boyhood.* New York: Random House, 1998.

4. Vincent, Norah. *Self-Made Man: One Woman's Year Disguised as a Man.* New York: Penguin Group, 2006.

5. Bly, Robert. *Iron John: A Book about Men.* New York: Perseus Books, 1990.

6. American Psychiatric Association. *Diagnostic and Statistical Manual of Mental Disorders,* Arlington, VA: American Psychiatric Association Publications, 2000.

7. Levy, Paul. *The Madness of George W. Bush: A Reflection of Our Collective Psychosis.* Bloomington, IN: AuthorHouse, 2006.

8. McGill, Michael. *The McGill Report on Male Intimacy.* New York: Henry Holt & Co., 1985.

9. Bergman, Stephen. "Men's Psychological Development: A Relational Perspective." Work in progress, Stone Center for Developmental Services and Studies, 1991.

10. Whyte, David and Angeles Arrien. *Embracing the Sacred Other: Celebrating the Masculine and the Feminine.* New Medicine Tapes, Berkeley, CA: Marion Civic Center, 1993.

11. Downey, Charles. "Secondhand Emotions: 'Catching' a Bad Mood." *Beliefnet,* http://www.beliefnet.com/healthandhealing/getcontent.aspx?cid=14265.

12. Larson, R.W. and Almeida D. M. "Secondhand Emotions: Emotional Transmission in Families," *Journal of Marriage and Family,* February 1999.

13. Walker, Mandy. "What the Longevity Project Tells Us about Divorce and Children," The blog, *Huff Post,* March 5, 2012.

14. Donaldson-Evans, Catherine. "Men Are Wired to Shut Down during Fights," *AOL Health,* October 5, 2010, http://www.yourtango.com/201084117/men-are-wired-shut-down-during-fights.

Chapter 12 Why Men Are Clueless in Relationships

1. Berger, Peter. *The Sacred Canopy: Elements of a Sociological Theory of Religion.* New York: Anchor Books, 1967.

2. Barrows, Sidney Biddle. *Mayflower Madam: The Secret Life of Sydney Biddle Barrows.* Westminster, MD: Arbor House, 1986.

3. Coward, Rosalind. *Our Treacherous Hearts: Why Women Let Men Get Their Way.* London: Faber and Faber, 1992.

4. Plato, "Allegory of the Cave." *Republic,* Book VII, 194ff.

5. "Who's Afraid of Couples Counseling—Stretching Your Comfort Zone." *Psychotherapy Networker,* November 2011.

6. Sheehy, Gail. *Understanding Men's Passages: Discovering the New Map of Men's Lives.* New York: Random House, 1998.

7. Goldberg, Steven. *Why Men Rule: A Theory of Male Dominance.* Chicago, IL: Open Court, 1999.

8. Gilmore, David. *Manhood in the Making: Cultural Concepts of Masculinity.* New Haven, CT: Yale University Press, 1991.

9. Faludi, Susan. *Stiffed: The Betrayal of the American Man.* New York: Harper Perennial, 2000.

10. Bergman, Stephen. "Men's Psychological Development: A Relational Perspective." Work in progress, Stone Center for Developmental Services and Studies,1991.

11. Jacobs, Tom. "Real Men Do Apologize," *Miller-McCune,* September 23, 2010, http://www.miller-mccune.com/blogs/news-blog/real-men-do-apologize-23241/.

12. Keen, Sam. *Fire in the Belly: On Being a Man.* New York: Bantam, 1991.

13. Goldberg, *Why Men Rule.*

14. Wilber, Ken. *A Brief History of Everything.* Boston, MA: Shambhala Publications, Inc., 2001.

Chapter 13 Her Advanced Knowing Matches New Perspectives

1. Arnold, Patrick M. *Wildmen, Warriors, and Kings: Masculine Spirituality and the Bible.* New York: Crossroad, 1991.

2. Hopkins, Patricia and Sherry Ruth Anderson. *The Feminine Face of God: The Unfolding of the Sacred in Women.* New York: Bantam Books, 1991.

3. Kastleman, Mark. "The Differences between the Male and Female Brain," *Net Nanny,* http://www.netnanny.com/learn_center/article/165

4. Hopkins and Anderson, *The Feminine Face of God.*

5. Woodman, Marion. *Leaving My Father's House: A Journey to Conscious Femininity.* Boston, MA: Shambhala Publications, Inc., 1992.

6. King, Theresa, ed. *The Spiral Path: Explorations of Women's Spirituality.* St. Paul, MN: Yes International Publishers, 1996.

7. Ibid.

8. Hoffman, Glynda Lee. *The Secret Dowry of Eve: Woman's Role in the Development of Consciousness.* Bethel, ME: Park Street Press, 2003.

9. Shlain, Leonard. *Sex, Time, and Power: How Women's Sexuality Shaped Human Evolution.* New York: Viking Adult, 2003.

10. *The Living Matrix: A Film on the New Science of Healing.* The Living Matrix, LTD and Becker Massey, LLC. 2009. DVD.

11. Cortwright, Brant. *Psychotherapy and Spirit: Theory and Practice in Transpersonal Psychotherapy.* New York: State University of New York Press, 1997.

12. Seligman, Martin. *Learned Optimism: How to Change Your Mind and Your Life.* New York: Vintage Press, 2006.

13. Grof, Stanislav. *Spiritual Emergency: When Personal Transformation Becomes a Crisis.* New York: Tarcher Books, Penguin Publishers, 1989.

14. Anderson, Walter Truett. *The Next Enlightenment: Integrating East and West in a New Vision of Human Evolution.* New York: St. Martin's Press, 2003.

15. Capra, Fritjof. *The Turning Point: Science, Society, and the Rising Culture.* New York: Simon and Schuster, 1982.

16. Campbell, Joseph. *The Hero with a Thousand Faces: Collected Works of Joseph Campbell.* New York: Pantheon Books, 1949.

Chapter 14 SHE-Q—The Wisdom of Women

1. Goleman, Daniel. *Emotional Intelligence: Why It Can Matter More than IQ.* New York: Bantam Books, 2005.

2. Winfrey, Oprah. Master Class with Gloria Steinem, OWN Network, March 13, 2012.

3. Dalai Lama. Vancouver Peace Summit 2009, September 27, 2009.

4. *The Living Matrix: A Film on the New Science of Healing.* The Living Matrix, LTD and Becker Massey, LLC. 2009. DVD.

5. Mundy, Lisa. *The Richer Sex: How the New Majority of Female Breadwinners is Transforming Sex, Love and Family.* New York: Simon and Schuster, 2012.

6. Rosin, Hanna. "The End of Men," *The Atlantic,* July 2010, http://www.theatlantic.com/magazine/archive/2010/07/the-end-of-men/8135/.

7. Gordon, Claire. "Young Women More Career-Driven Than Men, Study Says," *AOL Jobs,* April 20, 2012.

8. Goldberg, Steven. *Why Men Rule: A Theory of Male Dominance.* Chicago, IL: Open Court, 1999.

9. Carter, Jimmy. In *MoveOn.Org,* April 19, 2012.

10. Drexler, Peggy. "When Faith and Policy Trumps People," *The Huffington Post,* March 2, 2012, http://www.huffingtonpost.com/peggy-drexler/when-faith-and-policy-tru_b_1316008.html.

11. Flanagan, Caitlan. *Girl Land.* New York: Reagan Arthur Books, Little, Brown, and Company, 2012.

12. Weil, Andrew. "Creating a New Wisdom," *Psychotherapy Networker Conference.* Pre-conference mailer, March 22–25, 2012.

13. Cameron, David. "How We're Tackling Violence against Women: An Iceberg under the Surface of Society," *The Huffington Post,* March 3, 2012, http://www.huffingtonpost.co.uk/david-cameron/international-womens-day-david-cameron_b_1327807.html.

14. Rosenthal, Max. "Iraq War and Afghan Conflict Harmed the Economy, Study Says," *The Huffington Post,* March 1, 2012, http://www.huffingtonpost.com/2012/03/01/iraq-war-afghan-conflict-economy_n_1311717.html.

15. Carlton, Gretchen. "Women More Moral," *Huff Post* on AOL.com, March 18, 2012.

16. Searles, Rebecca. "Gelada Monkeys Miscarry When New Male Joins Group, Study Shows," *The Huffington Post,* February 28, 2012, http://www.huffingtonpost.com/2012/02/27/monkeys-miscarry-when-new-male-joins-group_n_1304320.html.

17. Caldwell, Leigh Ann. "Santorum: Obama's Worldview Upside-Down." *CBS News,* February 19, 2012, http://www.cbsnews.com/8301–3460_162–57381029/santorum-obamas-worldview-upside-down.

18. Hubbard, Barbara Marx. Documentary Video, http://www.thrivemovement.com/.

19. Darwin, Charles. *On the Origin of Species.* London: John Murray, 1859.

20. Goldberg, *Why Men Rule.*

21. Sheldrake, Rupert. *Morphic Resonance: The Nature of Formative Causation.* Bethel, ME: Park Street Press, 2009.

22. Clinton, Hillary. "Women in the World—2012," *The Daily Beast on the Daily Show,* Beast TV, April 9, 2012.

23. Myers, Wyatt. "7 Ways Marriage Helps Men's Health," *Everyday Health,* February 24, 2012, http://www.everydayhealth.com/mens-health-pictures/ways-marriage-helps-mens-health.aspx.

Chapter 15 Mentoring the Masculine

1. Hoffman, Glynda Lee. *The Secret Dowry of Eve: Woman's Role in the Development of Consciousness.* Bethel, ME: Park Street Press, 2003.

2. Macy, Joanna. *World as Lover, World as Self: Courage for Global Justice and Ecological Renewal.* Berkeley, CA: Parallax Press, 2007.

3. Levy, Paul. *The Madness of George W. Bush: A Reflection of Our Collective Psychosis.* Bloomington, IN: AuthorHouse, 2006.

4. Scarf, Maggie. *Intimate Partners: Patterns in Love and Marriage.* New York: Ballantine Books, 1988.

5. Gilligan, Carol, Jean Ward, Jill Mclean Taylor, and Betty Bardige. *Mapping the Moral Domain: A Contribution of Women's Thinking to Psychological Theory and Education.* Cambridge, MA: Harvard University Press, 1990.

6. Moore, Michael. *Stupid White Men: . . . and Other Sorry Excuses for the State of the Nation!* New York: Harper, 2002.

Chapter 16   The New Hero

1. Tarnas, Richard. *The Passion of the Western Mind: Understanding the Ideas that Have Shaped Our World View.* New York: Ballantine Books, 1991.

2. Shlain, Leonard. *Sex, Time, and Power: How Women's Sexuality Shaped Human Evolution.* New York: Viking Adult, 2003.

3. Sichel, Mark. "The Happiest Women Are Sexy and Have the Happiest Marriages," *Psychology Today,* August 2008.

4. Wilber, Ken. *A Brief History of Everything.* Boston, MA: Shambhala Publications, Inc., 2001. Keen, Sam. *Fire in the Belly: On Being a Man.* New York: Bantam Books, Bantam Doubleday Dell Publishing Group Inc, 1991.

5. Chance, Kenneth. *Confessions of a Closed Male: A Story of Spiritual Awakening.* Navarre, FL: Rojaketaka Publications, 1999.

6. Johnson, Robert. *The Fisher King and the Handless Maiden: Understanding the Wounded Feeling Function in Masculine and Feminine Psychology.* New York: HarperCollins, 1995.

7. Keen, Sam. *Inward Bound: Exploring the Geography of Your Emotions* New York: Bantam Books, Bantam Doubleday Dell Publishing Group Inc., 1992.

8. Harvey, Andrew. *The Return of the Mother.* New York: Penguin Putman, 1995.

9. Hoffman, Glynda Lee. *The Secret Dowry of Eve: Woman's Role in the Development of Consciousness.* Bethel, ME: Park Street Press, 2003.

10. Wilber, *A Brief History of Everything.*

11. McGill, Michael. *The McGill Report on Male Intimacy.* New York: Henry Holt & Co., 1985.

12. Levy, Paul. *The Madness of George W. Bush: A Reflection of Our Collective Psychosis.* Bloomington, IN: AuthorHouse, 2006

13. Tilin, Andrew. "Where Are All the Men?," *Yoga Journal,* http://www.yoga journal.com/lifestyle/2585.

14. Johnson, Robert. *HE: Understanding Masculine Psychology.* New York: HarperCollins, 1989.

15. Von Franz, Marie-Louise. *Alchemy: An Introduction to the Symbolism and the Psychology.* Canada: Inner City Books, 1981.

16. Hawking, Stephen. *A Brief History of Time.* New York: Bantam, 1998.

17. Von Goethe, Johann Wolfgang. *Goethe's Faust.* New York: Anchor Books, 1962.

18. Jung, Carl. *The Archetypes and the Collective Unconscious (Collected Works of C. G. Jung).* Princeton, NJ: Princeton University Press, 1981.

19. Ibid.

Chapter 17 A Balanced Future

1. Capra, Fritjof. *The Turning Point: Science, Society and Rising Culture.* New York: Simon and Schuster, 1982.

2. Bohm, David. *Wholeness and the Implicate Order.* London: Routledge, 1996.

3. Teilhard De Chardin in Tarnas, Richard. *The Passion of the Western Mind: Understanding the Ideas that Have Shaped Our World View.* New York: Ballantine Books, 1991.

4. Cooper, David. *God Is a Verb: Kabbalah and the Practice of Mystical Judaism.* New York: Riverhead Books, Berkeley Publishing Group, Penguin Putnam, Inc., 1998.

5. Wright, Frank Lloyd. In *Quote Magazine,* August 14, 1966.

6. Bly, Robert and Woodman, Marion. *The Maiden King—The Reunion of Masculine and Feminine.* New York: Henry Holt and Co., 1998.

7. Shlain, Leonard. *Sex, Time, and Power: How Women's Sexuality Shaped Human Evolution.* New York: Viking Adult, 2003.

Bibliography

Baron-Cohen, S. *The Essential Difference: Male and Female Brains and the Truth about Autism,* New York: Basic Books, Perseus Book Groups, 2003.

Berg, K. *God Wears Lipstick: Kabbalah for Women,* New York: The Kabbalah Center, 2005.

Bly, R., and Woodman, M. *The Maiden King: The Reunion of Masculine and Feminine,* New York: Henry Holt and Company, 1998.

Bohart, A., and Greenberg, L. *Empathy Reconsidered: New Directions in Psychotherapy,* Washington, DC, American Psychological Association, 1997.

Bolen, J. S. *Gods in Everyman: A New Psychology of Men's Lives and Loves,* New York: Harper San Francisco, 1989.

Bolen, J. S. *The Millionth Circle: How to Change Ourselves and the World,* York Beach, ME: Conari Press, 1999.

Borysenko, J. *Minding the Body, Mending the Mind,* New York: Bantam Books, Bantam Doubleday Dell Publishing Group, 1987.

Borysenko, J. *A Woman's Journey to God,* New York: Riverhead Books, Berkeley Publishing Group, Penguin Putnam, Inc., 1999.

Bragdon, E. *The Call of Spiritual Emergency,* New York: Harper San Francisco, 1990.

Braude, A. *Radical Spirits,* Boston, MA: Beacon Press, 1989.

Brussant, F., and Brussant, M. A. *Spiritual Literacy: Reading the Sacred in Everyday Life,* Scribner, 1996.

Campbell, J., Eisler, R., Gimbutas, M., and Muses, C. *In All Her Names,* New York: Harper San Francisco, 1992.

Carter, S., and Sokol, J. *Getting to Commitment: Overcoming the 8 Greatest Obstacles to Lasting Connection,* Lanham, MD: M. Evans and Company, Inc., 1998.

Collins, G. *When Everything Changed: The Amazing Journey of American Women from 1960 to the Present,* New York: Little, Brown and Company, 2009.

Connell, W. *Masculinities,* Berkeley, CA: University of California Press, 1995.

DiCarlo, R., ed. *Towards a New World View: Conversations at the Leading Edge,* Las Vegas, NV: Epic Publications, 1998.

Doyle, L. *The Surrendered Wife: A Practical Guide to Finding Intimacy, Passion, and Peace with a Man,* New York: Simon and Schuster, 1999.

Eisler, R. *The Chalice and the Blade: Our History, Our Future,* New York: Harper San Francisco, 1987.

Emoto, M. *The True Power of Water: Healing and Discovering Ourselves,* Hillsboro, OR: Beyond Words Publishing, 2005.

Flinders, C. L. *Rebalancing the World: Why Women Belong and Men Compete and How to Restore the Ancient Equilibrium,* New York: Harper San Francisco, 2000.

Gilligan, C. *The Birth of Pleasure,* New York: Alfred A. Knopf, Random House, 1999.

Gilmsan, P. G. *Herland,* Mineola, NY: Dover Publications, 1998.

Gimbutas, M. *The Living Goddess,* Berkeley, CA: University of California Press, 1999.

Goleman, D. *Working with Emotional Intelligence,* New York: Bantam Books, Bantam Doubleday Dell Publishing Group, 1998.

Griffith, E. *In Her Own Right: The Life of Elizabeth Cady Stanton,* New York: Oxford University Press, 1984.

Grof, S. *Ancient Wisdom and Modern Science,* Albany, NY: New York State University Press, 1984.

Grof, S., and Grof, C. *Spiritual Emergency,* New York: Jeremy Tarcher, Penguin Putnam, Inc., 1984.

Hagan, K. L., ed. *Women Respond to the Men's Movement,* New York: Harper & Row, 1992.

Hall, N., and Dawson, W. *Broodmales,* New York: Spring Publishing, 1989.

Harrison, S. *Doing Nothing: Coming to the End of the Spiritual Search,* New York: Jeremy P. Tarcher, Penguin Putnam, Inc., 1997.

Harrtis, S. *Letter to a Christian Nation,* New York: Alfred A. Knopf, Random House, 2006.

Hein, S. *Opening Minds: A Journey of Extraordinary Encounters, Crop Circles and Resonance,* Boulder, CO: Mount Baldy Press, Inc., 2002.

Hillman, J., and Ventura, M. *We've Had a Hundred Years of Psychotherapy and the World Is Getting Worse,* New York: Harper & Row, 1992.

Hitchens, C. *God Is Not Great: How Religion Poisons Everything,* New York: Twelve, Hatchett Book Group, Inc., 2007.

Hooks, B. *Feminist Theory: From Margin to Center,* Cambridge, MA: South End Press, 1984.

Hycner, R. *Between Person and Person: Toward a Dialogical Psychotherapy,* Gouldsboro, ME: The Gestalt Journal Press, 1993.

Iglehart, H. A. *Womanspirit: A Guide to Women's Wisdom,* New York: Harper & Row, 1983.

Johnson, A. G. *The Gender Knot: Unravelling Our Patriarchal Legacy,* Philadelphia, PA: Temple University Press, 1997.

Johnson, K. *The Grail Myth: Celtic Quest for the Self, The Quest,* Spring, 1995.

Justice, L. A. *What Women Really Want . . . and How They Can Get It,* New York: Carroll and Graf Publishers, Inc., 2000.

Kalsched, D. *The Inner World of Trauma: Archetypal Defenses of the Personal Spirit,* New York: Routledge, 2005.

Keepin, W. *Divine Duality: The Power of Reconciliation between Women and Men,* Chino Valley, AZ: Hohm Press, 2007.

Kiersey, D., and Bates, M. *Please Understand Me: Character and Temperament Types,* Del Mar, CA: Prometheus Nemesis Book Company, 1978.

Kingman, D. R. *The Men We Never Knew: Women's Role in the Evolution of a Gender,* Berkeley, CA: Conari Press, 1993.

Kornfield, J. *A Path with Heart: A Guide through the Perils and Promises of Spiritual Life,* New York: Bantam Books, Bantam Doubleday Dell Publishing Group, 1993.

Kvam, K., Schearing, L., and Ziegler, V., eds. *Eve and Adam: Jewish, Christian, and Muslim Readings on Genesis and Gender,* Bloomington, IN: Indiana University Press, 1999.

Lerner, G. *The Creation of Patriarchy,* New York: Oxford University Press, 1986.

Lipton, B. *The Biology of Belief: Unleashing the Power of Consciousness, Matter and Miracles,* Santa Rosa, CA: Mountain of Love/Elite Books, 2005.

Lipton, B., and Bhaerman, S. *Spontaneous Evolution: Our Positive Future and a Way to Get There from Here,* London: Hay House, 2009.

Luke, H. M. *The Way of Women: Awakening the Perennial Feminine,* New York: Bantam Doubleday Dell Publishing Group, Image Books, 1995.

MacKinnon, C. *Toward a Feminist Theory of the State,* Cambridge: Cambridge University Press, 1989.

Madison, G. B. *The Hermeneutics of Postmodernity: Figures and Themes,* Bloomington, IN: Indiana University Press, 1988.

Mandala, M., Vietgen, C., and Amorok, T. *Living Deeply: The Art and Science of Transformation in Everyday Life,* Oakland, CA: New Harbinger Publications, Inc., 2007.

Mariechild, D. *Mother Wit: A Feminist Guide to Psychic Development,* Freedom, CA: The Crossing Press, 1981.

May, R. *The Cry for Myth,* New York: W. W. Norton & Company, 1991.

Mayer, N. *The Male Mid-Life Crisis: Fresh Starts about 40,* New York: Signet Books, Penguin Books, 1978.

McTaggart, L. *The Field: The Quest for the Secret Force of the Universe,* New York: Harper Collins Publishers, Inc., 2001.

Mehrotra, R., ed. *The Essential Dalai Lama: His Important Teachings,* New York: Viking, Penguin Group, 2005.

Mencken, H. L. *In Defense of Women,* Mineola, NY: Dover Publications, 2004.

Miller J., and Stiver P. I. *The Healing Connection,* Boston, MA: Beacon Press, 1997.

Millet, K. *Sexual Politics,* Champaign, IL: University of Illinois Press, 2000.

Miners, S., ed. *A Spiritual Approach to Male/Female Relations,* Adyar, India: Theosophical Publishing House, 1984.

Monk, S. M. *The Dance of the Dissident Daughter,* New York: Harper San Francisco, 1992.

Moody, H., and Carroll, D. *The Five Stages of the Soul,* New York: Anchor Books, Random House, 1997.

Moore, R., and Gillette, D. *The Lover within: Accessing the Lover in the Male Psyche,* New York: HarperCollins Publishers, 1993.

Moore, T. *Care of the Soul: A Guide for Cultivating Depth and Sacredness in Everyday Life,* New York: HarperCollins Publishers, 1992.

Murcock, M. *The Heroine's Journey,* Boston, MA: Shambhala Publications Inc., 1990.

Muten, B., ed. *Return of the Great Goddess,* New York: Stewart, Tabori and Change, Abrams,1994.

Neumann, E. *The Great Mother: An Analysis of the Archetype,* Princeton, NJ: Princeton University Press, 1955.

Nicholson, S. *The Goddess Reawakening: The Feminine Principle Today,* Adyar, India: Theosophical Publishing House, 1989.

Nickles, E. *The Coming Matriarchy: How Women Will Gain the Balance of Power,* Adelaide, AU: Sea View Books, 1982.

O'Donohue, J. *Anam Cara: A Book of Celtic Wisdom,* New York: Cliff Street Books, HarperCollins Publishers, 1997.

Paglia, C. *Sex, Art, and American Culture,* New York: Vintage Books, Random House, 1992.

Pearson, C. S. *Awakening the Heroes Within,* New York: Harper San Francisco, 1991.

Pearson, C.S. *The Hero within: Six Archetypes We Live By,* New York: Harper San Francisco, 1986.

Prato, L. *From the Inside-Out: Shattering the Mental Illness Myth. A True Story,* Charleston, SC: BookSurge Publishing, 2009.

Rothschild, B. *The Body Remembers: The Psychophysiology of Trauma and Trauma Treatment,* New York: W.W. Norton & Company, 2000.

Ruether, R. R. *Gaia and God: An Ecofeminist Theology of Earth Healing,* New York: Harper San Francisco, 1992.

Ryan, W. *Blaming the Victim,* New York: Vintage Books, Random House, 1972.

Sanford, J. *Healing and Wholeness,* Mahwah, NJ: Paulist Press, 1966.

Sardello, R. *Love and the Soul,* New York: HarperCollins, 1995.

Schaef, A.W. *Women's Reality: An Emerging Female System in a White Male Society,* New York: Harper & Row, 1981.

Shem, S., and Surrey, J. *We Have To Talk: Healing Dialogues between Women and Men,* New York: Basic Books, Perseus Book Groups, 1998.

Sjoo, M., and Mor, B. *The Great Cosmic Mother: Rediscovering the Religion of the Earth,* New York: Harper San Francisco, 1987.

Sommers, C.H. *Who Stole Feminism: How Women Have Betrayed Women,* New York: Simon and Schuster, 1994.

Spangler, D. *The Call,* New York: Riverhead Books, The Berkley Publishing Group, Penguin Group, 1996.

Stanton, E. C. *Eighty Years and More: Reminiscences 1815–1897,* Amherst, NY: Humanity Books, 1993.

Starr, T. *The Natural Inferiority of Women: Outrageous Pronouncements of Misguided Males,* New York: Poseidon Press, 1981.

Tannen, D. *You Just Don't Understand: Women and Men in Conversation,* New York: Ballantine Books, 1999.

Targ, R., and Katra, J. *Miracles of Mind: Exploring Nonlocal Consciousness and Spiritual Healing,* Novato, CA: New World Library, 1998.

Tarnas, R. *Cosmos and Psyche: Intimations of a New World View,* New York: Viking, Penguin Group, 2006.

Tavris, C. *Mismeasure of Women,* New York: Simon and Schuster, 1992.

Taylor, J. B. *My Stoke of Insight: A Brain Scientist's Personal Journey,* New York: Viking, Penguin Group, 2009.

Thistlethwaite, S. B., ed. *Adam, Eve, and the Genome: The Human Genome Project and Theology,* Minneapolis, MN: Fortress Press, 2003.

Tiger, L. *The Decline of Males,* New York: St. Martin's Press, 1999.

Valian, V. *The Morning After: Sex, Fear and Feminism, on Campus,* New York: Little, Brown and Company, 1993.

Vaughan, F. *The Inward Arc,* New York: Shambhala Publications Inc., 1986.

Von Franz, M.-L. *Alchemy: An Introduction to the Symbolism and the Psychology,* Toronto: Inner City Books, 1980.

Walsh, R., and Vaughan, F., eds. *Paths beyond Ego: The Transpersonal Vision,* New York: Jeremy Tarcher, Penguin Putnam, Inc., 1993.

Warren, R. *Women's Lip,* Bridgeport, CT: Hysteria Publications: A Division of Sourcebooks, 1998.

Wilber, K. *The Spectrum of Consciousness,* Adyar, India: Theosophical Publishing House, 1987.

Wilber, K. *A Theory of Everything: An Integral Vision for Business, Politics, Science and Spirituality,* New York: Shambhala Publications Inc., 2000.

Wilber, K. *Up from Eden,* New York: Shambhala Publications Inc., 1981.

Wilk, S. R. *Medusa: Solving the Mystery of the Gorgon,* Oxford University Press, 2000.

Wolf, N. *Fire with Fire,* New York: Random House, 1993.

Zukav, G. *The Seat of the Soul,* New York: Simon and Schuster, 1990.

Zweig, C., ed. *To Be a Woman: The Birth of the Conscious Feminine,* New York: Jeremy Tarcher, Penguin Putnam, Inc., 1990.

Index

Adam and Eve, Gnostic version of, 126–27, 128

Aetiology of Hysteria (Freud), 61

Aggression, reducing male, 232–33

Alchemy: An Introduction to the Symbolism and the Psychology (Von Franz), 272

Alcoholics Anonymous, comparing male chauvinism to, 158

Allegory of the Cave (Plato), 194–96

Almeida, David, 183

Alphabet versus the Goddess, The (Shlain), 36

American Psychological Association (APA), 8

Anderson, Eric, 175

Anderson, Walter Truett, 216

Angel of the House movement, 16–17

Anima as feminine aspect of male, 271–76

Anthony, Susan B., 15, 16

Anti-essentialist theory, 14

Aphrodite, 37

Aquinas, Thomas, St., 37

Archetypal tales, women's identity and, 63–66

Aristotle, 24, 162–63

Arnold, Patrick, 203

Athena, 37

Balance and flow of opposites, 21–32; control of women and, 31–32; creativity of men *vs.* women and, 30–31; evolutionary process and, 24–25; morality of men *vs.* women and, 28–30; rationality of men *vs.* women and, 26–28; Yin and Yang concept of, 21–24

Balanced future, 277–87; concept of fairness and, 281–82; feminists concerns for, 279–80; masculine and feminine qualities for, 284–87; Nature and, 280–81; spiritual context for, 282–84; Tao concept of, 277–79

Barrows, Sydney Biddle, 190

Bartky, Sandra, 11–12

Belenky, Mary, 52

Berger, Peter, 190

Biological differences, imbalance and, 43–44

Blame placement and relationships, 132–39

Bly, Robert, 143–44, 148–49, 179; connecting with parents and, 181; naiveté of males and, 144; numbness of males and, 145–46; passivity of males and, 144–45, 254

Bohm, David, 278–79

Bolen, Jean Shinoda, 71, 116, 117

Bonobo chimpanzees, 232–33

Brief History of Time, A (Hawking), 272

Brizendine, Louann, 42

Bruce Effect, 234

Cameron, David, 232
Campbell, Joseph, 219
Capra, Fritjof, 218
Care: morality of, 97–102; rationality
    of women and, 85–86
Caretakers of Earth, women as, 233–35
Carter, Jimmy, 230
Cautious confirmers, men as, 154–56
Chalice and the Blade, The (Eisler), 4–5
Chance, Kenneth, 265
Chardin, Teilhard De, 282
Chauvinism explained, 159–60
Chesler, Phyllis, 8
Chromosomes, creativity of women
    and, 118–19
Clinton, Hillary, 239
Cluelessness of men, 187–202; answers
    to problem, 189–91; changing feel-
    ings and, 196; Maher on, 201–2;
    nature and nurture involvement
    in, 197–201; overview of, 187–88;
    problem explained, 189; responses
    to, 191–94
Codependence, 100–101
Collected Works (Jung), 275
Confessions of a Closed Male (Chance),
    265
Connecting with parents, boys, 180–81
Constructed knowing, 81
Cooper, David, 283
Cortwright, Brant, 213
Coward, Rosalind, 192
Creativity explained, 115
Creativity of women, 115–23; balance
    and flow of opposites and, 30–31;
    chromosomes and, 118–19; femi-
    nine principles and, 117–18, 121; *vs.*
    men, 120; mitochondrial DNA and,
    118–19; pregnancy as initiation and,
    116–17; Schuon model and, 121–22;
    sex of the divine and, 115–16; spiri-
    tual/religious context of, 122–23
Cultural feminism, 14

Dalai Lama, 240, 241
Daly, Mary, 14, 164
Darwin, Charles, 27
*Darwin Machines and the Nature of
    Knowledge* (Plotkin), 94
Dawkins, Richard, 230, 283
De Beauvoir, Simone, 128
Decision makers, women as, 82–83
Deep sleep, males and, 149
Depression among boys, 178–80, 199
Descartes, René, 27
Deutsch, Donnie, 249
Diagnostic and Statistical Manual
    (DSM), 53, 179
Divided Brain, The (McGilchrist), 90
Divorce rates, 111
Dukakis, Olivia, 197

Egophrenia, 271
Emotional evaders, men as, 154
Emotional Intelligence (Goleman), 77,
    79, 107, 137, 221–22
Emotional intelligence and morality of
    women, 107–8
Emotionally asleep men, 148–50
Emotions: feelings and, 191; rationality
    of women and, 78–80
Empathy: human relationships and,
    254–55; morality of women and,
    103–5
Epistemological framework, 3
Epistemology, 3
Equality, Band-Aid, 1–19; author's
    introduction to, 1–6; issues of, 6–8;
    New Choices program and, 8–10;
    politically correct, 18–19
Equality, women's studies and, 10–18;
    Angel of the House movement and,
    16–17; anti-essentialist theory and,
    14; feminism and, 14–15; Paglia
    and, 13; sexual harassment issues
    and, 10–11; victim psychology and,
    11–12

Erikson, Erik, 100
Essentialism, 14
Euripides, 64
Evolutionary process of women, 24–25

Faludi, Susan, 62–63, 199
Faust (Von Goethe), 272
Fear and Trembling (Kierkegaard), 163
Female Brain, The (Brizendine), 42, 66
Females as primary sex beliefs, SHE-Q and, 227–29
Feminine-based intelligence, SHE-Q as, 222–24
Feminine Face of God, The (Hopkins and Anderson), 204
Feminine principles, creativity of women and, 117–18, 121
Feminine self-esteem, women's identity and, 69–74
Feminine spirituality, SHE-Q and, 237–38
Feminism: anti-essentialist theory of, 14; concern of, 279–80; explained, 159–60; focuses of, 14–15; second-wave, 15–17
Fiorenza, Elizabeth, 16
Fire in the Belly, A (Keen), 58–59
Fluke, Sandra, 229
Freud, Sigmund, 29; self-esteem and, 61–62
From Time to Time (Tillich), 164

Gender, sex *vs.,* 40
Gender identity, altering, 44–45
Gender roles, 40. *See also* Imbalance between sexes; nature and, 41; sex act and women, 41–42
Gender War, Gender Peace (Kipnis and Herron), 63
Gilligan, Carol, 97–99
Gilmore, David, 197
Girl Land (Flanagan), 231

Gnostic version of Adam and Eve story, 126–27, 128
Goldberg, Steven, 39; feminists double standards and, 228–29; male domination and, 49; mature masculinity and, 201
Goleman, Daniel, 77–78, 137
Good males, connecting with, 240–41
Gordon, Claire, 226
Gray, John, 131–39, 146
Great Chain of Being concept, 25
Great Mother, 30
Greenspan, Miriam, 7
Grof, Stanislav, 215
Guilt, women and feelings of, 51
Gyn/Ecology (Daly), 164
Gynesapiens species concept, 70

Harvey, Andrew, 266
Hawking, Stephen, 272
Hera, 37
Hero, men as new, 261–76; anima as feminine aspect and, 271–76; hearing call to, 264–71; journey of, 261–64
Hierarchy, principle of, 158
Hieros gamos, 274, 285
Hoffman, Glenda Lee, 208–10
Home as final stage of journey, 284–87
Hormones and morality of women, 105–7
Hubbard, Barbara Marx, 235
Human learning, 94–95
Humor, SHE-Q and, 240
Hundredth Monkey phenomenon, 237
Hyde, Janet Shibley, 66

I AM (Shadyac documentary video), 67
Imbalance between sexes, 33–49; biological differences and, 43–44; factors impacting, 45–46; gender identity, altering, 44–45; history of,

33–35; language control and, 36–40; male immortality and, 46–49; maleness or femaleness and, 41–43; nurture, impact of, 44; sex, gender, and equality issues and, 40–41; status elevation by men and, 35–36
Individuation, Jung meaning of, 274
Inequality changes, SHE-Q and, 229–31
Instincts, defined, 94
Intelligent emotions, 78–80
Intimacy, men and, 153–54
Intimate Partners (Scarf), 254
Irwing, Paul, 66

Jnaneshwar (mystic), 283
Johnson, Robert, 272
Journey of life for women, 219–20
Jung, Carl, 65–66

Kant, Immanuel, 28–29, 31
Keen, Sam, 58–59; mature masculinity and, 200–201
Kierkegaard, Soren, 163
Knowing, stages of, 80–81
Knowledge, constructing of, 81–82
Kohlberg, Laurence, 3–4; morality of women and, 29–30, 97–98, 99
Kwan Yin, 283

Language control, imbalance between sexes and, 36–40
Law of Her Own, A (Forell and Matthews), 137
Left brain, explained, 92–93
Less Noble Sex, The (Tuana), 24
Levy, Paul, 179
Liberal feminism, 14–15
Limbaugh, Rush, 229
Liquid Trust, 105–6
Love Calling (Deutsch), 249
Lysistrata, 232

Macy, Joanna, 250, 280
Maher, Bill, 201–2
Male-bashing, 146–47
Male chauvinist pig, confessions of, 157–71; confrontational period and, 164–67; family of, 160–61; marriage and, 164; overview of, 157–60; philosophy and, 162–64; postconfrontational period and, 167–71; pre-confrontational period and, 160–64; religion and, 161–62
Male immortality, imbalance and, 46–49
"Male Naiveté and the Loss of the Kingdom" (Bly), 143–46
Male relational dread (MRD), 141–56; cautious confirmers, men as, 154–56; defined, 150–53; emotionally asleep men and, 148–50; intimacy and, 153–54; male-bashing and, 146–47; masculinity, rock of, 147–48; mystery/mastery behavior of, 156; naiveté and, 144; numbness and, 145–46; overview of, 141–44; passivity and, 144–45; reluctant revealers, men as, 154; Stone Center and, 150–53
Malignant egophrenia (ME), 179
Malleus Maleficarum, 38
Man, becoming a, 173–85; changes in traditional values and, 184–85; connecting with parents and, 180–81; crying and, 176–78; depression among boys and, 178–80; feelings and, 181–82; nature and nurture of, 183–84; negative emotions and, 182–83; overview of, 173–76
Manipulation, defined, 253–54
MARI (Mandala Assessment Research Instrument), 22
Masculine, mentoring, 243–59; changing others and, 250–51; empathy and, 254–55; female perspective of,

257–59; male perspective of, 255–57; overview of, 243–44; reasoning for mentoring, 249–50; talking as solution and, 252–53; understanding mentoring and, 244–49; woman's intentions for, 251–52; women manipulating men and, 253–54
Masculine/feminine qualities for balanced future, 284–87
Masculinity, rock, 147–48
Maslow, Abraham, 215
Masson, Jeffrey, 61
Mature love and relationships, 129
Mature masculinity, definitions of, 200
McGilchrist, Ian, 90, 93, 94, 95
McGill Report on Male Intimacy, The, 153–56
Medea, 64
Men and relationships, 187–202; changing feelings of, 196; connectedness, quest for, 189–96; Maher on, 201–2; nature and nurture of, 197–201; overview of, 187–88
Men Are from Mars, Women Are from Venus (Gray), 130, 131–39, 146
Men as new hero, 261–76; anima as feminine aspect and, 271–76; hearing call to, 264–71; journey of, 261–64
Mental health for women, good, 7
Mentoring: female perspective of, 257–59; male perspective of, 255–57; reasoning for, 249–50; understanding, 244–49
Mill, John Stuart, 163
Miller, Jean Baker, 88
Mirror neurons, 107
Mitochondrial DNA, 118–19
Mitochondrial Eve, 119
Monogamy, 175
Monological gaze, 268
Moore, Demi, 138

Moore, Michael, 255
Moral development, female, 101–2
Moral exemplars, 99
Morality of care, 97–102
Morality of women, 97–113; balance with others and, 28–30, 110–13; embodied sense of, 102–3; emotional intelligence and, 107–8; empathy and, 103–5; hormones and, 105–7; Kohlberg and, 29–30, 97–98, 99; mirror neurons and, 107; morality of care and, 97–102; overview of, 97; roots of, 105; self-in-relation concept and, 108–10
Moses, 37
Mundy, Lisa, 225
Mystery/mastery behavior, male, 156

Naiveté of males, 144
Namaste, 103
National American Women Suffrage Association, 16
Nature and nurture: culture and, 197–98; male psyche and, 183–84; testosterone levels and, 198–201
Neocortex, 208
New Approach to Women & Therapy, A (Greenspan), 7
New Choices program, 8–12, 59–61; focuses of, 8–9; sexual harassment issues and, 10–11; victim psychology and, 11–12
New Passages (Sheehy), 111, 148
Next Enlightenment, The (Anderson), 216
Nicholson, Jack, 141
Numbness of males, 145–46
Nurture. *See also* Nature and nurture: impact of, 44; importance of, hypothesis, 45–46; nature influence on, 43–44

One up/one down measurement, 155

Opposites, balance and flow of, 21–32; control of women and, 31–32; creativity of men *vs.* women and, 30–31; evolutionary process and, 24–25; morality of men *vs.* women and, 28–30; rationality of men *vs.* women and, 26–28; Yin and Yang concept of, 21–24

Optimism, emotional distress and, 108

Our Treacherous Hearts: Why Women Let Men Get Their Way (Coward), 192

Oxytocin, 105–7

Paglia, Camille, 13

Pandora, 37

Pappas, Stephanie, 119

Pasick, Robert, 149

Passages (Sheehy), 148

Passivity of males, 144–45

Patriarchal system, 158–59; death of, 184; in Japan, 160–61; philosophy and, 162–64; religion and, 161–62

Patriarchal values, Wilber and, 33

Patriarchy, romantic love and, 126

Perennial wisdom, 122

Peterson, Laci, 6

Philip, Prince, 280–81

Pintar, Judith, 126, 128–29

Plato, 26, 163

Plausibility structure, 190–91

Pleasantville (movie), 145

Politically correct equality, 18–19

Politically Incorrect (television show), 201

Politics (Aristotle), 162–63

Pollack, William, 176–77, 178, 258

Postmodern movement, 8

Prefrontal cortex, 208

Pregnancy, creativity of women and, 116–17

Printing presses, religious wars and, 38–39

Psychology: concepts in and rationality of women, 86–90; defined, 7; Stone Center challenges of, 87

Psychotherapy and Spirit (Cortwright), 213

Psychotherapy Networker (journal magazine), 152, 196

Radical feminism, 14

Rational, meanings of, 95–96

Rationality of women, 77–96; balance and flow of opposites and, 26–28; care and, 85–86; decision making and, 82–83; divided brain and, 90–92; emotions and, 78–80; knowledge, constructing of, 81–82; left brain and, 92–93; *vs.* morality, 97; overview of, 77–78; psychology, concepts in, 86–90; responsibility and, 85–86; right brain and, 93–96; stages of knowing and, 80–81; thinking from both sides of brain and, 83–85

Real Boys (Pollack), 176

Reasonable person standard, 136–37

Relational behavior, defined, 86–87

Relational dread, male, 141–56; cautious confirmers, men as, 154–56; defined, 150–53; emotionally asleep men and, 148–50; feelings, reluctant to disclose, 154; intimacy and, 153–54; literature concerning, 153; male-bashing and, 146–47; masculinity, rock of, 147–48; mystery/mastery behavior of, 156; naiveté and, 144; numbness and, 145–46; overview of, 141–44; passivity and, 144–45

Relational lie, 139–40

Relationships, reasons for failure of, 125–40. *See also* Men and relationships; blame placement as, 132–39; Dr. Phil advice and, 135–36;

inequality as, 138–39; male experience as standard and, 136–38; *Men Are from Mars, Women Are from Venus* and, 130, 131–35; overview of, 125–29; relational lie and, 139–40; war between sexes and, 129–31

Relationships, SHE-Q and, 242

Reluctant revealers, men as, 154

Republic, The (Plato), 163

Resentment flu, women and, 131

Responsibility and rationality of women, 85–86

Revolution from Within (Steinem), 11, 58

Richer Sex, The (Mundy), 225–26

Right brain, explained, 93–96

Roberts, Bernadette, 206

Romantic love and relationships, 125–29

Rosenthal, Max, 232

Rousseau, Jean-Jacques, 29

Sacred Canopy: Elements of a Sociological Theory of Religion, The (Berger), 190

Sagan, Carl, 278

Sahib, Bhai, 207

Santorum, Rick, 235

Scarf, Maggie, 254

Schuon model, 121–22

Schwarzkopf, Norman, Jr., 176

Second sex, women as, 67

Second-wave feminism, 15–17

Secret Dowry of Eve, The (Hoffman), 208

Self, defined, 86

Self-assertion, self-esteem and, 55–57

Self-esteem, women's identity and, 51–75; archetypal tales and, 63–66; changing views on, 53–54; feminine, concept of, 69–74; feminine knowing and, 74–75; Freud and, 61–62; literature concerning, 58–59; New Choices program and, 59–61; overview of, 51–52; self-assertion and, 55–57; separation of sexes on issues of, 67–69; solutions to, 52–53; steps to change views of, 57–58

Self-in-relation theory, 87–88, 108–10

Self-Made Man (Vincent), 179

Seligman, Martin, 214

Sexes, imbalance between, 33–49; biological differences and, 43–44; factors impacting, 45–46; gender identity, altering, 44–45; history of, 33–35; language control and, 36–40; male immortality and, 46–49; maleness or femaleness and, 41–43; nurture, impact of, 44; sex, gender, and equality issues and, 40–41; status elevation by men and, 35–36

Sexes, separation of on self-esteem issues, 67–69

Sex of the divine aspect, 115

Sexual abuse, SHE-Q and, 235–36

Sexual harassment, 10–11

Sex *vs.* gender, 40

Shadyac, Tom, 67

Sheehy, Gail, 111, 148, 197

Sheldrake, Rupert, 236–37

SHE-Q, 221–42; aggression, reducing male, 232–33; basis of, 224–25; caretakers of Earth, women as, 233–35; changes in workforce and, 225–27; connecting with good males and, 240–41; connecting women to women and, 236–37; corrective measures in, 241–42; explained, 222–24; females as primary sex beliefs and, 227–29; feminine spirituality and, 237–38; humor and, 240; inequality changes and, 229–31; knowledge and, construction of new, 238–40; overview of, 221–22;

relationships and, 242; sexual abuse and, 235–36

Shlain, Leonard, 36–37; first commandment and, 38; imbalance, end of, 286; language for sex and, 48; women and concept of time, 70

Smart Women, Foolish Choices (Kinder and Cowen), 58

Socialist feminism, 14

Spiral Path, The (Roberts), 206, 207

Spirituality of women, 203–20; belief and, 212–13; enlightenment experiences and, 216–17; female brain and, 208–11; journey of life for, 219–20; nature and nurture of, 205–6; overview of, 203–5; *vs.* religion, 206–7; Tao and, 207–8; transpersonal psychology and, 213–19

Stanton, Elizabeth Cady, 15–17, 203

Status elevation by men, imbalance and, 35–36

Steinem, Gloria, 11, 58, 59

Sternberg, Robert, 138–39

Stiffed (Faludi), 62–63

Stone Center at Harvard/Wellesley, 86, 87–90; disconnecting of boys theory of, 173–74; empathy and, 103–4; male relational dread and, 150–53

Stupid White Men (Moore), 255

Talking as solution, 252–53

Tannen, Deborah, 155–56

Tao: balanced future and, 277–79; spirituality of women and, 207–8; wholeness and, 21

Tarnas, Richard, 262–63

Tart, Charles, 149–50

Tell Me You Love Me (HBO series), 136

Tend and befriend response, 100

Ten Stupid Things Women Do to Mess Up Their Lives (Schlessinger), 58

Testosterone, 42–43

Thinking, right and left brain side, 83–85

Tillich, Hannah, 164

Tillich, Paul, 164

Tolle, Eckhart, 67

Toward a New Psychology of Women (Miller), 88

Trading Spouses (television series), 177

Transcendent function, 275

Transpersonal psychology, 213–19

Tuana, Nancy, 24, 28

Turning Point, The (Capra), 278

Understanding Masculine Psychology (Johnson), 272

Understanding Men's Passages (Sheehy), 148

Victim, perceptions of, 11

Victim psychology, 11–12

Vincent, Norah, 179

Von Franz, Marie-Louise, 272

Von Goethe, Johann Wolfgang, 272

Wade, Nicholas, 119

Wayne, John, 139, 146

Weil, Andrew, 232

Wholeness, 277–79

Why Men Rule (Goldberg), 39

Whyte, David, 182

Why You're Not Married (McMillan), 58

Wilber, Ken, 33, 180; mature masculinity and, 201; nature and, 59

Wisdom of women, 221–42. *See also* SHE-Q

Witches of Eastwick (movie), 141

Woman's Bible, The (Stanton), 16

Women: concept of time and, 70; control of, 31–32; creativity of, 115–23; morality of, 97–113; rationality of,

77–96; self-esteem and identity of, 51–75; SHE-Q as wisdom of, 221–42; spirituality of, 203–20; studies, equality and, 10–18

Women and Madness (Chesler), 8

Women's Ways of Knowing (Belenky), 52, 80

Women to women, connecting, 236–37

Women Who Love Too Much (Norwood), 58

Woodman, Marion, 205, 286

Workforce, changes in, 225–27

Wright, Frank Lloyd, 283

Yin-Yang: balanced future and, 277–79; balance of flow and, 21–24; concept of, 63; as masculine/feminine principle, 21; symbol of, 21, 22

Zak, Paul, 106

About the Author

MICHELE (SHELLEY) TAKEI holds a PhD in transpersonal psychology and women's studies from Union Institute. She has been a professor at numerous universities where she has taught courses in both traditional and transpersonal psychology. She retired recently from Atlantic University, where she was on faculty for 15 years. While at Atlantic, she developed and headed the concentration in "Feminine Psychology and Spirituality."

She has also worked with thousands of women as the director of a Single Parent and Homemaker Program, as well as in her private psychological practice.

Takei is the owner and trainer of MARI (Mandala Assessment Research Instrument), a reliable and accurate, Jungian-based psychological assessment based on symbols and colors.

She lives in Raleigh, North Carolina, with her husband of 46 years. Their three children and five granddaughters also live in Raleigh. From May through September, Shelley and Frank are residents of Lily Dale, New York, where they are owners of the Angel House, a popular guesthouse.